A Darkened Reading

A **Darkened** Reading

A RECEPTION HISTORY
OF THE BOOK OF ISAIAH
IN A DIVIDED CHURCH

ROBERT L. KNETSCH

☙PICKWICK *Publications* • Eugene, Oregon

A DARKENED READING
A Reception History of the Book of Isaiah in a Divided Church

Copyright © 2014 Robert L. Knetsch. All rights reserved. Except for brief quotations in critical publications or reviews, no part of this book may be reproduced in any manner without prior written permission from the publisher. Write: Permissions. Wipf and Stock Publishers, 199 W. 8th Ave., Suite 3, Eugene, OR 97401.

Pickwick Publications
An Imprint of Wipf and Stock Publishers
199 W. 8th Ave., Suite 3
Eugene, OR 97401

www.wipfandstock.com

ISBN 13: 978-1-62564-361-2

Cataloguing-in-Publication Data

Knetsch, Robert L.
    A darkened reading : a reception history of the book of Isaiah in a divided church / Robert L. Knetsch

    x + 264 p. ; 23 cm. Includes bibliographical references and index.

    ISBN 13: 978-1-62564-361-2

    1. Bible. Isaiah. Criticism, interpretation, etc.—History. 2. England—Church history—19th century. 3. Church of England—History—19th century. I. Title.

BR759 K627 2014

Manufactured in the U.S.A.

For Leila

Contents

Preface | ix

    Introduction: The Problem of Exegesis in a Divided Church | 1

1 The Scriptural Hermeneutic of Early Anglicanism: A Touchstone | 13

2 The Breakdown of Uniformity: Seventeenth- and Eighteenth-Century Competing Intra-Anglican Scriptural Visions | 42

3 Robert Payne Smith: Rescuing Isaiah from Its Opponents | 82

4 The Politics of Division: Christopher Wordsworth and the High Church Exegesis of Isaiah | 118

5 Skepticism Is the "Truest Piety": Thomas Kelly Cheyne and the Broad Church Exegesis of Isaiah | 155

6 English Roman Catholicism and Isaiah: Exegetical Minimalism in a State of Siege | 187

7 Conclusion: The Despair of Ecclesial Biblical Retrieval | 221

Bibliography | 243
Index | 255

Preface

THIS BOOK HAS EMERGED in its present form out of the research and writing I did for my dissertation during my time as a doctoral student at Wycliffe College, Toronto. The spark that initiated my thinking was Ephraim Radner's book, *The End of the Church*; its challenge to face head-on the deeply contested nature of many theological practices of the Church in the midst of its division overlapped with my desire to closely explore the relationship between theology and Scripture. As I say at the end of this book, what I have written is rather bleak, but it emerges out of my love for the Church and out of a desire to call the Church—not back to a putative pristine golden era, whenever and whatever that may be—but to its own Scriptures, the writings that have always been there. This book challenges various prevailing notions about "how we got here," suggesting that the neutral, objective universe that modernity trumpets is very much a part of the Church's history; they are also her worst enemies.

Wycliffe College has justly been noted as an eminent institute of theological education; it also provided a caring, stimulating environment for my studies. My studies began with Professor Joseph Mangina's astute and incisive teaching and Professor David Demson's wise and knowledgeable guidance. I had the immense honor to have Professor Ephraim Radner as my advisor. He is one of the most gifted and insightful theologians of our time. His loving but firm direction, and his writings that inspired this work, led me to think more deeply on matters of theology and the Church.

Many eyes have read various forms of this book, polishing its rough edges and finding my many errors; I am indebted to Judah Oudshoorn, Susy Kim, and Peter Genzinger for their readings of chapters. Peter, too, always offered a supportive and deeply meaningful friendship during my years of labors. The bulk of the proofreading effort, however, I credit to Katherine Dearlove, whose gifted and ever-vigilant skills caught many egregious mistakes.

Finally, and above all, I thank my family. My two daughters, Aliyah and Zara, were always a source of joy, love, and support during this process. Leila, my wife, was ever-patient, and kept me grounded. I dedicate this book to her for her never-failing love, for enduring many months of brooding over my research, and, above all, for believing in me.

Introduction

The Problem of Exegesis in A Divided Church

THE DARKNESS OF ECCLESIAL DIVISION: ANTAGONISTIC AND IRENIC EXEGESIS

This book aims to detail a kind of "microhistory" of the book of Isaiah's reading during a certain time period in order to make certain "macrohistorical" claims. Fundamentally, it tests the hypothesis that an inherently divisive ecclesial reality obscures the theological exegesis of Scripture in the nineteenth-century Church of England. This further suggests that the riven Church Universal—the Body of Christ—endures a kind of veil over her exegetical eyes. The Church of England serves both as the historical focus of this discussion, but also as a kind of parable of the deeply problematic nature of ecclesial division.

The tragedy of a divided Church[1] is, in one sense, an obvious reality since the Reformation. While the burgeoning ecumenical movement of the twentieth century attempted to take seriously this challenge to the creedal claim that the Church is "one" and "catholic," there is an important question placed before the Church during the past five hundred years. How has the once inseparable relationship between the Church and her sacred writings been sundered by what now appear to be irreversible differences in the very methods of scriptural interpretation? This book is more than a merely descriptive account of *what kinds of new readings* emerge and diverge, but *the way that multiple competing ecclesiologies are the engines that drive these innovations*.

---

1. I employ a distinction between the "Church," (capitalized) as the body that serves as the referent for the word in the Apostles' Creed; "church" (lower case), denotes a particular, local community.

A Darkened Reading

This discussion of a divided Church is not explicitly a study of current and specific trends in Anglican readings of the Bible. Rather, I consider the nineteenth century as emblematic of the confusion over the role of Scripture within the Church, the consequence of a combative matrix that dilutes Scripture's theologically and ecclesiastically preeminent role. A host of historical, political, and sociological accounts could be offered that describe the origin and development of contemporary controversial issues. This discussion, however, is situated strictly along theological lines since, as this is a discussion of the Church, the theological dimension is paramount, subordinating all other matters. Such an examination could, for instance, be carried out around the locus of "communion," but even this is a concept that is in peril, when applied to the Anglican Church today. There are competing claims as to what it means for one church to be in communion with another even *within* the bounds of particular Anglican Churches, now multiplied throughout the world.[2]

In *The End of the Church*, Ephraim Radner offers a pneumatological argument that that the structure of theological discourse by both Protestants and Roman Catholics is inherently divisive. He points out how unusual it is that the Church often finds it "normal" that the Bible can be read in contradictory ways. The claims of an Anglican "communion," are often asserted in a context where there is confusion about the theological role of Scripture in the Church. In his book *In The Ruins of the Church*, R. R. Reno argues, like Radner, that the Church in her divided condition reads Scripture dysfunctionally. Reno points to nineteenth-century thinkers who, in typical modernist fashion, use Scripture in such a way that it functions as a "hindering, limited, and ruined artifact of a now dead past"—a use Reno attributes to both "liberals" and "conservatives" who "flee from the body of received tradition."[3] Scripture is no longer the driving engine that shapes the providentially-ordered life of the *one* Church throughout history. Reno argues that it is not the historical-critical movement as such that tore the Bible from its ecclesial moorings, but a move away from the *askesis* of reading the Bible in common worship. I argue that this ascetic lack arose out of theological controversy and even violence, which bred modern ways of reading Scripture.

My intent is to add to Reno and Radner's work by considering the nature of *exegesis* within a particular historical time period: a "thick reading" of a certain reception history. Such focus grants greater resolution to

---

2. For instance, Turner and Radner indicate the Communion problematic in theological terms in *The Fate of Communion*.

3. Reno, *In the Ruins of the Church*, 18.

an exploration of the Church of England's struggle during a theologically pivotal time. It was during the nineteenth century that many of the various "wings" of the Church solidified, and this internal division generated a kind of identity crisis—though I also argue that this is the ineluctable product of ecclesial struggles of previous centuries.

Contemporary concerns of, for instance, sexual identity, the nature of marriage, and the challenge of "science" are epiphenomenal to much deeper issues related to the nature of the Church, which need to be explored within a specific historical context. This analysis asks questions of ecclesial identity within a specific, local Christian community, testing the hypothesis that confusion about the relationship between Scripture and the identity of the Church profoundly and negatively affects the practice of theological exegesis. The extent to which these conclusions can be subsequently transposed to a wider field of application I leave to the concluding chapter.

The competing factions within the Anglican Church are well known, and I describe them in the context of the nineteenth century in more detail at the end of the next chapter, but I outline them here very briefly. I consider the Low Church party as comprising those who identify with the Evangelical Movement. The High Church party, out of which the Oxford Movement arose, comprises those who attempt to construe the Church of England as inheritors of the historically constituted catholic Church. Finally, for the sake of simplicity, I regard the so-called Broad Church party as thinkers who adhere to a "liberal" perspective. This latter group, in my construal, affirms an engagement with Scripture that attempts to cohere with modern notions of textual analysis. But, much more than this exegetical dimension, there is an entire theological anthropology that serves as the substructure of their orientation to Scripture, and humanity in general. They tend to eschew dogmatic claims in favor of Christianity as an instance of a general "religious" characteristic inherent in human identity.

Many thinkers straddle the boundaries between any of these movements. This makes choosing appropriate exegetical exemplars difficult, and raising the risk of offering caricatures. For this reason, I have set a criterion of choice that each thinker has had significant engagement in work at an academic level, while at the same time being a good exemplar of his particular ecclesial perspective. All primary exemplars were appointed to a university position and offered a notable contribution to Isaiah scholarship during their tenure. At the same time, none of the central figures were considered founders of their respective movements.

Finally, all these thinkers thought of themselves as committed representatives of Protestant theology, and therefore the greatest catalyst for antagonistic thought was, in their minds, the ever-present specter of Roman

Catholicism. I attend to this oft-persecuted minority in England in Chapter 6. The Protestant attitude toward Roman Catholics often called for a defensive position by Catholic theologians, which played a major role in the combative matrix of theological exegesis. It was not until 1829, however, that legal restrictions on Roman Catholics were eased, and still quite some time before major English universities (Oxford and Cambridge) granted degrees to those who would not subscribe to the Articles of Religion of the Church of England. Therefore, it is much harder to find Catholic thinkers in England of equal academic stature to this study's chosen Anglican exemplars, and who are nonetheless fairly representative of Roman Catholicism. Since the Bible was the battleground of division amongst Protestant parties, the subsequent response by Roman Catholics was to *avoid* any serious exegetical engagement, beyond a superficial level. I show this by making use of academic periodicals, devotional literature and the writings of popular Catholic thinkers.

There are two primary categories under which I define the general phenomenon of "divisive exegesis." The first is an overt, "antagonistic" mode of interpretation within a particular context of attacks directed (whether explicitly or implicitly) against other parties within the Church. This is almost always present as a kind of patina over the reading of the Bible by Protestants against Roman Catholics, or vice versa. Whether this is an interpretation that sees the Beast of the Book of Revelation fulfilled in the Roman Catholic Pope, or the scattering of stars by the great dragon in Revelation 12 to be the work of Martin Luther's new Reformation, this antagonistic exegetical orientation is easily identifiable. It is by no means trivial in its effect on ecclesial division; often it gave some impetus for religious violence in Europe. However, partly out of this antagonistic exegesis emerged a more subtle and pervasive reading that is tethered to a web of philosophical commitments about the nature of the human, religion, God, and texts. I refer to this as an *irenic* mode of divisive reading.[4] This approach strives to move away from complexity and pluriformity of meaning in favor of certain "essences" of "religious" systems. It avoids particular dogmatic dogmatic claims as they are perceived as inhibitors to the expression of individual faith. Irenic exegesis esteems a critical orientation to the Bible that tends to be funded by a desire to rise above division, but in the end escapes from the idea of the Bible as *Scripture*. This is an exegetical orientation that regards the Bible in terms of historical and philological categories, with a

---

4. I speak more of irenic exegesis in the next chapter; I must mention that I am borrowing and expanding on this term from Michael Legaspi's *The Death of Scripture*. It serves as a significantly influential and helpful concept in this book.

view to avoiding the dogmatic dimension so key to exegesis for centuries before the Reformation.

METHODOLOGY: ANGLICANISM AND EXEGESIS

How the Anglican Church in the nineteenth century came to find itself in a position of exegetical plurality requires a tracing of its exegetical and theological history from the time of the Reformation. Here I briefly outline my analytical method by describing what it meant in the sixteenth and seventeenth centuries to read the Bible in the Church *in a uniquely Anglican way*. I expand on this in Chapter 1 as the analytic "touchstone" of my primary Isaiah exegetes.

My approach questions the sufficiency of narratives that describe new exegetical approaches to the Bible as mere reactions and accommodations to modern thinking. This overlooks serious theological matters that relate to modernism itself. In what follows, I dispute the view that nineteenth-century controversies such as the relation between science and theology, the protection of the autonomy of the individual, and the development of the scientific analysis of the Bible, *viz.*, historical criticism, provide the impetus for new exegetical approaches. Rather, they are best described as inevitable consequences to those changes in ways of reading Scripture that were antecedent to such theological bombshells as *Essays and Reviews* (1860). This study seeks to put to rest the myth that exegesis failed because of the external pressures of new scientific discoveries and the development of new methods of historical research.[5] The "new worldview" that arose, according to this myth, is all too often construed as an external, alien interjection of ideas that permeated Christian thought with respect to Scripture, resulting in the Bible's liberation (for "progressives") or its diminishment (for "conservatives"). In contrast, I suggest that *the vast changes in the very nature of reading and exegesis are epiphenomenal to ecclesial division.*

---

5. This is the implicit view taken, for instance, by New Testament scholar Bart Ehrman in his *The New Testament*, a popular text on the New Testament. His approach is a "historical" one. As such, "historians, as historians, have no privileged access to what happens in the supernatural realm; they have access only to what happens in this, our natural world" (Ehrman, *The New Testament*, 15). Despite Ehrman's supposed clarity in distinguishing between the "supernatural" and "natural" realm, this statement is indicative of his acceptance of a "natural" world and the ensuing scientific tools that precipitate from this assumption. Walter Brueggemann speaks to this notion more explicitly when he says, "the rise of science meant that the Bible came to occupy no privileged position of interpretation" (Brueggemann, *Theology of the Old Testament*). Most modern textbooks take it as a matter of fact that exegesis has been completely reoriented, shorn of "pre-critical" biases.

This account describes how new critical tools attempt to respond to religious conflict. Indeed, *most significant inroads into biblical criticism were done with an aim to help the Church*, even if the result was to undermine it. These critical tools were therefore children of the Church itself. Most critical pilgrims saw themselves as working toward the betterment of the Church, aiming to solve the intractability of division.[6] By the time of the nineteenth century, this desire for the improvement of religion was no different. Frederick Farrar's 1889 Bampton Lectures offer a progressivist account of the history of biblical interpretation. Farrar says, "my sole desire has been to defend the cause of Christianity by furthering the interests of truth."[7] Or John Tulloch's *Movements of Religious Thought in Britain during the Nineteenth Century* (1888) speaks of the genius of Coleridge's rejection of biblical infallibility in favor of the "divinity of scripture" which resides "not in the letter but in the spirit."[8] Tulloch found unquestionable the necessity to divide the "spirit" of the Bible from "dogma," for, "dogma splits rather than unites from its very nature."[9] This latter quotation is representative of what I claim is a common thread of irenic exegesis that runs through exegetical history. Farrar and Tulloch view the new exegetical environment quite positively, as the consequence of an advance in knowledge, and "nothing less than a new revelation of the ways and works of God."[10] Farrar and others conceive of the "newness" of the age as external to the Church, that is, *despite* the Church or *to spite* the Church. However, the form of exegesis I describe is, fundamentally, *ecclesially* derived, misshapen as it may have been, and the result of the Church's divisive climate.

Rowan Greer's position in *Anglican Approaches to Scripture*, one of the few recent treatments of Anglican hermeneutics, is characteristic of a positive view of modern exegetical confusion. Greer traces the multiple uses of the Bible through Anglicanism's development, and attempts to make the case that Samuel T. Coleridge (1772–1834), the Romantic literary critic, poet, and philosopher, provides the best paradigm for interpreting Scripture. He agrees with Coleridge's view that "orthodoxy" (read: a traditioned, ecclesial reading of Scripture) suppresses the many human voices in Scripture. If Greer has a hermeneutic, it is this: we cannot hear Scripture "as we move away from what is necessary to salvation or away from what will come to

---

6. For a detailed documentation of this claim, see Gregory, *The Unintended Reformation*.
7. Farrar, *History of Interpretation*, ix.
8. Tulloch, *Movements of Religious Thought*, 30.
9. Ibid., 335.
10. Farrar, *History of Interpretation*, ix.

be called the 'essence' of Christianity."[11] This view is an irenic form of early modern attempts to bypass exegetical debate and division by extracting and abstracting a particular essence against which the Scriptures themselves and their multiple interpreters are to be judged. The consequence is a turn away from the particularity of the scriptural text in favor of modes and tools of reading that seek to apprehend these essential meanings. The chosen tools, however, were multiple and varied, selected under the claim of an improved "certainty" of textual meaning, independent of confessional commitments.

Roman Catholic scholar Aidan Nichols in *The Panther and the Hind* offers a more trenchant critique of Anglicanism. He asserts that Anglicanism's theological pluralism is far from a coherent identity and in fact contributes to an inherent instability within Anglicanism. For Nichols, it is the historical development of the characteristically Anglican *via media* that exerts a disintegrating force on ecclesial identity. The *via media*, for Nichols, denotes a state of affairs in Anglicanism that attempts to forge a course between the extremes of Protestantism and Roman Catholicism, but in doing so, chooses to make no significantly identifiable doctrinal decisions. However, what, in Nichols' view, is the appearance of doctrinal ambiguity, is in fact a defining characteristic of early Anglicanism, in which Scripture shapes theological thought instead of subjecting it to definitive confessional statements. Whether his interpretation of the *via media* is an accurate one (and it is, at best, historically simplistic), the greatest lacuna in Nichols' work is a consistent discussion of how Scripture functions in the development of Anglican identity. I propose to argue that his conclusion regarding Anglican instability is correct; however, I ultimately suggest that this is the case of *all* hermeneutical schemes in the face of ecclesial breakdown, and, as such, they are projects of despair.

The four central chapters of this book (Chapters 3-6) comprise an exploration of Isaiah commentaries. Before embarking on this, however, for the purpose of greater clarity and precision, I begin in the next chapter with an outline of a uniquely Anglican vision of Scripture in terms of certain exegetical categories. While I would claim that this hermeneutical vision is in many ways "unique" to Anglican thought, the exercise serves a greater heuristic purpose. This biblical orientation's contours may indeed have homologous particulars with other Christian groups of the time, but attending closely to its peculiarly "Anglican" nature allows for a "thick analysis" of this reception history.

In addition to outlining this reading of the Bible, I briefly describe three intellectual "movements" of sorts that exert a force on and are driven

11. Greer, *Anglican Approaches to Scripture*, xi.

by a divisive ecclesial reality: humanism, skepticism, and various spiritualist traditions. I regard these throughout this dissertation as the tools that contribute to exegetical disintegration. They often play an important part of the "standard" account of early modern history. This account, however, often neglects their role in ecclesial division. Each commentator or set of commentators align themselves with more prominence along one of the three axes of humanism, spiritualism, and skepticism.

I describe the uniquely Anglican hermeneutical vision of the Bible in terms of the Church's central thinkers: Thomas Cranmer (1489–1556), John Whitgift (*c.* 1530–1604) and Richard Hooker (1554–1600). The three categories that guide the analysis of Isaiah commentaries are: (1) The relation between Scripture and the ecclesial community as a whole, vis-à-vis the individual; (2) the claim that Scripture functions as the *one* Word of God, that is, as a single canon, given its unity by virtue of its ultimate author, namely, God; and (3) the christological hermeneutic demanded by Scripture; that is, that the ultimate textual referent has to do with Jesus of Nazareth, not just in terms of prophetic prediction, but by way of figuralism and typology. These categories are not *per se* unique as regards a Protestant hermeneutic. What I present, however, is how they manifest in an Anglican mode. I am not arguing for the normativity of Cranmer, Whitgift and Hooker's original vision of Scripture's place in Anglicanism. However, I demonstrate how the nineteenth century's variegated and divisive exegesis is not only incongruent with, but *subversive* of this foundational scriptural framework. This Anglican framework, as it is rooted in the use of the Prayer Book, continues to exert a kind of counter-witness to the increasingly incoherent exegetical efforts of Anglican scriptural expositors. At times, this is an exertion in the form of a negative shadow over exegetical experimentation, never entirely losing its sway. Considering this form of Anglican hermeneutics as a "touchstone" for a distinctly ecclesial scriptural orientation, a well-defined methodology is therefore formulated to carry out the analysis of Isaiah commentaries.

I give attention to the nineteenth century in order to test the fruits of modern scriptural obscurity, not only among and between Protestants and Catholics, but within the putative Anglican Communion itself. The modern Church has no coherent, unifying, and conceptual framework that clarifies the hearing of Scripture. Philosophically validated standards of interpretation and competing ways of reading the text within vying Christian communities begin to function as the engines of exegetical labors. The categories of ecclesiology, canonicity and christology become theologically muddled in the nineteenth-century response to humanism, skepticism and spiritualist traditions.

THE IMPORTANCE OF ISAIAH AS AN EXEGETICAL LENS

This book examines commentaries on the book of the Prophet Isaiah to explore the ways in which the ecclesial context of nineteenth-century England impacts Anglican exegesis. This choice is by no means a random one: Isaiah is an ideal book through which to answer larger questions of biblical exegetical styles. My contention is that a person's interpretation of Isaiah sheds light on understanding his or her interpretive approach of *all* of Scripture. This is because, right from the origins of Christianity, Isaiah functions as a central "bridge" between the two Testaments. This section briefly describes the impact of this important book on the early Church.

The texts of the New Testament reveal a tradition in which Isaiah itself bears witness to New Testament realities. Brevard Childs and John F. A. Sawyer each provide an excellent outline of the presence of Isaianic themes and quotations within the New Testament.[12] For instance, consider how the following passages bear witness to Isaiah's impact on the early Church. Taking the generally accepted view that Paul's genuine letters pre-date the Synoptic Gospels, in Rom 9, from one of Paul's earliest letters, he references six citations of Isa (1:9, 8:14, 1:22,23, 28:16, 29:16, and 45:9). In 1 Cor 14–15, Paul also quotes from Isa 28:11–13, and from 25:8. These letters are usually dated from approximately the sixth decade of the first century. Furthermore, Sawyer lists nine passages from Mark's Gospel itself—thought to be the earliest written Gospel—in which the author explicitly cites or alludes to texts from Isaiah. All four Gospels quote from Isa 4:3 with regard to John the Baptist, as well as from 6:9–10, which also appears in Acts 28. The tradition also offers Jesus' description of his own ministry in the famous passage of Luke 4:

> [Jesus] went to Nazareth, where he had been brought up. . . . He stood up to read, and the scroll of the prophet Isaiah was handed to him. Unrolling it, he found the place where it is written:
>
> "The Spirit of the Lord is on me,
> because he has anointed me
> to proclaim good news to the poor.
> He has sent me to proclaim freedom for the prisoners
> and recovery of sight for the blind,
> to set the oppressed free,
> to proclaim the year of the Lord's favor."

In this case, Jesus directly applies Isa 61:1,2 to himself.

12. Childs, *The Struggle to Understand Isaiah*, 5–19; Sawyer, *The Fifth Gospel*, 21–41.

Finally, the book of Revelation is saturated with Isaianic imagery, which I will not detail. Note that none of the passages I cite refer to the more traditional verses such as that of the Virgin Birth (Isa 7:14) or of the Suffering Servant (Isa 53). All in all, "many of the most familiar themes and quotations from the 'Fifth Gospel' owe that familiarity to their appearance already in early Christian scripture as much as to the Church's use of the original book of Isaiah. They had already received their Christian meaning, in other words, almost before the Church came into existence."[13] Childs notes that "The United Bible Society's Greek New Testament estimates that there are more than four hundred quotations, paraphrases, or allusions to the book of Isaiah in the New Testament" and that the distribution is "remarkably even."[14] Isaiah's central position in Christian scriptural exegesis continued in subsequent centuries. The Church Fathers often used Isaiah as part of the theological articulation of the faith for liturgical inspiration. Angela Christman and Michael Hollerich draw primarily on the commentaries of four early Church Fathers, as well as less frequent quotations from sermons and other writings of John Chrysostom, Origen, Irenaeus of Lyons, Tertullian, and Gregory of Nyssa in *Isaiah: Interpreted by Early Christian and Medieval Commentators*. The result is a rich tapestry of tradition in which Isaiah functions as a key exegetical connection between the two Testaments. It ought to also be noted that there was pluriformity and controversy in interpretations; there were not (usually) multiple ecclesial communities competing with one another, yet interpretation was by no means uniform or static.

Since Isaiah was such a central book for New Testament authors as well as for the Church Fathers, it is also a fundamental text for the development of the relation between the two Testaments. For this reason, an analysis of a specific reader's approach to Isaiah will indicate his or her view of Isaiah's place within the Church, the connection between the Old and New Testaments, as well as the nature of a christological hermeneutic. The way in which a particular exegete upholds, defends, deviates, or challenges certain aspects of this reception history reveals the exegete's particular theological commitments.

---

13. Sawyer, *The Fifth Gospel*, 29. Though Sawyer refers to Isaiah as the "Fifth Gospel," he has no historical source for this claim. It is not, as far as I can tell, a denotation that is explicitly used by the early Church Fathers. The closest is a passage from Jerome, who says, "Isaiah is an evangelist and an apostle as well as a prophet" (Christman and Hollerich, *Isaiah*, 6).

14. Childs, *The Struggle to Understand Isaiah*, 5.

THE PROBLEM OF "THEOLOGICAL EXEGESIS"

I frequently use the term "theological exegesis" or "theological interpretation" in this project, a concept that is notoriously difficult to define, as numerous thinkers are in conflict over its essential features. Indeed, this conflict is precisely part of the problem: exegetes of all stripes consider their various commentaries as appropriate *theological* engagement with the Bible. Many writers on the subject refrain from defining the concept. For instance, Daniel Treier speaks of how theological interpretation declined "due to the rise of 'critical biblical scholarship,'" only to be recovered by the exegesis of Karl Barth.[15] Elsewhere he speaks of theological interpretation as being theological when "Christians read the Bible as Scripture, authoritative as God's Word for faith and life; thus, to encounter Scripture [is] to encounter God."[16] Clearly Treier believes that the task in which many present-day interpreters are engaging is not proper theological exegesis. This is not to suggest that Trier's work does not raise several laudable suggestions for moving beyond the critical work of nineteenth-century scholars. Yet he misses the point that these same scholars thought that by, for instance, uncovering the diachronic shape of the text, and exposing its redactional layers, exegesis, and even the Church, was all the better for it. Moreover, the aspects of particularly "theological" interpretation that Treier commends are not necessarily consistent with those of others. In a contribution to a book on theological interpretation, Stephen Fowl says "the key to interpreting theologically lies in keeping theological concerns primary to all others. In this way, theology becomes a form of exegesis, not its result."[17] This is in distinction to having any kind of "governing hermeneutic" in interpretation. *Whose* "theological concerns" are primary? For Walter Brueggemann, it is the Church who performs this interpretive task; yet "the Church" must determine "how to practice the normativeness of scripture in a way that lets all . . . interpreters listen and submit their readings to the judgment of the whole church . . ."[18] It is often very difficult to render any concrete particularity to the phrase "the judgment of the whole church" as it is unclear who the Church is. Other "keys" to proper theological interpretation are legion: narrative, feminist, semiotic, canonical.

The quandary, therefore, is how to employ a term for which giving a definition would bring it into irresolvable conflict with others; it is a "party"

---

15. Treier, *Introducing Theological Interpretation of Scripture*, 11.
16. Ibid., 13.
17. Fowl, "Further Thoughts on Theological Interpretation," 127.
18. Brueggemann, *The Book That Breathes New Life*, 39.

word. This is precisely the theme of this project: ecclesial division renders theological interpretation highly problematic. For this reason, I can only provide a historical work that takes a particular case, the Church of England, and I present a peculiarly Anglican vision of what it means to read Scripture. Surely this does not mean that this model is a sufficient definition, but I suggest that it adequately holds together several strands, such as the centrality of the Church in not only *performing* the interpretation, but also being the one to whom, or even *against* whom, Scripture speaks. It accepts that the central creeds of the Church give guidance to this interpretation and that the two Testaments are held together because they bear witness to Jesus Christ. Any interpretation that does not have these elements intrinsic to exegesis is not, strictly speaking, theological, *in terms of the Anglican vision I explicate*, and whose fate I explore.

For each Isaiah commentary I present findings that emerge from the analysis. My claims are rather bleak, namely, that the divisiveness of the Church has made theological exegesis inherently incoherent. Since the Church's own identity is confused, and Scripture is the very Word of God to the Church, then the Word is misunderstood, misconstrued, or just unheard.

1

The Scriptural Hermeneutic of Early Anglicanism

A Touchstone

INTRODUCTION: A HERMENEUTICAL MODEL

THIS CHAPTER SITUATES THE context of my discussion of an enervated biblical exegesis by describing a uniquely Anglican reading of the Bible. This vision of reading Scripture is the organizing principle, or "touchstone," for the analysis of various competing exegetical approaches to Isaiah in subsequent chapters. It also provides helpful categories for assessing the similarities and differences *within* the Church of England as well as that between Anglicans and Roman Catholics. The intent is not to prescribe this hermeneutical vision as normative *per se*, but to employ it as a heuristic for exegetical analysis, based on historical and theological data. While the vision that emerges in early Anglicanism was a unique one, it did not survive intact; nonetheless, its impact continues to be perceived, however evanescent.

The foundational theological figures who shape this touchstone are Thomas Cranmer (1489–1556), John Whitgift (1530–1604) and Richard Hooker (1554–1600). I attend to each of these insofar as their thought impacts a particular vision of reading Scripture. Three central categories help to define this exegetical touchstone:

(1) the relation between the Bible, the Church, and the individual;

(2) the way that each book of the Bible participates in the *canon* of Scripture as the *one* word of God; and

(3) the nature of a *christological* reading of the Bible, which pertains to how Old Testament is related to the New.

I should note the asymmetrical nature of my discussion; the first category—the communal nature of reading Scripture—is the most distinct one in Anglicanism and I give it the most space. It is also the one category most closely bound to the identity of the Church. The christological reading of Scripture and the claim that the entire Bible comprises the one Word of God are not *per se* unique to Anglicanism but does manifest certain peculiarly Anglican modalities of expression. In the discussion below, where I attend to the christological reading of Isaiah, I detail some specific uses of the Old Testament in general, and Isaiah specifically, in the Prayer Book.

THE TOOLS OF DIVISION: HUMANISM, SPIRITUALIST TRADITIONS, AND SKEPTICISM

It is instructive to outline some challenges and competing options amidst the various factions within the Church before and after the Reformation. These movements were instruments of division, though they were not themselves a direct cause of it. Often I show that a certain "party" within the Church identifies with one of these new ways of thinking of thinking.

I challenge the contention that the emergence of new hermeneutical options, particularly in a highly critical form, are primarily (though not exclusively) *external* rather than *internal* ecclesial phenomena. Indeed, many new approaches to the Bible arose for the purpose of edifying the Church rather than for destroying it. The standard account, as represented, for instance, by Roy Harrisville and Walter Sundberg, suggests that "the doctrinal conflict between historical criticism and the dogmatic tradition" is "nothing less than a war between two worldviews of faith: the worldview of modern critical awareness originating in the Enlightenment and the inherited Augustinian worldview of the Western church."[1] Again, Gadamer states that "Enlightenment critique is primarily directed against the religious tradition of Christianity—i.e., the Bible.... This is the real radicality of the modern Enlightenment compared to all other movements of enlightenment: it must assert itself against the Bible and dogmatic interpretations of it."[2] This story, in which new hermeneutical approaches emerged because of external

---

1. Sundberg and Harrisville, *The Bible in Modern Culture*, 5.
2. Gadamer, *Truth and Method*, 272.

challenges to traditional doctrine, is mistaken, or at least too simplistic, based as it is on the presupposition that the Church is distinct from the rest of society. While such a distinction can perhaps be made today in the post-Christian West, the Reformation and its antecedents occurred in the midst of "christendom," an era during which most people rarely had any other option than to be steeped in Christian beliefs. The typical narrative of ecclesial dissolution suggests that changes were imposed externally on the Church, as the "enemy" of a putatively "Augustinian worldview." The debates between those who read the Bible in a traditional mode—one which attempts to reflect on the theological claims of the Church—and those who interpret by the use of historical-critical tools cannot, in my view, be effectively distinguished from each other as representations of two "worldviews of faith." Instead, *they issue out of the same Christian tradition.* New modern interpretations are, in fact, the offspring of the Church, however misshapen and corrosive.³ They emerged in response to the divided Church's claims on Scripture and were birthed through division and fragmentation. My account, therefore, is a theological and historical description of how this change in reading the Bible emerges *internally* to the Church, despite the claims of thinkers such as Harrisville and Sundberg, who characterize it as an external assault on the Church's traditional doctrines by those who whose goal was to attack "the Church" itself.

H. G. Reventlow outlines the effect of spiritualism on Puritanism, which impacted Scripture's interpretation in England.⁴ It would be beyond

---

3. What I mean by "modernity" is not the development of new scientific methodologies and rational systems in themselves, i.e., Newtonian mechanistic science and Cartesian epistemology. Rather, it is the universalization of these methodologies to *all* human enterprises as sufficiently valid tools that informs my employment of "modernity." In this I am following Stephen Toulmin's argument in Toulmin, *Cosmopolis*. See also Gillespie, *The Theological Origins of Modernity* in which Gillespie argues against the common story that modernity was the ushering in of an age that surpassed the need for religion and religious language, but rather, that modernity was a theologically/metaphysically derived phenomenon.

4. Numerous movements prior to the Reformation can be denoted as "spiritualist," characterized by their particular view of history. Joachim of Fiore (c. 1135–1202) was an exemplar of this Spiritualist position, which can be discussed only briefly (see Reventlow, *The Authority of the Bible*, 25–31) but there were many other groups such as the Brethren of the Common Life and Girolamo Savonarola's (1452–1498) quasi-theocratic republic (Gillespie, *The Theological Origins of Modernity*, 88–89). Fiore and his followers envisioned the flowering of a new age of the Spirit in eschatological terms that saw the materiality of the world as unnecessary. Fiore did not repudiate Scripture, but the important point for my purposes is that for spiritualist followers, "the sacraments become superfluous, the priesthood is unnecessary, [and] the significance of Scripture is in fact evacuated" (Reventlow, *The Authority of the Bible*, 27).

Theologically, in spiritualist traditions external matters assume a diminished role

the task of this chapter to enter into the history of spiritualism in general. My more modest claim is that the Puritan discourse—taken up by the Evangelical movement in later centuries—takes on a spiritualist tenor, adopting spiritualist "traditions," rather than being direct descendants of spiritualist thinkers of the twelfth and thirteenth centuries. The primary characteristic of this tradition (or, better, set of traditions) is a focus on the inner life of the *individual* and a minimization of the Church's concrete particularity. Its contribution to division is the tendency to think of the Church as playing a variegated but diminishing role within theological discourse in favor of more "spiritual" ideas that are detached from concrete embodiment. In Protestantism, there came to be many manifestations of this spiritualist tendency, one of which was a distinction in the Church between the "visible" and "invisible" Church, the latter of which is the set of those who are the "elect" or the "saved." It is the non-visible Church which, ironically, came to be seen as the "embodied" one.

Humanism is an intellectual and cultural phenomenon with a complex history, but its impact generates a series of movements, which in turn influence biblical exegesis. I characterize this impact as one that results in a desire for a *repristination* of the Church and a concern for the moral life of the individual believer. It is the former that had a greater impact on ecclesial division, as ecclesial repristination suggests a desire to move theological and biblical discourse *ad fontes* and a tendency toward criticizing the era following the patristic period.

Finally, I follow Popkin's account of skepticism's impact during the Reformation as formative for theological discourse and the context out of which modern thinking developed.[5] For instance, the agitation of William Tyndale (1494–1536) generated new rhetorical modes of disputation, as argued by Peter Auksi. While it may to some extent be a generalization, Auksi's analysis of the debate between Tyndale and Thomas More (1478–1535) reveals that the Catholic history of *disputatio* led to rhetoric in which (at least for More) "verbal expressions which religious certitude makes possible become conflated with or analogous to mathematical exactitude."[6] In Tyndale's mind, Catholic focus on logical syllogisms, distinctions between terms with agonizing exactitude and hyper-rational sophistry insufficiently

---

in salvation. For some, this means arguing that the sacraments are unnecessary. The interest in the inner dimension of the individual human before God becomes determinative for a thought pattern that "sees man himself, his spiritual quality and his ethical conduct, as the decisive factor for salvation" (Reventlow, *The Authority of the Bible*, 25).

5. See Popkin, *The History of Scepticism from Erasmus to Descartes*.
6. Auksi, "Reason and Feeling as Evidence," 13.

account for the affective or experiential mode of human sensation.[7] No longer do these modalities reflect the simple message of Scripture; rather, they actively obscure it. Tyndale regards scholasticism as a belletristic veiling of Christianity's truth, the result being the severe occlusion of its affective power. Thinkers like Tyndale, however, found new ways to argue their case against the rigorous scholasticism of Roman Catholic opponents. More's reliance on the tradition of disputational methodology is countered by Tyndale's appeal to the experience and feelings of the individual believer—the "heart" being the catch-all phrase—to prove the veracity of his arguments. In Tyndale's debate with More, targeting what he sees as dry scholasticism, he appeals to feeling, "because it indicates the crucial presence of the Spirit" and the labyrinth of Catholic scholastic argumentation is a Sisyphean effort that produces an empty faith: "The children of light . . . have empirical subjective experience of the internal, rejuvenating power of a 'feeling faith' which lies beyond the manipulations of reason and the authority of others."[8] This shift in discursive modality from the scholastic-disputational to the affective-emotional is indicative of a crisis of thought in religious belief, arising directly from disputes within a dividing Church, rather than an intentional and conspiratorial attempt to usurp Christendom. Popkin describes the time of the Reformation as an "intellectual crisis" during which thinkers sought for means of achieving certainty. This intellectual crisis led to a rise of skepticism, a mode of thought that continues to dominate Western thinking. The resulting skeptical attitude accords with Tyndale's approach.

This skeptical attitude led someone like Luther to seek absolute certainty, a quest that fails if it relies on the dictates of the Church. In turn, "the rule of faith for the Reformers . . . appears to have been subjective certainty, the compulsion of one's conscience."[9] While Luther does not resort as directly to feeling and personal experience as Tyndale, both attempt to solve the epistemological crisis in similar ways. The ensuing perennial Pyrrhonic problem brings into question new epistemological approaches to the Christian faith, out of which emerge further methods to validate the new method, resulting in an infinite regress of methodological skepticism. The

7. Consider Tyndale's mocking of Catholic methodology: "First, they nosel them in sophistry and in *benefundatum*. And there corrupt they their judgements with apparent arguments, and with alleging unto them texts of logic, of natural *philautia*, of metaphysic, and moral philosophy, and of all manner books of Aristotle, and of all manner doctors which they yet never saw . . . one holdeth this, another that; one is a Real, another a Nominal. What wonderful dreams have they of their predicaments, universals, second intentions, *quiddities, haecceities*, and relatives" (Tyndale, *The Obedience of a Christian Man*, 22–23).

8. Auksi, "Reason and Feeling as Evidence," 14.

9. Popkin, *The History of Scepticism from Erasmus to Descartes*, 8.

discussion shifts from a concern about the meaning of the biblical texts to that of *method*: each party therefore identifies with a particular school and its respective claims to certainty.

AN ECCLESIAL READING OF THE BIBLE

The first dimension of a uniquely Anglican reading of the Bible is an *ecclesial reading*, which has to do with several important hermeneutical themes unique to Anglicanism. This exegetical aspect is distinct from Roman Catholic practice (at least, from that of most of the late Middle Ages) in the Anglican "laicization" of not only the Bible, but also of the liturgical practice of the entire Church in England, aiming at one "common" worship. While an episcopal structure remained that "imposed" various doctrines on parishioners, the aim is conformance for the common good of the Church. The perils of individualism are avoided, while at the same time, private reading, if not private interpretation, is encouraged only *within* this common structure.[10]

The rise of spiritualist and humanist traditions within the intellectual milieu of the Middle Ages had the ecclesial consequence of placing an emphasis on the inner life of the individual believer. By the commencement of the Reformation, these traditions also had an effect on the liturgical life of the Church by decoupling the connection between liturgical practice and

---

10. I deny the contention popular claim that Anglicanism, in its inception, and thus in its scriptural vision, is a *via media* between Protestantism and Roman Catholicism, and thus that it was somehow "half-reformed." This myth is promulgated by many, such as Roman Catholic Aidan Nichols. He argues that the *via media* is the source of Anglican instability. Nichols asserts the *via media* that developed "corresponded to the demands of realistic politics when Elizabeth came to the throne in 1558" (Nichols, *The Panther and the Hind*, 38). The consequence of the *via media* is the comprehensive nature of the Anglican Church, a kind of permissive large tent that allows for a wide spectrum of beliefs, the source of his contention that there is an unstable diversity that undermines Church unity. In comparison to the Roman Catholic Church, the Church of England, as such, has no unique doctrinal standard or creed which gives it a formative and unique identity. This is not an uncommon perspective. This oft repeated idea has recently come under increased scrutiny. Despite the popular use of the term *via media*, early shapers of Anglicanism aimed for a truly Catholic Church within England, an *Ecclesia Anglicana*. To cast Anglican identity as an entity that emerged out of a phenomenon of Henrician and Elizabethan *realpolitik* does not accurately take into account the theological dimension and scriptural vision of major thinkers in the Church of England. Dewey Wallace's reassessment of the so-called Anglican *via media* in "Via Media? A Paradigm Shift." makes the salient point that later Anglicanism, following thinkers like the Caroline Divines, might rightly be thought in its later development as a *via media*, but not in its early form under Elizabeth and its culmination in the work of Richard Hooker.

the Bible. Structurally, immediately after Henry VIII's break with Rome, much remained the same within the Church of England and it took several decades to solidify something recognizably "Anglican." Many Anglican divines saw the separation and independence from Rome, both politically and ecclesiastically, as an inheritance and continuation of the rights that were afforded England in the past. In the *Act in Restraint of Appeals* of 1533, Henry argued that the King was the "Supreme Head" of the Church because England was not a mere subject of the Pope, but an *"empire*—or as we should say today, a nation-state, fully self-sufficient in its single sovereignty. In this nation state the King . . . is furnished by the goodness of Almighty God with plenary and entire authority and jurisdiction."[11]

Thomas Cranmer, the Archbishop of Canterbury during Henry VIII's reign, began the process of developing the Anglican scriptural vision. Numerous writings of Roman Catholic, Calvinist, and Lutheran perspectives were disseminated and the new Church of England had to find a way of navigating them. Upon Henry VIII's death, the radical element succeeded in despoiling shrines, removing monasteries, and stripping away numerous aspects of the liturgy. Increased permissiveness for reform allowed Cranmer to bring about several changes. Cranmer was the primary writer of the first Prayer Book and it was part of the Act of Uniformity in 1549, permitting the use of only one liturgy. For the first time, Mass was also said in English, rather than in Latin.

The theological ancestors of the Puritans borrowed ideas from Zwingli and Calvin, raising challenges to Cranmer's Prayer Book as timid and falling short of removing the ceremonies they saw as superstitious practices unwarranted by Scripture. Two central Puritan biblical perspectives vis-à-vis ceremonies and practices can be generally described:

(1) practices that were commanded or described in Scripture (e.g., baptism), are to be "repristinated" in a form that is the least "papist." This approach usually urged a reduction or elimination of liturgical action and a more spiritualist interpretation of the practice; and

(2) that all ceremonies not so explicitly outlined in the Bible were considered superstitious and therefore proscribed.

In response to these looming challenges to the ecclesial form of life formulated by the Archbishop of Canterbury, in 1547 Cranmer and other notable thinkers issued a set of sermons to be publicly read.[12] The first of

---

11. Dawley, *John Whitgift and the Reformation*, 11.

12. The low level of education of the average priest and the extent to which Reformed theology had yet to permeate all of England necessitated a common set of sermons to be preached to ensure a smooth transition to the new regime. See Miller, "The

these so-called Edwardine Homilies was Cranmer's "A Fruitful Exhortation to the Reading and Knowledge of Holy Scripture." In it we can readily obtain an understanding of his view of Scripture.[13] For Cranmer, a personal familiarity with Scripture is important and he affirms the importance of duty and right behavior. However, while the countenancing of the vernacular can appear to suggest a perspective that encourages a purely individualist reading of Scripture for moral formation, Cranmer's vision is directed toward the *common* good, and as such his sermon describes a vision of Scripture that differs from his opponents' who offered other perspectives of the Bible. For instance, Scripture, says Cranmer, is more than that which must be read; it is the very Word of God, and "there is . . . abundantly enough, both for men to eat, and children to sucke. There is, whatsoever is meet for all ages, and for all degrees and sorts of men."[14] Scripture is food and constitutive not only of the individual, but also the commonwealth. Reading the Bible in the Church is like sitting down to a family meal. As the Word of God, Scripture has its own power to transform all who read it: "he that is most turned into [the Bible], that is most inspired with the Holy Ghost, most in his heart and life altered and changed into that thing which he readeth."[15] The use of the term "Word of God" with respect to Scripture is notable, for "holy scripture is the 'true word of God;' the phrases, 'word of God,' 'God's word,' 'scripture,' and 'holy Scripture,' are, in fact, interchangeable in the homily."[16]

One reason why everyone should read Scripture, and the implicit aim of this sermon, is that they are to be steeped in this word of God, fully engaged not only in terms of reading, but participating in habitual, even repetitive, practice. There is to be a "continual reading of God's word"[17] "where holy scripture's use is characterized as reading, hearing, searching and studying"[18] since, as the word of God, Scripture is the source of all theology. Cranmer's sermon cannot be seen as an injunction to an individualist, private reading of the text:

First Book of Homilies and the Doctrine of Holy Scripture."

13. I use the version printed in Leith, "A Fruitful Exhortation," reprinted from *Certain Sermons appointed by the Queen's Majesty to be declared and read by all Parsons, Vicars, and Curates every Sunday and Holy Day in their Churches* (1623). I make the not entirely proven assumption that Cranmer was the author of this homily, which has only been agreed to by a consensus opinion.

14. Leith, "A Fruitful Exhortation," 233.

15. Ibid., 234.

16. Miller, "The First Book of Homilies," 446

17. Leith, "A Fruitful Exhortation," 234.

18. Miller, "The First Book of Homilies," 451.

The fact that [this sermon] appears in an approved, sanctioned homily of the institutional hierarchy of the church belies such as notion. Rather, what is contended [by the homilist] is that because the Bible is God's word to his people and his church, it warrants direct use by all its people.[19]

Most importantly, any individualistic tenor of *A Fruitful Exhortation* must be understood in the light of the Prayer Book, the central participative element of this early Anglican hermeneutic. The Prayer Book is Cranmer's legacy, as its structure points to his ecclesiology and his understanding of the role of Scripture.

In the Prayer Book, Cranmer aims for a reformation in England that "is less a triumphant embrace of the individual's private and invisible self than a concerted effort to shape the otherwise *uncontrollable and unreliable internal sphere* through common acts of devotion."[20] Ramie Targoff makes the rather startling and counterintuitive claim that Cranmer's support for an English service and a Bible available to all was to counter the danger of *Roman Catholic* interiority. Roman Catholic opposition to common liturgical practices in the "vulgar" tongue engenders a greater push for Roman Catholics to engage in individualist piety. "For sixteenth-century Catholics, the challenge of public devotion was not to promote a shared and collective liturgical language, but instead to encourage the worshippers to perform their own private devotions during the priest's service."[21] There was in Catholic practice a sharp dichotomy between the bodily actions of ordained ministers and the interior devotional life of the laity, of whom it was expected to find their own means to engage in devotional acts. Targoff's contention therefore is that Catholic worship for the laity was more individualistic than that suggested by Roman Catholic polemicists themselves.

It is not that Cranmer was unconcerned about personal piety and the inner life; like any reformer, Cranmer believes ultimately in the importance of personal faith for salvation.[22] His construal of this faith, however, is not so neatly described as the inner disposition of the individual, and here Cranmer significantly diverges from using feeling and experience as "proof" of the certainty of a person's faith. The state of an individual's inner life, in fact, is unknowable ("uncontrollable and unreliable"). Therefore, bodily

---

19. Ibid., 450.
20. Targoff, *Common Prayer*, 6, italics mine.
21. Ibid., 14.
22. See Null, "Thomas Cranmer's Theology of the Heart," in which he outlines Cranmer's use of the term "heart" in the Prayer Book. In my view, Null attempts too strongly to cast Cranmer in Evangelical terms, zeroing in on the language of the "heart."

practices of common liturgical acts tame the chaotic feelings and emotions *of priest and laity alike*. It is for this reason that Cranmer focuses on the idea of *common* prayer and for *conformity* to a shared devotional language.

Consider as examples the prayers and responses for Morning Prayer. In the 1549 Prayer Book, the text, just like Psalm 51 from which it is taken, is in the first person. The priest says "O Lord, open thou my lips," to which the people respond, "And my mouth shall show forth thy praise." By the time of the 1552 Prayer Book, however, the singular "my" is altered to "our."[23] Moreover, while Cranmer accepts that people who are "grieved in conscience" may wish to speak to a priest and make a confession Cranmer urges a common (or "general") confession during which all members of the congregation pray together:

> Gone is all attention to the relationship between the individual and his conscience: the focus falls instead on the harmony of social relations. What had become a personal, confidential confession from the worshipper to the priest becomes a public admission made before the entire congregation.... The "satisfaction" of the collective group, not the "quietness" of the inner self, renders the aspiring communicant worthy of admission.[24]

The modern discomfort with "conformity" conceived in terms of bland homogeneity would be unintelligible to Cranmer whose liturgical aims were "to restructure corporate worship so that it is entirely compatible with, as well as conducive to, the practice of personal devotion."[25] This approach to prayer is linked to the shape of the Prayer Book and thus to the reading of Scripture; while people can most certainly read it on their own, when they are gathered for worship, reading the Bible together is the primary task.

Cranmer's Prayer Book is a nascent Anglican approach to Scripture and the embodiment of an Anglican way of reading the Bible. With the Prayer Book, people habitually engage Scripture: prayer, worship, and a lectionary. The call to uniformity therefore should be seen as a call to commonality and community in which the words and language of Scripture shape and inform each liturgical act. The role of the Church, under the authority of Scripture alone, is to be the teacher of Scripture. As I show below, one of these ways can be preaching, but this is not the sole mode by which people learn the faith and engage the Bible.

---

23. See Targoff, *Common Prayer*, 29–35 for more of Cranmer's changes to more corporate language in the Prayer Book.

24. Ibid., 33.

25. Ibid., 35.

There is also an incarnational motif in Cranmer's view of Scripture. As the Church is shaped by the power of Scripture, it conforms to the incarnated Word. Rather than having an undue concern for personal, individualist piety, Cranmer, like Luther, sees the inherent pridefulness of a will turned inward. The Continental Reformers were highly influential on Cranmer. His more Zwinglian understanding of the Eucharist later in life, as well as his equally Zwinglian iconoclastic fervor under his archbishopric, indicate some affinities with a Swiss version of reform thought.[26] However, Cranmer's distinguishing characteristic is the use of corporate language and the development of the Prayer Book as the constitutive element of this corporality. And the Prayer Book itself was generative of debates and controversies in subsequent centuries. Cranmer, therefore, cannot be seen as the "inventor" of the Anglican vision of Scripture, but his vision is an important step along the way.

An important theme that is suggested by this shaping of the Church by the power of Scripture is that the Church is *under the judgment of Scripture*. That is to say, while the Church does not always faithfully say what the Bible says, this is nonetheless her calling. And when she fails, the Bible as the Word of God is the judge. This is what pre-eminently makes the Church of England a "Protestant" Church right from its inception.

When Queen Elizabeth ascended the throne of her Roman Catholic half-sister Mary, she once again brought the country into firm Protestant territory. Out of the terrors of Queen Mary arose a new group (or, rather, groups) of individuals who were eventually called "Puritans," but who went under other names such as "Vestiarians" and "Disciplinarians." This newly-emerging party tended to view the sufficiency and perspicacity of Scripture in a way that vitiated against "externals," such as the use of the Prayer Book and the episcopacy. They regarded these not only as unnecessary but as indicative of remaining latent "papist" tendencies within the Church of England. Queen Elizabeth and the theologians of her time had to find a way to navigate between a Cranmerian approach and the challenges of the Puritans.

The rather standard account of the so-called "Elizabethan settlement" of 1559, however, is problematic. It is usually seen as a "middle way" that encouraged comprehensiveness and moderation.[27] Rather, the intent was for a true *Ecclesia Anglicana*, formulated to meet the unique character of the English people and political situation. The more accurate version of the

---

26. Bromiley, *Thomas Cranmer, Theologian*, 69–70.

27. This is the view of many. E.g., Dawley argues that "the unique and creative feature of the Elizabethan settlement proved to be its comprehensiveness" (Dawley, *John Whitgift and the Reformation*, 47–48).

so-named *via media* is a path of careful navigation between what Elizabeth and her advisors viewed as *Protestant* extremes. Whereas the old enemies were Continental Protestants and Roman Catholics, the new battle was between Puritans and the Established Church of England.[28] In terms of a strict accounting of theological propositions, "'Puritans' and 'Anglicans' appeared difficult to distinguish theologically."[29] After all, Puritans were not originally a separatist sect in England but were full members of the Church of England. Peter Lake shows that the "struggle [between established Anglicans and the Puritan party] was conducted within what amounted to a formal doctrinal consensus between the two sides."[30] It was not Calvin as a thinker who threatened the Church under Elizabeth but the political and ecclesial agitations for reform that some of his followers so strongly urged. And all of these emerged out of competing visions of reading Scripture.

The following offers an account of Puritan thought and Whitgift's response to it within the context of this dimension of an ecclesial reading of the Bible. I consider the two *Admonitions*, written by John Field and Thomas Wilcox (first *Admonition*) and the great Puritan Thomas Cartwright (*A Second Admonition to Parliament*), to which is also attached *A View of Popishe Abuses*, also written by Field. I focus only on those which pertain to these Puritans' reading of Scripture and some secondary concerns that arise from such a reading.

The central Puritan argument is that the Church must follow Scripture in such a way that any practice not directly supported by reference to the Bible must be *ipso facto* eschewed. The options, for them, are very clear: "Either must we have right ministerie of God, & a right government of his church, according to the scriptures sette up (bothe whiche we lack [in the Church of England] or else there can be no right religion."[31] The Church of England is the true Church or it is not, and the only judge is Scripture, construed in a particularly Puritan way. The *true* church is an invisible one, the Church of the elect of God, whose assurance of salvation leads to the

---

28. The view that Anglicanism can be seen in terms of a *via media* between extremes is ably challenged by Dewey D. Wallace Jr.'s reassessment of the so-called Anglican *via media* in "Via Media?" The work of Richard Hooker, which was much more Calvinist and in close *theological* agreement with Puritans, but differed with regard to ecclesial governance. And, as Lake suggests, "Ultimately these divergent interpretations were grounded on fundamentally different premises about the nature of church government, premises which were presented as different readings of scripture" (Lake and Dowling, "Presbyterianism," 209). Later Anglicans who urged a *via media* would be uncomfortable with how Calvinist Whitgift and Hooker were.

29. Wallace, "Via Media?," 4.

30. Lake, *Anglicans and Puritans?*, 25.

31. Frere and Douglas, *Puritan Manifestoes*, 6.

practice of good works. Or, to put it in terms that correspond with spiritualist traditions, the true Church is "spiritual." Thus, there is not one visible Church but a series of small communities of believing churches of the elect, or even sub-groups within such local churches. *Already worked into their ecclesiology is a theology of a visibly divided Church.* Oneness or catholicity is imperceptible by any external, physical signifiers. For Puritans concerned about the "papist" threat to England, such external practices are often themselves indicative of a false church.

Establishment theologians rejected such a form of ecclesiology that saw no inherent worth in the visible, external practices of the Anglican system. For Whitgift, these external practices, along with word and sacrament, draw the elect to God.[32] In other words, the Church is, in Augustinian parlance, a *corpus permixtum*, a mixed body of the elect and reprobate.[33] While one cannot fully know who is a member of the elect, the practices of the common life of the Church, shaped by the Prayer Book, work toward bringing the elect to God. Politically, this means no formal distinction between the Church and the commonwealth,[34] but the theological impetus for this is an ecclesiology that conceives of the *commonality* of church life. Peter Lake points out that part of the reason for this is Whitgift's "dour Calvinism," which regards human nature so "riven with sin to cast doubt on the effectiveness of any popular government."[35] Cartwright's typically Puritan suggestion that the "good men" of the congregation can democratically comprise ecclesial governance goes against this view.

In the *Admonitions*, Field, Wilcox, and Cartwright have essentially two complaints that relate to the Bible and ecclesiology, both of which are closely linked to their anti-Catholicism. First, their view is that the Church of England, while having made some motions toward becoming a truly reformed church, falls short as a result of "popish remnants both in ceremonies and regiment."[36] The second concern has to do with the "reading ministry" of Scripture, to which I attend later. The prime motivator for their worries, perhaps rightly in light of their recent history with Queen Mary, is fear of a return to romanist heresy, the "religion of the Anti-Christ." The authors consider the use of vestments and other such shared practices with Roman Catholics as those which "come from the Pope, as oute of the Troian horses

---

32. Lake, *Anglicans and Puritans?*, 50
33. See, e.g., Augustine, *On Christian Doctrine*, §XXXII
34. Lake, *Anglicans and Puritans?*, 50.
35. Ibid., 61.
36. Frere and Douglas, *Puritan Manifestoes*, 8.

bellye, to the destruction of God's kingdome."[37] At fault, and the central aim of their criticism, is the Prayer Book, "an imperfecte book, culled & picked out of that popishe dunghill the Masse booke full of all abhominations."[38] They reject the continuation of such liturgical movements as celebrating saints' days, the "jewish" practice of the churching of women, and kneeling during communion. This relates to Scripture for the simple reason, in the eyes of the Puritans, that none of these practices are to be found in the Bible's literal depiction of the early Christian Church. The Puritan form of primitivism and repristination seeks to return the Church to a form that is explicitly endorsed by Scriptural injunction, or at least one that can be discerned from the New Testament Church. Anything else is the false Church of Antichrist.

John Whitgift, who eventually became Archbishop of Canterbury in 1583, responded to the charges made in the *Admonitions*.[39] He made not only *one* reply, but two, as Cartwright very quickly published his own rejoinder to Whitgift, to which Whitgift also responded.[40] While not a systematic theologian in the mode of Richard Hooker, "perhaps more than any other he made possible the growth of the distinctive ethos of Anglicanism."[41] In Whitgift's view, "the scripture is most untolerably abused, and unlearnedly applied"[42] by the writers of the *Admonitions*. A defining matter for Whitgift is that of ecclesial (and, to a lesser extent, social) order, and he quotes Continental reformers such as Zwingi to show that the discord Puritans were sowing threatens the peace of the Church.[43] He in turn shows that Puritans risk betraying Anabaptist tendencies. There are for Whitgift numerous ecclesial practices that contribute to the edification of the people and are things indifferent, devised for the sake of the peace and good order of the commonwealth and of the Church. In his view, it is absurd to oppose something based on the absence of express endorsement in Scripture:

> Such and such things were not in the apostles' time; *ergo*, they ought not to be now. Which kind of argument is very deceitful,

---

37. Ibid., 32.
38. Ibid., 21.
39. Strype, *The Life and Acts of John Whitgift*, 1:54–79.
40. The first is Whitgift, *An Answere to a Certain Libel Intituled* and the second, rather awkwardly, Whitgift, *The Defense of the Answere to the Admonition Against the Reply of TC*. I cite from Whitgift, *The Works of John Whitgift* in which both Whitgift's and Cartwright's rejoinders are interwoven.
41. Dawley, *John Whitgift and the Reformation*, 165.
42. Whitgift, *Works*, 1:58.
43. Ibid., 1:125–39.

and the mother and well-spring of many old and new schisms; of old, as of them that called themselves *Apostolicos*, and of the Aërians; of new, as of the anabaptists, who, considering neither the diversity of times concerning the external ecclesiastical policy, nor the true liberty of the christian religion in extern rites ... have boldly enterprised to stir up many and heinous errors.[44]

The Bible, therefore, cannot be a rule book for a single ecclesiastical system. The vicissitudes of history provide new contexts in which the Church must live out its calling. The resemblance of certain practices to Roman Catholicism does not immediately disqualify their use. Whitgift, with great rhetorical flourish, suggests that the Puritans, in arguing against anything remotely "popish," err in a manner similar to that of the Arians of the fourth century:

> The self-same reasons moved the Aërians to forsake the order of the church and to command their disciples to do the contrary of that that the church did. We borrow good laws of the gentiles; and we use the churches, bells, pulpits, and many other things used of papists, &c.[45]

Whitgift's construal maintains a respect for tradition, not for its own sake, but for the purpose of maintaining the order of service that a radical liturgical transformation would disrupt, insofar as Scripture is not opposed. He also does not want to conceive of a Church unconnected with its history as the people and community of God. If there are aspects of the Church that have existed for centuries, then barring any scriptural injunction against them, they are *a fortiori* to be commended.

Whitgift wrote in a highly charged atmosphere in which his rhetorical skill and incisive turn of phrase, alongside his highly effectual administrative abilities, essentially resulted in him "winning" the battle, according to Dawley.[46] His considerable contribution to an Anglican biblical hermeneutic is the continuity and extension of Cranmer's notion of the Church in which the Bible is read communally. Reading Scripture as individuals is not in opposition to the claims of the Church, but as a reflection on Church teaching. He construes the liturgical shape of Church practice not only as a means to maintain order and minimize individualist thinking: these liturgical, external practices within the *corpus permixtum*, and the *one, visible* body, are what draw the elect to God. The Bible is recited within a normative series of habits that discipline the laity. Attempts to repristinate the Church

---

44. Ibid., 1:60–61.
45. Ibid., 1:66–67.
46. Dawley, *John Whitgift and the Reformation*, 186–87.

based on ideas of what the early Church did generate an unstable state of affairs since the shape of this "primitive" community is unclear.

Whitgift's contributions to an Anglican vision of Scripture are not always explicitly laid out in his writings. Peter Lake argues that Richard Hooker is the grand synthesizer of the numerous and disparate ideas of Cranmer, Whitgift, and others. Lake makes the controversial claim that Hooker *invented* Anglicanism in his *Laws of Ecclesiastical Polity*.[47] The magnitude and scope of Hooker's *Laws* preclude anything other than a brief examination of his innovative approach here. I briefly outline how Hooker addresses the problem of ritual prescribed by the Church of England, particularly those not explicitly described in Scripture. I illustrate his continuity with Whitgift and Cranmer's vision of reading the Bible, and that engaging in common liturgical practices forms and shapes the inner life of believers.

There are several practices loathed by the authors of the *Admonitions* that are not explicitly outlined in the Bible, such as kneeling, the use of the cross, and vestments. Hooker takes a measured and careful position in favor of conformity. It is noteworthy that Hooker rejects the inherently antagonistic argument that requires the Church to define itself over-against the practices of Rome:

> That extreme dissimilitude which they urge upon us, is now commended as our best and safest policie. . . . The ground of which politique position is, that *Evils must be cured by their contraries*, and therefore the cure of the Church infected with the poyson of Antichristianitie must be done by that which is therunto as contrary as may be.[48]

Hooker is aware that there is more than a strict biblicism occurring here—Puritans surely knew that the Bible said nothing of numerous practices in which both the Church of England and the non-Conformists engaged. Hooker's opponents, rather, reject the notion that external practices common to the Established Church and the Roman Catholic Church have any efficacy on the inner spiritual life of the individual. This is a denial of the importance of a *communal* participation of ecclesial activities.

I would prefer to ameliorate the image of Hooker as one who merely *reasons* his way through a defense of the Church, by appending the concept of *wisdom*. Order in the Church is achieved only by a wise recourse to a careful discernment of those practices that are not directly laid out in Scripture, so as to decide what is of benefit to the whole, not merely to the individual. With respect to any good law, says Hooker, "A law therefore generally taken,

---

47. Lake, *Anglicans and Puritans?*, 227.
48. Hooker, *Laws*, IV.vii.viii, 298.

is a directive rule unto goodness of operation. The rule of divine operation outward, is the definitive appointment of God's owne wisedom set down within himself. The rule of naturall agents that worke by simple necessity, is the determination of the wisedom of God."[49] When searching the Scriptures, then, it is wisdom that directs the reader:

> Whereas they allege *the wisedom* doth teach *every good way*; and have thereupon inferred, that no way is good in any kind of action, unless wisedom do by scripture leade unto it: see they not plainely how they restraine the manifold wayes which wisedom hath to teach men by, unto one only way of teaching, which is by scripture? The bounds of wisedom are large, and within them much is contayned. Wisedom was *Adams* instructor in Paradise: wisdom indued the fathers, who lived before the law ... by the wisedome of the law of God, *David* attayned to excell others in understanding; and *Salomon* likewise to excell *David* by the selfe same wisedom of God.[50]

Hooker's use of wisdom shows more than just a concept of reasoned prudence, but a trust that, just as the Holy Spirit (which I suggest is linked to his use of wisdom in this passage) guides biblical characters, he also guides those who read the Bible. This is not to deny Hooker's appeal to the "light of reason" given to people, but I suggest that this rationality has not yet been through the grist of Cartesian epistemological doubt, which searches for certainty along the lines of a geometric proof. Hooker urges a reasoned reading of Scripture that is to be led by the wisdom of God.

Hooker contends that the carefully preserved ancient practices in the Church are not suffused with superstition. Maintaining an awareness of the distinction between the inward and outward dichotomy emerging from the Puritan preference for the former, he argues that

> There is an inward reasonable, and there is a sollemne outward serviceable worship belonginge unto God. Of the former kind are all manner of vertuous duties that each man in reason and conscience to Godward oweth.... It is the later of these two whereupon our present question groweth.[51]

The principle that guides Hooker's acceptance of certain practices is their "conveniencie and fittnes, in regarde of the use for which they should

---

49. Ibid., I.i.viii, 84.
50. Ibid., II.i.iv, 147.
51. Ibid., V.iv.iii, 31.

serve."[52] Hooker avers that, "that which inwardlie each man should be, the Church outwardlie ought to testifie. And therefore the duties of our religion which are seene must be such as that affection which is unseen ought to be."[53] By "conforming" to these outward acts, the inner life of the believer comes to take on the shape of this outward behavior, a concept that coheres with Targoff's thesis regarding the common life of the Church. More than mere *adiaphora* to be decided by the Queen, outward ceremony "was essential to the worship of God because it held so much significance for the Christian in his [outward] devotion."[54]

Starting with Cranmer, developed by Whitgift, and synthesized by Hooker, this concept of an ecclesial reading of Scripture therefore sheds light on an Anglican biblical hermeneutic. The extent to which the Bible was translated into English illustrates the belief that *all* should have access to Holy Scripture. Yet, from the beginning, Anglican thinkers worked against an individualistic view of the faith in which Scripture has to do with the inner life and personal edification, but a common, ecclesial spiritual formation. These ideas became embodied in the Prayer Book as a kind of guide to this spiritual formation.

THE CANON OF SCRIPTURE: THE POWER OF THE WORD READ AND SPOKEN

It is a traditional doctrine that both the Old and the New Testament comprise the *one* word of God. This section outlines the ramification of this doctrine in Anglican practice, which has to do not just with the *canonicity* of the specific books, but with the sufficiency of these books *in themselves* as the word of God.

A central tenet bearing on the reading of Scripture in the Prayer Book is Article 6 of the Articles of Religion:

> Holy Scripture containeth all things necessary to salvation. . . . In the name of the Holy Scripture we do understand those canonical Books of the Old and New Testament, of whose authority was never any doubt in the Church.

It is neither the Church nor its traditions that comprise faith, but the Scriptures, which, it should be noted, are explicitly defined as "those canonical Books of the Old and New Testament." The Article continues to name

52. Ibid., V.vi.i, 33.
53. Ibid., V.i.ii, 33.
54. Lane, "Before Hooker," 347.

precisely which books are canonical. Cranmer's vision of Anglicanism was therefore profoundly influenced by an appreciation of Scripture:

> The new Anglican piety was thoroughly Biblical. In this context *offices, sacrament, and the sermon all embodied the living Word of God*. The unique feature of the English Reformation at this point, moreover, is that Bible and Church were not set one against the other.... This firm grasp upon the centrality of the Scriptures within the life of the Church brought to Anglicanism its precious freedom from the restraints of sixteenth-century confessional dogma.[55]

Because the Bible, comprising equally the Old and New Testaments, is the Word of God, and since its reading is deeply connected to the Church itself, the Bible cannot be decoupled from ecclesial offices and sacraments, nor especially from preaching. It is this latter concept that illustrates the canonicity of Scripture in a distinctly Anglican light. A major agitation of Puritans was the lack of frequent preaching in the Church of England. In the Puritan view, the Prayer Book errs by encouraging a liturgical service that merely urges a "bare reading" of Scripture without need for explication. For the Puritans, "the word of God" means more than Scripture: "by the word of God, it is an offyce of preaching, they [the supporters of the Established Church] make it an offyce of reading.... [But] reading is not feeding, but it is an evil as playing upon a stage, and worse too."[56] What then is meant by the "word of God," therefore, is in dispute. Unlike Cranmer's image of ingesting Scripture by reading, no longer is this sufficient for the believer to be "fed."

A defining aspect of Puritan worship was a rigorous explication of Scripture, influenced by Ramism, as handed down by the French philosopher-logician Pierre de la Ramée.[57] The basic concept of Ramism was "arranging concepts in such a fashion as to make them understandable and memorable."[58] With respect to preaching, the result is the division and subdivision of concepts related to the appointed text. This presents a close reading of the passage, out of which the preacher extracts essential principles, laid out in an easily organized way. More than just a highly methodical approach to the Biblical text, the aim was to so explicate it that each hearer fully understands the text's meaning. For the Puritans, the "bare" reading of Scripture was entirely insufficient. This Ramist approach to preaching "provided the theoretical framework by which the preacher could impart

55. Dawley, *John Whitgift and the Reformation*, 118, emphasis mine.
56. Frere and Douglas, *Puritan Manifestoes*, 22.
57. See Sprunger, "John Yates of Norfolk," and McKim, "Functions of Ramism."
58. McKim, "Functions of Ramism," 504.

information as well as instruct and correct the lives of the hearers."[59] The bare reading was thus insufficient in allowing the text to be effective without a preacher.

Puritans were also opposed to how the Prayer Book liturgy used the words of Scripture as the basis for congregational prayer. For instance, the *Admonition* refers to the churching of women after childbirth when the mother recites Psalm 116 as if it were her own prayer. For the Puritan, this is "abusing the psalm to her,"[60] as if what was said by the psalmist thousands of years earlier can somehow be also said by a woman today. Many prayers in the Book of Common Prayer work in a similar fashion: the *Nunc Dimittis* comes from Luke 2, not to mention that the entire Book of Psalms is placed in the Prayer Book, organized for daily reading. In addition, many of the prayers that were penned by Cranmer were saturated with scriptural imagery.[61] For the Puritans, this saying of the Psalms, often antiphonally, is a misrepresentation of the text in which "they tosse the Psalms in most places like tennis balles."[62] If a biblical prayer were to be used verbatim, the Lord's Prayer would be acceptable since its form was explicitly endorsed by Jesus. Scripture must be properly located in its historical context and not used in such a way that the congregation takes on the hypocritical "role" of the biblical character. Puritan prayer urges spontaneity, and utterances that are "from the heart." For Puritan sympathizers,

> the 'perfect Gift' of God lies in the unpremeditated devotional voice, the 'freedom of speech' that each individual ought by right to possess. To worship according to the 'outward dictates of men' instead of the inward 'sanctifying spirit' means to prefer humanly authored texts to divine ordination—to commit the act of idolatry.[63]

Whitgift defends this concept of a "reading ministry," or the "bare reading" of Scripture. The theological principles that underlie this aspect of Anglicanism reveal a radical discontinuity between Puritan and Conformist perspectives on the Bible. For Whitgift, Cartwright's argument that a reading ministry is insufficient itself belies a "popish" inclination, for it implies

---

59. Ibid., 511–12.

60. Frere and Douglas, *Puritan Manifestoes*, 21.

61. Cranmer's arrangement of the Psalms in this manner moved the task of performing the daily offices by priests to the common layperson. The Prayer Book was to be "'common,' but only in the sense that the priest and people attended to the same aspects of the liturgy together" (Maltby, *Prayer Book and People*, 41).

62. Frere and Douglas, *Puritan Manifestoes*, 29.

63. Targoff, *Common Prayer*, 37.

that there is an obscurity to the reading of Scripture that must be removed by preaching:

> What is this else but together with the papists to condemn the scriptures of obscurity, as though all things necessary to salvation were not plainly and clearly expressed in them? ... I grant you that every man understandeth them not; for it is the Spirit of God that openeth the heart of man both to understand the scriptures read and preached.[64]

By no means does Whitgift deny the importance of preaching but rather considers it as ancillary to the hearing of Scripture. At stake for him was the very power of the words of Scripture themselves to convert. In other words, *the reading of Scripture is itself an act of preaching.* Puritan demands for textual explication as part of the reading of the Word of God in order to guarantee biblical effectiveness denigrates Scripture's own inherent canonical power as the Word of God. To make preaching the *sine qua non* of the proper use of the Bible is to add to the power of God's word, as the "papist" does:

> Do you think that there cometh no more knowledge or profit by reading the scriptures than doth by "beholding of God's creatures?" Then let us have images again, that they may be laymen's books, as the papists call them; no doubt attributing as much to the external and visible creatures as they did to the reading of the eternal word of God; wherein you join with them, for anything that I yet see.[65]

Whitgift's theological point is a distinctive position in early Anglicanism, which is that God's Spirit alone speaks through the words of Scripture. A sermon can no doubt mediate this utterance of the Spirit but to demand that the sermon serve as the singular medium of the Spirit's power is to denigrate the power of God's word.

Part of what contributes to Whitgift's rather "passive" view of God's work in the reading of the Bible is his Calvinism. Whatever means God deploys are God's prerogative. Quoting 1 Cor 3:6, Whitgift avers that,

> St. Paul saith: "I have planted: Apollos watered; but God gave the increase;" *ergo*, "there is no salvation without preaching;" ... St. Paul there declareth that the preaching of the word is not effectual, except God give the increase, that we ought not to attribute our salvation to the ministers of the word, but only to God. He

---

64. Whitgift, *Works*, 3:37.
65. Ibid., 3:32.

makes no comparison betwixt reading and preaching; neither is there anything there spoken . . . which may not be applied to attentive and diligent reading. . . . It may be that God doth not only work faith by reading; but it is commonly so . . . for God worketh by both.[66]

Whitgift also mistrusts the spontaneous prayers of the preacher to which the people were expected to say "amen." In other words, Puritans are "insisting that the minister ought to serve as 'the mouth of the people' . . . [which] Cranmer and his fellow liturgists sought to avoid."[67] To suppose that there must be more required than the canonical Scriptures, opposes the idea of a communal reading of Scripture and of praying in which there is no distinction between the people and the priest. In Whitgift's view, to locate the minister as the focus of preaching and praying is not in line with a reformed church but a reversion to "papist" sensibilities in which the priest is distinct from public worship. Like the Roman Catholics, the words of the preacher, in Whitgift's construal of Puritanism, take on equal footing with the Bible. Instead, the Prayer Book, steeped in biblical language, and using set prayers, ensures that the worship of the congregation is independent of the whims of the preacher. Thus, the words of the Bible are eminently more trustworthy for the use of prayers than human spontaneity.

Hooker's writings agree with Whitgift on this point: "The Church as a wittnesse preacheth his meere revealed truth by *reading* publiquely the sacred scripture. So that a seconde kind of preaching is the readinge of holie writ."[68] Hooker uses the example of the Jews, who read Scripture in the midst of the community, arguing that there is no Old Testament evidence for sermons. In Hooker's view, the Puritans only consider the reading of Scripture as a mere prelude to the sermon:

> For with us the readinge of scripture in the Church is a parte of our Church litourgie, a speciall portion of the service which we doe to God, and not an exercise to spend the time, when one doth waite for an others comminge, till the assemblie of them that shall afterwardes worship him be complete. Wherefore the forme of our public service is not voluntarie, so neither are the partes thereof left uncertaine, but they are all set down in such order . . . as hath in the wisdome of the Church seemed best to

---

66. Ibid., 3:35.
67. Targoff, *Common Prayer*, 40.
68. Hooker, *Laws*, V.xix.i, 67.

concurre . . . with the generall purpose which we have to glorifie God.[69]

Clearly, for Hooker, "we therefore have no *word of God* but the Scripture."[70]

Hooker disregards Ramist categories, but considers Scripture in terms of the "end" to which it is oriented, that is salvation.[71] But, despite his opposition to Puritan Calvinism, Hooker firmly maintains a Reformed outlook with respect to Scripture, namely, that the Bible is essential to knowledge of God apart from mere reason. Moreover, the Church is under its authority, and the Bible does not receive its authentication from the Church; the work of the Holy Spirit is essential to saving faith, and there is a place for reason aided by grace.[72] Where Hooker differs from many of his Puritan opponents is that he does not regard Scripture as self-authenticating merely in terms of the text, apart from the Holy Spirit. While Scripture is sufficient with regard to the end for which it was devised, "when of things necessarie the verie chiefest is to know what bookes wee are bound to esteeme holie, which poynt is confest impossible for the scripture it selfe to teach."[73] But the power of the word of God is not found by some first principle by which Scripture can be judged. Rather Hooker affirms the mystery of the faith:

> Wee are not therefore ashamed of the gospell of our Lord Jesus Christ because miscreants in scorne have upbraided us, that the highest point of our wisdom is *Believe*. That which is true and neither can be discerned by sense, nor concluded by meere naturall principles, must have principles of revealed truth whereupon to build it selfe, and an habit of faith in us wherewith principles of that kind are apprehended. The mysteries of our religion are above the reach of our understanding, above discorse of mans reason, above all that any creature can comprehend. Therefore the first thinge required of him which standeth for admission into Christes familie is beliefe.[74]

Hooker avoids reducing Scripture to a book of moral and dogmatic propositions; rather, he is a careful thinker:

> Hooker realized clearly and yet critically that our understanding of even basic principles is subject to change . . . He knew at first

---

69. Ibid., V.xix.v, 71.
70. Ibid., V.xxi.ii, 84.
71. Lake, *Anglicans and Puritans?*, 227.
72. Voak, "Richard Hooker," 121–26.
73. Hooker, *Laws*, I.xiv.1, 125. See also Voak, "Richard Hooker," 127–28.
74. Hooker, *Laws*, V.lxiii.i, 290.

hand that the study of Scripture is an ongoing process. His own attempts to understand biblical revelation are informed by sympathetic acquaintance with previous efforts in many periods, including his own. Some of his harshest words are for those who would throw away centuries of devout and learned hermeneutics in order to insist arrogantly on the exclusive and obvious truth of their own party's reading.[75]

In his own way, Hooker rejects the search for absolute certainty, the quest that ends in the *crise pyrrhonienne*. Instead he argues for "habits of faith" that alone nourish belief. These shared practices are closely connected to Scripture and shape the life of the community. There is no infallible evidence for Scripture's veracity, apart from those reasons given in the context of belief, "the highest point of our wisdom." What makes Hooker distinct is that his "intent was to be a faithful interpreter of the Reformation principle of *sola scriptura* in a historical and polemical context very different from the early sixteenth-century arguments between Protestant reformers and Roman Catholic apologists."[76] When Hooker speaks of reason, the term is often perceived in categories that accord with Enlightenment perspectives that see reason as a purely human faculty. However, if instead "Hooker refused to see the internal testimony of the Spirit in opposition to reason," then we can discern a much grander synthesis in his unique description of Anglicanism.[77] A bifurcation between rationalism and affective modes of thought is a false dichotomy in Hooker's way of thinking.

Therefore, regarding the theme of the canon of Scripture, I present Whitgift and Hooker not just as proponents of the unity of the two testaments, Rather, they argue that all the words of Scripture have their own power working through a "reading ministry." Preaching is only one way for that the Bible to be properly heard. Faith, the summit of wisdom, calls the reader to remain in the text without seeking external modes of authentication. Puritan opponents saw the Word of God in need of supplementary apparatus that curtail the power of a reading ministry, and thus also that of the Bible as canon.

A CHRISTOLOGICAL READING OF SCRIPTURE

As with a canonical reading of the Bible, the concept of a christologically permeated text is far from innovative, historically speaking. None of the

---

75. McGrade, "Richard Hooker," 423.
76. Ingalls, "Richard Hooker" 353.
77. Ibid., 365.

combatants in early Anglicanism found it problematic, for instance, to interpret Isa 53 christologically. My intent in this section is to bring together the notion of an ecclesial reading of the Bible with the fact that both the Old and New Testaments comprise the *one* Word of God because of a christological hermeneutic of Scripture.

In the Anglican view, worship has a *shape*, which itself molds the worshipper into the image of Christ; there is therefore very little in early Anglicanism that is governed specifically by anything overtly confessional: "Other churches may be anchored in confessional documents, or doctrinal formularies, or a systematically articulated theology, or the pronouncements of magisterial authorities. . . . The Anglican anchor is worship, whereby *worship* is meant the Book of Common Prayer."[78] Whereas Lutherans had the *Augsburg Confession*, or Puritans the *Heidelberg Catechism*, Cranmer assembled the Prayer Book under the governance of Scripture, which itself shapes the Church to the form of Christ. There is no centrally formulated creed unique to the Anglican Church, notwithstanding the Thirty-Nine Articles, which do not comprise a creed as such.[79] This does not suggest an absence of doctrine, but Anglicanism can be regarded in its uniqueness not by specific doctrinal propositions, but by an *ethos*. Since Christ is everywhere in Scripture, then all prayers and practices are shaped by the same Scripture. The specific impact this vision has can be seen implicitly. If Christ's work in the Church has more than a merely interior effect on an individual believer, then Christ must especially impact external worship.

As an example, consider a sermon by a contemporary of Whitgift and Hooker, Lancelot Andrewes (1555–1626), called "A Summary View of the Government both of the Old and New Testament." Andrewes focuses on various Old Testament figures as being theologically descriptive of proper Church polity. Seeing Israel, perhaps anachronistically, as a "commonwealth,"[80] Andrewes traces the pattern of religious and civil government in Israel from the time of Moses and Aaron to that of the kings of Israel to the time of captivity under Nehemiah. Thus, for example, he can list the hierarchical form of the "Church" of Israel under Aaron as follows:

    α. Aaron was the high priest

---

78. Hefling and Shattuck, "Introduction," 3.

79. It is important to note that historic creeds such as the Apostles' Creed *do* function quite crucially in the liturgy, and therefore, the Church of England is indeed "creedal."

80. See, e.g., Andrewes, "A Summary View," 339.

> β. under him Eleazar; who, as he had his peculiar charge to look unto, so he was generally to rule both Ithamar's jurisdiction and his own;
>
> γ. under him Ithamar, over two families;
>
> δ. under him three prelates;
>
> ε. under each of them, their several chief fathers … as they were termed [in] Exod. vi. 25; under Elizaphan four, under Eliasaph two, under Zuriel two, Numb. iii. 18 &c.;
>
> ζ. under these, the several persons of their kindreds.
>
> There is worth here noting that albeit it be granted that Aaron was the type of Christ, and so we forbear to take any argument from him; yet Eleazar, who was no type, nor ever so deemed by any writer, will serve sufficiently to shew such superiority as is pleaded for; that is, a personal jurisdiction in one man resiant over the heads or rulers of divers charges.[81]

Andrewes views the Israelite theological/political structure as an exemplary form of Church government that the Church of England is to continue. It is rooted in Aaron as a "type" of Christ. He shows that the New Testament does not deviate from this pattern, calling for the office of Apostle, prophet, evangelist, bishop, doctor, and diaconus.[82] In response to the Puritan practice of seeing the Old Testament as typifying Christ in a merely spiritual (meaning non-material or external) manner, the Established Church appeals to the episcopal structure of the Church. Similarly, Puritans saw their presbyterian or congregationalist model equally biblical. Both ecclesial perspectives arise out of how the Bible was interpreted, and therefore it is essential to show the above distinctions between these competing hermeneutical options.

In addition, however, and central to this christological hermeneutic, is an account of the dual referent for the term "word of God," which is also part of the liturgical phraseology with respect to Scripture in the Prayer Book. The Word, the λογοσ, or *verbum* from John 1, is a central christological theme, closely connected to Scripture since at least the time of Origen. That is, the Incarnation of the Word, the second person of the Trinity, funds a view of the Bible as God's "speech" to humanity as a recapitulation of what Mihai Niculescu calls the "sojourning" of the Logos:

> Unlike modern hermeneutics, Origen does not construe the advent of the biblical Logos according to the existential historicity

---

81. Ibid., 341–42.
82. Ibid., 351.

of the human receptor, but rather according to the immemorial historicity of the Logos Himself. The Logos claims or elects the receptor by biblically addressing him or rather, He is the advent of a biblical address, which claims the receptor as an immemorially called addressee.... Biblical figures and images speak to the reader morally and physically (prophetically) only insofar as the Logos spells them out historically to us or, insofar as the Logos addresses us figuratively and iconically in the Bible as the Bible.[83]

Thus, Christ, as the Word, "speaks" the Scripture, not only in a wooden "dictation" model but as a constant presence within the text. The Logos is therefore mediated textually, but he also shapes and governs this mediation. There is a kind of sacramentality in the engagement of Scripture. Christ, the Logos himself, is participative of this mediation.

In my analysis of Isaiah commentaries, it is therefore important to consider to what extent this christological hermeneutic is connected to the Incarnation of the Son in history. In other words, to what extent is the word, or text, related to or participates in the "Word," the Logos?

THE OLD TESTAMENT AND ISAIAH IN THE PRAYER BOOK

It is helpful to end this chapter with some useful illustrations of how the Prayer Book uses the Old Testament and Isaiah to bring to life this discussion of an Anglican reading of the Bible. Given what has been outlined thus far, it goes without saying that the Prayer Book enjoins reading the Old Testament as frequently as the New. The Psalms, most of all, are such an important part of the Prayer Book that Coverdale's translation of them appears as a separate section of the text, and in fact the Psalms remain in that format in all English updated forms of the Prayer Book to this day. Their arrangement is such that the reader prays a Psalm or a portion of a Psalm in the morning and evening. Just as the Psalms serve as the "prayer book" of Israel, so too are they for the Church. This is not only for ecclesial reasons, but because the Psalms contain the figure of Christ within them. They do not serve a merely predictive function of, for instance, Christ's cry of dereliction (Psalm 22). Rather, Christ functions as the agent who participates in the act of prayer, and therefore all who are members of his body are to pray this way.

It is also significant that the Table of Lessons for daily prayer always includes a reading from each of the Old and New Testaments. The intent

---

83. Niculescu, *The Spell of the Logos*, 55.

of the lectionary is to set up a schedule by which all of the Old Testament is read once a year and the New twice a year. This is more than intending an "ordered" approach to the Bible, but an aim to submit the Church to a scriptural pattern, which is itself shaped by Christ as the incarnated Word of God. In what follows, I look briefly at the organization of the lectionary in terms of a christologically shaped pattern, including Isaiah's place within this pattern, after which I consider the use of Isaiah in the liturgy proper.

Isaiah plays a particularly important role in the liturgy of holy days. There is, of course, the traditional use of Isa 9 on Christmas day, and of Isa 52:13–53 at the beginning of Passion Week (Palm Sunday), as well as for the evening prayer of Good Friday. From the first Sunday in Advent and for three Sundays after Epiphany, a chapter from Isaiah is appointed to be read both at Matins and Evensong. The first Sunday of Advent has a reading from Isa 1, which says, "Heare the worde of the LORDE ye tyrauntes of Sodom: and herken vnto the lawe of oure God, thou people of Gomorra," which is hardly a proclamation of Christmas cheer.[84] Yet, further in the chapter is written, "Though youre synnes be as read [sic] as scarlet, shal they not be whyter then snowe? And though they were like purple, shall they not be like whyte woll?" (v. 18), which connotes the cleansing of sin by Christ's true sacrifice, rather than the false festivals decried in this chapter. On Trinity Sunday, the lectionary appoints Isa 6, in which there is the thrice-chanted prayer of "holy, holy, holy" by the creatures before the throne. On Whitsunday, Isa 11 points not just to a fulfillment that "Then shal the Gentiles enquere after the rote of Iesse (which shalbe set vp for a token vnto the Gentiles) for his dwellinge shalbe glorious," but also to the mission and hope of the Church.

In addition to these readings of Isaiah appointed for use on Sundays and holy days, the liturgy itself uses Isaiah as part of the prayers and exhortations read in and by the Church. See, for instance, the *Te Deum* (which is also found in the Roman Catholic office): "To thee all Angels cry aloud . . . Holy, Holy, Holy: Lord God of Sabaoth," which refers to Isa 6. On the Monday before Easter, the liturgy lists Isa 63, which speaks on the one hand of the vengeance of God, who comes to "tread down the people in mine anger," and yet "in all their affliction he was afflicted, and the angel of his presence saved them." This was appointed to teach of God as judge to a people who have forgotten him, yet also of God as a savior who redeems.

As with all readings, the liturgy appoints other corresponding passages from the New Testament: a portion of Isa 50 on the Tuesday before Easter, Isa 7:10 on Annunciation day, and Isa 40 for St. John the Baptist day. However, it is important to note that Isaiah does not boast of a particularly

---

84. I use Coverdale's translation, the most common version during Cranmer's time.

more central position in the Prayer Book, but, rather, it is woven into the liturgy as an important part of the canon as the one word of God and bears witness to Christ. Such a hermeneutic does not merely rely upon a concept of prediction, but also of figuration and allusive images that evoke christological concepts. For this reason, Isaiah does not stand on its own but participates in a grand vision of Scripture in which not only Isaiah, but all of the Old Testament and the Bible speak in some way of Christ.

CONCLUSION

This discussion shows that the uniquely Anglican biblical hermeneutic, which I describe in terms developed by Cranmer, Whitgift, and Hooker, can be articulated by using the three categories of ecclesiology, canon, and christology. I show how, while these terms also inform other ecclesial traditions, they describe the landscape of an Anglican vision of Scripture that evoke its distinctiveness. With respect to the Church, a liturgically shaped community reads the Bible for the purpose of a form of "laicization" in which all are called to read the Bible as a *visible* ecclesial community marked by equally visible practices. This vision seeks, therefore, to oppose the centrality of an individualist interpretation, without discouraging personal use. Regarding the canon, while preaching serves an important part of this liturgical shape, it is not the *sine qua non* of proper reading of the Bible, for if the entire Bible comprises the *one* Word of God, then even the "bare" reading is sufficient to enact the words in which the Word, the Logos, recapitulates the Incarnation. Finally, regarding the christological shape of the Bible, the Old and New Testaments are both central in the reading ministry precisely because Christ is the *telos* of the text, governing and upholding it. Just as the Incarnation was a concrete, physical event, Old Testament interpretation is not only to be carried out in "spiritual" terms. As we see exemplified in Andrewes' sermon, it can contribute to an understanding of, for instance, Church polity.

The primary intent of outlining a peculiarly Anglican way of reading Scripture is to maintain a consistent focus on the historic basis of biblical hermeneutics in the Church of England. The categories provide an analytic heuristic for the purpose of comparing nineteenth-century Anglican exegetes with one another and with this biblical vision. Moreover, despite the tectonic shift in exegetical approaches to the Bible by nineteenth century, this uniquely Anglican vision never entirely loses its hold.

2

The Breakdown of Uniformity
Seventeenth- and Eighteenth-Century Competing Intra-Anglican Scriptural Visions

THE ENLIGHTENMENT, CHILLINGWORTH, AND LATITUDINARIANISM: A NEW ERA BEGINS

THE HERMENEUTICAL LEGACY OF Cranmer, Whitgift, and Hooker, out of which emerged a uniquely Anglican way of reading Scripture, did not succeed in placating the complaints of Puritans or those of the growing number of breakaway groups that formed, particularly during and after the English Civil War(s). It is questionable whether the imposition of uniformity was ever successful in England; perhaps its ultimate failure as government policy was the passing of the Act of Toleration in 1689. The execution of Charles I, the Interregnum, and the Glorious Revolution precipitated a renegotiation of the relationship between the Bible, a fractious Church, the canon, and Christ's incarnational presence within the text. This re-evaluation brought the Church of England under the influence of a number of competing hermeneutical visions at a level never seen before. Yet the unique Anglican approach to the Bible was not a mere chimera; it continued to exert a pressure, albeit often muted, in the form of the Prayer Book.

Several scriptural exegetes represent new visions arising out of the crucible of division, providing a comparative context for my discussion of nineteenth-century interpreters. What I refer to as "irenic" readings of the

Bible are orientations to the text that, in an effort to avoid and minimize division, concomitantly minimize theological exegesis, or change the nature of the "religion" to which this theology points.[1] The impact of this approach to Scripture is "theological minimization," whereby *technique, methodology,* and the *textualization* of Scripture become dominant at the expense of deeper theological themes of Church, canon, and christology.

However, this failure was by no means total. John Rogerson argues that the influence of German scholarship on England was slow for geographical and cultural reasons. I suggest, on the other hand, that one of the factors impeding the rise of critical exegesis was the "pressure" of the Book of Common Prayer, and not merely a fear of the German "rationalism," as Rogerson argues, though this was a very real fear.[2] The Cranmerian vision of Scripture continued to exert its power, mitigated as it was, and it continues to do so today.[3]

This chapter focuses on England and hermeneutical changes concomitant with the Enlightenment and its particular relation to ecclesial division, using Isaiah as the focal point. There are numerous historical strands that account for the emergence of this new "age." I give prominence to that of the struggle to make sense of Scripture in the midst of religious conflict. In this sense, I construe the Enlightenment as a *response* to the turmoil and violence of the Thirty Years War and the English Civil War, out of which derive competing theological visions.

It is helpful to begin with the figure of William Chillingworth (1602–44), who represents of new ways of thinking of Scripture originating in

---

1. Legaspi, *The Death of Scripture* offers a very similar argument to that of this project with respect to a rise in an "irenic" reading of Scripture that attempts to treat the Bible as something other than what it is, namely "Scripture," in favor of what Legaspi calls "academic," "moral," or "literary" biblical alternatives. Whereas his treatment primarily focuses on Germany and Michaelis, the parallels between aspects of my argument and his are close. In part, my argument suggests that what happens with more vigor in Germany is the repetition of a process already initiated in England. Legaspi is nonetheless influential on this project as I apply his term—an "irenic" reading of Scripture—in the context of England, rather than Germany.

2. I employ the term "critical" here to denote any mode of reading the text to which is appended "at the expense of," "in distinction from," or "separate from" a theological reading of the text. For instance, philological methods came to be used independent from theological exegesis. With regard to the "fear" of German thinkers, Crowther writes, "because the most famous freethinkers in England encouraged the spread of German literature, the Anglican Church became increasingly suspicious of it" (Crowther, *Church Embattled*, 48–49).

3. Rogerson is right to note the important influence of German Old Testament scholarship. But he also acknowledges that the critical method in fact derived from the English deists, who in turn impacted German innovators such as Reimarus (Rogerson, *Old Testament Criticism in the Nineteenth Century*, 10).

the seventeenth century. Chillingworth is emblematic of a broad tendency toward doctrinal "minimization." This tendency is the direct result of the violent upheavals of seventeenth-century England, many of which were the result of theological conflict. This was the era out of which emerged deism and latitudinarianism. Chillingworth and his colleagues at the Great Tew initiated a new perspective on religion that produced exegetes like Richard Stafford and William Day, whom I consider below, in this "project" of the minimization of theological exegesis.[4] The rise of what is often called latitudinarianism corresponds to the idea of natural religion in a strong form, whose purpose was to avoid the perceived problems of theological or "dogmatic" readings that constrain the individual appropriation of Scripture. With the success of Newtonian science, for instance, religion came to be cast in a new way. There was a minimization of the importance of dogmatic claims in favor of setting up a simple set of moral laws that were as easy to apprehend and predict as those of gravity. Each person has the lights of reason *and* of Scripture for guidance—yet "one begins to suspect . . . that the two lights were not entirely equal."[5]

Chillingworth is best known for his work *The Religion of Protestants: A Safe Way to Salvation*, written during the reign of Charles I.[6] It was written for the purpose of arguing against Roman Catholics—particularly the Jesuits—for the purpose of showing, first, that Scripture is the only necessary sacred document for salvation and, second, that each individual can and should have the right to interpret it. It was written directly against *Charity Maintained by Catholics* by the Jesuit Edward Knott.

Some themes in *The Religion of Protestants* resemble Puritan themes, particularly with respect to the idea of the repristination of Christianity. Moreover, despite his putative acceptance of the Thirty-Nine Articles, Chillingworth clearly moves away from a uniquely Anglican biblical hermeneutic in that he is suspicious of any ecclesial presence in biblical interpretation. This arises out of his dislike for Roman Catholicism. Rejecting the traditions of the Roman Catholic Church, Chillingworth's view is that

> the Church of Rome, to establish her tyranny over men's consciences, needed not either to abolish or corrupt Holy Scriptures,

---

4. The Great Tew was an estate near Oxford and at which many faculty met informally. The group associated with Chillingworth came to be called the Great Tew Circle, out of which his ideas and others with him "served as a centrepiece of Latitudinarian thought" (Pfizenmaier, *The Trinitarian Theology of Samuel Clarke*, 43). Pfizenmaier regards Chillingworth's ideas with respect to epistemology a "rationalization of divinity" (44).

5. Greer, *Anglican Approaches to Scripture*, 71.

6. I employ the 1888 edited version of Chillingworth, *The Religion of Protestants*.

> the pillars and supporters of Christian liberty.... But the more expedite way ... was to gain the opinions and esteem of the public and authorised interpreter of them, and the authority of adding to them what doctrines she pleased, under the title of traditions.[7]

Chillingworth's emphasis on "conscience" and a strong eschewing of the traditions of the Roman Catholic Church reveal a great deal about his orientation toward the relation between Scripture and the Church. He regards "tradition" as having been added in a dictatorial and conspiratorial manner that suffocated the primitive Church. In language that aims to avoid even the more minimal "tradition" of Protestantism, he proclaims in perhaps his most well-known passage:

> by the "religion of Protestants," I do not understand the doctrine of Luther, of Calvin, or Melancthon; nor the confession of Augusta, or Geneva ... nor the Articles of the Church of England.... But that wherein they all agree, and which they all subscribe with a greater harmony, as a perfect rule for their faith and actions, that is the BIBLE. The BIBLE, I say, the BIBLE only, is the religion of Protestants![8]

On its surface, this statement may appear to be rather innocuous, mirroring the traditional Protestant *sola scriptura* principle. But the theological hermeneutic of "the BIBLE" must be considered in the context of how it attests to ever-widening cracks in the sway of a uniquely Anglican reading of Scripture.

First, Chillingworth's assertion is the consequence of seeing "that there are popes against popes, councils against councils, some fathers against others, the same fathers against themselves."[9] Such a combative, divisive atmosphere leads him to seek a kind of "textual" repristination of Christianity—nothing need be sought elsewhere than this one text, and no authority can dictate otherwise. Despite Chillingworth's Anglicanism, it is clear that by this time, various spiritualist and humanist traditions entered into the minds of the religious elite in the face of religious division.[10] Whereas the

7. Chillingworth, *The Religion of Protestants*, 90.
8. Ibid., 463.
9. Ibid., 463.

10. The fact cannot be inconsequential that Chillingworth's views were most certainly forged by his own vacillation between the Roman Catholic and Anglican Churches, finally choosing the latter. A constant thread running through his religious struggles, is his search for flexibility and "intellectual speculation" rather than a simplistic quest for an infallible authority. See Orr, *Reason and Authority*, 14–20.

Roman Catholic Church claimed infallibility in the magisterium, Chillingworth formulates what appears to be a strict form of *sola scriptura* to bypass claims to an infallible human authority. As Reventlow argues, "in its polemical aim, *The Religion of Protestants* is directed against precisely this claim to infallibility."[11]

Second, Chillingworth speaks to what it means to be an *agent* of interpretation. While the Bible alone is the religion of Protestants, it is under the interpretive agency of rational credibility. But it is a certain *kind* of rationality, for Chillingworth rejected the notion that religion provides certainty of salvation by means of dogmatic systems, often embedded within ecclesial structures. Rather,

> upon men of temper and moderation, such [men] will oppose nothing because you maintain it, but will draw as near to you, that they may draw you to them, as the truth will suffer them; such as *require of Christians to believe only in Christ.*[12]

For Chillingworth, what is important for "men of temper and moderation" is to believe only the simplest of things. Against doctrine, Chillingworth directs his attention to the moral and ethical aspects of religion, since, without the kind of certainty inherent within strict Puritan predestinarian theology, Christianity has only a *moral* certainty.[13] Therefore, "the strength of faith required of a Christian for salvation was meagre."[14] The rational credibility of the Bible becomes defined in the context of conceiving of Scripture not as a book that provides the tools for building dogmatic structures, for these are mere human constructs repugnant to true faith. Rather, "God is not defective in things necessary; neither will he leave himself without witness, nor the world without means of knowing his will and doing it."[15] The conscience of the individual adjudicates the meaning of Scripture: "every man is to judge and choose; *and the rule whereby he is to guide his choice, if he be a natural man, is reason.*"[16] There is, then, an "authority" parallel with Scripture—"natural reason"—that determines what Scripture is to mean.

It warrants repeating that out of the crucible of division comes this search for common rationality, as the bonds of ecclesial communion shatter. This "common reason" is not just a faculty of the interpreter, but is

---

11. Reventlow, *The Authority of the Bible*, 149.
12. Chillingworth, *The Religion of Protestants*, 13, italics mine.
13. Orr, *Reason and Authority*, 80.
14. Ibid., 81.
15. Chillingworth, *The Religion of Protestants*, 124.
16. Ibid., 95, italics mine.

determinative of biblical interpretation. For instance, Chillingworth makes a distinction between those texts which are problematic and those which are "so plain and evident, that no man of ordinary sense can mistake the sense of them."[17] The latter are therefore to be preferred, sundering a cohesive canonical vision of the text. Because God is good and requires little to believe, the Bible is not to be read coercively; thus, the religion of Protestants is "safe."[18] The individual interpreter is free from the pressures of external coercion, as a dogmatic tradition is a "restraining of the word of God from that latitude and generality, and the understandings of men from that liberty, wherein Christ and his apostles left them; is and hath been the only fountain of all the schisms of the church."[19] It is schism, therefore, that compels someone like Chillingworth to minimize the doctrinal centrality of Scripture and to magnify the indispensability of reason in private interpretation.

I consider this to be what is a called a "latitudinarian" perspective" on Scripture, part of which is that the Bible confirms what humanity can already know by reason. With the Bible placed, at most, at equal parity with autonomous reason, the perceived violent dogmatism of earlier years is regarded as capable of avoidance. While Chillingworth does not directly speak to the issue of prophecy and Isaiah, we can make some observations on his thought and that of others who came to think similarly. First, this theological minimization subjects the reading of Scripture to a simplified approach. This is in opposition not to textual difficulty or opacity, but its complexity, or as I call it, its theological *fecundity*, a web of interconnected referents that are tied together christologically. Second, the importance of the Old Testament is canonically relegated to a secondary canonical status. Many latitudinarian thinkers tended to favor the New Testament, particularly in the moral teachings of Jesus. This is in distinction to a hermeneutic that assumes the presence of Christ, the Word, within *all* of Scripture, rather than regarding the moral precepts of Christ's earthly teachings to be the biblical center.

Chillingworth, however, only sets the scene. It was not until the eighteenth century that Anthony Collins (1676–1729) challenged the belief that the Old Testament predicted the coming of Christ. Collins is representative of latitudinarianism's culmination, which is deism. He argues that predictive prophecy is a misreading of the text. In 1727, he published *The Scheme of Literal Prophecy Considered*, in which he opposes the notion of an expected Messiah in Jewish thought at the time of Jesus; rather,

---

17. Ibid., 183.
18. Orr, *Reason and Authority*, 91.
19. Chillingworth, *The Religion of Protestants*, 250.

> it is reasonable to believe, that as the Jews, during the existence of their ... monarchy, and for a long while after the captivity, were all *Letter Men*; so it is no less reasonable to imagine, that when they began to Hellenize, and to allegorize their Scriptures, they had a constant opposition from some *Letter Men* among them, to that scheme and way of thinking.[20]

Collins' heroes, the "letter men," were those who read the Scriptures "literally." It was the contamination of Hellenist allegorization that caused a breakdown in reading the Old Testament—such a breakdown being defined as a Christian reading that considers Isaiah in messianic terms. Collins maintains that traditionally christological texts, such as the virgin birth in Isa 7:14, or the vicarious suffering of Christ in Isa 53, do not refer to anything other than local, historical events in the life of Israel.[21] Collins' hermeneutic was a historical one, whereby he examined Jewish texts such as the *Targum* to conclude that the use of "allegory," by which he means reading Scripture in a way other than according to a literal meaning, was essentially a category error that smothered the original meaning of the text. Even more, however, was that the effect, by pointing out that the Old Testament bears no prophetic relation to the New, was that the Old Testament serves no useful function for a newly baptized "natural" form of Christianity.

I want to focus on two central motivations for new critical exegetical approaches to Scripture that began in England. The first arose using new philological (humanist) tools that had already been employed by Erasmus, which questioned biblical interpretations that favored trinitarian doctrine, among others.[22] This opens the door to a host of Protestants (primarily) who initiate a repristination project to recover the "lost" Christian faith. Stephen Nye (c.1648–1719), for instance, a clergyman of the Church of England, challenged the traditional doctrine of the Trinity and contributed to the rise of Unitarianism in England. He based his views of the Trinity on his interpretation of the Bible, in which "the Doctrines of the Trinity and Incarnation have no solid or good Foundation in *Revelation*, or Holy Scripture."[23] He argued that the entire structure of Christian doctrine was one of spurious additions and traditions based on ideas that are "of *suspected* Authority

---

20. Collins, *The Scheme of Literal Prophecy Considered*, 22.

21. See, e.g., ibid., 146–48, 308.

22. The most famous of these is especially relevant for my discussion below of Stephen Nye. Erasmus omitted the *Comma Johanneum* in his 1517 edition of the Greek New Testament, based on textual-critical grounds that it was a spurious addition. See Metzger and Ehrman, *The Text of the New Testament*, 101–2.

23. Nye, *A Letter of Resolution*, 1.

and Credit in the Original."[24] Thus, just as with the Trinity, Nye dispensed with the doctrine of Mary as *theotokos*, the use of images, and the reliance on authoritative statements of ecumenical councils. As Nye argued, "these Doctrines are not Traditions from the Ancients, but Novelties, and Corruptions, and Depravations of genuine Christianity."[25] Any early texts that do support the doctrine of the Trinity are "certainly spurious or forged."[26]

Nye, and others like him, worked with a form of Puritan sentiment that regarded tradition, hierarchy, and ecclesial political power to be so deeply ingrained in the historical development of Christianity that the "true" faith had for centuries been eclipsed by forgeries and the misguided assertion of a fitness between tradition and the Bible. This parallels Chillingworth's philosophical form of theological minimization. Nye even goes so far as to suggest that Islam is closer to the truth regarding the oneness of God than historical Christianity.[27] This project was therefore one which aimed to clear away these heretical accretions.

The second motivation for new critical approaches to the text, also shared with anti-trinitarians such as Nye, speaks more to *motive* than method, which is to likewise strip away various accretions precisely *because they are the cause of division*. In Nye's view, the problem is the existence of such "fundamental doctrines" as the Trinity:

> the Doctrines under Consideration, have so divided the Churches after the Name of Christ; that there is no Agreement ... The Orthodox (as they call themselves) are so *multifariously* divided that they are not (perhaps) ten of them in a Party.... And the Dissent among them is so bitter and unreconcilable, that the *Anathema's* [sic] fly as thick and fast at one another as at the Unitarians.[28]

Nye's view, therefore, is that *the cause of division is doctrine itself*, especially its close tethering to Scripture.

This negative view of doctrine led others, such as the deists, to construe the phenomenon of "religion" anew. It was not done in a consistent or methodological way; thinkers like Herbert of Cherbury, Anthony Collins, and Matthew Tindal sought for a form of religion that eschewed what they saw as irrational interpretations of the text.[29] The driving force was

24. Ibid., 2.
25. Ibid., 11.
26. Ibid.
27. Ibid., 18.
28. Ibid., 7–8.
29. Herbert of Cherbury (1583–1648) and Matthew Tindal (1657–1733) were,

"toleration," within a milieu of humanism, which maintained "a basic form of Christianity that could be accepted in private, without the tyranny of a State Church."[30] John Rogerson, in accord with Reventlow, notes that "there was also a Puritan element among certain liberal thinkers, which attacked the clericalism and ritual of the Church of England by attacking those parts of the Old Testament devoted to priesthood and ritual."[31] Thus, despite the aim of "toleration," the root of much radical thought in the seventeenth and eighteenth centuries was a reading of Scripture that challenged the Anglican view of the ecclesially constitutive aspect of theological exegesis *precisely because of its close relation to theology*, which was seen to be avoided due to its tendency toward causing violence and confusion.

Moreover, as Marcus Walsh notes, within the milieu of Roman Catholic and Protestant conflicts over scriptural authority, Anglican divines eventually came to see themselves as "professional interpreters":

> For these Anglican divines valid interpretation of the Bible, as of other books, was substantially dependent on the bringing to bear of relevant knowledges, linguistic, cultural, and historical. Because scriptural interpretation is therefore necessarily knowledge-based, the clergy must be the best interpreters because of their scripture-directed professional training.[32]

This is consonant with Legaspi's characterization of a theological change in how Scripture was read in Germany—though this also applies to England:

> By the middle of the eighteenth century, masters of text—philologists, classicists, and orientalists—emerged as leaders in the new academic biblical sciences. As scholars focused on textual disorder, the authority of the Bible as an obligatory touchstone for contemporary life also weakened. The Bible became, instead, an exotic "resource." . . . Instead of looking *through* the Bible in order to understand *the truth about the world*, eighteenth-century scholars looked directly at the text, endeavoring to find new, ever more satisfactory frames of cultural and historical reference by which to understand *the meaning of the text*.[33]

---

with Collins, representatives of deist beliefs. Tindal is particularly well known for his pressing of the point regarding "natural religion" in Tindal, *Christianity as Old as the Creation*.

30. Rogerson, *Old Testament Criticism in the Nineteenth Century*, 147.
31. Ibid.
32. Walsh, "Profession and Authority," 388.
33. Legaspi, *The Death of Scripture*, 26, italics in original.

Rather than approving of the Church's service in some way as constitutively necessary for interpretation (and as the *subject* of interpretation), an impossible task when the Church was unable to present itself as a unified entity, interpreters began to consider the Bible in terms of *a textual problem*.

SEVENTEENTH- AND EIGHTEENTH-CENTURY COMMENTARIES ON ISAIAH

This section considers several exegetes of Isaiah and the way in which they represent an evolving hermeneutic. I present them thematically, with the intent to illustrate some of the exegetical issues I discussed above with regard to Chillingworth and latitudinarianism, particularly in the way that the process of exegesis becomes less concerned with theological matters and more directed to textual issues. The consequence is a reading of Isaiah almost exclusively in terms of its poetic or literary force that reveals the primitive "Hebrew" religious impulse, whose aesthetic power speaks to the affective dimension of human religion.

Most of the following commentaries have little direct impact on exegesis today (Robert Lowth is an obvious exception). However, they serve as helpful signposts on the way to the exegetical state of affairs in nineteenth-century England, often beyond the purview of general public perception.

Brevard Childs makes a useful distinction between two Continental Isaiah commentators who had an influence on English exegetes: Hugo Grotius (1583–1645) and Abraham Calov (1612–86). Childs uses these exegetes as representative of two kinds of exegesis; I categorize my exegetes more narrowly.[34] Grotius read Isaiah philologically, assembling all available Hebrew and Greek texts. He functioned in a way that untethered theology from exegesis and his analysis tended to lead him to historical conclusions in which he down-played any reading of the Old Testament informed by the New Testament. He aimed to "treat the biblical text purely as a scientific object to be critically analyzed."[35] Childs argues that it was only as a concession to his readers that he acknowledged some form of "mystical" reading, once all historical meaning was extracted from the text, hovering abstractly above Isaiah's words. On the other hand, Abraham Calov, as an orthodox Lutheran, strongly opposed and was appalled by Grotius's approach to Isaiah. The result was "a dogmatic hardening never present either with Luther

---

34. These two modes are outlined by Childs, *The Struggle to Understand Isaiah as Christian Scripture*, 230–35.

35. Ibid., 231.

or Calvin."[36] Calov accused his opponents of being "Judaizers," which he defines as any Christian who reads the Old Testament seeking only proximal, historical referents. The impact of the divisive exegesis of Grotius and Calov is that "a profoundly Christian exegetical tradition present in both the Church Fathers and Reformers is missing in both protagonists."[37]

I arrange various seventeenth- and eighteenth-century exegetes as an unfolding of the phenomenon of theological minimization in exegesis. The first exegete, Nehemiah Rogers (1593–1660), stands as the best representative of an interpretation of Isaiah that corresponds with my construal of the Anglican hermeneutical touchstone. All subsequent interpreters participate in theological minimization in various ways. William Day (1605–84) exemplifies a stark departure from Rogers' reading in a rhetorical textual analysis that pushes the theological referents of Isaiah to a secondary level of exegesis. The exegesis of Samuel White (c.1677–1716), in his debate with William Whiston (1667–1752) in the eighteenth century, is an extension of Day's interpretive strategy. That of Richard Stafford's (*bap.* 1663–1703) attempts to speak to English dissenters as one of privatization of belief, unconnected with any concrete ecclesial body, *despite* his aim to bring dissenters back into the Church of England. Richard Kidder (1633–1703) functions in a mode akin to that of Calov, highly apologetic, and anti-Jewish. I also briefly consider the commentary on Isaiah by William Lowth (1660–1732) in Simon Patrick's *Critical Commentary* as representative of this exegetical mode. Finally, I end with Robert Lowth (1710–87), the son of William, as heralding a new synthesis of many of the above modes in a proto-romantic exegetical style in which he "discovers" the structures of "Hebrew" poetry. He construes Isaiah in terms of its aesthetic style and in terms of its power to elicit the affective capacity of the religious person.

Nehemiah Rogers: The Song of the Vineyard

Nehemiah Rogers' 1632 work, *The Wild Vine*, is indicative of a richly theological reading of Isaiah that most closely corresponds to an Anglican reading. Rogers was a strong Royalist when being so was still relatively safe. Archbishop Laud viewed him with favor, referring to Rogers as "a man of good note."[38] It can be assumed, therefore, that Rogers did not have particular sympathy for the Puritans. It would be a mistake, however, to view Rogers as parroting a bland Establishment perspective of Scripture.

36. Ibid., 232.
37. Ibid., 235.
38. Laud, *The Works of the Most Reverend Father*, vii, 242.

What is striking about *The Wild Vine* is that it is an exposition only of Isa 5:1–7, the "Song of the Vineyard," and yet this is a work that is almost 320 pages long. But more than Rogers' prolixity is of note; the breadth of theological discourse that imbues his reading of merely seven verses indicates how closely Rogers sees the connection between theology and the entire canon of Scripture centered on Christ. And the presence of the Church is never far off. For instance, in his discussion of v. 1, "my welbeloued hath a vineyard," he says,

> And by *vineyard* he meaneth the Church visible, as in the application of verse 7 we may see. By which similitude the nature and condition of the Church is usually set forth in Scripture, and by none more: For indeed there is no earthly thing that doth better resemble it, than a *vineyard* doth.[39]

This is typical of Rogers' approach to the text. Even though he fully understands that the "proximate" interpretation of v. 7 is a reference to Israel and Judah, the passage is yet in theological continuity with the Church of the New Testament. Rogers makes no distinction between the two and does not get caught up in seeking out a univocal referent for the text. The Church is a figure of Israel and vice versa.

Rogers has a keen sense of the Church as not only divided, but as one that *suffers*. Maintaining the image of the Church as a vine, he notes that "there are many branches in the root, yet all make but one Vine: so all the faithful in the congregation, and all the congregations of the faithfull in the whole world make but only one Church."[40] However, rather than appealing to the concept of one "true" or "invisible" Church, Rogers recognizes the unavoidable truth that the Church has become fractured, and he attempts to account for this:

> All the branches of a Vine . . . are not alike fruitful, neither doe they all draw sap and moysture from the root; for as some are fruitfull and flourish, so some againe are barren and wither, which are cut off and cast into the fire: Thus is it in the Church visible; all the members thereof are not alike incorporated into the root, through the invisible bonds of the Spirit, neither doe they *bring forth fruit in him*. Some there are who are only *externally grafted*; others there are who are also *internally*. The former sort are such members of the Church visible, who by externall baptisme haue given their names to Christ, and so entered into

39. Rogers, *The Wild Vine*, 73.
40. Ibid., 76.

the profession; yet indeed are not Christs, because they haue not the Spirit of Christ.[41]

Rogers reserves judgment on the ecclesial worth of the various Protestant sects, though it is important to note that although he wrote in the midst of the Thirty Years War, a similar level of religious violence (relatively speaking) had yet to be seen in England.[42] For him, "albeit a Church bee corrupted with error and idolatry, yet it is still to be accounted Gods Church, till he haue diuorced and forsaken her."[43] The divisiveness and tendency of many Protestants in England to dissent concerned him: "Those therefore that condemne the Church of *England* for a No-church, and make a separation from it in regard of the errours and corruptions that are in it, are farre from the Spirit of *Christ*, and the *Prophets* and *Apostles*, who neuer made any schismaticall and bodily separation from any true Church."[44] Rogers, despite being an "establishment man" (or could be construed as such), was aware of numerous corruptions in the Church of England, but "the beholding of *tares and weeds* in the field, may instruct us of the state and condition of the Church militant."[45] It is precisely *because* the Isaiah passage interprets itself as being about Israel and Judah that he can use this image to speak of the nature of the Church. Just as Israel experiences the suffering and the judgment of God, so too does the Church. This is particularly evident as he explores vv. 5–6, which say, "I will take away the hedge thereof, and it shall bee eaten up . . ." The history of Israel illustrates what results from God's judgment, which is the removal of "Gods *diuine protection*, which was as a *hedge* or *wall* about them, and whereof they should be now depriued."[46] Rogers moves back and forth between Israel as the "original" historical referent to a theological interpretation that points to the Church. Rogers asks, "why then are wee smitten, plagued, punished?"[47] in connection with this same discussion. His ecclesiology is deeply connected to the view that, while there may be a "false" Church, there is no ideal or perfect Church

---

41. Ibid., 76–77.

42. This reserve of judgment is notwithstanding a forthright assessment of the state of the Roman Catholic Church, of which he proclaims, "the Church of Rome doth wilfully and obstinately destroy the foundation itselfe, and therefore may be concluded for no Church of God" (ibid., 98).

43. Ibid., 95.

44. Ibid., 96.

45. Ibid., 84.

46. Ibid., 206.

47. Ibid., 211.

but rather one that is embedded in the historical contingencies of God's providential rule.

It is also notable that Rogers exemplifies a very rare kind of ecclesial reading, though he more closely embodies a "Protestant" interpretation, in his understanding of the Bible as a presiding judge over the Church. An "ecclesial" reading is not merely an assertion that the Bible is read in and by the Church, nor that the Church is the only interpreter of Scripture. Rather, in this passage, Rogers sees Scripture referring to the fire of God who purifies an imperfect Church. Despite this being a necessary aspect of *sola scriptura*, and can be perceived incipiently in early Anglican theologians, *no other exegete I consider exegetes Isaiah in this way*. Moreover, while not in itself uniquely "Anglican," the way in which the Church and Israel are theologically tethered speaks to the concrete reality of the Church. In other words, just as Scripture speaks to corporate, or *corporeal* Israel, Israel as a people are a referent of more than a merely spiritual, invisible Church.

The canonical and christological aspects of Rogers' exegesis can be seen in his discussion of the image of the vine and its theological connection to John 15. This is by no means the only biblical connection that Rogers makes to the rest of Scripture; he links his discussion to a wide variety of biblical passages, both from the Old and New Testaments, always with a view that within Isaiah, Christ, and the Church inherently participate in the text's meaning. For instance, he observes the horrors of the war on the Continent: "Our brethren in France and Germany are whirled about in these bloudie tumults; there heare the dismall cries of cruell aduersaries, crying *kill, kill*; the shrikes of women and infants; the thundering of those murdering peeces in their eares,"[48] and uses the words of Amos 6:4–6 to indicate the relative safety of the English from such tumult.[49]

William Day and Samuel White: Heralds of a New Protestant Poetics

Scant decades after Rogers' work, in 1654, William Day penned *An Exposition of the Book of the Prophet Isaiah*. I present Day's exegesis, and its distinct difference from Rogers,' as presaging a host of new exegetical strategies that

---

48. Ibid., 269.

49. I say *relative* safety, as there were by that time considerable factions within the Church of England; the Puritans were still a significant force, as well as the Arminians (whom I would prefer to call proto-High Church or, more unwieldingly, "non-predestinarians.") The fateful reign of Charles I had also begun seven years before the publication of *The Wild Vine*.

characterize the era. I locate Day within the exegetical milieu as participative of exegetical tools that emerge from an irenic approach to Scripture. That is, despite William Day's traditional faith commitments, the primary mode of exegesis becomes transposed from one that I describe in the Anglican vision to a methodological analysis of rhetorical tropes, from which the "spiritual" is seen as exegetically distinct. I end this section by giving an account of Samuel White's engagement with William Whiston and how, by the next century, Day's rather novel approach to Isaiah became the standard exegetical orientation.

A king's scholar at Eton who received his M.A. in 1632, Day's rhetorical/textual methodology and his theological commitments reveal a discontinuity between them right from the preface to his work. This new perspective (described below) on reading the Bible becomes important for my analysis of both Robert Payne Smith in Chapter 3 and Thomas Kelly Cheyne in Chapter 5. Day's preface suggests a view that does not appear to be innovative. He gives a summary of the intent of Isaiah, "the most *Evangelical* of the prophets." It is, in his view, exemplary in its ability to foretell Christ, for Isaiah "hath many excellent prophecies of Christ."[50] Jews were unable to understand the predictions of Christ in Isaiah, because prophets like Isaiah

> did either speak of it in Parables, and dark Speeches, and Allegories, or because they spoke of it under the Types and shadows of other things: And under [these] doth our prophet speak of the *Gospel*. . . . For he prophesieth first of things to come in times nearer to his own times. . . . Many places of the holy Writers of the Old Testament, and especially of the Prophets, carry with them a double sense; One concerning terrene and corporall things, and things to come to passe before the days of the Meβiah: another concerning spiritual and heavenly things. . . . The first sense I may call, the *First*, or *Literal*, or *Historical*, or *meaner Sense*: The second sense I may call the *Second*, or the *Mystical*, or *Sublime Sense*.[51]

This hermeneutical construal is rather orthodox at a superficial level. Numerous exegetes attest to a "double sense" of the text whereby the historical sense mediates a meaning that accords with a christological referent. But Day's exegesis is compartmentalized: there are *two different ways of reading the text* in such a way that the "first" sense enjoys exegetical privilege. Thus,

50. Day, *An Exposition of Isaiah*, i. The preface does not offer page numbers, so I supply them.
51. Ibid., iii.

> Now by what has been spoken, it is easie to conjecture, which of the two . . . is the *Thorow-sense, that is,* which of the two senses . . . is that, which is continued and carried word by word through an whole History or Prophecie. . . . Certainly it is the *First, Literal, Historical* or *Meaner sense*; and for the marriage through of this. . . . I have bent my poor labours in this work. . . . But (you will say) to take paines about [this first sense] is to favor *Judaisme*; and to make the heart of the *Jew* (which is obstinate enough) yet more obstinate towards the *Gospel* and *Christianity*. . . . I answer, That to take paines for the finding out of the *Literal* sense is no whit to favor *Judaisme*, but to seek out the Truth; and if the seeking of the Truth, makes the *Jew* obstinate towards the *Gospel* . . . it doth but *occasionally,* and the very best things may be an *occasion* of the worst of evils.[52]

This passage reveals much of what Day seeks "in a place of much difficulty and controversie,"[53] where the search for this historical, "first," sense is in terms of a *primary* meaning that reveals the "truth." In such a quest for the ultimate meaning of the text, however, there can no longer be any appeal to a constitutive theological dimension that funds this "truth." Rather, such a theological truth is secondary to it, even exegetically optional. This secondary, "spiritual," meaning is by no means unimportant to Day, but functions at an ahistorical, allusive level.

It is remarkable how Day's exegetical orientation forms his categorization of the literary tropes present in Isaiah. This is his explicit intent, given that between the preface and main body of *An Exposition of the Book of Isaiah*, he has a section that gives "An Explanation of those Termes of Art, and Rhetoricall Tropes and Figures Which most frequently occurre in this Book,"[54] namely, such terms as anthropopathia, enallage, hypallage, synechdoche, and various types of metonymy. A significant portion of Day's exegesis categorizes the text in terms of Isaiah's use of such literary-rhetorical forms. For instance, Isaiah 30:27 says "Behold the Name of the Lord cometh." Day avers, "The Prophets puts [sic] *the Name of the Lord* for *the Lord himself,* after the Hebrew manner *per Metonymiam Adjuncti: q.d.* The Lord cometh."[55] A significant allotment of his commentary is dedicated to indicating such literary forms, as well as paraphrasing or restating what the verse means, rather than a *commentary* (or even an exposition) as such along the lines Rogers.'

52. Ibid., x.
53. Ibid., viii.
54. Ibid., xv-xxii.
55. Ibid., 2:90.

Some important passages in Day's work indicate how he differs from Nehemiah Rogers. Consider Isa 5, the Song of the Beloved. For v. 7, which was so central to Rogers ("For the Vineyard of the Lord of Hosts is the house of Israel"), Day says

> This Conjunction *For*, if it be a *Causal*, and so taken, sheweth that there is an ἔλλειψις here, and that something is to be understood: That therefore which is to be understood here, is this, or the like, *q d. Now therefore the Lord will forsake his People, the house of* Israel *and the men of* Judah *and will leave them to be spoiled by their enemies and will not help them, for that which is meant by the Vineyard of the Lord of Hosts, is the house of* Israel.[56]

Day's analysis, which explores the meanings of words and the rhetorical categorization of phrases, is his common exegetical approach. When it comes to any kind of theological interpretation of this passage of Isaiah, he says

> This verse telleth us, that what the Prophet sang of the Vineyard in the former verses, was a *Parable*: Now although it be not necessary that whatsoever is contened in a *Parable*, should have its application (because many things are spoken to make up the narration, and many things are added to adorne it). And although it might seem enough to make this *Parable* and the *Apodosis* thereof to meet to say, that, as this Vineyard had all things requisite to make it fruitfull: So had the *Jewes* whatsoever was needful to make them good: And yet for all that, as the Vineyard prooved naught: so did the *Jewes*.[57]

Day does not make any references to deeper theological issues in the text. There is certainly no connection to or intimation of the Church.

It is helpful to investigate Day's analysis of Isa 7 as the traditionally christological passage that refers to *almah* and Emmanuel, and which is also important for my analysis in subsequent chapters. Day commences by giving a historical overview of King Ahaz's fear of the army of Rezin of Syria, then he paraphrases the passage until he reaches the verse "Behold a virgin," which Day interprets as meaning "Behold one who is now a Virgin.... To speak of this place in its first sense is most probably thought to be that Prophetesse, which our Prophet took to wife." As for the appellation *Immanuel* of this child, he suggests,

> This name *Immanuel* signifieth *God with us. Matth. 1. v. 23.* And it was given unto this Child, to signifie, that God would be with

56. Ibid., 1:39.
57. Ibid., 1:40.

the *Jewes*. . . . Probable it is (as I said) that this *Immanuel* was the Sonne of the Prophetesse, which is mentioned *Chap 8. v. 3*.

He continues, however, by adding,

> Yet in a second and more sublime sense, the *Virgin Mary* is here signified, who was a Virgin and a Mother both *in sensu Composito* (as the Schoole speaks) that is, a Virgin even when she was a Mother. . . . For he was true God, who being made Man, dwelt with us, and among us, *Matth. 1. 23*. and was our Salvation, of which *Immanuel, Immanuel* the Sonne of *Isaiah* was but a type.[58]

Day is here invoking Abelard's distinction between *in sensu composito* and *in sensu diviso*, and it is not clear how this contributes to his argument. What is clear, however, is that his interpretation does not emerge out of an explicitly theological context (though an implicit one is certainly present). For instance, given the deeply christological history of Isaiah's theological reception, Day's connections to Jesus are sparse, "secondary," and are certainly not central to his analysis. Rather, his exposition hinges on a semantic analysis in order to justify the dual meaning of Mary and the Prophetess as referents. In other words, less dogmatically-based tools come into play in Day's analysis that, however conservative their conclusions, eschew a basis in a theological history.

Even in Day's consideration of Isa 53, while he accepts is fulfilled by Jesus of Nazareth, the exegetically relevant issues have less to do with theology, the Church, or a conception of Scripture's christological coherence. Rather, philological discourse drives his discussion:

> Note that whereas many passages of this book have a twofold sense. . . . And this Prophecy relateth both to *Jeremy* as the *Type*, and to *Christ* as the *Antitype*: And whereas the words in the *Hebrew* Text are so ordered and chosen, as that they do signifie both these senses, which cannot so well be expressed in any other language as this: The Translators of our Bible aymed more at that sense which immediately concerned *Christ* (as being more sublime, and as it were the kernel, whereas the other is but as it were the shell) then at the other. Wherefore they not having words to signifie both senses, so fit as they are signified in the *Hebrew*, chose words which signified what is immediately prophecyed of *Christ* the Antitype, rather than what is prophecyed of the *Type*.[59]

58. Ibid., 1:60–61.
59. Ibid., 3:111.

This is representative of a minimization of the theological dimension of the text, looking for the intent of the author on the one hand, while maintaining a "sublime" or "second" sense that justifies the preservation of theological meaning on the other. There is nothing new in taking recourse to philology to resolve theological issues—philology being one among many exegetical tools available to the interpreter. What I am highlighting is that it has become the *primary* recourse to theological conundrums within the biblical text. Despite the fact that Day is not heterodox in his theological commitments, *Christ is not of central concern to his exegesis of Isaiah 7, nor that of 53*. While he maintains that the Holy Spirit is the "author" of the Bible and does not question the historical accuracy of the text, Day yet exemplifies, in comparison with Rogers, is *a new meaning of exegesis*. Early Anglican exegesis considered the Bible as not merely a text with only one referent. Rather, the object to which the text points can have several levels of meaning. In other words, "[m]ultiple meanings emerge from allegorical readings of texts because the things to which the words literally refer have themselves further multiple references."[60] Because people like Day saw the exegesis of Scripture as a *textual* effort, such older theological schemata were avoided so that the world of signs in which the Bible participates flattens into a theory of textual correspondence. Once this becomes the method, when theology functions as a merely "secondary" mode of reading Scripture, it can be dispensed with, or treated at a level that is more residual than secondary.

There is therefore a stark difference between the exegesis of William Day and that of Nehemiah Rogers. Rogers' interpretive approach most closely corresponds to the Anglican touchstone of Chapter 1. That is, the Church as a corporate body is a central textual referent, just as much as Christ is, *because* he is corporeally present in the text. What is of central concern for Rogers is pushed to a "secondary" or spiritual mode of reading the text in Day's exegetical approach, overtaken by an interest in philological, rhetorical and textual analyses. For Day, interpretation has become methodical, not theological.[61]

The major difference between Day and Rogers, therefore, is that Rogers affirms a polysemous quality of the text, funded by a deep appreciation of typological signs and figural allusions, whereas for Day, there are, at most, two textual/theological referents. Yet, despite the stark exegetical differences between the two, both would ascribe to similar, if not identical, theological

---

60. Harrison, *The Bible, Protestantism*, 28.

61. I appreciate that most of the interpreters with whom I engage think that what they are doing is "theological exegesis." Despite this, Cranmer, Whitgift, and Hooker would find the exegetical approaches of these later figures to be unrecognizable because of a difference in theological commitments regarding the nature of Scripture itself.

the breakdown of uniformity 61

propositions. Their exegetical dissimilarity is especially interesting given the short span between the times during which the two thinkers wrote. I suggest there are two reasons for these almost opposing exegetical methods that contribute to my central claim: first is the intervening English Civil War (and, of less impact, the Thirty Years War on the Continent), which heightened the fear of violence generated by theological debate. The result was to seek out non-theological textual methodologies, which I denote as an irenic mode of exegesis. Second is that during the seventeenth century, there emerged a form of "Protestant poetics," as Barbara Lewalski calls it. I construe this in exegetically antagonistic terms by its characteristic as an interpretation that shuns what was seen as excessive allegorization by Roman Catholics. Both of these important facets offer a coherent account of the difference between two exegetes like Rogers and Day, even though neither of them as individual exegetes explicitly invokes either reason.

In terms of irenic exegesis, part of the central claim of this project is that a fissiparous Church brings about a new exegetical state of affairs. In the mid-seventeenth century, England witnessed two major wars—the Civil War and the Thirty Years War—each of which precipitated a great deal of violence. More importantly, they were regarded as conflicts that came about because of opposition between religious parties. Like Richard Popkin, Stephen Toulmin invokes the concept of certainty to support the thesis that the result of the Thirty Years War was this: "[t]he longer fighting continued, the less plausible it was that Protestants would admit the 'certainty' of Catholic doctrines, let alone that devout Catholics would concede the 'certainty' of Protestant heresies."[62] While theological arguments had to do with such issues as justification by faith and the intercession of the saints, the orbital center was the interpretation of Scripture. As Peter Harrison argues, "the Reformation stood as a challenge to authority as such, replacing the authority of the institution with that of scripture, or in the case of the more radical reformers, with that of the individual."[63] If certainty could no longer be achieved by theological and scriptural discourse, then "the only other thing thinking people could do was to look for a new way of establishing their central truths and ideas; one that was independent of, and neutral between, particular religious loyalties."[64] Thus, exegesis gravitated toward methodological edifices that sought to be non-theological. The Bible came to be read in the context of a Quest for Methodology, independent of "priestcraft"

---

62. Toulmin, *Cosmopolis*, 55.
63. Harrison, *The Bible, Protestantism*, 99.
64. Toulmin, *Cosmopolis*, 70.

and perceived institutional oppression. In the context of the Enlightenment University in eighteenth-century Germany, Legaspi suggests

> this approach to the Bible, which relied heavily upon empirical models of linguistic and historical study borrowed from classic philology, lent shape and support to the larger project of recovering a scholarly, nonconfessional Bible. The ideal of an academic ecumenism, by which scholars of various religious persuasions could work cooperatively to produce interpretations of the Bible in accord with the canons of modern rationality, became modern criticism's leading light.[65]

While Legaspi's work revolves around events in Germany in the eighteenth century, Day's exegesis gives evidence that, in seventeenth-century England, this kind of approach is in its nascent stage. In fact, I am pushing back Legaspi's argument, suggesting that this methodological transformation happened in England, albeit less robustly, *before* it did in Germany. Day is one of the first to transform Scripture into the "literary Bible," a consequence of this irenic "academic ecumenism." In the case of Day and his exegetical successors, I suggest that the Thirty Years War had less of an impact on English divines than the more immediate catastrophic events of the English Civil War.[66] At the level of lay scriptural interpretation, the result was a highly antagonistic atmosphere in which the English despised the previously "papist" king (i.e., Charles I), from whom they were freed. For Establishment

---

65. Legaspi, *The Death of Scripture*, 33.

66. In 1632, Charles I had been king for seven years, and there was plenty of unrest fomented by his various political machinations. Nonetheless, while frustrations were mounting, there was a policy of non-enforcement of laws against recusants, and a flowering of High Church activity by the so-called Caroline Divines, which raised the suspicions of Puritan thinkers regarding Charles' intentions. By the time of Day's commentary in 1654, he wrote after events of such calamity that many saw it not only as the end of an era, but of time itself. After Charles' death, with almost apocalyptic zeal for the ushering in of the Kingdom of Heaven, the Puritan Oliver Cromwell was placed as Lord Protector over England. But the effect was chilling, for "the soldiers may have cheered when Charles's head rolled from the block, but upon the country as a whole there settles a sense of horror, of guilt, of shame" (Moorman, *A History of the Church in England*, 243). The developing pietistic Puritanism that took hold did not impose a single form of church governance; for them, conscience was more important, and therefore no formal creed was imposed on English subjects—except that they confess faith in Jesus Christ. Whereas in one sense this was toleration, it may be more accurate to call it "enforced minimalism," and this minimalist view of Christianity and the Bible can be seen in the less religiously robust forms of latitudinarianism and deism. Furthermore, as Paul Boyer observes, "[w]ith the defeat of Charles I in 1646 and his beheading in 1649, apocalyptic speculation surged among English radicals, largely drawn from society`s lower ranks, who saw an egalitarian new order on the horizon" (Boyer, *When Time Shall Be No More*, 65).

theologians like Day, the tendency was to distance themselves from an overly creedal biblical interpretation. Day marks the beginning of a process whereby exegesis means something other than it had once been, and this is the result of a divided (and often violent) Church. This process treats of deeply held theological commitments such that they are less influential on the task of exegesis.[67]

Second, in more general hermeneutical terms, a uniquely Protestant mode of exegesis flowered in the seventeenth century, precisely because it aimed to distance itself from its medieval roots. Such roots were often conflated with Roman Catholicism. Pre-Reformation exegesis advocated for the four-fold reading of Scripture—literal/historical, allegorical, tropological and anagogical—which was a systemization of many exegetical strategies that began with the Church Fathers to Augustine and Hugh of St. Victor, and was more or less given its final structure by Thomas Aquinas.[68] For Protestants, "the literal meaning of scripture is often conveyed through figurative language and so can be properly apprehended through rhetorical and poetic analysis." It was a rejection, primarily given impetus by Puritan concerns, of the "ecclesiastic 'scenery' of the medieval Church."[69] The emphasis on *sola scriptura* implies that no external exegetical structures were permissible. The key to biblical interpretation, therefore, must be inherent within the Scriptures. Moreover, since the Bible is a *text*, then only textual strategies are sufficient for determining biblical meaning: "Tropes are now perceived as God's chosen formulations of his revealed truths, which man must strive to understand rightly, in themselves, and not as a stimulus to a higher vision."[70] This is a shift away from the allegorical and toward the

---

67. With respect to the division between Protestants and Catholics, there were increased challenges to the reliability of the Vulgate, encouraged by the discovery of new collections of texts that made their way into England. For instance, England was able to convince the Greek Patriarch of Constantinople, Cyrillos Lucaris (1570–1638), to relinquish what came to be called the Codex Alexandrinus. Protestants began to prefer more ancient Hebrew codices and devised new tools to compare various manuscripts in order to determine the most probable "original" words. This preference was dual in nature: it reflected the humanist desire to reclaim the work of the "ancients," but it also was polemical in that it challenged Roman Catholic views of the "fixed" and reliable text of the Vulgate. Many, such as Richard Bentley (1662–1742), Master of Trinity College, Cambridge, aimed at producing an edition of the New Testament that would most closely approach that of the Council of Nicaea (Katz, *God's Last Words*, 189–91). As we saw, one consequence was a rejection of the so-called Trinity "proof-text" of 1 John 5:7, which Bentley rejected as spurious. See also Mandelbrote, "English Scholarship," 76.

68. Dickson, "The Complexities of Biblical Typology," 257. The actual deployment of all four senses discretely was rare.

69. Lewalski, *Protestant Poetics*, 72.

70. Ibid., 77.

"literal," meaning the textual *form* of the passage itself: "Once the text was freed from the interpretive constraints of its context, there seemed to be no way of governing how the texts could signify; and they attributed the excesses of patristic allegory to just such privatistic readings."[71] This led to a situation in which "Protestants intensified and systematized the study of the rhetorical tropes and schemes in scripture. . . . This emphasis urged the skills of the literary critic upon the reader of the Bible."[72] This was a uniquely Protestant move that "promoted in sixteenth- and seventeenth-century England a specifically biblical poetics . . . under the influence of Protestant theology and the new literary and philological interests of the period."[73] This is not to suggest that the poetic form of Scripture inhibited exegesis *per se*, but that this process of systemization and rather rigid categorization delimited its fecundity. The new textual focus produced a series of handbooks that listed the numerous literary tropes of Scripture to help decipher its "code." Examples include John Smith's *The Mystery of Rhetorique Unvail'd* and the English sourcebook for typology, Benjamin Keach's *Tropologia: A Key to Open Scripture Metaphors*. In the Protestant view, the focus was on *types* versus what they regarded as ahistorical allegories: "the mistake of the Gothic monkish allegorists . . . had been to remove the sign from its historical context in the literal narrative of Scripture, which had led to unlimited semiosis: any sign could have any number of referents, unless there was a way to predict or control the process of signification. The historicity of types gave an evidentiary value to Protestant hermeneutics that allegory did not have."[74]

William Day's exegesis reflects this ever-more central tendency in the seventeenth century and beyond. Even though the original intent of Protestant biblical poetics was to reveal Scripture's deep typological and theological meaning, Day's constant attention to the task of categorization shifts attention to identifying literary tropes. He mirrors the Protestant aim to

---

71. Dickson, "The Complexities of Biblical Typology," 266. Dickson does point out that, while the seventeenth century brought about a new kind of Protestant typological/rhetorical rigidity, this is not to suggest that there was an absence of deep exegesis whose exegetical layering has affinities with medieval approaches. Dickson's poignant example of Donne's "Hymne to God my God, in my sicknesse" is exemplary (Dickson, "The Complexities of Biblical Typology," 267). However, despite the complexity in Protestant exegesis, the fact is that it is *different*, and becomes more so, in that it *tended* to avoid allegorical modes (or, to put it perhaps another way, used allegory differently than Catholics did) *and* directed their attention to rhetorical tropes as an antagonistic response to Catholic categories.

72. Lewalski, *Protestant Poetics*, 78.

73. Ibid., 8.

74. Dickson, "The Complexities of Biblical Typology," 259.

disdain the allegorical in favor of the literal, yet functions at a highly systematic level, essentially cataloguing literary tropes, suggesting that, in doing so, the greater part of exegesis is complete. Moreover, implicitly, this developing Protestant poetics places Scripture on the road to becoming another kind of text than *Scripture*. Robert Lowth's thought (see below) is representative of the culmination of (Old Testament) Scripture as a kind of primitive Hebrew poesy. The central relevant point for this project, however, is that the root of this development is that it is a uniquely Protestant form of exegesis carried out in opposition to earlier Roman Catholic exegetical practices.

I now turn to the exegesis of Samuel White whose work bears a close resemblance to that of William Day. White's influence is Hugo Grotius, so it is unsurprising that, given my above summary of Continental exegetes, his approach bears a similarity to Grotius' in its concern, broadly speaking, with philological matters. I present him in the context of his debate with the Arian William Whiston, who was one of White's main interlocutors. White wrote *A Commentary on the Prophet Isaiah, wherein the literal sense of the prophecy is briefly explained* in 1709, and which I regard as a continuation of the "textualization" process that William Day initiates.

William Whiston's Boyle Lectures, entitled *The Accomplishment of Scripture Prophecies*, spurred White to give an account of prophecy in Scripture. Whiston and White were contemporaries who were in conflict over the nature of prophetic interpretation. However, the contours of their discourse are entirely "modern" in that their debate concerning the nature of prophetic referents and textual analyses eclipsed the Anglican vision of reading the Bible. There was no longer a comprehensive theological vision of *how* Scripture functions. Like Isaac Newton, Whiston was keenly interested in prophecy and his Boyle lectures were an attempt to show with the clarity of mathematical exactitude:

> (1) the certainty of the Spirit of Prophecy from the beginning of the World; (2) the Divine Authority of those sacred writings, which have all along contain'd the Predictions of future Events, no way within the reach of natural Foresight; (3) the certain truth of the Christian Religion, as it is confirm'd from those ancient Prophecies, fulfilled in our blessed Saviour; and (4) the just reasons we have thence to expect the completion of those other Prophecies, which are not a few, whose Periods are yet to come.[75]

With respect to prophecy, Whiston

---

75. Whiston, *The Accomplishment of Scripture Prophecies*, 6.

argued that prophecies in the Old Testament could only have a single meaning: either they referred to later events in the Old Testament itself, or they predicted something that would occur only at the time of Jesus. The notion of typology was unacceptable to him: a prophecy could not refer simultaneously to two different events.[76]

Samuel White argues against Whiston's view, as he believes that it leads to numerous confusing readings; for instance, two consecutive verses could refer to two different events in time.

Whiston and White can be placed in the same "free-thinker" category as that of Matthew Collins (see above), notwithstanding the fact that they were not as controversial in their writings. I argue this because Whiston's freedom from theological history leads him to his anti-Trinitarian thought and White, more subtly, moved to a mode of exegesis akin to Day's in which figuralism, textual fecundity, and the presence of the Word within the text become acutely minimized. For White is critical of not only Whiston, but also of St. Jerome and "a Jesuit" (Cornelius à Lapide) who interprets the "Moab" reference in the passage as the Devil. Even more troublesome to him, is the interpretation of "the mountain of the Lord's House" as the Church. For "the generality of Commentators overlook the genuine signification of single Words and make them like so many Puppets [to] just speak as they please."[77] Thus, like many of his academic contemporaries, White disdains the received tradition of the Church in favor of a reassessment of the "real" meaning of the text and a desire to find the most original sources. White is a "free-thinker" as his view is that "the spectacular lack of agreement by religious authorities should alone convince us that each individual believer should approach the text armed with reason rather than prejudice."[78] He has his own set of non-dogmatic rules for interpretation which, true to an irenic intent, directs the interpretive efforts toward conclusions that avoid controversy.

In contrast to Whiston, White often does not accept a unitary textual referent, because doing so errs by forcing a pastiche of confusing indicators within a single passage; in such a model, one text would refer to a historically proximate event, while the next to a future one. White argues that there are dual textual referents, signifying an interpretive change to a narrowing of which texts can refer to more than one event, and a reduction of meaning to (at most) two referents. With regard to the former, White states that

---

76. Katz, *God's Last Words*, 144.
77. White, *A Commentary on the Prophet Isaiah*, iii.
78. Katz, *God's Last Words*, 144.

only in such Places as are quoted in the *New Testament* a double Sense is to be allow'd; and have for that very Reason gone out of the common Road of Interpreters, because I found that the greatest part of them more sollicitous about fast'ning their own Sense on his Words, than giving the Sense he design'd by them.[79]

The notion of dual textual referents in Scripture is not new; the theological concept of typology is a means of understanding how Christ is the center of all of Scripture. However, in his attempt to avoid spurious interpretations, White retreats from the Anglican hermeneutic that holds up Scripture as a fecund web of interconnected meanings.

Turning our attention back to White's exegesis of Isaiah, consider his interpretation of Isa 53, a central passage in the history of theology. He dissents from Grotius' interpretation that this is about the suffering of Jeremiah and says "this Chapter is to be understood solely of *Christ*, as all interpreters agree,"[80] himself abstaining from applying his own rule of dual interpretation. For White, "the Application of this to our *Saviour* is so obvious that every *Christian* Reader cannot fail to make it, as soon as he reads the Words."[81] Two points are of note, however. The first is his assertion of the clarity of a univocal textual referent. It is "obvious" to anyone who is a Christian. Yet, by this time there were numerous thinkers—Grotius being a prime example—who by no means considered this an obvious interpretation of the Suffering Servant. Secondly, White does not as such appeal to the tradition of the Church, or any particularly *theological* understanding of Scripture; in fact, he argues that "any one who has any knowledge of the *Hebrew* Language will at first sight discover, what violence is offer'd to the Original Expressions by this Interpretation of *Grotius*, and how exactly every Character here agrees with the circumstances of our *Saviour's* Death and Passion, in the first literal allow'd Sense of the Words."[82] The appeal is not directed toward or within a theological/hermeneutical structure, but to a proper knowledge of Hebrew and the "original" meaning of the text, that is, by an appeal to philology.

White, however, is less univocal in his interpretation of one of the most central prophetic passages in Christian theological history, Isa 9. For each chapter, White offers a small preface, in this case entitled "The Argument of Chapter IX," comprising a précis of the central concerns of the passage. In White's outline of the argument, Christ is no longer the central referent of Isa 9. There is, in fact, no mention of Christ, but a mere summary of the

79. White, *A Commentary on the Prophet Isaiah*, xl.
80. Ibid., 371.
81. Ibid., 373.
82. Ibid., 381.

historical events that gave rise to a need for the comfort that the passage offers. Thus "the people that walked in darkness, have seen a great light" refers to "the Jews shut up in *Jerusalem*, surrounded by a Great Army, and by the *Light* . . . their marvellous deliverance from an Enemy." Once White, however, reaches that most central passage, verse 6, he is more in agreement with Grotius that this

> must be understood in the first literal sense as *Hezekiah*. . . . Whereas the Birth of Christ so many Hundred Years after could have no influence on the Time of their present Distress . . . but the Words are so chosen that in their utmost and full Import they are more applicable to our Saviour than to *Hezekiah*, of whom the Jews are not to be blam'd for interpreting these Two Verses, since the Connexion necessarily requires it; but their Fault is . . . that they will not allow any one else to be design'd by the Prophet, tho' the Words plainly shew he had a greater Person in his Eye.[83]

Also in contrast to his interpretation of Isa 53, which White interprets christologically, he is similarly univocal in his interpretation of Isa 11 ("a rod out of the stem of Jesse"), by almost completely avoiding any christological referent. His preface begins with the rather harsh claim that "This Chapter is by the *Jews* understood of the *Messiah*, as they vainly fancy, yet to come, and with these fatally blind Wretches I find *Mr. Whiston* concurs."[84] He is resolute to interpret Isaiah 11 in terms of Israel's need for a just ruler over them at the time of the Assyrian invasion. White does acknowledge Paul's use in Rom 15:12 of Isa 11:10, and therefore it would appear that the New Testament regards this as a christological passage. His response is rather enigmatic:

> The Christian Interpreters understand the Prophet of the *Messiah* already come, finding the 10th Verse apply'd by St. *Paul* to our Saviour, and therefore, says *Zach. Ursin.* [Zacharias Ursinus], the rest of this Chapter must be apply'd to *Christ* and the calling of the Gentiles: and I would very willingly allow the Consequence, were it possible to make Sense of the Prophet without straining his Words.[85]

However, once he arrives at the point of commenting on Isa 11:10, he neglects to mention any Christian interpretation. His antipathy for

83. Ibid., 69.
84. Ibid., 85.
85. Ibid., 86.

Whiston's interpretation trumps his dual referent rule, even though the New Testament provides justification for another meaning to prophecies. What stirs him to such opposition is Whiston's interpretation of v. 12, which suggests there would be a future restoration of the Jews to their own land. Not only does his interpretation of the text become clouded by his dislike of Whiston, but his problem with such an interpretation is that to read Isaiah in this way would no longer be *historical*. Rather, it would mean there are prophecies yet to be fulfilled. Whatever the case, White is neither consistent in his interpretive methodology nor is he free from the influence of the numerous controversies that had arisen during his time.

Of equal importance, however, is that White presumptively maintains a thin form of typology and predictive value to Isaiah. But his more pressing concerns for historical and philological reconstructions of the world of the Prophet eclipse the rich theological landscape that informs the early Anglican hermeneutic, of which Nehemiah Rogers is representative. Through Samuel White, the irenic exegesis of Day flowers into a more robust form of critical reading that conspicuously minimizes a correspondence between Scripture and the proclamation of the Church.

Richard Stafford: Ecumenical Minimalism and Religious Privatization

Richard Stafford (*bap.* 1663–1703) was a committed member of the Church of England who worked to see dissenters come back into the fold. While he is an *apparent* proponent of the Church of England, Stafford continues the process of theological minimization. I begin with some of his more general works, followed by a series of sermons that speak on Isa 38:2, 3. Stafford stands on the cusp of the eighteenth century, when critical exegesis began its ascendancy. Stafford is, however, a transitional figure, by no means challenging the historicity of the Bible. Rather, he functions on the other side of the coin forged by Day, whereby he speaks to the *kinds of belief* that one should hold. In 1695 Stafford wrote *An Exhortation to all Dissenters to Return to the Church of England*, and in 1699 he issued the tract *The Cause and Cure of Divisions*. His sermons on Isa 38:2, 3 also show his use of the Bible and Isaiah to support his arguments.

One could suppose that a work with the former title would be a plea that the Church of England is the "true" Church and for all dissenters to turn toward her for salvation. This is not the case; indeed, he is highly critical of the Church of England, saying "what is called the National Church, or the Church of *England*, hath truly Ordinances or Ceremonies of Divine

Service, and a Worldly kind of Religion, modelled after the fashion of and according to the Course of this World."[86] He bemoans the fact that "the Pure, Primitive Christianity, and that Way of Worship which was used in the Days of the Apostles, and First Christians, is now in a manner lost from among us. . . . If ever God had a true Church in the World (as he hath always) most certainly he had at that time."[87] This is an ideal instance of a call for the humanist-inspired repristination of the Church. Despite Stafford's call to remain in the Church, he, Puritan-like, urges the Church of England back to an unadulterated, "original" form. Indeed, in *The Cause and Cure of Divisions*, the "cause" is that this pure form has been sullied by the dross of superstitious invention:

> But Alas! Herein Man hath found out many Inventions. *In their setting of their threshold by my thresholds, and their Post by my Posts,* Ezek. 43:8. He hath intermingled and added many things into the Worship of God, which *God never Commanded, nor came they into his mind*, as himself saith by his Prophet Jeremiah.[88]

What, then, is his "cure" for all the divisions in the Church?

> There should yet be a further Reformation even in our Reformed Churches, that is, to bring them up or back again into a Greater Degree of Spirituality and Truth; And to do all things according to the Pattern shewed to us in the Gospel. For then only Primitive times would return.[89]

It is a subtle but significant point that Stafford refers here to the gospels as the source of this "pattern," rather than all of Scripture. Recall that earlier Anglican divines such as Lancelot Andrewes deployed a figural Aaronic priesthood for the priestly and episcopal structure of the Church of England, based on the text's christological center. In Stafford's case, there is a kind of "gospel within the gospel" based on John 4:23, where Jesus proclaims that believers would worship "in the Spirit and in truth." Stafford's goal is a "spiritualization" of the faith that minimizes "Liturgies, Rites, Ceremonies, Traditions and Institutions of our own. . . . So that is not the worship of the true God, which is the *Circumcision made with hands*."[90] His ambition is for an inward, private faith: "nor yet doth the true worship of God stand or

---

86. Stafford, *The Cause and Cure of Divisions*, 6.
87. Stafford, *An Exhortation*, 6.
88. Stafford, *The Cause and Cure of Divisions*, 3–4.
89. Ibid., 8.
90. Ibid., 11.

consist so much in Divers Bowings and Cringings, or Gestures, but it is an inward thing; for what is Spiritual or in Spirit, is inward."[91]

Turning to matters bearing on matters related to the Old Testament, we find similar spiritualist themes that reject the "cunning corrupt *Romish* priests."[92] Stafford's focus is on individual morality:

> Notwithstanding all controversies, Disputes and different Congregations which are now in the Nation and throughout Christendom; yet as to this the Rule is safe, herein to do as *Moses did, who was admonished of God when he was about to make the tabernacle. For see (saith he) that thou make all Things according to the Pattern shewed to thee in the Mount.* And now that the Old Dispensation is abolished we are to see that we Order all Things in our Worship *according to the pattern shewed to us in the Gospel.* . . . I do believe and speak after my Judgment, that there is not a way of Worship now in this nation, nor yet on the Earth which is exactly according to the Scriptures of Truth in all things, and in all things according to the Pattern shewed in the Gospel.[93]

It is *not* "notwithstanding" the disputes of groups with numerous creedal commitments that emerged out of the Civil War and its aftermath, but precisely because of them that thinkers from Day, to Stafford and beyond, brought to completion a project to compartmentalize theology, personal faith commitment, and liturgical practice from biblical exegesis. Note that this is concurrent with a devaluation of the abolished "Old Dispensation," by which Stafford means the structure of external rites and practices. Even while defending the Church of England, Stafford betrays its hermeneutical vision, opting to reject the view of common worship held by Cranmer, Whitgift, and Hooker, replacing it with a now-familiar private faith. Day's approach is a change in methodology, and Stafford's is that of general *religious disposition*.

Richard Kidder and William Lowth: Defending Scripture

Since Christianity's origins, the perceived fulfillment of the Bible's prophetic claims has been used as part of the apologetic to justify its truth. Yet, with the rise of rhetorical, philological, and historical tools as constitutive of the exegetical process, this apologetic orientation toward Scripture became a

91. Ibid., 12.
92. Stafford, *Comfort and Benefit*, 12.
93. Ibid. 48–49.

particularly dominant counter-reaction, even in the midst of deploying these tools. The Bible has value in terms of its apologetic effectiveness on the basis of its probative validation of Christianity. I employ William Lowth and Richard Kidder as exemplars of this perspective.

William Lowth, father of the more-famous Robert Lowth, criticizes Samuel White in the Isaiah portion of Simon Patrick's *Critical Commentary and Paraphrase of the Old and New Testament*, a highly popular volume that was originally published in the early eighteenth century. In it, Patrick *et. al.* give a running commentary on the entire Scriptures. However, it is clear that by the eighteenth century, the authors perceive a need to "vindicate [the prophetical texts] from some novel expositions, which tend to deprive Christian religion of the benefit of so considerable a testimony."[94] Lowth reacts against Samuel White's interpretation, which "supposes that the far greatest part of this prophecy relates only to the times in which the prophet lived."[95] This raises a perennial question about prophecy in general as the "critical" era begins: to what extent is Isaiah predictive of events beyond his immediate historical horizon?

Many have analyzed Isaiah for its ability—or lack of it—to have correctly, sufficiently, and clearly predicted the coming of Jesus of Nazareth as the Messiah. An interesting case in point is the 1699 writing of Richard Kidder, entitled *A Demonstration of the Messias, In which the Truth of the Christian Religion is defended, especially against the Jews*. This work gives a clear picture of such apologetic exegesis, whereas Lowth's work, aside from some comments I mention above, is directed toward more textual concerns. Given the title, one would justly wonder why Kidder would write a work so directed toward *Jewish* arguments against Christianity, since their presence in England was not particularly significant. While Kidder mostly concentrates on Jewish arguments about the meaning of Scripture, his worry is that increasingly popular critical readings of the Bible had parallels with to those historically offered by Jewish thinkers. A gifted Hebrew scholar, Kidder claims to "take all possible Care to inform my self what it is that the Jews have to object against Christianity." And yet, he also complains that

> Atheism and Contempt of all Revealed Religion have prevailed of late Years. We have lived to see Moses derided, and his History ridiculed and exposed; and the Writings of the New Testament made the Matter of Drollery and profane Contempt. . . . I have to do with the Jews in the following Papers, who impugn

---

94. Patrick and Lowth, *A Critical Commentary*, iii, 223.

95. Ibid., iii, 225.

Christianity, and object against the Writers of the New Testament. Some among us use the same Objections.[96]

Who does Kidder have in mind as his interlocutors, aside from the Jews? Perhaps he is referring to, as one of those "deriding" Moses, the philosopher (and Jew, albeit an excommunicated one) Baruch Spinoza, whose *Theologico-Political Treatise* was so critical of the traditional perspective of the Old Testament that it was banned for many years. Yet Kidder does not explicitly name any of his Jewish interlocutors, so one can only speculate.[97]

Isaiah is foundational to Kidder's argument. For instance, the unbelief of the Jews is fulfilled by Isa 6:9, and Jesus is the obvious referent for the "root of Jesse" in Isa 11:1 and, of course, he stands as the Suffering Servant in Isa 53.[98] Kidder's arguments also include those that support the use of typology of a sort, but usually in a rather wooden manner whereby types properly fulfill their role as argumentative buttresses for predictive prophecy, rather than as participants in a comprehensive theological vision of how Scripture relates to the world, or indeed, as the interpreter of the world to the Church.

This apologetic reading is problematic, if exegesis is not to become a process of shaping passages into merely defensible propositional statements. Thinkers like Kidder believe that engaging with Scripture as such is a theological task, whereas I argue this is merely a continuation of theological minimization. The reason for this minimization is that the perceived attack on Scripture results in an equally antagonistic response in the context of "proving" the Bible's truth instead of its theological content.

---

96. Kidder, *A Demonstration of the Messias*, iv. Page numbers of this preface to Kidder's work are not in the original work and are provided by me.

97. Many of the Jews were considered foreigners and Amsterdam was a key enclave of European Jewry, seen as an economic foreign threat to England. Jews like Spinoza, however, were also regarded as presenting various "intellectual" threats from the Continent. James II offered the Jews what Katz refers to as "what amounted to a Declaration of Indulgence" (Katz, *The Jews in the History of England*, 151). Also politically connected to Holland, these Dutch Jews were "heavily involved" in William of Orange's accession to the throne during the Glorious Revolution (ibid., 157), whereas the English Jews were rather passive recipients of the new regime. In terms of population, however, there simply was no real threat beyond that which was illusory: the population of Jews in the late seventeenth century was about 550–660 (ibid., 162). These disproportionate attacks, I contend, are because the Jews "continued to be used as an extreme [negative] example when the question of religious toleration came up" (ibid., 175). *Rhetorically*, to associate an argument with those of the Jews was very effective at disarming its power.

98. Kidder, *A Demonstration of the Messias*, 72, 172, 173.

Robert Lowth and Proto-Romanticism

Theological minimization culminates in this account in Robert Lowth, and, via a transformation of philology into poetics, and religious apologetics into affective aesthetics, his critical work on Isaiah and the Bible is the fruition of exegetical irenicism. Published in 1778, Robert Lowth's work became the standard of Isaiah scholarship in England arguably until that of S. R. Driver. Lowth did not merely offer a commentary, but a new translation of Isaiah, and for the most part he limits his remarks to issues pertaining to philology. For instance, in his comments on Isa 53, Lowth quotes the Hutchinsonian Benjamin Kennicott's analysis of Origen's debate with Jews on this passage.[99] The point of contention is whether v. 8, rendered in the LXX as "εἰς θάνατον, unto death" was part of the original text. The adjudication of this depended on the fact that Origen, as the author of the Hexapla, must know the "original" better, and is therefore more trustworthy. Kennicott and many others of his time represent a perspective in England that Katz calls the "apotheosis of the author," a view that leads Lowth and others to seek various methods of "textual repristination." One result is "cutting the Jews out of the inheritance of Scripture by claiming to have discovered a method of textual criticism which would reveal God's message in its pristine Sinaitic glory.... Kennicott wanted to restore the *original* text of a *divine* author."[100] The vagaries of historical turbulence that muddy the *urtext* of the original authorial genius must be sifted by a process of textual archaeology.

But Lowth's primary concern, and his greatest influence on biblical criticism, was to bring to light the aesthetic of Hebrew literature and "modern understandings of prophecy as literature."[101] While Lowth's work initially had a greater effect in Germany than in England, it continued to be widely published for over a century.[102] His ideas were built on those established in his earlier and more famous work *Lectures on the Sacred Poetry of the Hebrews*, in which he notes the similarity between the writing style in the Psalms, Isaiah, and other prophets.[103] Lowth was also strict about providing an accurate translation "upon just principles of criticism, in a rational method of interpretation." Otherwise, the results would be flights of fancy for which he chides the Church Fathers: "such strange and absurd deductions of notions and ideas ... was the case of the generality of the Fathers of the

---

99. Lowth, *Isaiah*, 241–42. More on Hutchinsonianism is detailed in chapter 4.
100. Katz, *God's Last Words*, 210–11.
101. Hayes and Prussner, *Old Testament Theology*, 50.
102. McGinnis and Tull, "The Poet's Prophet," 224.
103. Ibid., 226.

Christian Church, who wrote comments on the Old Testament: and it is no wonder, that we find them of little service in leading us into the true meaning and the deep sense of the prophetical writings."[104] Lowth bemoans the dearth of Hebrew knowledge, and he explicitly rejects the Council of Trent's declaration enshrining the authenticity of the Vulgate.[105] He also implicitly criticizes his own Church of England and other traditions for not maintaining an accurate translation of the Scripture. Lowth in principle does not let the Church or any doctrinal perspective determine textual meaning; only critical translation, presumably one which he (as Bishop and one who was "professionally trained,") can properly expound, determines meaning.

Lowth mostly consulted scholars from the Continent, particularly Michaelis' commentary on the Old Testament, "an illustrious monument to the learning, judgment, and indefatigable industry of that excellent person" (and Michaelis himself made use of Lowth's ideas of biblical poetry in his work).[106] Lowth also refers to Vitringa, "to whom the world is greatly indebted for his learned labours on the Prophet."[107] Walsh argues that Lowth exemplifies the professional scholar, who, in his *Lectures on the Sacred Poetry of the Hebrews*, produced "a work essentially secular in method, deliberately avoiding theological issues, based on formal, stylistic, and metrical analysis and historical scholarship."[108] Or, as Ian Balfour suggests, Lowth engages in "a procedure that from the start places the psalmist, the prophet and the pagan poet all on the same level."[109] Thus, as poetry, and as a *literary* text, a book like Isaiah bears evidence of certain literary modes of speech, such as prosopopoeia, in which the human author has merely "attributed" certain words to God.[110] In the end, Lowth's impact was such that

> The Bible became, to a significant extent, one text among others. . . . The path Lowth charted led in two directions: his

---

104. Lowth, *Isaiah*, xliii.

105. Ibid., xlv.

106. Ibid., lvi, and also O'Neill, *The Bible's Authority*, 29. In chapter 5 of Legaspi, *The Death of Scripture*, Legaspi indicates the indebtedness of Lowth and Michaelis on each other. Each had their own peculiar effect on their respective academic cultures; but both, in Legaspi's account, "invent" the idea of biblical poetry.

107. Lowth, *Isaiah*, 131.

108. Walsh, "Profession and Authority," 393. This is not an entirely fair assessment of Lowth, for there is by no means an absence of theological concern. Prickett is more careful, noting Lowth's conservatism: "The Bible was still regarded by Lowth as having 'one common author'—in the person of the Holy Spirit. . . . We are still a long way from the world of Eichhorn, Lessing, and Herder" (Prickett, *Words and the Word*, 111).

109. Balfour, *The Rhetoric of Romantic Prophecy*, 56.

110. Ibid., 64–65.

> historical criticism helped unsettle the status of the literal sense of the Bible as an index of actual history, while his elucidation of the aesthetics of Scripture helped open the sacred text to the powerful revisionary readings undertaken by the Romantic poets.[111]

Lowth's critical work heralds a change in the definition of *prophecy*. Even the Hebrew word *Nabi* is recast in this aesthetic context as having a broad interpretations, such as "a Prophet, a Poet, or a Musician, under the influence of divine inspiration."[112] There is a shift away from a theological notion of prophet toward ideas consonant with concepts in neoclassical literature. Lowth also makes great use of the concept of the biblical text's *sublimity* as a category describing the affective, mysterious power of prophetic utterance, arising from a mind possessed by the genius of enthusiasm. Thus, says Stephen Prickett, "through Lowth's influence the Bible was to become for the Romantics not merely the model of sublimity, but also a source of style and a touchstone of true feeling."[113]

Lowth's critical impact was somewhat halted in England because of the strength of the peculiarly Anglican hermeneutic that made "non-theological" reading of the Bible difficult. Yet Lowth's contributions took form on the Continent.[114] Thus this "invention of biblical poetry" accomplished by Lowth is, as I construe it, not a development arising spontaneously or in a vacuum. Rather, following in the tradition of Day and White, he seeks new hermeneutical, non-dogmatic approaches to unlock the text that the divided Church was unable to do. However, *none of these figures see themselves as doing anything other than theological exegesis*, for each considers that there was within the Bible the means for Christianity's vindication (Kidder) or by which religious feeling can be evoked (Lowth). Nor are they particularly damaging in and of themselves with respect to, for instance, revisioning Isaianic authorship. However, Lowth's work stands as a marker in a tradition which was to

> offer a radically new frame of reference. . . . The idea of biblical poetry emerged precisely when theological definitions were receding to the margins of exegetical discourse. The concept

---

111. Ibid., 77.

112. Lowth, *Lectures on the Sacred Poetry of the Hebrews*, ii, 12.

113. Prickett, *Words and the Word*, 109. The concept of biblical sublimity is not a new one. But what is new is the emphasis upon the non-pneumatically defined characteristic of its affective impact on the reader by virtue of its textual (albeit divinely-inspired) structure.

114. Ibid., 115.

allowed interpreters direct access to the Bible, independent of the 'grand narratives' of the 'canonical tradition.' As a result, the point of contact ... was not identity in a community of faith united by canon but rather faculties of aesthetic judgment.[115]

Legaspi's description of the canon and the community as constitutive elements of Scripture are analogous to my account of early Anglican formulations of biblical hermeneutics. And, given the fact that all of those with whom I have engaged were devoted Christians (Lowth was no less than the Bishop of London), another of Legaspi's points must be emphasized: none of these figures by any means repudiate the importance of the Bible but in fact *are attempting to reclaim it and make it relevant*. If the Bible can be rescued from the impotent and divisive clutches of a divided Church via a project of cultural and academic revivification, then they saw themselves as participating in a very religious project indeed. Lowth and his successors—Broad Church and Evangelical alike—essentially abandoned the Cranmerian vision of Scripture and followed a path that, albeit in a more attenuated form, was also practiced with more enthusiasm in Germany, as sketched out by Legaspi:

> The harsh and violent realities of religious division in the centuries following the Reformation featured sharp criticisms of traditional belief, on the one hand, and intensification of confessional interpretation and polemical theology on the other. What developed in the mid-eighteenth century was . . . the realization that the Bible was no longer intelligible as scripture. . . . If the Bible was to find a place in a new political order committed to the unifying power of the state, it would have to do so as a common cultural inheritance.[116]

This is part of the vision of the "romantic university" that includes the Bible as an essential aspect of culture, and as a "classic" text, but not necessarily as *Scripture*.[117]

CONCLUSION AND AN OUTLINE OF NINETEENTH CENTURY ANGLICAN PARTIES

Protestant exegesis often aimed to avoid the perceived pitfalls of the allegorical exegesis of someone like Nehemiah Rogers. There is an inevitable

---

115. Legaspi, *The Death of Scripture*, 127–28.
116. Ibid., 5.
117. See also Hofstetter, *The Romantic Idea of a University*.

movement toward a literary reading of the text and led to the close connection between "the identification of the meaning of a text with its author's intention, and the privileged status of scientific discourse."[118] It emerges out of the Protestant anti-"romish" views of Scripture that appears to too freely engage in allegorical readings that justified the entire Roman Catholic system. Note, too, that the centrality of authorial intent is also problematic to Protestantism's own biblicism, as it risks disallowing the power of the *inspired* Word to operate at a level that may surpass that of the original author.

It was *de rigeur* for Protestants in the nineteenth century engage in this more "antagonistic," anti-Catholic form of reading. But William Day personifies a more subtle, "irenic" hermeneutic that is markedly different from that of Rogers. The religious violence of the English Civil War urged a reading of the Bible that avoids the divisiveness of dogmatic interpretation. Basic Christian tenets are not necessarily denied, but theology is no longer closely connected to the text of Scripture.

During this time, exegetes sought a *method* of reading the text. One way was the kind of "rationalist" approach of philology and textual repristination that the new "Protestant poetics" called for. Other methods paralleled that of Robert Lowth, who "rescues" the Bible both from a theological and a purely rationalist approach to identify within the text a distinctly "Hebrew" poetic impulse whose aesthetic impact on the reader is so important for how religion is conceived in Romanticism.

In what remains of this chapter, I would like to sketch out the contours of the various competing parties in the Church of England of the nineteenth century. Furthermore, I begin to indicate how each party stands in continuity with certain aspects of biblical approaches from the previous centuries. In 1855, William Conybeare wrote *Essays Ecclesiastical and Social* in which he describes three forms of church "parties" within the Anglican Church: the Low Church, the High Church and the Broad Church.[119] His is a helpful place to begin, as there is a general congruence between my designations and that of Conybeare's, though his is further subdivided. Like Conybeare, I use the term "Low Church" to represent the Evangelical party within the Church of England. By the time of the nineteenth century, this was one of the most influential parties in England, but its antecedents are present in the ideas of the Puritans. Its most defining moment came in the eighteenth century with the ministry of the Wesley brothers and the revivalist movements that swept through England had an enormous impact on English

---

118. Harrison, *The Bible, Protestantism*, 266.
119. Conybeare, *Essays Ecclesiastical and Social*, 57–164.

piety that remains to this day.[120] As with the Puritans, there is a deep suspicion of external practices that appear to be "popish," and there is a focus on inner piety and individual experience. Many of the revivalist movements split from the Church of England; I focus only on those Evangelicals of the Church of England. Of the four types I consider, the Low Church party is, as a rule, most concerned with the Bible as the source of faith, practice, moral, and ecclesial life and are nervous of any challenges to the emerging scholarly findings which, for instance, questioned the Mosaic authorship of the Pentateuch or the historical veracity of biblical events.

As Tod Jones expresses it, the Broad Church is "'not a party,' 'not a group,' 'not a faction,' and 'not an organised alliance,.' . . . By parts consisting of rational and emotional elements, by description as comprehensive, radical, and conservative."[121] It may be that Jones' description renders definition impossible, but I more narrowly attend to the Broad Church as a movement whereby historical-critical study of the Bible as a primary means of exegesis is seen as not only acceptable, but even necessary, and often an end in itself. They are the "liberal" wing of the Church of England, who seek a "progressive" application of Scripture to the life of the Church. Moreover, they are by far the most influential party in the current state of the Anglican Church in the West. For many of the Broad Church, their approach to Scripture enables one to rise above the perceived repressive power of church dogma. It would be inaccurate to argue that they *tout court* accept the critical stance toward Scripture already well-defined by a majority of biblical scholars in Germany in the nineteenth century—far from it. Broad Church members shared with Low Church Evangelicals a strong dislike for anything "romish," but they did not accept the Bible as the only source for dogma. Therefore, they were in a sense fighting on two fronts—the perceived Roman Catholic threat of the Tractarians, and the "enthusiasm" of the Evangelical wing. Yet, by the end of the century, the Broad Church became a significant aspect of the Church of England.

The High Church/Tractarian party descends in some part from the reign of Charles I and his Archbishop William Laud. Tractarians reject personal and private interpretation of Scripture more strongly than the older High Church party does. But the exegetical practices of High Church adherents in the nineteenth century have some similarities with the Tractarians. I focus, however, on the more parochial, political interpretation of the old High Church wing, as I argue that the Tractarians more closely resemble

---

120. The extent to which the nineteenth century was a time of lost faith and the waning of Evangelical fervor is adroitly challenged in Larsen, *Crisis of Doubt*.

121. Jones, *The Broad Church*, 1.

Evangelicals in terms of their desire to become ecclesially unmoored from the state, and as a reactionary movement against "liberalism."

Finally, I attend to English Roman Catholic biblical perspectives in the nineteenth century. They are, of course, the perennial catalysts for numerous upheavals in English history, but their history is too complex to treat with as much detail as that of the Church of England. They comprised an entire social community unto themselves for centuries, at times triumphant, but most often powerless at the hands of Anglican persecutions. But once Protestants had a firm grip on political power, Catholics had to flee (like the Puritans, many went to France) or to live in isolated communities. For this reason, many of these communities functioned in a "sectarian" manner.[122] During the reign of Queen Elizabeth I, some continued to give their allegiance to Rome and they were called recusants and the Anglican establishment tended to view them with deep suspicion. But Roman Catholics also had their own vigorous responses to the Protestant claim on all sides of *sola scriptura*, as they saw this as being the same thing as "private interpretation." Catholics were often ready to point out that the same Bible that was used by all parties resulted in numerous heretical developments. While the Roman Catholic "threat" did not emerge in the nineteenth century as it did during the reign of James II, the antagonistic perspective of the other parties resulted in no emancipation for Roman Catholics until 1829. The Union with Ireland Act of 1800 did not help in allaying fears, as many Roman Catholics moved from Ireland to England, and, eventually, Roman Catholic members of parliament became a reality.

Roman Catholic biblical exegesis in the nineteenth century was generally impacted by the Counter-Reformation, which produced the Council of Trent.[123] The Council rejected the idea of *sola scriptura*, seeing it as equivalent to private interpretation, a view not usually denied by Protestants. Since *sola scriptura* was conceived within the antagonistic matrix of Protestant-Catholic animosity, it was viewed as a negatively construed term. For Protestants, "Bible alone" was not, in other words, merely a positive statement on the power of Scripture alone for salvation, but a doctrine that negated the power of any mediatory figure, such as a priest, or the Church in general. *Sola scriptura*, therefore, was for the most part a doctrine that developed as direct fallout of the divisive context of sixteenth-century Europe. Several Council of Trent decrees made it difficult for Roman Catholics to engage in biblical exegesis in the same manner as Protestants. Individual, personal reading of Scripture was not strictly proscribed, but was virtually impossible, as ver-

---

122. Questier, *Catholicism and Community*, 3.
123. See Bedouelle, "Biblical Interpretation," 428–49.

nacular translations were rarely made available. When the Douay-Reims version was finally published (the full version in 1610), few could afford it. And the work of Protestant translation was viewed with intense suspicion, as they (rightly) noted that even from the time of Tyndale, these translations were developed with Protestant biases and, in the view of Catholics, resulted in changing the very words of God. Such a task could only be done by the institution in which the Holy Spirit works.[124]

The theologically minimalist field of discourse is the context in which exegetical debates of the nineteenth century occur. Thus, Evangelicals like Robert Payne Smith (Chapter 3) do not offer a markedly different methodology from that of a Broad Churchman like T.K. Cheyne (Chapter 5). Even a High Church thinker like Christopher Wordsworth (Chapter 4) employs certain exegetical categories that have been developed by those who attempt to relate the Bible to immediate problems of ecclesiological or human existence. As the subsequent chapters show, all these latter exegetes are deeply interested in "theological" matters, defined in various ways, but the theological quality of the text is an *optional* mode of discourse and not constitutive of the Bible as the word of God.

---

124. One important Catholic thinker who must at least be mentioned is Antoine Augustin Calmet (1672-1757). Although he resided in France, this French Benedictine wrote *Commentaire Littéral sur tous Les Livres L'Ancien* in 8 volumes from 1707-16. This was a work that, like that of Simon Patrick, commented on the entire Bible and was admired by Protestants and Roman Catholics alike. In many ways it was a rather traditional Roman Catholic approach. It should be noted, however, that there were some divergences from typical Roman Catholic exegesis. First, Calmet tends to move away from single proof-texts—the traditional messianic texts, for instance—and "argues that one cannot understand the figure of the Messiah from a single passage . . . But the interpreter must take into consideration the whole range of passages within the larger narrative context" (Childs, *The Struggle to Understand Isaiah*, 257). Second, Calmet is fully willing to concede to a proximate, historical referent to a passage like that of Isa 7:14, but he also argues that there is a "spiritual" sense of the text beyond the merely historical, and the two have a very close connection to each other. This single verse is part of a greater temporal sequence that participates in the grand hope of Israel for redemption, and hence that same hope for all of humanity. In other words, Calmet did not read these texts in two discrete ways, but allowed the historical and the spiritual senses of the text to flow into each other. I mention Calmet—a non-English theologian—because of his influence on Roman Catholics in England, which extended across educational and professional lines. He also, regrettably, represents one of the rare occurrences of Roman Catholic exegesis that had any impact on English Roman Catholics.

3

Robert Payne Smith
Rescuing Isaiah from Its Opponents

INTRODUCTION: COUNTERACTING "MODERN INFIDELITY"

AFTER THESE PREPARATORY CHAPTERS, we can finally begin with the process of a close reading of representative Isaiah commentaries. I have selected Robert Payne Smith (1819–95) as representative of scholarly Evangelicalism and also one of the few Anglican Evangelicals engaging in debates surrounding Isaiah. In this chapter I show that Smith embodies a highly individualistic methodology, which *ipso facto* leaves little space for an ecclesially- and christologically-embodied hermeneutic. Instead, Smith opts for a "modernist," reading that eschews, for instance, the concrete reality of Israel in favor of a "spiritual" interpretation.[1] He selectively chooses methodology that emerged out of the irenic mode of exegesis, but antagonistically directs them against his interlocutors, who are primarily those of a "liberal" persuasion, who in many cases he considers unbelievers.

---

1. One certainly cannot expect Smith to do anything other than a "modern" reading, just as Aquinas' was "medieval." The extent, however, to which an interpreter claims to have abrogated and rendered irrelevant earlier interpretations—a particularly common mentality in the modern era—speaks to the way in which they are members of a kind of "party." Therefore, in this chapter, despite Smith's relative orthodoxy, his is a "modernist," at least methodologically.

I examine how ecclesial division implacts Smith's exegesis using the two categories I introduced at the beginning of this book of antagonistic exegesis, and a seemingly more passive, irenic exegesis.[2] The active, antagonistic mode is one where, in Smith's case, exegesis becomes governed by a rigorous apologetic such that the text is read and interpreted *against* that of others. With regard to the former, Smith's antagonism is against those who, in his mind, denigrate the sanctity of the Bible. The divisive context of the historical-critical method and the need for "facts," "objective" interpretation, and "proof" compel his readings to be shaped by such terminology. Indeed, while Smith's exegesis aims at certain doctrinal matters, he seeks to use these putatively non-theological tools to uncover doctrinal truth. Such tools, however, seldom differ from those of his opponents. In other words, the erosion of the uniquely Anglican reading of Scripture drove thinkers like Smith to read Scripture in ways that are not methodologically different than those of his opponents. I organize my analysis with respect to this Anglican hermeneutical "touchstone" of Chapter 1 to bring into relief these two aspects of division with respect to theological exegesis.

Smith was one of the founders of Wycliffe Hall, Oxford, in 1877, and of Ridley Hall, Cambridge, in 1881, both schools with a strong Evangelical perspective. He was assistant master at Edinburgh Academy (1847–53), headmaster of Kensington Proprietary School (1853–57), sub-Librarian at the Bodleian (1857–65), Regius Professor of Divinity at Oxford (1865–71), and dean of Canterbury (1871–95.) He is best known for his monumental work on the *Thesaurus Syriacus* (eventually translated into English as *A Compendious Syriac Dictionary*), though he published on numerous issues, arguing on behalf of an Evangelical, conservative position. This included *Daniel I-VI: An Exposition of the Historical Portion of the Writings of the Prophet Daniel* and a translation from Syriac of *The Third Part of the Ecclesiastical History of John Bishop of Ephesus*. He also penned prefaces for various popular pamphlets that defend an Evangelical perspective. An interesting case is that of *Modern Infidelity and the Best Methods of Counteracting It*. The pamphlet argues that

> the most effectual method of combating *unbelief in individuals* is the *moral isagogic*, *i.e.,* that by which the conscience is touched, the religious need awakened, and salvation in Christ heartily and lovingly testified, from personal experience. . . . In combating *systems of unbelief*, success is only to be hoped for from a

---

2. As I am about to engage directly with an exegete here, it should be noted that the danger is that I am implying that ecclesial division is the singular cause of various biblical "burdens." It is not necessarily an "either-or" case, in which the Church would not experience confusion had the Reformation not occurred.

really *scientific* method of defence [and]. . . a constant employment of the ever-improving apparatus of modern investigation.³

Although Smith did not write this passage, his moral imprimatur of this work in the preface suggests that his approach to combating "modern" readings is similar. Indeed, the above passage is a fit summary of Smith's position, namely, an affective mode of engagement with the text, and an aim to be scientific and objective.

As an orientalist, Smith knew Arabic, Hebrew, and Syriac and was interested in matters related to the Old Testament. However, he also wrote on clerical education, and was committed to setting up schools for boys and girls, aligned along Evangelical convictions. Although originally influenced by the Oxford Movement, he eventually moved toward an Evangelical position, sympathetic to non-conformists, though he remained an Anglican.⁴

With respect to Isaiah, Smith did not write a commentary on the book, as such. He did, however, write two works that are relevant to the present discussion and represent a typically Evangelical perspective. The first is a series of nine sermons that he preached at Oxford entitled *The Authenticity and Messianic Interpretation of the Prophecies of Isaiah Vindicated in a Course of Sermons*. While the title implies that they are sermons, it is clear that, at least in the published version, they are most accurately to be regarded as lectures designed to make a scholarly case for the prophetic ("messianic") character of Isaiah. Smith also gave the Bampton Lectures in 1870, entitled *Prophecy: a Preparation for Christ*, which were "preached" at Oxford. The subject of this latter work is not Isaiah as such, but the prophet figures rather prominently in the preface, as he assesses the newest scholarship on the book. Although my analysis focusses more on *The Authenticity and Messianic Interpretation*, Smith's discussion of Isaiah in his Bampton Lectures helpfully complements my own. Both publications are part of his larger project with respect to how the Old Testament is to be read as Christian Scripture and how theology is related to the Bible. His shorter and earlier work, *The Mosaic Authorship and Credibility of the Pentateuch* (1838) also indicates his rather polemical endeavor to argue against new scholarship with respect to authorship, in favor of the "credibility" of the Old Testament.

My analysis first gives an overview of his method of reading Isaiah that comoes out of *The Authenticity and Messianic Interpretation of the Prophecies of Isaiah Vindicated* and *Prophecy: a Preparation for Christ*. I follow this by discussing the theological ramifications of his work and his attempts to

---

3. Christlieb, *Modern Infidelity*, 5.

4. Simpson, "Smith, Robert Payne (1818–1895)"; Harris, *Evangelicals and Education*, 348–49.

read Isaiah "theologically." I order my analysis with respect to the distinctly Anglican vision of reading Scripture from Chapter 1. Thus, I consider Smith's reading in terms of ecclesiology and individuality, the wholeness of Scripture, and how christology functions to hold the two Testaments together, such as figuration and his construal of the meaning of prophecy.

ANGLICAN ISAIAH SCHOLARSHIP IN THE NINETEENTH CENTURY: A NEGLECTED PROPHET?

This section briefly outlines the exegetical context of Smith's contribution to work on Isaiah. Commentaries and new research on Isaiah abounded in the eighteenth and nineteenth centuries. For the most part, however, aside from Robert Lowth's (1710-87) commentary on Isaiah, much of the work was done by Continental scholars, most notably Campegius Vitringa (1659-1722), Wilhelm Gesenius (1786-1842) and Bernhard Duhm (1847-1928.) These earlier scholars approached Isaiah in the form of critical philological studies, not unlike that of seventeenth-century interpreter William Day in Chapter 2, though Day's exegetical method was less formalized. Whereas the reception history of Isaiah from the beginning located the book in a highly "christianized" context, "the new concern to get back to what the original Hebrew meant . . . was especially challenging in the case of Isaiah" and it became one of the central books that functioned as a "test case" for the historical-critical method.[5]

Though these Continental authors' work on Isaiah was well known in England, there were also some English-language commentaries that were popular in Smith's day, but very few were carried out by Anglicans. In England, greater attention was typically given to other Old Testament books than Isaiah. In fact, aside from Christopher Wordsworth and Thomas Kelly Cheyne (Chapters 4 and 5), there is a notable absence of scholarly work in the form of a proper commentary on Isaiah during the nineteenth century, and the few existing discussions and intellectual studies tended to revolve around textual "problems," such as authorship, dating, and the verifiability of the recounted historical events. Of course, at a more public level, pastors continued to preach from Isaiah and there were numerous commentaries with which preachers consulted, such as Rawlinson's work on Isaiah in the *Pulpit Commentary*, though this was a late nineteenth-century contribution. There was marginally more interest in Isaiah from nonconformist thinkers, such as Joseph Addison Alexander, who wrote a commentary in 1851, George Adam Smith in Scotland in two volumes (1888, 1890), and

---

5. Sawyer, *The Fifth Gospel*, 178.

Ebenezer Henderson. All were aware of the work that was done in Germany to question, for instance, unitary authorship, and in many of their commentaries attended to these issues.

By the nineteenth century, and following upon work by the aforementioned Continental thinkers, a new "critical" approach to the Bible and the Old Testament in particular arose. For instance, many scholars used Thomas Hartwell Horne's popular three-volume *An Introduction to the Critical Study and Knowledge of the Holy Scriptures*. With respect to doctrinal propositions, Horne's text had a very conservative orientation to the Bible. At the same time, his rather modernist notions can at times be perceived, such as when he argues that in interpretation, "the only way by which to understand the meaning of the sacred writers, and to distinguish between true and false doctrines, is, to lay aside all preconceived modern notions and systems.... Only an unbiased mind can attain the true and genuine sense of Scripture."[6] Regarding prophecy, Horne defines it as "the highest evidence that can be given, of supernatural communion with the Deity."[7] This idea of "proof" figures prominently in his *Introduction*, and all miracles recorded in Scripture are proofs of the text's divine origin, which has echoes of Richard Kidder's reading of Isaiah that we saw in the last chapter. For Horne, prophecy is an event, a subcategory of miracle.[8] Horne's analysis of Isaiah relies heavily on Robert Lowth's work, as well as that of Vitringa. He also references other less-known people who wrote pamphlets on Isaiah, as well as another Bible handbook by Robert Gray.[9] However, Horne does not address issues of authorship and considers it unquestionable that Christ is clearly predicted in the book.[10] The similarity of Horne's *Introduction* to that of Robert Payne Smith is made clear further in this chapter. I mention Horne for the purpose of indicating the kind of intellectual language that was common in the nineteenth century defense of prophecy.

SMITH'S EXEGETICAL METHODOLOGY

I begin with a brief note on Smith's overall methodology. His approach to Scripture is governed by a need to argue against other readings. This is particularly evident in his argument for a preservation of the miraculous

6. Horne, *Introduction*, 2:663–4.

7. Ibid., 2:641.

8. See ibid., 1:231–495, in which the concepts of "proof" and "evidence" figure strongly.

9. Gray, *A Key to the Old Testament and Apocrypha*.

10. Horne, *Introduction*, 4:159.

quality of the text, which can be revealed by philological and textual analysis. Moreover, I describe how Smith views the task of exegesis and the way that the Bible does not cohere with the Anglican touchstone, and in fact works against it.

A simple examination of the titles of Smith's works reveals the highly apologetic aim of his writings. Even a cursory reading quickly indicates that Smith's purpose is to defend Isaiah against those who attempt to read the book in ways that deny the evidentiary power of prophecy as proof of the truth of the Christian faith. For the most part, his interlocutors are those of the "new scholarship," primarily German, whose work on Isaiah and much of the Old Testament, in Smith's view, brought the book into question in terms of its predictive power, its unitary authorship, and its cohesion. Therefore, it is certainly the case that Smith's approach is funded by an interecclesial divisive context: he is not reading Isaiah for the purpose of exegesis on Isaiah's terms but in a defensive mode that sees the Bible as an embattled text, under siege by approaches that were beginning to gain currency in the nineteenth century.

The preface to *Prophecy: a Preparation for Christ* is a good example of the form of Smith's apologetic method. He focuses particularly on Isaiah and shows what he sees as laughable inconsistencies between biblical scholars. For example, Smith says

> The book is a mere collection of fragments, of all dates, written by a confused horde of nameless personages, many of them mere imitators, whose effusions have been patched together upon no other principle than that of filling up the skins of parchment. And yet this *olla podrida*, this hotch-potch, in which are jumbled together the fragments of writers ... is the book in which Hebrew genius reaches the summit alike of strength and beauty.[11]

The German scholars whom Smith references, from Ewald to Gesenius, from Augusti to Koppe, all argue for an Isaiah that comprises a patchwork of unrelated textual fragments, yet it is, illogically, their claim that it is simultaneously a work of Hebrew literary genius (certainly impacted by Lowth's work.) This disingenuous argument is not sustainable for Smith on logical grounds. He continues to show how one scholar such as Movers argues that Isaiah 23 was written by Jeremiah, while Ewald meanwhile makes the case that it was written by a disciple of Isaiah. Yet, according to Bleek, Isaiah was composed by the time of Jeremiah.[12] This cacophonous and disparate list

11. Smith, *A Preparation for Christ*, xviii.
12. Ibid., xx.

of scholars reveals, to Smith, a contradictory, and hence unreliable, state of affairs that renders any of their findings suspect.

The findings of these "negative critics," as he calls them, are problematic above all because of their *presuppositions* in approaching the book, namely, that "prophecy has no supernatural element."[13] This category of the "supernatural," is fundamental to a correct reading of Isaiah and the Bible in general. For Smith, "prophecy is a miracle; the very thing for which we argue is a supernatural presence of God in the words and actions of certain persons who claimed to speak in God's name."[14] The negative critics "start with the denial of the possibility of God speaking to man at all. . . . They are bound to affirm that every precise prophecy is either an imposture or an artifice."[15] While these critics may have come to contradictory conclusions regarding the date or authorship of Isaiah, the primary problem is that they all agree that such a "supernatural" element in Scripture cannot exist and therefore they must find a way to explain it away via a "natural" explanation.

Smith's perspective on the Isaiah conceives of it as a book in which the predictions contained in it were "so marvellously fulfilled in Christianity," and their value to prove the truth of the Christian faith must be employed to their fullest extent.[16] A book as important as Isaiah must be regarded in terms of its evidentiary value. That is, the Old Testament in general functions as a "preparation" for the coming of Christ, and as such, must bear evidence of "proof." The purpose of the "preparatory dispensation" of the Old Testament was to prepare humanity for "true religion," the contours of which is

> the bestowal of sufficient aid to enable us to fulfil our obligations to God, and of some means for the purification of the conscience from the stain of sin, and for the raising of the soul from its present degradation to a fitness for the reception of God's mercies. We assert that Christianity is the sole religion upon earth which fulfils these necessary conditions; and, farther, that God has given us the sole satisfactory proof that it is the true religion.[17]

This perspective is the governing motif of Smith's exegesis of Isaiah. As such, his view of the Old Testament is that it serves a rather minimal function, which is defined in terms of its apologetic and evidentiary force via its narration of supernatural events that prove its miraculous power. If Isaiah were

13. Ibid., xxiv.
14. Ibid., xii.
15. Ibid.
16. Ibid., xv.
17. Ibid., viii.

not to have this quality, if it were merely a collection of disconnected texts by anonymous sources, then it no longer could be relied upon to provide evidence of God's communication to humanity and preparation for Christianity—that is, true religion.

Smith's methodology reveals that he is as much a scholar of the nineteenth century and an inheritor of new readings of Scripture as those against whom he writes. Indeed, while it is clear that his presuppositions with respect to the "supernatural" character of Scripture differ from his opponents,' *he engages in the debate in terms defined by his own interlocutors*. Moreover, following on the developments of the previous century, the analysis of the Bible is a *textual* matter, meaning the application of whatever scientific, historical, and philological apparatus that can uncover its meaning is necessary.

There are two central points that indicate the deeply modernist mode in which Smith engages Scripture. First, the use of the term "supernatural" as a category that implies an explicit opposition to the "natural realm" is a relatively recent theological phenomenon, especially the way that Smith uses it. Such theological discourse makes dualistic distinctions between that which is "natural" and a further "realm" or state of being that stands above the natural world, to which are attributed aspects of the divine. Yet, the use of "supernatural" as a term meant to stake out the realm of divine causation was almost unused until the thirteenth century.[18] However, this discourse of the work of God as "supernatural" became particularly ascendant after the Reformation. The "natural" world came to be seen as that region in which the world could be described in terms of immanent material causation. I regard the ascendancy of this perspective after the Reformation, in broad terms, as a *theological* process precisely because it is also parallels the *hermeneutical* shifting of biblical textual referents in strictly material terms. The rejection of the supernatural, thus defined, was not because of an atheistic impulse *per se* but because the supernatural was thought of as a source of disorder to a naturally ordered world, viewed as a kind of theurgic act, which was *theologically* unacceptable for those who yet maintained belief in a perfect and immutable God. Thus, exegetes could in principle accept "supernatural" occurrences, but, as we saw with William Day, most considered them as separate interpretations of a natural occurrence.

---

18. See Bartlett, *The Natural and the Supernatural in the Middle Ages*, 15. C. S. Watkins shows the use of the supernatural in a specifically English context. For instance, he shows how, in the Middle Ages, miracle was not thought of in terms that accept a strong dichotomy. See, e.g, his discusson of William of Malmesbury (Watkins, *History and the Supernatural in Medieval England*, 45).

For Smith, this supernatural interruption of the natural realm, far from producing disorder—despite the unpredictability of such disruptions—was the proof of this other "realm" of being that oversaw its shaping. These miraculous events provide clues to—and certainty of—this other realm. However, the fact that Smith employs the category of "supernatural" suggests that he buys into a dualist perspective that would have been rather foreign to earlier readers of Scripture. In the twentieth century, Henri de Lubac, for instance, aimed to recover a sense of the supernatural, which "is the whole order of realities that are related to our final end in the beatific vision. Thus he could affirm that the supernatural designates the divine order of things in its contradistinction from, but in union with, the human order."[19] Proofs of the veracity of the Bible build a case in a quasi-judicial form. Charles Taylor, using Max Weber's well-known categories, describes the process whereby the "sacred" and "secular" are divided along materialist/spiritual lines in terms of a change from an "enchanted" to a "disenchanted" world:

> ... the enchanted world, in which nature and social life were interwoven with higher times, left little room for unbelief. Theologians distinguished between the natural and the supernatural level, but it was not possible to live experientially with one's awareness confined to the first. Spirit, forces, powers, higher times were always obtruding ... With the disenchantment of the world ... this kind of extrusion of the higher became in principle possible.[20]

Taylor argues also that this distinction between the natural and supernatural during the early modern period was made precisely for the purposes for which Smith uses the term, namely "to establish the sovereign power of God, whose judgments made right and wrong, and could not be chained by the bent of 'nature.'"[21] Therefore, this separation of God's providential ordering of the world from the realm of "natural" or material causes (which is also the very basis of the scientific method) was not an idea imposed by malicious forces outside of ecclesial boundaries, but a theological category

---

19. Moloney, "De Lubac and Lonergan," 514. John Milbank also credits Kant with this ontological bifurcation: "orthodoxy requires that we understand the universe in vitalist and panpsychic terms ... precisely because the natural is ontologically inseparable from the lure of the supernatural. Ockham's theology ... within whose lineage Kant's philosophy still falls ... by requiring a sharp separation of reason from will, as of reason from faith ... ensured the corralling of nature and reason in the sterile hall of mirrors which is the epistemological universe of representation" (Milbank, "Hume Versus Kant," 289).

20. Taylor, *A Secular Age*, 375.

21. Ibid., 542.

(given force by nominalist argumentation against Thomistic "realism"[22]) that Smith unconsciously, but wholeheartedly, adopts and uses.

Second, while on the surface Smith views the Bible as *sui generis*, his methodology employs categories developed in the modern period and that have little to do with an Anglican vision of Scripture. This parallels the work being done by other Evangelicals at the time. For instance, there was the "Christian Evidence Society," which was started by Anglicans, and was presided over by various Archbishops (the first being Tait.) This organization was dedicated to providing, as would be expected, various proofs for the veracity of the Christian faith in the face of perceived attacks:

> For a defence they appealed to the "evidences" of Christianity, the long-standing apologetic tool of both Anglicans and Nonconformists, derived from Locke, Butler, Paley and others within the empirical tradition of English theology. In this tradition biblical miracles and the fulfilment of biblical prophecy in Jesus had provided objective support for the claim that Christianity has a supernatural origin. . . . This emphasis found links later in the century with an Evangelical tradition which despite its emphasis on the experience of the heart had also seen the need to defend the authenticity of the Bible and Christian truth in an objectively certain way.[23]

Since this Society was formed by Anglicans and Nonconformists, one can see even within its Evangelical commitments a microcosm of the ease toward which the irenic reading of Scripture obtains, for "although based on a Trinitarian understanding, *it would studiously avoid all discussions of distinctive doctrines and not commit itself to any particular view of inspiration.*"[24] The uniquely Anglican mode of reading the Bible could not hold sway; rather, a new hermeneutic had to emerge in the face of competing visions such that

> while there were both internal and external evidences for Christianity, the internal took a distinctly secondary position in the

---

22. Ibid.

23. Johnson, "Popular Apologetics in Late Victorian England," 560. I have found no evidence that Smith was a member of this society, only that there are very strong parallels between it and his apologetic approach to the Bible. I should also mention the recent work, Penner, *The End of Apologetics*, which is a trenchant critique of the whole apologetic process' deeply modern cast. My only critique of Penner on this score is his acceptance of the common narrative of modernity as extrinsically related to the Church, rather than the Church's significant participation in, and contribution to, modernity's development.

24. Johnson, "Popular Apologetics in Late Victorian England," 561, italics mine.

argument with unbelief to the "facts" provided by the external: the person and character of Jesus Christ, the realities of fulfilled prophecy and miracles, the evidences provided in the history and spread of Christianity of its supernatural origins, and its adaptation to human nature.[25]

Smith's orientation vis-à-vis Isaiah accords very closely with this description and he and his opponents share a common language and philosophical-theological commitments. Smith is willing to "play by their rules" in terms of what is acceptable evidence and proper mode of argumentation. In other words, despite their incorrect assumptions regarding the supernatural, he accepts that it is in theory possible to make the case for specious Old Testament predictions based on a common logical structure:

> Let the critics, then, disprove the real inner unity between the two Testaments; let them show that the Christian Church does not answer to, and complete ... the earlier dispensation. Till they do this, it is in vain to put forward the negative criticisms as fairly commensurate with the greatness of the thesis which it undertakes to prove. The Bible, it says, is an ordinary book; its miracles are contrary to science; its prophecies the record of facts that have already happened. But they assume all this; they do not attempt to prove it.[26]

All matters of Scripture are valid objects of logical disputation irrespective of ecclesial location and theological commitment for Smith. He attempts to argue that the most "natural" explanation for the prophecies in the Old Testament is their miraculous fulfillment in Jesus. The meaning of the Suffering Servant in Isa 53 is "clearly" Jesus because it is the best explanation of the literal and logical meaning of the text; those who cannot see this are deliberately ignoring it because they are blinded by their anti-supernaturalistic presuppositions. However, by using terms that imply a certain inherent clarity of the literal meaning of the text, Smith accepts that, while he and his opponents do not share certain fundamental conclusions, they share enough common language and philosophical assumptions with respect to the use of "evidence" that they should succeed in disassembling the texts of the Old Testament. The only difference is that he considers his own arguments to be more persuasive.

Smith's family resemblance to his opponents is in sharp distinction to my construal of the hermeneutical vision of early Anglicanism. Indeed, it is

---

25. Ibid., 568.
26. Smith, *A Preparation for Christ*, xv.

not at all clear how Smith's theology of Scripture is "Anglican" in any way; he is, rather, Evangelical-in-general, as there is no reference to the Anglican Church. Like his contemporaries, Smith aims to read Scripture in a way that is commensurate with the critical tools that were developed in the midst of controversy. There is no ecclesiology that funds his exegesis. Therefore, his particular apologetic form, and hence divisive mode of reading Isaiah, *requires that he enter into a debate that is already shaped by those whom he opposes*. As strident and combative as Smith attempts to be in his lectures, he has no distinctive vision of Scripture. Instead, he is a sign of the reality of a divided Church, and hence of the minimization of the much deeper vision of the Bible inscribed by Cranmer, Whitgift, and Hooker.

By employing the categories related to the Anglican touchstone of Chapter 1, in what follows I expand on the differences between Smith and this Anglican hermeneutical vision, as well as how his exegesis is shaped by divisiveness. In each case, aside from the instances where Smith is directly opposing certain readings, because of his apologetic approach, he takes on the various assumptions of his modern audience and is only different from them in degree, but not in kind.

THE BIBLE, THE CHURCH, AND THE INDIVIDUAL

Like many of his Evangelical contemporaries, Smith, I argue, urges an approach to the Bible that is non-mediatory, that is, one in which the individual has a direct relationship with God via the Scriptures and their personal experiences, usually expressed in terms of the affectations of the "heart." This gives evidence to the effect of a divisive reading in that such an exegetical perspective avoids the problem of giving the Church—a divided and fractious institution—any pride of place in the exegetical process. By Smith's time, a reading tethered to the particularity of an ecclesial community would be a "denominational" one, rather than personal.[27] Evangelicals

---

27. The High Church party took the precisely opposite view in light of the so-called "Western Schism" in which a whole section of Evangelically-minded West Country Anglicans seceded from the Established Church, based on their reading of Scripture with respect to the Trinity. The High Church Party saw this as "the predictable outcome of the rejection of episcopal authority, and a dangerous distortion of the right of private judgement" (Carter, *Anglican Evangelicals*, 149). See also Zabriskie, *Anglican Evangelicals*, 83–86 and Jay, *The Evangelical and Oxford Movements*, 5. Carter describes the "primacy of the individual experience" in the Evangelical movement. Many Establishment Evangelicals did not explicitly argue against a role for the Church in the exegesis of Scripture and they were as a rule positive toward the Prayer Book (see, e.g., Carter, *Anglican Evangelicals*, 2). Their interpretation of the Prayer Book (and Cranmer) would be an Evangelical one, of which Ashley Null's would be a good modern-day example

regarded the union of Church and State in terms of an Old Testament biblical model, but ecclesial structures were no more than the mere *bene esse* of the Church, since the "real" Church was that of the invisible elect.[28] Primacy was given to Scripture in a more individualist mode; the power of its "bare reading" within the Church was attenuated. The result was, as with Puritanism, a greater focus on preaching; this produced giants like Charles Simeon, but there was also an associated diminution of interest in the communal nature of faith.

In Chapter 1, the Anglican "touchstone" describes how the Church plays a central role in theological exegesis. Attendant to the rise of ecclesial division since the time of Hooker was the detachment of the Church from such a reading, and we saw this disintegration in Chapter 2. The following examines how Smith's hermeneutic is emblematic of a highly individualist reality that virtually ignores any concrete role for the Church as a particular, visible reality. I contend that this approach to Scripture parallels that of thinkers such as Chillingworth, whose exegetical approach arose out of an equivalence made between a dogmatic and an ecclesial reading. And an ecclesial reading is problematic because of the perception that it leads not only to division and controversy, but also violence. New, non-theological methodologies fund new readings of the text. The attempt itself to move away from division generated this new latitudinarian disposition that was, in effect, another party from whom many thinkers borrowed (often unconsciously) numerous exegetical strategies that read Scripture against the Church.

The working out of these ideas can be seen in Smith's exegesis of Isaiah. Despite the need for certain fundamental assumptions regarding the "supernatural" aspect of the Bible, the reader can obtain a correct understanding of the text if he or she can, with more or less objectivity, interpret the text aright. As Smith argues, "a fair judgment can be arrived at only by an examination of the evidence which [the Bible] offers in support of its claims, and this inquiry should be arrived on in a judicial frame of mind."[29] The negative critics do not possess this "judicial frame of mind" in their examination of the evidence, and thus their arguments fail. This is not to say that Smith rejects any element of prior antecedent faith, for he argues that "if the Bible be the Word of God, our duty is to bow our wills humbly and obediently before it"—and yet, he adds, "but a being made in God's image

---

(Null, "Thomas Cranmer's Theology of the Heart"; Null, "Thomas Cranmer and the Anglican Way of Reading Scripture.")

28. Carter, *Anglican Evangelicals,* 29–30.
29. Smith, *A Preparation for Christ,* xv.

has no right to abandon his self-mastery except upon the clearest *evidence*."[30] In the preface to his Bampton Lectures, Smith says, "there are prophecies which refer simply to our Lord, and which no straightforward criticism can interpret otherwise.... The balance of evidence is so entirely in favour of the Messianic interpretation."[31] This reveals that Smith's loyalties reside in two camps: he maintains a certain veneer of theological language with respect to Scripture, but firmly accepts that the individual must be convinced by "clear evidence" before submitting to its words.

A corollary to this need for clear evidence and an impartial mind in the reader's approach to Scripture is a very clear individualist tendency, so central to modern interpretative approaches. There is a very minimal role for the Church as a corporate body in Smith's exegesis: the individual reader approaches the text to mine it for its evidentiary value in order to find proof for "true religion" and self-certainty. In his first sermon on *The Authenticity and Messianic Interpretation of the Prophecies of Isaiah*, he attempts to argue against a "Roman" view of Scripture as opposed to the right of "private judgment." Smith states that "[Protestant] theologians have been apt to speak chiefly of the 'right' of private judgment; and those who have taken less controversial ground have described it as a 'duty.' *Truly it is neither one nor the other, but a necessity: men must choose.*"[32] The importance of free will is discussed further in this chapter, but for now I merely indicate that it plays a central role in Smith's exegesis of Scripture. The implication of an approach to Scripture that argues for clear evidence is that individuals must apprehend and make their own judgment about whether to accept it or not.

Smith also appeals to another aspect of the individual that is equally important in the nineteenth century—the affections and emotional disposition. We saw this above in the language of the Christian Evidence Society. Such thinking about faith is the fruit of the new methodology inherited from many in the previous century—of which Robert Lowth is emblematic (see Chapter 2). Though the affective aspect of exegesis is more muted in the works I examine here, Smith does appeal to the "heart," a term often used by both Evangelicals and Broad Churchmen alike. Smith says,

> in [the Bible] ... men find what they need,—it supplies a want, a craving in their own natures ... Call it, if you will, fanaticism, but as a matter of fact it is this internal conviction which supports and upholds the true Christian. It is man's own heart at last, taught by the Holy Ghost, which convinces him that he

---

30. Ibid., xi, emphasis mine.
31. Smith, *The Authenticity and Messianic Interpretation of Isaiah*, xxvi.
32. Ibid., 4, emphasis mine.

> needs a Saviour, and that Jesus of Nazareth both can and will save him.[33]

> Christianity ever has claimed, and still claims, the heart, and demands of those who profess it, that they should submit even their inmost wills to the pure and holy will of God.[34]

This language is classically Evangelical, with its appeal to the "heart," as is an aim to convince people of their need of, and "craving" for, something missing in life, a craving which only Jesus can fulfill. But the language of the heart and of the affections are not the sole province of Evangelical piety, but also of more liberal thinkers like S. T. Coleridge for whom the experiential dimension of religion is key.[35]

For Smith, therefore, the exegesis of Scripture is best accomplished by the exercise of the individual believer and the Church serves in a secondary capacity. While the Church is a referent for various prophecies in terms of its prefiguration by the nation of Israel for Smith, she does not appear to exercise any function with respect to the exegetical *process* itself. She serves as a kind of extradiegetic point, without any connection to the biblical story. While his opponents often read Scripture against the tradition of the Church as a sign of the victory of the individual against the dominance of Church authority, Smith's more subtle version of this tendency places him in closer affinity with them than he may wish to explicitly affirm. While most of his conclusions are in agreement with historical Christianity and the Creeds, his exegetical method, which favours the personal judgment of the individual reader of the text, by no means guarantees that such conclusions ensue.

A theologically central concept to Smith's individualist construal is "free will." Free will is a gift given by God and is inherent within each person. In Smith's understanding of prophecy, he is therefore careful to avoid a rigorous form of necessary fulfillment and even argues that some deliberately added confusion had been inserted in the text to elicit curiosity.

> There may be, perhaps, in his words some slight degree of ambiguity, some slight veiling of his meaning, for such was usually the case with the answers of the prophets as to their outer form,

---

33. Smith, *A Preparation for Christ*, 46–47.
34. Smith, *The Authenticity and Messianic Interpretation of Isaiah*, 240.
35. See, e.g, Barbeau, "Coleridge, Christology, and the Language of Redemption," 263–82, where we can see how Coleridge is deeply interested in the language of theology for its evocative power.

yet so as only to arouse the curiosity of the people to penetrate into their inner meaning.[36]

This arousal of curiosity works within the individual and influences the exercise of the will to move beyond the possible ambiguities in the text toward faith in its core message. At the same time, because of the way that Smith emphasizes the importance of free will, when prophecies were given, they were not necessarily going to be carried out: "the declarations of the prophets might fail of their accomplishment if men truly repented, and thereby obtained mercy of the Lord."[37] Prophetic speech has an aspect of "foretelling," but so "as not to interfere with [people's] free will."[38] The driving force of history, therefore, is not primarily in terms of God's providential ordering—and certainly not in terms of earlier Anglicanism acceptance of predestination—but as driven by the aggregate of individuals exercising free will over time. Smith is by no means the only one for whom free will was an important category; the centrality of free choice and the exercise of the conscience of the individual is a hallmark of modern thought. What this shows, however, is that Smith is as much a part of this mode of thinking whereby the individual is given precedence over the Church. If, instead of viewing history as driven by the aggregate of human free choice, the Church was conceived as the locus of God's providential shaping of history, then Smith would have to grant more to a corporate understanding of authority and *how Scripture itself is read* in such a corporate body.

However, given Robert Payne Smith's modernist sensibilities, his exegetical practice shifts from the ecclesially defined hermeneutic that was so central for Hooker, Cranmer, and Whitgift. This leaves the Church ill-defined, its divided existence accepted as an unproblematic fact.

THE CANON OF SCRIPTURE

Along with the close relationship between the Church and the common liturgical reading of Scripture is the early Anglican vision of the Bible in which the Old and New Testaments comprise the *one* word of God given to the Church. While it is doubtful that Smith would disagree with the principle of this idea, his approach is, once again, emblematic of a modernist reading in several ways. My overall claim is that Smith's thought is a product of, and deeply indebted to, the previous two centuries of exegetical changes

---

36. Smith, *The Authenticity and Messianic Interpretation of Isaiah*, 24.
37. Ibid., 256.
38. Ibid.

that emerged as a result of violence and division. The most overt way that division shapes Smith's exegesis can be seen in his antipathy toward "liberal" scholars. However, the more far-reaching influence is that of tools that arose out of an irenic orientation, which shies away from "dogma" and moves toward supposedly less contentious themes of history and philology. Smith, however, attempts to retain these tools, while re-injecting some form of theological method into the text via his apologetic project.

In the context of biblical canonicity, the modernist quality of Smith's exegesis shows itself in two ways. First, he reads the prophet as a unique "genius" figure. Rather than a view of Isaiah as a one elected by God to speak to Israel, Smith considers him as an admirable individual, a kind of "holy hero," uniquely gifted to speak of spiritual things. Since Smith is concerned with Isaiah as an individual, the exegesis of the book requires an attendant search for the inner mind of the prophet himself. Second, the relationship between the two Testaments is one of abrogation; there is little beyond its merely predictive "messianic" function that has continued bearing on the Church. As with the previous section, Smith's apologetic and divisively-informed reading places him in a position that seeks the "spiritual" and predictive senses of the Old Testament, devoid of Israel's particularity and "Jewishness." In this sense, Smith stands within the tradition of the "Protestant poetics," that we saw in Chapter 2; that is, Scripture becomes denuded of its fecund web of interconnected referents, all centered on the One who dwells within it, that is, Christ. Instead, there emerges a much more wooden, linear, and often univocal relationship between referents.

In terms of Smith's view of the prophet as a kind of religious hero, he follows a relatively new approach to reading the prophets. which is a kind of reconstruction of Isaiah. Smith claims to be able to describe the character and thoughts of the prophet—that is, the intention of the author. While this aspect of his work can also speak to his methodology, it illustrates his *theological* understanding of the nature of a prophetic document. This focus on the prophet *qua* historical figure is a subtle but important exegetical move that differs from the early Anglican approach to exegesis. The prophet comes to be seen in terms of a heroic figure, an individual with preternatural abilities who stood apart from the people to whom he spoke. Isaiah, Jeremiah, or Ezekiel thus came to be studied as people whose uniqueness meant that they did not need to be read in continuity or context with the levitical ceremonies, for instance, nor in terms of the age that came after them. This is where the loss of a canonical approach is most acutely felt, for if Isaiah is connected, for instance, to the Torah as a part of a greater whole, then there is inherently more cohesiveness to the faith of which it speaks. As Christopher Seitz says, "arguments portraying all the non-Mosaic books as diverse and wide ranging misunderstand the achievement of the Prophets and the relationship of this achievement to the Law as a single and foundational grammar."[39] This "misunderstanding" was dominant in nineteenth-century hermeneutical practice and is (perhaps) only recently changing.[40]

Interpretation that is impacted by a focus on the prophet as a figure of individual genius generates several exegetical consequences. For people such as T. K. Cheyne in Chapter 5, the book of Isaiah must be read only in historical terms, as a text produced from a certain culture, which is therefore indicative of that culture's form of "religion," and only perhaps obliquely our own. Smith does not read Isaiah as only a mere product of Israelite religion; however, his focus on the character and mind of the prophet serves to bolster his points, and in so doing, he is happy to engage—at however minimal a level—in the same practices as his opponents.

On the one hand, Smith accepts that Isaiah (and any other prophet) is bound by his historical context—that is, language and forms of thought can only be borrowed from the surrounding culture.[41] This speaks to his understanding of the use of language that a prophet may use, whether it is allegorical or literal. Yet, in order to protect Isaiah (and his book) from being read in an all-too-human way, Smith surmises a kind of mechanism by which the Holy Spirit works through the prophet.

> [Isaiah] felt himself, indeed, borne along by an irresistible influence, and was conscious that what he spake came from God; and subsequently, as he recalled his words to mind, he must have known that much that he had spoken referred really to the Messiah's advent; but probably he would altogether have been unable to distinguish between what was temporary and what eternal, or to tell what mysteries of redemption lay concealed under the veil of allusions to contemporaneous events.[42]

However unsure the prophet may have been vis-à-vis present and eternal time, what Isaiah wrote "referred really to the Messiah's advent." To suppose that Isaiah had a "conscious" knowledge of the coming of the Messiah, for Smith, is necessary in order to contest arguments that propose that Isaiah meant to refer only to chronologically proximal events. True, Smith

---

39. Seitz, *The Goodly Fellowship of the Prophets*, 129.

40. Ibid., 41–42 refers to a steady increase in recent times in reading the prophets as a *collection*, but also notes that there is a "time lag" between this new (but in many ways, old) approach to the Old Testament as a canonical collection and an incorporation of this view into published literature.

41. Smith, *The Authenticity and Messianic Interpretation of Isaiah*, 250.

42. Ibid., 12.

concedes, "the prophet was often thinking of some minor event, and his words have a true reference to it;" however, "they also pass beyond."[43] The prophet is more than a mere person but a necessary "infallible authority" in order to provide for Israel an "increase of knowledge . . .[and] more truth and greater illumination" that allow them to reach "fresh stages" of revealed truth.[44] The *prophet* as well as the *text* was for Smith an infallible guide, albeit a temporary one.

I do not claim Smith is being simplistic on this point, as he admits that "they probably did not themselves fully understand all they said."[45] But Smith does *not* want to suggest that, for instance, in Isaiah's *almah* prophecy of 7:14 there was a contemporaneous event that the prophet had in mind, overshadowing the spiritual referent: "the fervour of inspiration often carried them onwards into future times."[46] Smith attempts to prove that in such a passage, the intended meaning of Isaiah was the Messiah. First, he situates the historical context of the prophet as a time of imminent danger of invasion by a foreign power. Second, Smith surmises that his audience was the "common people."[47] His role was to be their comforter in such a time, since King Ahaz was beginning to seek help from Assyria. According to Smith's logic, since the text speaks of a virgin who will give birth to a son who would be called "the Mighty God, the Everlasting Father" (Isa 9:6), then it could not be possible that his prophecy referred only to the son of just any young woman. Smith insists, as part of his argument for the "established grammatical rule which prevails throughout all the prophetical books"[48] that his translation of the Hebrew word *almah* as "virgin" is a necessary one, despite Jewish (and "rationalist") interpretations otherwise. For Smith, his reading is the most "obvious" one, "a translation which would naturally suggest itself to every reader at first sight, and which only an elaborate criticism, bent upon the overthrow of all ancient landmarks, would venture to dispute."[49] The prophet's intended meaning, therefore, is clearly accessible to any reader.

I do not attend to the current hermeneutical problematic of surmising "authorial intent," but rather I seek to point out that this *method* is akin to Smith's contemporary liberal interpreters with respect to the "literal" meaning of such Old Testament passages, yet whose conclusions are

43. Ibid., 268.
44. Ibid., xix.
45. Smith, *A Preparation for Christ*, xxii.
46. Ibid., 15.
47. Ibid., 20.
48. Ibid., 25.
49. Ibid., 47.

nonetheless contrary to his. For instance, about a century and a half earlier, Anthony Collins, the famous Anglican eighteenth-century deist, published *The Scheme of Literal Prophecy Considered* in which he argues in minute detail that nowhere in the Old Testament was a future messiah predicted. Collins does so with the same approach as Smith wherein his reading is "obvious" and that he can penetrate into the mind of the prophet. As Hans Frei says, Collins's approach meant proceeding "first, by taking into account of the human author's intention *as an independent factor*."[50] With respect to Isaiah and many other prophetic books, Collins quotes biblical passages, alongside of which he provides a "paraphrase" that gives his view of what the prophet "literally" meant. This is, in Collins' view, the plain sense of the text. He cannot accept that Jesus was the one predicted in Isaiah in a literal sense; he rejects

> Men's endeavours to find that [interpretation] in them, which the Prophets themselves had no imagination of, and which is manifestly without the least foundation in the literal sense. It is necessary to confound the Prophets, and to reduce their prophecies to nothing, or to an unintelligible state, before an interpretation remote from the sense of the Prophets can be introduced.[51]

With respect to the specific prophecy of Isa 7 and of the *almah* conceiving a son, Collins concludes that the true meaning of the prophecy was that "the immediate *conception* of a *male child* is promised as a *sign* to Ahaz, as the conception of a male child 800 years after was improper."[52] It is "improper" because, since Ahaz wanted a sign from Isaiah, it would be a matter of little import to King Ahaz to receive a promise so far in the future. His conclusion, therefore, is that Isaiah was referring to his own son, Shear-jashub and that Isaiah's wife was the *almah*.

What we have, therefore, are two interpreters whose arguments deploy similar historical methods and approaches, claiming knowledge of the intention of the prophet Isaiah and who reconstruct a historical situation that serves their respective polemical interests. Both appeal to the "clear" and "obvious" meaning of the text. Yet they each come to radically different conclusions. Thinkers like Collins and a great majority of people after him were faced with a common set of rules of engagement with Scripture, despite the level of orthodoxy they may or may not possess. As Frei notes

---

50. Frei, *The Eclipse of Biblical Narrative*, 78.
51. Collins, *The Scheme of Literal Prophecy Considered*, 270–71.
52. Ibid., 308, italics in the original.

> Collins has placed his opponents in a most unenviable quandary by putting before them two, and only two, alternatives. One either admits the applicability of rules for literal interpretation . . . in which case the New Testament claims concerning the meaning of Old Testament passages . . . are demonstrably false; or one says that the rules . . . are those for nonliteral [i.e., typological, mystical or figural] interpretation, which is equivalent to saying that the interpretation is meaningless because it has nothing to do with the words of the text of the prophecies. Literal and false, or typological and meaningless; those were his alternatives.[53]

Smith by no means rejects a typological interpretive method, but such an approach is only warranted once the "proof" of the literal meaning of the text has been assured. And the means by which this proof is obtained is via "subsuming literal meaning under the dominance of independent criterion."[54] For exegetes like Smith, the figure of the prophet was as a character whose "intention" can be discerned using hermeneutical rules external to the Bible and alien to earlier Anglican readings of Scripture in which authorship was indissolubly linked to God as the agent of textual development. By accepting such rules, those in continuity with thinkers in Collins' tradition could find Smith's "proofs" entirely unconvincing.

It is important to note again how this separation of Isaiah within its canonical context is relevant to my assertion regarding a divided Church and the impact of such division on exegesis. It must be repeated that there is little similarity between Smith's approach and that of the early Anglican vision of the Bible. In the latter perspective, the canon of Scripture views the entire corpus as the word of God, funded by a conviction that the theological substrate of the Bible is an interconnected web of theological links and polysemous referents; this is seen paradigmatically in the exegesis of Nehemiah Rogers in Chapter 3. Yet Smith's exegesis moves beyond (or behind) the text in order to determine the historical context and the mind of the author as the means of interpretation. This is the product of division in the sense that we can regard Smith as standing on the shoulders of exegetes like William Day and Richard Kidder, who prescind from a close theological connection within the word of God in terms of the former and toward an apologetic analysis with respect to the latter.

---

53. Frei, *The Eclipse of Biblical Narrative*, 70. Frei continues to show that this dual choice was by no means accepted by all (his description of Sherlock's rejoinder to Collins is a fine example), but he does make clear that this was the governing approach in general. The die had already been cast in the eighteenth century.

54. Ibid., 76.

I now turn to the problem of Smith's abrogation of the Old Testament in his interpretation of the text. His reading can be seen as inheriting a "spiritualist" tenor, which is often the result of an abrogative orientation. I am not suggesting that Smith rejects a connection between the two Testaments; indeed, a central part of his project is to defend it. But by allowing himself to be drawn into modern concerns with the prophet as an individual and by viewing the relationship between the Testaments as merely one of abrogation and prediction much is lost in Smith's exegesis.

Above, I discussed how the role of the Church in the process of scriptural interpretation is virtually non-existent in Smith's account. However, the function of prophecy in *predicting* the Church plays a role as central as that of the Suffering Servant and the vicarious suffering of Christ. This is one of the most detailed accounts of Smith's figural mode of reading the Old Testament. It therefore serves well here as an exemplar of how figuralism functions in his exegesis, and also reveals much about Smith's theology of the Church and the Old Testament, which is relevant to a discussion of the canonical connection between the two Testaments.

Smith's view of the Old Testament, which he often calls the "Jewish Scriptures," is governed by a theology of abrogation; the coming of Jesus Christ has superseded the Jewish ceremonies prescribed in the levitical ceremonies. Sermons VIII and IX of *The Authenticity of the Messianic Interpretation of the Prophecies of Isaiah* are dedicated exclusively to Isaiah 65:17: "Behold, I create new heavens and a new earth: and the former shall not be remembered, nor come into mind." Traditionally, the interpretation of this passage is an eschatological one of the future consummation of the Church and all of history. Smith, however, takes a quasi-preterist perspective of this text. He applies it to the age of the Church which has surpassed that of old (Jewish) dispensation. His exegesis of the Old Testament orients and defines it in functional terms whereby Jewish particularity is abrogated in favour of its "spiritual" core.[55] In doing so, Smith avoids, to some extent, the problem of the non-linearity and historically problematic stories of the Old Testament. The Old Testament is to be read primarily in terms of its central

---

55. I should mention that many of the quotations that follow are redolent with what twenty-first century eyes would view as patently anti-Semitic terms. I will not be critiquing his anti-Semitism *per se*, but only his theology with respect to the Old Testament, of which his harsh words are to some extent merely epiphenomenal. However, it was not unusual to avoid reading the Scripture in the same way that Jews do. We also see this in the previous chapter with Kidder, who attempts to refute numerous "Jewish" arguments against Christianity. By Smith's time, as with Kidder, not only were these arguments employed by his liberal opponents, but I would suggest that arguments in favour of Jewish particularity, aside from the problem of the culture's general repugnance of Semitic people, were too "physical" and "embodied" and thus not "spiritual" enough.

spiritual message.[56] But the means by which thinkers like Smith attempt to avoid divisiveness by this argument—which is often raised only at convenient moments—results in moving the exegesis out of textual particularity into the realm of general ideas.

I do not suggest that Smith consciously conceives of the Old Testament as somehow less a part of Scripture, for he says in *Prophecy: a Preparation for Christ* that

> The difference . . . between revelation in Christ and in the prophets is not that the words of the one are more God's words than those of the others. . . . We must not, then, draw distinctions between the Old Testament and the New, as though they differed in authority, or in the nature and extent of their authority.

Yet, in the very next sentence, Smith says

> The distinction which the Apostle [in Hebrews 1:1,2] draws is in the manner of the revelation, the different way in which it was given, not in the degree of it. In the Old Testament it was partial, gradual, progressive; in the New, it is full, perfect, final, complete.[57]

Aside from a potential contradiction between Smith's aim to make no distinction between the Testaments and his approval of the Apostle doing so, it is also not obvious how the incompleteness of the Old Testament is not overshadowed by the perfection of the New. I aim to show that what makes the Old Testament "incomplete" for Smith are the *carnal* elements of Jewish practice that hide its spiritual message.

Smith argues that the meaning of Isaiah 65:17 is "the substitution of the Christian in the place of the Jewish Church."[58] The prophet Isaiah's "intention" was to speak against any national desires and in favour of a universal religion ushered in by the coming of the Messiah. This is a historical process of development whereby the latter supersedes the former: "as the Jewish and Christian Churches represent the same one divine institution in different stages of its development, they naturally are closely interwoven in the Prophet's mind."[59] Judaism (which to Smith is equivalent to the Jewish nation, Israel) is a merely transient phenomenon that was to be replaced by the Church, the permanent institution of God's people. Jewish practice was

---

56. This therefore parallels some of the spiritualist traditions that I outline in chapter 1 in which physical concreteness is shorn in favour of a non-material spiritual core.
57. Smith, *A Preparation for Christ*, 61.
58. Smith, *The Authenticity and Messianic Interpretation of Isaiah*, 223.
59. Ibid., 227.

a mere placeholder for something greater and more permanent. In the end "the lineal Israel shall be rejected"[60] as a result of Jewish moral failure in following God's law. This rejection of Israel means that "she must abandon all that was local, and temporary, and distinctively Jewish in her law; that she must adapt herself to a wider and nobler sphere, and cast off the trammels and imperfections of a mere preparatory stage."[61] The function of the Old Testament for Smith, and the theological principle behind reading it, is an understanding of a kind of pedagogical age that advances the human race to a point of readiness for the coming of a new religion. The loss of particularity (of Israel, of various cultic practices, etc.) in the move toward a universal religion corresponds to the idea of a religion that is less concerned about external actions; but "at the most holy rite of our religion we recite its moral precepts; and its truths, separated from all temporary and local admixture, are the subject of our creeds and articles."[62]

These moral precepts, the dictates of the inner life, are what maintain the unity between the first "Church" of the Jews and the final Church of the Christians. Smith claims that "ever has the Church retained all that was essential to Judaism."[63] Christ ushers in an age from which the external husk of a primitive, nationalist religion has been removed in favour of a universally enlightened humanity who have achieved the light of advanced morality. While the Church continues to read the Scriptures and maintain the Sabbath, says Smith, "no longer is it a bondage, but . . . subservient to our moral and spiritual good."[64]

My claim, therefore, is that Smith does not see Scripture as bearing a dual witness in the Old and New Testaments; instead, the former merely points *functionally* to the latter for its legitimization. Smith conceives of the solution to the "problem" of the Old and New Testament portions of Scripture by taking "the live option of understanding the canon's constitutively twofold character as *development*."[65] Smith, however, is not representative only of the Evangelical Movement on this point, but of the theological shape of much nineteenth-century Anglican thought with respect to Scripture. *Development* was a congenial concept to the modern idea of a movement of humanity to a more enlightened stage and a universal religion. This development via Christianity is proven by the fact that "the principles

60. Ibid., 231.
61. Ibid. 235.
62. Ibid., 236.
63. Ibid., 238.
64. Ibid., 238–39.
65. Seitz, *Figured Out*, 109.

which [Christianity] enunciates have directed the whole course of modern thought and progress. Even erroneous views of the doctrines of Christianity have retained something of the vigour of the parent stock."[66] In other words, Christianity—even Christianity-in-general as a kind of ideological movement that may or may not be orthodox—bears a positive moral force in the life of all cultures throughout the world, enabling the successes of human advancement.

In Smith's interpretation of Isaiah, the rejection of Jesus of Nazareth by the Jewish Sanhedrin in the gospels, and their concomitant rejection of him as the Messiah was predicted in their own Scriptures, leading to God's rejection of the Jewish people. The "remnant" that Isaiah refers to in such passages as Isaiah 10:20–21 and Paul in Romans 9–11 is about the small selection of believing Jews out of whom the Church of Christ was called by God's election. Even more, in Smith's view, "God saw fit to remove a danger out of the Church's path by the complete obliteration of the Jewish polity and priesthood,"[67] and in order to "clear the way," as it were, God destroyed the Jewish nation in A.D. 70. The only solution for remaining Jews was to accept the new dispensation, "a spiritual religion, from which all the gross and material elements of their old faith have been purged away."[68] The Jewish dispensation is "carnal," whereas the Christian Church heralds a spiritual age, "embracing . . . both Jew and Gentile within her fold, upon equal terms, and with all distinction and disparity removed. . . . The Jew retains no right by reason of his lineage."[69]

The concepts of typology and figuration also inform Smith's understanding of this older dispensation: "For to the Jew truth was given in shadow, and outline, and prophecy; to the Christian it has been given in substance."[70] Once again, the Christian Church's existence as the full perfec-

---

66. Smith, *The Authenticity and Messianic Interpretation of Isaiah*, 240.

67. Ibid., 244.

68. Ibid. This writing was prior to the rise of a form of dispensationalism that viewed the return of "carnal" Israel to the Holy Land as part of God's prophetic plan, which would culminate in the eschaton. It should be noted that one aspect of Smith's argument in Sermons VIII and IX, to which I am not attending, is his disagreement with those Evangelicals who view the coming of a millennial dispensation (he does not mention Darbyism, but I suspect he has it in mind, though it was an eschatological claim that had been in existence since at least the seventeenth century); for Smith, the Church is the full and final fulfillment of prophecy, whereas for others there is yet to come another age of even greater perfection. For Smith, "a millennium would be but an intermediate purgatory" (ibid., 266), and would void the perfection of what was brought about by the coming of the Messiah.

69. Ibid., 252.

70. Ibid., 253.

tion of Jewish hope means that there is no longer a need for the ongoing use of figuration for interpretation of the text beyond its participation as a historical tool for apologetics. What remains is a rather static view of typology and prophecy whereby once the tools of prediction and/or figuration have done their job, they are no longer germane to theological exegesis of the present reality of the Church but have given way to historical modes of reconstruction. There is an ostensive attempt to preserve a belief in the *one* canon of Scripture by attempting to hold the two Testaments together by a rather wooden mode of spiritual figuration. At the same time, Smith's exegesis indicates a clear inequality between the two Testaments. The Old Testament serves the function of pointing chronologically to a distant referent, Jesus of Nazareth, and renders the events in terms of codified, non-concrete referents that, once uncovered, have served their purpose.

While Smith interprets Scripture in a way that the Church is the perfection of Jewish Scripture, there is little that can be gleaned from his writings with respect to *what* he means when he refers to the entity he calls "Church." He tends to argue that the Church has gained what the Jews have lost, but only in its "spiritual" essence, which all Jewish practices were meant to "mean." Smith's view of the Church is not a sectarian one; he is not arguing that he can distinguish between a "true" and a "visible" Church. Rather, he agrees with earlier Anglicanism that "the Church visible has possession of the promises because it contains the Church invisible" and prefers "leaving the separation between the true and the false to the unerring Judge above."[71] But his ecclesial perspective is rather stunted beyond this point; the remainder of his limited discussion on the Church is directed toward the role of individuals in "working out their probation."[72] His account argues that, despite the perfection of prophecy by the institution of the Church, the Christian life marks a time in which individuals live out their lives in preparation for the next:

> The promises of the New Testament are not earthly blessings and bodily enjoyment, but earthly trial and the subjection of the body, and unceasing labour, and patient waiting, by which the soul is prepared for heavenly blessedness. . . . Christian men find their solace, not in being allowed to combine earthly success with the discipline which fits them for heaven, but in the foretaste of spiritual joys even here; "for the kingdom of heaven is within you."[73]

71. Ibid., 254–55.
72. Ibid., 255.
73. Ibid., 258–59.

The earthly life is the life of the individual, in the Church no doubt, but in a Church that Smith defines in very broad terms. The Church merely indicates a "spiritual" age for which the Jewish "Church" was a mere preparation.

SMITH'S CHRISTOLOGICAL AND SPIRITUAL HERMENEUTIC

In this final section, I consider Robert Payne Smith's exegesis of Isaiah in comparison with the christological shape of the uniquely Anglican vision of the Bible. My argument is that the extent to which Smith conceives of Isaiah christologically is matched only to the extent that it can function predictively. This is a corollary of his functionalist use of the Old Testament in general. I also show how his reading of the book speaks to his theological account of the relationship between the two testaments; in this case, a christological reading is directly connected to one that is "spiritual," shorn of carnal particularity in favour of abstract spiritual/moral principles. Finally, I assess how he relates "the word and the Word," the incarnated Logos, to the text.

Smith's reading of Isaiah is intensely centred on proving that the book's prophecies accurately predict the coming of Jesus; he calls the nature of these prophecies "messianic." Yet, it is important for Smith that the relationship between the Old and New Testaments be a "spiritual" one. His apologetic stance demands that he work in the mode of his opponents, which leads him to use his own form of textual criticism to reconstruct the historical events surrounding various texts. At other times, he moves to a "spiritual" interpretation, bypassing the "historical." This results in a ramified exegesis, in which a christological hermeneutic is unclear. In order to provide evidence and proof against his opponents, therefore, Smith's reading of Isaiah is a rather wooden one. It is the attempt to prove the truth of the book—that is, his engagement in a divisive reading—that drives his mode of theological exegesis.

While much of what Smith writes in *Prophecy: a Preparation for Christ* and *The Authenticity and Messianic Interpretation* indicates a strong belief in prophecy as a literal description and prediction of figures and events that were to occur in the future at the coming of Jesus, Smith describes Old Testament prophecy in more subtle terms. The prophets, he says, "were God's representatives on earth, and the mediators between Him and man."[74] As such, they were people who did not merely speak of the future but were "to appear for God whenever any step was to be taken forward in the

---

74. Smith, *A Preparation for Christ*, ix.

accomplishment of God's purpose."[75] They spoke on behalf of God and participated in God's plan to prepare the people of Israel for the coming of the Messiah. The means by which God communicated himself to the prophets was through the Spirit, who "was with [the prophets] in a higher way than in His ordinary and natural workings," and what they taught "was revealed to them directly by God and not attained to by the unaided workings of their mental powers."[76] Since this communication was so direct and, by all accounts unmediated, the inspiration of the Bible is such that it cannot be treated like any other book.[77] He putatively disallows any attempt to subject the Bible to the level of textual scrutiny that is afforded other classic texts, for the subject and genre of the Bible are "question[s] upon which we have years ago come, upon sufficient evidence, to a definite conclusion."[78] Nonetheless, when it suits his purposes, Smith does deign to employ a low-level form criticism of Isaiah. For this reason, Smith's hermeneutic is not a consistent one, particularly since his interpretation is driven not by theological exegesis, but by an apologetic urge to prove that the Evangelical position is the right one.

Even though Smith attempts to add subtlety to his definition of prophecy as being more than mere prediction, his apologetic approach rarely goes beyond the fitness between certain prophecies and the person of Jesus of Nazareth. One of the key arguments that "vindicates" the book of Isaiah is the way that the book lends support for the central tenets of the Christian faith, hence "proving" it is the true religion. In order to succeed, Smith sees it as his task to construct the historical context of Isaiah's prophetic utterances and to show that his predictions were fulfilled only in the person of Jesus of Nazareth. His exegesis is done in a rather bifurcated manner, in which he can apply all the rules of low-level historical criticism on the one hand, yet on the other hand make exegetical moves toward a typological mode when he deems it necessary (and convenient) to support his argument. Smith's exegetical approach is in marked distinction not only to the ancient Fathers who read the Bible, but also to more restrained Protestants like John Calvin, who did not consider the Old Testament as a mere "history of Israel," but saw the events that the Bible describes as shaped by God's providential ordering.

---

75. Ibid., ix.

76. Ibid., x.

77. Ibid. It is likely here that Smith is indirectly arguing against Benjamin Jowett's comments in *Essays and Reviews* (1860) that Scripture should be "interpreted like other books" (Jowett, "On The Interpretation of Scripture," 404). Despite the uproar that Jowett's comments generated, this was actually not a novel idea, even in more-conservative England.

78. Smith, *A Preparation for Christ*, xi.

Each word, phrase, and event has inherent theological fecundity that cannot be exhausted by the extraction of historical data. This latter method was the means by which early Anglicans read Scripture (see Chapter 1), part of which included figuration, typology, and, indeed, real historical events. This "pre-critical" method was constructed in an entirely different theological understanding of what the Bible *is*, which is a text permeated by the presence of the Logos in a recapitulation of the Incarnation via textual mediation. There was rarely a sharp distinction between history and figuration because the entire text was superintended by the "Word of God." This Word providentially shaped the text (and the history it recounts), which must be understood within a grander scriptural vision, an economy in which the Church participates. This did not discount prophetic prediction, nor figuration or typology, but each was a part of correct scriptural reading.[79] This exegetical fecundity is not apparent in Smith's exegesis but has been sharply attenuated by the ever-present need to prove Scripture's veracity.

Robert Payne Smith's worry is that "negative critics" reject any predictive or typological value to the Old Testament. It is of utmost theological importance that it be demonstrated that Isaiah's prophecies refer to Jesus of Nazareth:

> No slight matter is at stake; for if the virgin's child is a son of Ahaz or a son of Isaiah . . .what the Church loses is not merely the confirmation of prophecy to the Messiah's advent, but the doctrines connected with His being the Virgin-born. . . . It is the same in the interpretation of the fifty-third chapter [of Isaiah]. . . . If it be proved that the chapter does not refer to our Lord . . . the belief of all Christian men from the earliest ages to the present day in the efficacy of our Saviour's death ceases to have a foundation.[80]

---

79. The distinction between figuration, typology, and allegory are notoriously difficult. I define figuration as the theological principle whereby the shape of events described in the text participate in a common ontological framework and pattern whereby God's providential lordship in history can be discerned. Typology refers to *figures*, that is, unique people or things whose character and identity foreshadow a greater figure or event. Typology almost always refers in some way to Christ in Scripture; e.g., in John 3:14, Jesus indicates a link between the serpent lifted up by Moses and himself. In both figuration and typology, events and figures that occur centuries apart participate in a "time" that is not the same as "historical time." Finally, allegory tends to refer to other "spiritual" interpretations that may be moral or anagogical. Yet, for so-called "pre-critical" readers, such conceptions are not always articulated with such categorical detail; all ways of reading Scripture contribute to its "literal" sense if one attends to the theological *res* of the text.

80. Smith, *The Authenticity and Messianic Interpretation of Isaiah*, 2.

These stakes fund Smith's urgency to "vindicate" the prophet from his detractors, and are what drives his exegesis. While he is astute enough to note prior to the passage above that faith does not rest on any single verse, the material shape of his argumentation is to narrow in on certain texts to show that their necessary referent is Jesus of Nazareth. We can see how Smith's reading comports with Frei's description of the "Supernaturalist" position in which

> [the text's] explicative meaning is the historian's reconstruction of the historical occurrence to which they refer, and that reconstructed fact either is or is closely related to their abiding meaningfulness.[81]

While Smith believed in Christ's centrality in all connections between the two Testaments, the textual referent is not intrinsic to the text, nor funded by a consideration of the utterance of the Logos within it.

Smith concludes that the scholars whom he opposes come to contradictory conclusions because they mistakenly misread the text in the same way that Jewish readers had throughout history: they read it *too literally*.[82] Both rationalist and Jew twist the text in such a way that its "natural" reading is suppressed: "as the Jew grants the necessity of every prophecy being fulfilled, he is often reduced to the most puerile shifts by difficulties which the rationalist, who denies the supernatural element of prophecy, escapes."[83] For instance, Smith mocks the Jewish view that the prophecy of Isa 11:7 ("the lion shall eat straw like the ox") means that "the physical conformation of that animal shall undergo a reconstruction."[84] It is clear to him that such a passage is allegorical, that the coming of the Messiah will result in peace between people, not a reconstituted digestive system for lions.

Smith grants that the prophecy of Isa 7:14 may indeed "allude" to a child that was to be born in Israel but the proximate event is merely a contingent one that serves the greater purpose of moving "from the temporary to the universal; from the fortunes of the carnal Israel to the Christian

---

81. Frei, *The Eclipse of Biblical Narrative*, 119.

82. It is worth noting Smith's often scathing attacks against the Jews as being primitive and "narrow-minded, prejudiced against foreigners, devoid of all cosmopolitan tendencies [!], not versatile enough to win any general favour" (Smith, *A Preparation for Christ*, 81). While perhaps this is merely a reflection of British disfavor towards Jews, I would also argue that it is the result of his frustration that his opponents often appeared to employ "Jewish" arguments with which the Church had already dealt in the first few centuries.

83. Smith, *The Authenticity and Messianic Interpretation of Isaiah*, 13.

84. Ibid., 14.

Church."⁸⁵ At first glance, this can perhaps be seen as a traditional argument for a typological interpretation, but what funds Smith's approach is an acceptance of the historical method that "proves" that the prophecy's meaning could not have been merely local.

> That the prophecy was not finally fulfilled in contemporaneous events we may, I think, infer from the consideration that plainly it was committed to writing long after its temporary use had passed away ... *the form in which [such prophecies] have come down to us is evidently the work of a later period*.⁸⁶

Here we have Smith engaging in his own kind of "form criticism." The "plain" and "evident" nature of the text indicates that the event anticipated by Jewish interpretation was to have occurred only as a sign to Ahaz and would have already taken place when Isaiah was compiled. For if it was "plainly" written after the fact, then for what reason was the prophecy written? In this case, he accepts an attenuated form of textual criticism and historical reconstruction, using them for apologetic purposes when it suits him.

Smith's exegesis of the song of the Suffering Servant, beginning at Isa 52:13, is also an important consideration as it figures so centrally, not only in the history of exegesis, but as the subject of Sermons VI and VII in *The Authenticity and Messianic Interpretation of Isaiah*. For Smith, this prophecy contains sufficient detail that it can speak of no other figure than Jesus of Nazareth and his Passion. Moreover, he contends that it is such a central text for the Christian Church that "if this passage be taken from us, we have lost the strongest bulwark and defence of the argument from prophecy as a whole."⁸⁷ Doctrinally, Isaiah is central to Christian teaching:

> The prophecy [of Isaiah 53] is the foundation therefore upon which the doctrine of the Atonement is built; and as it thus becomes the chief and most important of all the prophetic writings, we may well rejoice that it is also the most plain.⁸⁸

Smith rejects "modern critics" for whom "it follows, according to their theory, that the prophets, as mere poets and preachers, must adhere to the national idea of the Messiah."⁸⁹ Their interpretation of supposed messianic texts considers the referents to such texts as purely local, without remainder. Yet it is the very fact that this figure suffers and is humiliated that Smith

85. Ibid., 16.
86. Ibid., emphasis mine.
87. Ibid., 171.
88. Ibid., 222.
89. Ibid., 164.

finds most convincing, for if the purpose of the messianic writings were written to comfort the people of Israel, how could a suffering king provide this function?

Again, Smith's mode of reading this text is to start with a historical reconstruction of the events that surround the prophecy. Isa 52:13 urges Israel to regard her deliverer and is freed from the bonds of slavery; the remnant has returned to Jerusalem and the Babylonian captives are told to depart. Smith reminds his hearers of Isa 49:6, in which the Servant will be a "light to the Gentiles," and then argues that the song of the Suffering Servant begins to speak of the details of the life of this Servant, "from his humble birth to His ignominious death, and in the reference which follows to His Resurrection."[90] These details are to be read in their literal, historical sense. Israel was indeed to return to the land, released from their Babylonian captivity. Yet, once the texts have described the suffering of God's Servant, Smith says, "plainly, must we not apply these words to a more spiritual deliverance?"[91] Smith shifts from a "historical" to a "spiritual" mode of reading the text, enabling him to bypass the problems presented by his opponents, whose interpretations are incorrect because they are *too* literal. Smith surrounds his argument with other "messianic" texts of the Old Testament, namely the so-called "proto-gospel" of Gen 3:15. This "spiritual" interpretation of the text is essential to Smith's argument, for he says, "Christians are not at liberty to deny the spiritual interpretation of the Old Testament. . . . They are not mere facts of history, but lessons, teaching sometimes moral truths, but more frequently the mystery of the Gospel."[92]

Smith acknowledges that the necessity of a spiritual interpretation not only leads to controversy and debate, but is often the cause of it:

> A Church with no commission from God, no authority, no revealed truth, no inspired Word, would be doubtless a very peaceful Church, would stir up no controversies, and occasion no heart-burnings; but she would influence no minds, awake no sympathies, gain no friends, make no enemies, do no good, and be powerless even for evil.[93]

Thus, the very presence of these "negative critics," who reject the spiritual reading of the text and oppose the traditional reading of books like Isaiah, is not only necessary for the Church; such divisiveness also guarantees the truth of what he propounds. Without divisiveness, Scripture would be shorn

90. Ibid., 160.
91. Ibid., 162.
92. Ibid., 167.
93. Ibid., 166–67.

of its value and would be no more than an interesting book. Smith, therefore, welcomes the combative atmosphere that permeates biblical exegesis as being indicative of how important Scripture really is. To some extent, the reality of division in the Church is itself proof of the centrality and truth of the Bible.

Therefore, a spiritual reading of the text is a necessary mode of exegesis to which his rationalist critics refuse to go; they remain at the merely "literal" level and therefore miss the true meaning of what the prophet intends to convey. This, says Smith, was also the problem with the history of Jewish interpretation of Isaiah, and, like Richard Kidder from the last chapter, he devotes most of Sermon VI to an outline of this history. His purpose is to show the hopelessness and absurdity of such a task. In Smith's view, Jewish interpreters have had to invent numerous incredible explanations to account for the humiliation of the Servant figure of Isa 53, deliberately avoiding what he sees as the most obvious meaning of the text.

In general, the Jewish theory interprets the figure in the Song of the Suffering Servant as the nation of Israel, who must suffer for a time before she is to enjoy the peace of God. For Smith, the grammatical meaning of the text, however, does not allow for such an interpretation but rather demands a typological reading:

> All these passages are clearly irreconcilable with the theory that He was also the nation, or identical with any select portion of it.... There are, indeed, parts of the Messiah's office which his Church shared with Him: but there are others peculiar to him; as, for instance, that He suffers a vicarious death; that He makes intercession for sinners ... that He is a covenant of the people; and after His humiliation is worshipped by kings and princes, restores Israel, and is the salvation also of the Gentiles and the whole world.[94]

Since the grammar of the text describes an individual, and distinguishes this person from the people of Israel, then it follows that all of the attributes and actions given to this figure must reside in one person, and therefore must be the Messiah. Since this Messiah can only be Christ, it follows that the text must, where necessary, be read typologically and predictively. We see here a kind of syllogism that leads Smith out of the "merely literal" into a spiritual interpretation, which is the "messianic" or (superficially) the christological reading.

Smith's theological understanding of typology and prophecy is relatively traditional. The Jewish Scriptures reveal a "material" religion whose

---

94. Ibid., 189.

spiritual "core" is what remains essential across time. Some practices have ceased to exist. Some, such as sacrifice, "typify" Christ, and others are things indifferent. Prophecy often has only one meaning but can in certain instances have a double referent whereby the future event is the "fullest" fulfillment of the prophecy. But the existence of the "single meaning" type of prophecy is what funds Smith's form of argument and exegesis:

> The words have a true reference to some occurrence in Jewish or contemporaneous history; but a still truer reference to something Christian and spiritual. Not, indeed, always so; some prophecies seem to have no double meaning; *and the higher use of these perhaps is to give us some neutral ground on which to test the reality of prediction.*[95]

Therefore, while Smith argues strongly that the Bible is a unique book, authored by God, and even agrees that others may view the acceptance of prophecy as "irrational,"[96] he nonetheless concurs that there is some form of "neutral ground" that permits a reading that takes prediction, typology and allegory into account.

Smith's apologetic hermeneutic employs the text as a kind of launching pad for his own doctrinal arguments. He employs a dual reading of the text: a scientific one that happily participates in all the newly-developed modes of exegesis and a spiritual one that applies the text to a meaning that is outside the text—often in reference to Christ. An Anglican form of interpretation is eviscerated by his use of modern historical reconstructions that avoid a reading in which Christ is deeply present within the very words of the text. The "spiritual" referent hovers above the text, emerging only when his apologetic methodology is applied.

CONCLUSION

Robert Payne Smith intends that an interpretation of Isaiah be a theological activity. Within Smith's purview, to be theological, however, means that Isaiah must be read in a highly apologetic context where there is often little distinction between a theological and an apologetic exegesis. For the most part, Smith engages in the latter, to show that the Old Testament in general, and Isaiah in particular, can be used to "prove" the truth of Christian doctrine.

Part of theological exegesis, for Smith, is to consider the prophet as a unique, heroic figure, from whom thoughts and intentions can be discerned.

---

95. Ibid., 269, italics mine.
96. Ibid.

Moreover, Smith employs his own mode of historical reconstruction and textual criticism, but only to the extent that they support his apologetic aims. Smith is not unique in this regard. Brevard Childs notes that many conservatives in the nineteenth century often moved in a reactive mode. Non-Anglican J. A. Alexander, for instance, wrote one of the most definitive scholarly works on Isaiah in the English-speaking world at the time. He followed his teacher, the conservative German E. W. Hegstenberg, in his method, which was "largely an apologetic attempt to refute the critical approaches of the preceding two centuries. . . . Using the same tools—philological, historical and literary—he mounts a logical case for the traditional reading of the Old Testament prophets, especially Isaiah."[97] Like Alexander, Smith accepts the validity of the tools used for biblical exegesis only to the extent that he can turn them against his opponents, and it is the first of two ways in which I consider Smith's reading to be in an antagonistic mode. The second, irenic mode of divisive exegesis informs and shapes interpretation in the history of a divisive environment, out of which arose non-ecclesial, non-dogmatic, individualist readings of Scripture that purport to be objective.

This chapter shows how Smith's exegesis sharply differs from a uniquely Anglican biblical hermeneutic and is a symptom of the divisive reality of theological exegesis. Much of Smith's work takes on a highly apologetic, and even downright polemical, form as he aims to argue that modern "negative" critics err in their presuppositions regarding the supernatural nature of Scripture. They end up using "Jewish" arguments that deny any predictive element in biblical prophecy. But by entering into an apologetic and argumentative mode, his own theological suppositions and conclusions arise out of the crucible of ecclesial division to avoid any kind of reading that can be discerned as in accordance with anything uniquely Anglican.

Most notable is a stark absence of how the Church as a whole participates in the exegesis of Scripture; Smith is concerned primarily with individual appropriation of Scripture's spiritual message, apprehended by the "heart." Second, we should ask, as Brevard Childs does in more general terms, in what sense are Isaiah and the Old Testament constitutive of *Christian* Scripture? It is at this point that Smith is rather contradictory. On the one hand, he affirms that all Scripture is inspired and no "distinction" should be made between the Old and New Testaments. Yet, he is also clear that there *is* to be a kind of distinction, as the Old Testament comprises an older dispensation that is abrogated by the coming of Jesus. Therefore, the Old Testament is theologically valuable less for its particularity and as a unique witness to God's work in history, and more for its "spiritual"

---

97. Childs, *The Struggle to Understand Isaiah*, 267.

message. Little, however, is said with regard to the nature of this spiritual message aside from its reference to Christ and the Church in general or something that the individual must perceive and grasp with the "heart" and the exercise of free will.

Smith's exegesis of Isaiah also gives little consideration to the place of Isaiah in its final form within the canon. His theology of the Old Testament does not permit him to do this as he regards history as the gradual progression of humanity from a primitive, unenlightened state, enmeshed in external (Jewish) practices, to a one of enlightened, "spiritual," faith. As such, exegesis is to shed this carnal veil and aim at highlighting only those aspects of the text that comport with the New Testament. It is for this reason that so much of what Smith says of Isaiah is with regard to its capacity in providing "proof" of its relation to Jesus and the New Testament. He narrows his focus on those texts from Isaiah that permit him to do this.[98] Aside from this probative function, Smith does not attempt to locate Isaiah with respect to all of Scripture and its specific place within it. Rather, Smith has opted to choose a second option: "a history-of-religions approach [that] attempts to reconstruct a history according to the widely accepted categories of the Enlightenment as a scientifically objective analysis according to the rules of critical research prescribed by common human experience."[99] His brief attempts to state that the Bible is not to be read "like any other book" are not supported by the methods that he employs and reveal a rather conflicted view of Scripture; he wants at once to protect it from the negative critics who seek to devalue it, while employing the same methods these critics use in order to rescue it.

---

98. I concede that the intent of his sermons at Oxford was to assert the authenticity of a messianic interpretation of the book; but he is also clear about the importance of sustaining this argument to the edifice of Christian doctrine. Therefore, some texts are more important than others. Nonetheless, there are limitations to my argument, since we cannot consider the entire sweep of Smith's exegesis of Isaiah.

99. Childs, *The Struggle to Understand Isaiah*, 321.

4

The Politics of Division
Christopher Wordsworth and the High Church Exegesis of Isaiah

THIS CHAPTER INVESTIGATES THE High Church party of the nineteenth century in terms of its continuity with various seventeenth- and eighteenth-century like-minded thinkers. Christopher Wordsworth (1807–85, and nephew of the poet, William Wordsworth) is the central subject of this chapter. He was Bishop of Lincoln, a prolific author of books, commentaries, hymns, and poems, and had affinities with the general sweep of High Church opinion. He did not, however, participate in the *Tracts for the Times*, and was not associated with the Tractarians. While his exegesis of Isaiah is the focus of discussion in this chapter, I also consider the scriptural orientation of some Oxford Movement leaders for purposes of comparison, particularly of John Henry Newman (1801–90) and Edward Bouverie Pusey (1800–82).

My central claim is that Wordsworth represents a High Church perspective in which the Establishment Church of England, *qua* Establishment, is an instance of the "ideal" Church to which Scripture points. An exploration of Wordsworth's understanding of a text's ecclesial interpretation can be found by attending to his theological understanding of the Church. The greatest impact on his exegesis, and which distinguishes the High Church party over against that of the Oxford Movement, is an ecclesio-political vision of the Established Church of England, not merely in terms of Establishment for its own sake, but *as a response itself to division*. I consider this in distinction to the general anti-Establishment perspective of the Oxford

Movement. This chapter therefore attends to the central *political* motif of High Church theology—a vision of the English Church, which itself emerges out of the matrix of ecclesial division. Wordsworth's exegesis maintains much of the uniquely Anglican way of reading Scripture of Chapter 1 in comparison with many other exegetes in this book. He urges a deeply ecclesial reading of the text and sees Isaiah as intrinsically linked to all of Scripture as the one Word of God. Almost every verse bears witness to the presence of Christ and he connects Isaiah to the New Testament by typology and figuration. Wordsworth also rejects the Evangelical and Broad Church primacy of private interpretation. However, the means by which division impacts his reading of Isaiah are often revealed in terms that are by now rather familiar: his exegesis requires a certain kind of entrenchment and selectivity of sources that aim to "prove" that his interpretive conclusions are the only valid ones for Christians, and he is vehemently anti-Roman. Though he reads the text with considerably more sophistication than Robert Payne Smith, they share a similar orientation that does not consider Isaiah in a deeply figurative mode *because that is how Scripture is to be read*, but as a tool that provides evidence for its inspiration.

In order to make the case that a particularly pernicious form of ecclesial politics funds Wordsworth's exegesis, the following offers a brief historical background to the High Church party of the eighteenth century, ending with the "Hackney Phalanx" with which Wordsworth identifies. This offers a context for his interpretation of Isaiah and also identifies moments in his exegesis that indicate the impact of this political perspective. For Wordsworth, Scripture abounds in its testimony to Christ, but equally so to the Church as the locus of scriptural interpretation. However, Wordsworth appropriates a similar role as that of his heroes, the early Church Fathers, for whom the idea of coexisting, yet divided, "churches" was rare. His reading therefore has little consideration of the reality of a Church divided. Rather, it asserts a studious avoidance of this state of affairs by a perspective that implicitly assumes that the English Church is the only "true" Church, or at least the only true Church within the Kingdom, which accords with High Church ecclesiology. One of the central verses that gave biblical warrant for High Church royalism, and particularly relevant for my purposes, was Isaiah 49:23: "And Kings shall be thy nursing fathers and their queens thy nursing mothers." Nockles argues that "the text was interpreted to justify an understanding of the Royal Supremacy that was consciously anti-Erastian. Thus, for traditional High Churchmen, the Supremacy was but a reflection of the sacral, quasi-religious character of the office of a monarch."[1] I show the importance Wordsworth also places on this passage in my analysis of his exegesis below.

THE ECCLESIO-POLITICAL VISION OF THE HIGH CHURCH PARTY

As F.C. Mather notes, "however much importance has been assigned to High Churchmanship as a form of political behaviour ... this has been usually kept quite separate from High Church theology and High Church theory, which have not been allowed to count for much in eighteenth century Church and society."[2] My aim in this section is to address this omission by outlining several threads of this political vision and to show how it is intrinsic to High Church theology and exegesis. I also employ some exegetical remarks by Oxford Movement divines to indicate similarities and distinctions.

In general, all High Church adherents saw themselves as inheritors of an Anglicanism that harkened back to the Caroline divines, the anti-Calvinism of Archbishop Laud, the *iure divino* of the episcopacy and, in general, the more elaborate liturgical practices that paralleled or even mimicked the form of Roman Catholic rites. However, by the time of the eighteenth century, particularly with the accession of George III in 1760, High Church thought emerged as a significant position within the Church of England, for it "enabled High Churchmen for the first time since 1714 to focus their theoretical royalist sentiments once more on the person of a living monarch."[3] Additionally, the French Revolution incited jingoistic, monarchical political theories, particularly ones against the idea of a republic. As often as High Churchmen were suspected of being Jacobites, they were suspicious that others were sympathetic with Jacobins: "revision, or at least widespread discussion, of the religious status quo was on the agenda of deists, Arians and others, who were suspicious of 'priestcraft.' . . . [They] were perceived by High-Churchmen as evidence of 'the infidel spirit of the times.'"[4]

---

1. Nockles, *The Oxford Movement in Context*, 57.
2. Mather, *High Church Prophet*, 2.
3. Nockles, *The Oxford Movement in Context*, 58. George III was the first of the Hanovarian kings who was both born in England and whose first language was English.
4. Aston, "Horne and Heterodoxy," 896. Aston is quoting a letter from the Hutchinsonian George Horne, to whom I attend below.

It is instructive to briefly mention two influential forms of eighteenth-century High Churchmanship that provide an important context for the Oxford Movement as well as for the exegesis of Wordsworth. The Hutchinsonians were a kind of eighteenth-century High Church "movement," whose intellectual orientation descended from the rather eccentric writings of John Hutchinson (1674–1737). In response to Isaac Newton's grand system, which redefined the way people perceived the universe, Hutchinson "devised his own system of the world, the first part of which he published in 1724, under the title *Moses's Principia*," a clear attempt to challenge Newton's own *Principia*.[5] A central aspect to Hutchinson's thought was a peculiar approach to the Bible: since he considered it as the infallible word of God *interpreted in a certain way*, he could use it to develop his own theory of knowledge and science, which he believed people like Newton challenged. His focus was on Hebrew root words and grammar, and he accomplished his work as an autodidact of the language.[6] He ultimately sought to use the Bible—and the Old Testament in particular—as an apologetic device to prove the truth of Christianity, particularly with respect to the Trinity. He considered unpointed Hebrew as the original human language, and his abiding fascination with Hebrew was carried on by many of his followers, who maintained an interest in the Old Testament.

Hutchinson also "articulated High Church anxieties about the anthropocentric individualism of much rationalist theology," as well as a disdain for *a priori* arguments for the existence of God, and saw the idea of "natural religion" as an oxymoron, as true religion can only be based on the revelation of God.[7] Moreover, "Hutchinsonians were leading exponents in the eighteenth century Church of England of a revival of the Orthodox political theology associated with the Caroline Divines."[8] They can therefore be categorized biblically and politically as "anti-Enlightenment," of a specifically Newtonian sort, and certainly a reactionary movement.[9]

---

5. English, "Hutchinson's Critique," 582. One aspect of Newtonian science that particularly agitated theologians and scientists alike was how his gravitational model suggested objects can act "at a distance" on others without any direct bodily contact. Hutchinson's *theological* problem with this was the suggestion that inert matter can *act*; to him, this leads to a form of pantheism: "lying behind Hutchinson's question was the belief that matter was inherently passive. Spirit alone was essentially active. To attribute agency to matter was to ascribe divine attributes to it" (English, "Hutchinson's Critique," 585).

6. Ibid., 588–89.

7. Varley, *The Last of the Prince Bishops*, 41.

8. Nockles, *The Oxford Movement in Context*, 45.

9. Several important figures were associated with the Hutchinsonians, such as William Jones of Nayland (1726–1800), Alexander Catcott (1725–79), and George

While Hutchinsonianism as a distinct movement did not endure, some of its ideas fed into the ecclesio-political outlook of the so-called Hackney Phalanx, also known as the Clapton Sect. While they were intellectual inheritors of certain dimensions of Hutchinsonianism, this group minimized the anti-Newtonian rhetoric and opted for a more conventional approach to Hebrew and Old Testament linguistic studies. Even so, they "were uncompromising in their avowals of anti-Erastianism and on that basis attacked the theories of Warburton and Paley."[10] Important for my purpose, and in continuity with the Hutchinsonians, the royal office was viewed in a quasi-sacral manner, serving the needs of the Established Church.

By the time of Christopher Wordsworth, the dramatic activities of the Oxford Movement had overshadowed the Hackney Phalanx. However, it was a highly influential prelude to the Oxford Movement. The political events of the late 1820's surrounding Catholic Emancipation gave additional impetus

---

Horne (1730–92), bishops of Norwich. The latter figure serves as a good transitional figure between the Hutchinsonians and those of the later Hackney Phalanx. Horne, who became president of Magdalen College in 1768, was in his early life an ardent Hutchinsonian. However, for many who studied at Oxford, such as Horne, Jones, and Catcott, "the combination of a full-blooded system of thought with uncompromisingly confrontational followers did not help the reputation of Hutchinsonians in its early stages" (Gurses, "Academic Hutchinsonians," 411). Many gave up their strident anti-Newtonian stance as well as Hutchinson's idiosyncratic linguistic methods, if not an interest in Hebrew in general. An abiding theme that remained for these "moderates" was the political aspect of their thought, which saw the defence of Christian principles and the Established Church of England as essentially one and the same.

Horne's Hutchinsonian perspective "confirmed his essentially typological view of the Bible" (Aston, "Horne and Heterodoxy," 900). We can see how Horne applies this typological approach to the Old Testament, in particular the Psalms, in the preface to his *Commentary on the Psalms* (1776). If Isaiah has traditionally been given the appellation of "the Fifth Gospel," then the Psalter in Horne's description functions as a kind of sixth, for he regards it as "the Manual of the Son of God, in the days of his flesh" because of how often Jesus of Nazareth uses it (Horne, *A Commentary on the Book of Psalms*, iv). He also enumerates every instance in the New Testament in which the Psalms are employed. The words of the Psalms, because of their close connection to Christ, can be seen as "proceeding from the mouth of Christ, or of the church, or of both, considered as one mystical person" (Horne, *A Commentary on the Book of Psalms*, ix). As regards signification, interpretation is not merely about an ephemeral "spiritual" referent, but a movement: "on one side Canaan, and a national prosperity; on the other. heaven, and human happiness: on one side, a redemption from Egyptian servitude, and national evils; on the other, a redemption of the whole human race from absolute evil. . . . It is impossible, therefore, that God can say anything to David, under the quality of king of this chosen nation, which he does not speak, at the same time, to Jesus Christ, as King of all the elect" (Horne, *A Commentary on the Book of Psalms*, xvii).

10. Nockles, *The Oxford Movement in Context*, 58. These later figures, Warburton and Paley considered the Church of England as part of a larger "civil" entity, without any significant theological (or biblical) articulation.

to rethink the nature of the Church in the midst of a nation in which the Church was merely one among many Christian societies. So,

> by 1845, the question dividing High Churchmen was whether to oppose the government's secularising policy by, on the one hand, reasserting the Church of England's constitutional claims as they were prior to 1828, or, on the other hand, by arguing that the state's duties to the church were individual and that a restriction of those duties might be a price worth paying for the church's freedom. The former view was upheld by the Hackney remnant, including the Wordsworths; that latter represented the position of the Tractarian rump.[11]

It is this latter point that politically distinguishes the old High Church party from the Tractarians.[12] The Hutchinsonians and the Hackney Phalanx were the vanguard against the perceived attacks by latitudinarians, deists, and a secularizing government that appeared incapable of living up to the idea of the nursing parent of Isa 49:23. For the Tractarians, the solution was a relinquishment of a sacrosanct monarchy, while non-Tractarian High Church thinkers just as doggedly maintained the Caroline model. Indeed, its strengthening would be a salve for the encroachment of dissenters. While Wordsworth's political vision was less self-consciously aimed at maintaining a "party perspective" than that of the Oxford Movement, the High Church wing of the Church of England—Tractarian or otherwise—had to struggle with what it meant for the Church to *be* the Church in a fragmenting and rapidly secularizing society. My focus on the exegesis of Christopher Wordsworth is to show how his ecclesio-political perspective, itself a response to the problem of ecclesial identity, bears upon his reading of Isaiah.

George Horne (1730–92) and Samuel Horsley (1733–1806), two pre-Tractarian High Church exemplars, illustrate this theopolitical dimension and its hermeneutical impact. Committed High Churchman and moderate Hutchinsonian George Horne preached a sermon on 1 Pet 2:21 ("Leaving us an example, that ye should follow his steps"), entitled "The Christian King." In a figural move that bespeaks of his yearning for a close connection

---

11. Ibid., 90–91.

12. Nockles does note that some important leaders in the Oxford Movement, among them Newman and Pusey, initially held Establishment principles (Nockles, *The Oxford Movement in Context*, 72–79). Eventually, however, the Tractarians consciously distanced themselves from the old High Church party. They derisively referred to them as the "Zs," and sought to cast the old High Church party as "high and dry," a dying movement of stiff and staid worshippers who exhibited questionable zeal for the Apostolic faith. To some extent, this became an accepted fiction in the nineteenth-century mind.

between King and Church, Horne shifts from speaking of the horror of the suffering of Christ, to numbering Charles I as one of the martyrs who participate in the Passion of Christ,

> from righteous *Abel* to the blessed martyr of this day; upon whose unparalleled murder though we cannot reflect but with horror and astonishment, yet most gratefully are we ever bound to commemorate the glories of God's grace, which he made the villainy of the most abandoned miscreants an occasion of calling forth and displaying to mankind in the person of his anointed, who "left him an example, that he should follow his steps."[13]

Recognizing that such a comparison of the "royal martyr" to Christ could be unpopular, Horne asks, "why should it be thought a thing incredible, that the character of a Christian king should bear a resemblance to Christ . . . when we all know that the characters of some of the kings of *Israel* bore so near a resemblance, that they had the honour to prefigure him before his coming?"[14] Thus, Horne shows he is an archetype of High Church Caroline (literally) opinion by considering Charles I as a kind of "postfigural" image of Christ.

Samuel Horsley, bishop of Rochester, was a significant precursor to the Oxford Movement in that he "familiarized the Church of his day with the doctrine of apostolical succession, rescuing it from becoming the exclusive property of the Nonjurors."[15] While he died too early to be identified with the Hackney Phalanx, Horsley shares many of their perspectives, particularly vis-à-vis politics.[16] In terms of exegesis, I mention Horsley because his eschatological focus is an important concomitant mode of reading the Bible, influenced by his political commitments. Consider his *Critical Disquisitions on the Eighteenth Chapter of Isaiah* (1799). While he agrees that Isa 18 is "one of the most obscure passages of the ancient Prophets,"[17] he nonetheless does not shy from using it to speak of political events of his time and their relation to the eschaton. The passage refers to a time when God, "immediately

---

13. Horne, *Sixteen Sermons*, 5. While it is true that Charles was the only canonized saint of the Church of England, it was predominantly the High Church party that participated in his veneration.

14. Horne, *Sixteen Sermons*, 14.

15. Mather, *High Church Prophet*, 306.

16. Horsley also represents what Mather sees as a new "split" in the Church of England, no longer between the High Church party and the deists/latitudinarians, but the former and the Evangelicals (Mather, *High Church Prophet*, 308). The reason for this was his remarkable liberality toward Roman Catholic recusants, while remaining doggedly against dissenters, an opposite perspective to that of Evangelicals.

17. Horsley, *Critical Disquisitions*, 10.

before the final gathering of his elect from the four winds of Heaven, will purify his church ... and ... strike all nations with religious awe.... That purification ... is not at all inconsistent with the seeming prosperity of the affairs of the atheistical confederacy."[18] The "atheistical confederacy" he has in mind here is revolutionary France. Though he is somewhat circumspect in this identification, the political challenge of radical revolution in France clearly impacts his perspective on reading this chapter in Isaiah in that there was at least a nascency of Antichrist:

> His [Antichrist's] rise, strictly speaking, the beginning of the monster, was in the apostolic age. For it were easy to trace the pedigree of French Philosophy, Jacobinism, and Bavarian Illumination, up to the first heretics. But it is now we see the *adolescence* of that man of sin, or rather of lawlessness, who is to throw off all the restraints of religion, morality, and custom, and undo the bands of civil society.... That son of perdition who shall neither be a Protestant, nor a Papist; neither Christian, Jew, nor Heathen.[19]

Despite the general antipathy of English Protestants toward "papists," Horsley here no longer takes that more common position that the Pope was Antichrist. Rather, the Antichrist is identified by his irreligious policies. Relevant for the present matter is Horsley's identification of this atheistic system with France. Thus, by "direct denigration of the French the British national cause was enhanced in righteousness."[20] It is worth mentioning that, in general, this eschatological imminence in exegesis is not generally a hallmark of Tractarian reading. The Oxford Movement also made less direct prophetic interpretations of current events.[21]

In distinction to the ecclesially-centered, monarchical vision of the Church, the later Oxford Movement was equally concerned with ecclesial integrity, but in a political atmosphere that sought *independence* from the

18. Ibid., 84.
19. Ibid., 98.
20. Mather, *High Church Prophet*, 267

21. Note in particular Newman's Tract 83 on Antichrist In it, there is also no identification of Antichrist with Rome, and Newman is in agreement with Horsley that the coming reign of the Man of Sin would comport with the rise of liberalism; yet, they differ in that Newman no longer connected this interpretation to contemporary political realities. Rather, he identifies it with the very reality of a divided Church: "It is his policy to split us up and divide us, to dislodge us gradually from our rock of strength. And if there is to be a persecution, perhaps it will be then ... when we are all of us in all parts of Christendom so divided, and so reduced, so full of schism, so close upon heresy" (Newman, "Tract 83," 52.)

state. Approaches to exegesis for both parties often overlap, but the biblical support that the Oxford Movement sought for shifted away from the use of such passages as Isa 49:23, or that of the hierarchical priestly form of Andrewes (see Chapter 1). The Oxford Movement blamed the breakdown of the Church on "liberal" forces within and without, and fought their battles on these terms. The Church was no less a concrete, embodied reality within the world, but in the Tractarian vision, it became decoupled from the state.

Like many with a High Church orientation, Newman and Pusey found the ecclesiology of the spiritualist traditions as represented by both Evangelicals and Broad Church thinkers as hopelessly disembodied—and ultimately destructive—notions of the Church and Scripture. While their opponents regarded High Churchmen and Tractarians alike espousing "romish ritual," it was because of the "spiritualizing" of many Evangelical and Broad Churchmen that they aimed at a Church in which there was a concrete realization of the Church's bodily existence in the world.[22] Both Newman and Pusey urged a "literal" reading of the text, which *included* a Church figurally embodied in the people of Israel.[23]

---

22. This can be seen in Newman's discussion on the nature of prophecy in his sermons "The Christian Church a Continuation of the Jewish" and "The Principle of Continuity Between the Jewish and Christian Churches." Newman makes use of the notion of the "remnant" in Isa 37:31 to explore its fulfillment. He explicitly rejects the argument that there is an as yet future fulfillment as argued, for instance, by the Millenarians; but he also opposes a "spiritual" fulfillment, "that the promised reign of Christ upon the earth has been nothing more than the influence of the Gospel over the souls of men, the triumph of Divine Grace, the privileges enjoyed by faith, and the conversion of the elect" (Newman, "The Christian Church," 180–81).

23. With respect to Newman's understanding of the term "literal," I have already mentioned his more "carnal" understanding of the word. Much conjecture has abounded regarding Romanticism and its impact on the Oxford Movement, especially with respect to aesthetics and the imagination. However, the Movement's rootedness in the world and its focus on liturgy and embodied acts is better accounted for on the basis of its understanding of the Incarnation. In an otherwise fine and illuminating essay on Pusey, for instance, David Jasper suggests that in Pusey "it is the imagination which recognizes that the key to the profane is sacred history" (Jasper, "Pusey's 'Lectures,'" 60). Yet, the quote from Pusey's lectures that immediately follows to support his argument makes no mention of the "imagination." Jasper inaccurately attempts to link Pusey to Coleridge's Romanticism. It would be more correct to argue that Pusey, in his understanding of typology, approaches history theologically that urges a kind of analogy of faith where what can be known of sacred history is by the eyes of faith. This is not to say that those same forces that drove Romanticism were not present in the Oxford Movement, but the impact of Romanticism does not give sufficient explanatory power to many of their theological positions, certainly not in *Pusey's* writing. For many in the Oxford Movement, and Newman especially, their view of the world is "centred upon the mystery of the Incarnation, seen as providing the key both to the sacramental understanding of the universe, and to an understanding of the Church wholly centred upon the person and work of Christ, the redeemer" (Allchin, "The Theological Vision

One area of exegetical overlap between the old High Church party and the Oxford Movement is their appreciation of the exegesis of the Church Fathers. The Tractarians aimed at a more vigorous retrieval of the Fathers' approach to the Bible as a salve for the caustic impact of encroaching liberalism. Many, particularly liberals, saw the Oxford Movement in terms of the old High Church party, namely, as an attempt at domination and control, a retrieval of an era of Church tyranny. This was often the result of a misunderstanding of the difference between the aims of the Tractarians and the political goals of the old High Church party.

The old High Church party also challenged the tendency to make christological connections within a rather wooden predictive "prophetic" framework and this is another point of overlap with the Oxford Movement. Consider E. B. Pusey's view of prophecy and the Old Testament. I attend specifically to his "Lectures on Types and Prophecies of the Old Testament" of 1836. Unfortunately, these lectures are as yet unpublished, so I rely on Allchin's article on "The Theological Vision of the Old Testament" and Jasper's article "Pusey's Lectures and Types of Prophecies," as well as Timothy Larsen's *A People of One Book*, in which the first chapter is devoted to Pusey. For all that later in life Pusey often took a more strident and argumentative stand with respect to Scripture, it would be too strong to suggest that there was a conversion of sorts from the early, German-influenced Pusey to the hard-nosed and sometimes off-putting conservative who was the visible leader of the Oxford Movement. Since, as Larsen puts it so succinctly, "it is important to keep in mind how much E. B. Pusey . . . was hated,"[24] accounts of him must be considered in this context.[25]

---

of the Oxford Movement," 54). As Pusey himself says, "the whole system of religion, contemplative and practical, is one of God's condescension: God cometh down to us, not we mount up to God. Its cornerstone and characteristic is 'God manifest in the flesh'" (Douglas, "Pusey's 'Lectures,'" 16). Since Christ came in the body of a human—the One who is himself truly "carnal"—then this affirmation of created reality is to be followed by the Church, itself the body of Christ.

24. Larsen, *A People of One Book*, 11.

25. For instance, it is often suggested that Pusey's *Daniel the Prophet* is a work of an intransigent conservative, fighting a losing battle in favor of the sixth-century authorship of the book of Daniel. Larsen, however, convincingly shows that, on the basis of the depth of scholarship as well as the positive reception of this work, Pusey's *Daniel* was, in its time, a work that was unsurpassed for its level of argumentation until S. R. Driver's commentary in 1900 (Larsen, *A People of One Book*, 27–39). In his rehabilitation of Pusey's work, Larsen convincingly shows the extent to which Pusey *as a scholar of the Bible* has been suppressed in the many years since his death. At the same time, the level at which division figures in his Daniel commentary is revealed when he says, "Pusey's goal in this book 'is to meet the pseudo-criticism on its own grounds.' In other words, he will beat them at their own game with their acknowledged weapons; he will advance

Pusey's "Lectures on Types and Prophecies of the Old Testament" are instructive for his view of the relationship between the two Testaments, as well as that of prophecy. This was a time during which Pusey was working on the Library of the Fathers, and patristic exegesis strongly informs his view of Scripture. Significantly, at this time of his life, Pusey is critical of the way that the interpretation of prophecy is often in the context of what he refers to as "orthodoxism." This is an articulation of the Christian faith in terms that are simplified into what today would be called a "propositional" orientation to doctrine.[26] Regarding biblical exegesis, Pusey's critique is that

> We are anxious indeed, to trace up fulfilments of prophecy, but in a way wholly distinct; we wish to find predictions clear, apparent and undeniable, which we more sort with the events, and which on the very surface shall indisputably correspond.[27]

---

arguments that are built upon presuppositions or that employ methods which his opponents share" (Larsen, *A People of One Book*, 27). It is for this reason that, in the end, despite its level of scholarship, *Daniel the Prophet* is filled with "almost impenetrable rationalism" (Seitz, *Figured Out,* 17). Like Robert Payne Smith, the divisive context forces Pusey into this rationalistic corner. While Larsen is correct to note that Pusey's work is under-appreciated for its scholarship, this work—and the response it generated—was judged for its ability to *convince* and not to exegete.

26. I am alluding here to the language of George Lindbeck from *The Nature of Doctrine*, in which he distinguishes between cognitive-propositional and experiential-expressive modes of religious discourse. While I am clearly being anachronistic, I would argue that Pusey presaged a similar line of thought as that of Lindbeck. Jasper errs by characterizing Pusey's rejection of "orthodoxism" in "experiential-expressive" terms and aligns him with Coleridge and (William) Wordsworth. Pusey's approach can perhaps be thought of in a "cultural-linguistic" manner *avant la lettre*.

27. Quoted in Jasper, "Pusey's 'Lectures,'" 52 as p. 10 of the Pusey MS. Here, Pusey is reflecting a concept that is common to the thinkers within the Oxford movement, which is the notion of "reserve," as expounded by Isaac Williams (1802–65) in Tracts 80 and 87 in *Tracts for the Times*. Williams challenges what he saw as a simplistic mode of interpretation, including the cherished Protestant doctrine of scriptural clarity. As Williams says in Tract 80, "there appears in God's manifestations of Himself to mankind, in conjunction with an exceeding desire to communicate that knowledge, a tendency to conceal, and throw a veil over it, as if it were injurious to us unless we were of a certain disposition to receive it" (Williams, *On Reserve*, 2). Whereas Williams urges the notion of reserve in opposition to simplistic propositional doctrine, Pusey applies it with more focus on Scripture. Part of the reason for this apophatic moment of Tractarian theology is the apologetic context in which much of the Bible—especially prophecy—was too often read. As Pusey says, "the notion, and uses of Prophecy have, in these latter days, been much narrowed and obscured by the apologetic character which our Theology has so largely assumed" (quoted in Jasper, "Pusey's 'Lectures,'" 52, from Pusey's MS, p. 1.). This apologetic urge, which attempts to make clear what God had revealed under a veil, in fact contributes to an even greater obfuscation of God's revelation, as it reduces prophecy merely to a predictive function. In Pusey's view, the ancient Church regarded Scripture as infinitely fecund, full of meaning, at times hidden, but ever-generative in

Scripturally, Pusey sees it as essential that its center is Christ. However, God also uses the natural world in the process of revelation. Like the Fathers, Pusey and many of those of the Oxford Movement are informed by a platonic metaphysic in which the symbol, or "emblem," as Pusey calls it, ontologically participates in the referent:

> It is through the medium of these figures that we understand (as far as we do understand) the reality.... He who would lay aside these types and typical language, and understand the mysteries of God without them, will be acting contrary to the teaching of Scripture and so very wrongly and foolishly. Men think that they gain in clearness, but they lose in depth; they will employ definite terms, in order to comprehend that which is infinite![28]

Every biblical term, even in its potential obscurity and hiddenness, has been chosen by God. "Reserve" and "veiling" are important theological terms, as they protect the transcendental sacredness of Scripture and theological language from the enervation of simplistic language and external methodologies. He illustrates the way the Bible speaks of future things in the Old Testament by using the image of a child. The way a child speaks is constantly "typical" of the future-developed being: "they speak greater truth than they themselves (the outward organ of that truth) know: they speak it in reference to some particular occasion but indefinitely."[29] There is, then, a hidden meaning that is necessarily attaches to the words, which tradition calls the *sensus plenior*. Therefore, to engage in a new rendering of words by either simplifying or reducing them in categories of probative function is to strip off these layers of potential significance. Like Christ himself, they may not always be understood, but also like Christ, it is only these words and no others that God has chosen to participate in the reality of sacred history.

In this claim to hidden meaning within the text, Pusey has his sights aimed at both Evangelicals and Broad Churchmen, which he refers to respectively as the "pseudo-spiritualist" and the "carnal man." With respect to the Eucharist, though analogous with Scripture:

---

its revelatory power: "The Fathers, instead of following their own predilections, were prepared to 'follow out the hints which God has given,' and learn from apostolic teaching, putting Christ and not themselves at the centre" (Jasper, "Pusey's 'Lectures,'" 55, quoting from p. 12 of the Pusey MS). This does not mean that Scripture is obscure or opaque, but that the approach to it can only be valid through faith and through the means of God's self-revelation.

28. Quoted in Jasper, "Pusey's 'Lectures,'" 58 as Pusey's MS, p. 24.
29. Quoted in ibid., 58 as Pusey's MS p. 14.

> The pseudo-spiritualist and the carnal man alike see in the water, the bread or the wine nothing but the base element, and thereby each alike deprives himself of the benefit intended for him: the carnal will live on bread alone, the pseudospiritualist without it: the carnal mistakes the clouds and darkness for him who is enshrouded within it, the pseudo-spiritualist would behold Him whom 'man cannot see and live,' the 'light inapproachable whom no man hath seen or can see'; the carnal neglects the revelation, the pseudo-spiritual will know the unrevealed God.[30]

Neither Pusey nor Newman was merely nostalgic for a so-called "pre-critical" interpretation of Scripture, *per se*. They were familiar with the newest critical approaches (mainly coming from Germany) of the Bible. They did not ignore such writings, particularly Pusey, who had travelled to Germany in 1825 where he studied many German thinkers with appreciation.[31] What remains constant in Pusey's thought is a rigid rejection of the "orthodoxy" that simplifies the Christian faith into a purely propositional form.

Although there are areas of overlap between the Tractarians and the old High Church movement, the former is a more prominent retrieval project of patristic exegesis for the purpose of aiming at a "primitive" form of Christianity. In this, there is a similarity between the Oxford Movement and Evangelicalism, as opposed as they were to each other. For instance, the old High Church party was more amenable to employing more traditional "evidences" for the Christian faith.[32] Both, however, embarked on a

---

30. Quoted in ibid., 63 from p. 23 of the Pusey MS.

31. He studied August Tholuck (1799–1877) and Karl Immanuel Nitzsch (1787–1868) who represented the *Vermittelungstheologie* emerging from Friedrich Schleiermacher (1768–1834), which aimed to bring together traditional Christian doctrine with modern scientific thought. However, he was also engaged with more conservative scholars such as Ernst Hengstenberg (1802–1869), who participated in apologetic retrievals of the Bible, and, notably, of Isaiah itself, in the face of the scholarship of his German peers. Out of this experience came Pusey, *An Historical Enquiry*. At this point, he was not yet involved with the Oxford Movement, and in fact the book was written as a response to the High Churchman Hugh James Rose, whose own book (Rose, *The State of the Protestant Religion in Germany*, 1825) was a rather poor assessment of German theology.

Pusey was in a state of intellectual transition at that time, and critical of scholastic orthodoxy. Given that his influences at the time were more liberal theologians such as Tholuck, the account was reflective of their mediating theology. However, it is a mistake to view this as the more "free thinking" Pusey, whose perspectives were snuffed out by the conservatism of the Oxford Movement. It is true that, in the end, Pusey wrote rather "incautiously" and would later come to regret some of the conclusions of his work. See Frappel, "'Science' in the Service of Orthodoxy," 1–33.

32. This is one major issue on which Newman and Rose differed. See Nockles, *The Oxford Movement in Context*, 205.

vision of primitivism. The peculiarity of the old High Church movement, is a uniquely *English* political vision.

The end of the story of Pusey and Newman is well-known. Newman converted to Rome and Pusey narrowed his perspective on Scripture by entering into the battle arenas in which it fought. As with Cranmer, Whitgift, and Hooker, one can ask whether the deeply holistic scriptural vision of the High Church party was sufficiently stable to survive. The existence of a radically divided Church ineluctably renders such a scriptural vision untenable and forces it to define itself over-against its opponents. But the old High Church conception of Scripture was so tied to ecclesial embodiment yet the specificity of such a body is ill-defined or deeply contested. When divisiveness becomes endemic in the Church, this view of Scripture inevitably devolves into more simplistic categories of, for instance, "ritualism," "liturgy," or "pre-critical exegesis." How can an ecclesially and concretely embodied exegesis exist when such a body is fragmented?

WORDSWORTH AND HIS HERMENEUTICAL ORIENTATION

Wordsworth was not unfamiliar with controversy. When *Essays and Reviews* came out in 1860, he was one of the respondents, especially to the most notorious of the essays, "On the Interpretation of Scripture" by Benjamin Jowett. His reply, among that of other respondents, was published in *Replies to "Essays and Reviews"* in 1862.[33] As Rogerson puts it, his riposte was "polemical, sarcastic and at times unscrupulous;"[34] arguing that the "Evil Spirit which stirred up the first false teachers to corrupt the sense of Scripture"[35] continues to work today to lead people to the pitfalls of heterodoxy. Indeed, he states that the very fact of divisions and arguments over Scripture is a "proof of the divine truth of Scripture warning us that it would be so."[36]

Wordsworth was not known, as were Newman and Pusey, for being too comfortable with Roman Catholic thinking. Also unlike Pusey, and Newman, Wordsworth did not become branded as a "Romanizer" or a "friend to the Pope."[37] Unlike Pusey and Newman, Wordsworth wrote a commentary on most of the books of the Bible, a project that began with

---

33. Jowett, "On The Interpretation of Scripture," 330–433; Goulburn et al., *Replies to "Essays and Reviews."*
34. Rogerson, *Old Testament Criticism*, 217.
35. Goulburn et al., *Replies to "Essays and Reviews,"* 412.
36. Ibid., 417.
37. See Greenfield, "'Such a Friend to the Pope,'" 162–84.

the New Testament in 1856 and finished with the Minor Prophets in 1870. He shared certain basic commitments with Evangelicals, such as their views on perceived attacks on biblical trustworthiness by liberals, to say nothing of the use of radical German criticism by Unitarians. But Wordsworth remained, as his daughter Elizabeth notes, one with strong High Church affinities.[38]

As a representative of the old High Church faction, Wordsworth deploys Isaiah in his theological legitimization the National Church of England. The Church is the body that sprouted out of the soil of "literal Israel." The lack of any detailed particularity in his discussion of the Church leads only to the speculation that when he refers to the Church, he has the Established Church of England in mind. As concrete and embodied as High Church thinkers wanted it to be, it is hard to discern in Wordsworth's exegesis how any aspect of the Church was truly "one" or "catholic."

With respect to Wordsworth's overall view of Scripture, although his commentary is based on the Authorized Version (AV), he freely makes comments that suggest better translations of certain words: he does not consider the AV as sacrosanct. It is similar to the commentary style of Cheyne's that we will see in the next chapter in that it provides the text of Isaiah with a running commentary in small print. The Bible is of central importance to Wordsworth, and he considers his High Church principles fully congruent with Scripture. For two years in a row (1847–8) he gave the Hulsean Lectures at Cambridge, both of which speak to scriptural matters. A rather concise account of his view of Scripture in general can be found in the revised edition of these Hulsean Lectures called *On the Inspiration of the Holy Scripture*. Most of these lectures focus on the "inspiration and authorship" of various parts of the Bible, such as the letters of Paul and the Apocalypse. Not unusual is the strongly apologetic tenor of these lectures, but, perhaps surprisingly, his first mention of opponents to Scripture (disregarding the brief preface) is *not* the critics of the Bible, but Roman Catholics and some orthodox Protestants. The Roman Catholic claim is that the Scripture of the Protestants is neither sufficient, for it does not include the Apocrypha, nor was it fully canonized until the fourth century. Using this as his entry point, Wordsworth enters into his discussion on "The Foundation on which

---

38. See Overton and Wordsworth, *Christopher Wordsworth, Bishop of Lincoln*. It is of interest to note the role that many women played in the Oxford Movement. As Rebecca Idestrom notes, Elizabeth Wordsworth (1840–1933), Christopher's daughter, played a significant role as his chief assistant in writing the commentaries, but also made suggestions and gave considerable input. This contributed to her own depth of knowledge of the Bible, leading her to lecture to women and publish works on the Bible. See Idestrom, "Elizabeth Wordsworth," 181–200.

the Canon of Scripture Rests."[39] As an indication that his view of Scripture differs from that of other Protestants, he explicitly rejects Article V of the Belgic confession, which states that "we believe without a doubt all things contained in [the Scriptures]—not so much because the church receives and approves them as such but above all because the Holy Spirit testifies in our hearts that they are from God . . ." Wordsworth faults the Confession for conceiving of the Holy Spirit testifying in the heart of the individual as highly subjective and providing insufficient foundation for the truth of Scripture. As he says, "we are *forbidden* in Scripture to believe *every* spirit, and are there commended to *try the spirits, whether they be of God;* and we have *no* way of trying them, except by the *Word of God*. We must, therefore, *first* be sure that we *have* the *Word*, before we can ascertain whether we possess the *Spirit* of God."[40] The implication of relying on one's own sense of internal conviction is to ask, "what claims would the Bible have above those of the Koran?"[41] In his view, many of the continental Reformers were "betrayed by an arbitrary abuse of private judgment."[42] Moreover, this statement in the Belgic Confession denies the Church a determinative role in the canon of the Bible; the agency of the Spirit is thus resident in the conviction of the individual rather than that of the Church.

Wordsworth, conversely, affirms the central role of the Church in relation to Scripture. He begins by rejecting the Roman Catholic view that the Church affirmed and recognized what the Scriptures are, and, rather tautologically, this recognition is what makes them the Scriptures. This is where we can see how the principle of primitivism informs his argument. The problem with Roman Catholic claims to the ancient provenance of their practices is that "they confound the *present* Church of Rome, which is only a *part*, and a *corrupt* part, of the Church, with the *primitive* Church *Catholic*. . . . We revere the testimony of the primitive Catholic Church, namely, that of CHRIST Himself, that we cannot accept the Canon of the present Church of Rome."[43] This is the typically Protestant aim of repristination that claims a time of ecclesial deterioration during the Middle Ages, necessitating the Reformation to bring the Church back to its primitive roots. The problem, of course, is that the argument becomes almost a purely historical question: what aspects of the early Church are truly "primitive?" Who are its representatives?

39. Wordsworth, *On the Inspiration of the Holy Scripture*, 2–28.
40. Ibid., 14.
41. Ibid., 15.
42. Ibid.
43. Ibid., 20.

In the end, however, the Church does not function to validate or make Scripture what it is merely by naming it as such; rather, using the analogy of road sign, Wordsworth asserts that the Church is a sign. Thus,

> the sign is *more visible* than the city, but it does not *make* the city; and, if it were destroyed, the city would still remain; and when the traveller arrives at the city, the city proves itself to be the place which the sign indicated, and thus proves the credibility of the sign. So, the Christian Church, it is true *directs* us to Scripture, but she does not *make* Scripture, nor *give* authority to it.[44]

As with Pusey, material signification is important in High Church thought. The Church is more than a mere sign: the believer cannot apprehend Scripture without the direction of the Church. At the same time, the Church does not have priority over Scripture. Since the sign participates in the thing to which it refers, then the Church is also shaped by the economy of salvation recounted in the Bible.

In order to know if the referent is inspired by the Holy Spirit, Wordsworth does not appeal to anything external to the Church itself:

> We reply, it is an indubitable *fact* that a religious Society, known by the name of the Church, exists, and has existed in this country since the time of the Apostles: and this Society exercises a visible authority, and discharges certain public offices in Prayer, and Preaching, and the Ministry of Sacraments, in public buildings called churches, throughout the Realm. This Society appeals to the eye and to the ear of all. . . . The Church presents us with a Volume, called the HOLY BIBLE, containing writings which she affirms to be inspired by God.[45]

This is a curious claim: one wonders if Wordsworth really believes that Christianity was present in England during the Apostolic era, if by this he is referring to the first century. Myths of a very early primitive Christianity coming to England were not unheard of, and perhaps Wordsworth had some of them in mind.[46] The important point is that there is no sense by

---

44. Ibid., 20–21.

45. Ibid., 23.

46. During Wordsworth's time, there was Rundle, *The Early Dawn; or, Sketches of Christian Life in England in the Olden Time*. Rundle was associated with the Oxford Movement; the first chapter of *The Early Dawn* tells of a meeting in England between a Druid, a Jew, and a Christian. While the story is mythical, she presents it as part of an account of the Church in England, leading to Wycliffe. There is also the more popular, and equally unsubstantiated myth, of Joseph of Arimathea coming to England, which

which the individual believer justifies the veracity of the Bible in Wordsworth's account. He regards the Church of England as the best representative of the primitive Church, which has faithfully presented the Bible to the people of the world.

In terms of the relation between the Church and Scripture, Wordsworth argues that

> the primitive Apostolic Church of Christ exercised a fourfold office: first, that of a contemporary Witness to its genuineness and authenticity; next, that of a Guardian of its integrity; next, that of a Herald, by public reading and interpretation of it in her religious assemblies ... and finally that of a Judge, by vindicating its divine character, and by distinguishing it from all supposititious writings claiming to be inspired.[47]

This fourfold office of the Church can be articulated as a unique High Church form of a *via media*, but vastly different than that of the Broad Church. In the case of the latter, the *via media* is construed as a kind of prudent, functional (and emaciated) golden mean, carefully maneuvering between dogmatism and complete unbelief. By invoking the primitive Church, Wordsworth on the one hand rejects the assertion that Scripture obtains its credibility by virtue a claim by the Church, as in Roman Catholicism. On the other hand, he denies the so-called "right to private judgment" that is the hallmark of Evangelical and liberal perspectives.

It is noteworthy that of all the commentators I consider in this dissertation, Wordsworth is the most hostile to Roman Catholics. This is not unusual, for it is often those of High Church proclivities that tend to feel the need to defend their perspective against those who accuse them of "romanizing" tendencies. Particularly relevant for this chapter, they often saw Roman Catholics as not truly "English" and unable to maintain allegiance to

---

eventually becomes mixed with the legend of the Holy Grail. One can only speculate, however, what Wordsworth has in mind. Lest it is supposed that Wordsworth's claim that there was a Church in England at the time of the Apostles is an aberration, he repeats this claim on p. 29.

Such pro-English theology is not just the purview of High Church theologians. Two notable examples are worth mentioning. The famous hymn writer Isaac Watts (1674-1748) is well known not only for popular hymns, but for his replacement of references to Israel and Judah with that of "Britain" or "Great Britain" in his *Psalms of David* (1719) (see Hull, "Isaac Watts," 59–79). Similarly, there is the well-known poem "Jerusalem" by the artist and poet William Blake (1757-1827), which became a hymn in the Church of England that begins: "And did those feet in ancient time / Walk upon Englands mountains green: / And was the holy Lamb of God / On Englands pleasant pastures seen!"

47. Wordsworth, *On the Inspiration of the Holy Scripture*, 25.

the Crown. They were seen as a kind of foreign presence in England, opposing the High Church theopolitical scheme. The result is that Wordsworth's exegesis of Scripture is directly impacted by this antagonistic state of affairs. His essay on "Union with Rome" is illustrative of how vicious his discourse can be. He argues ultimately that "now the prophecy became clear, clear as noon-day; and we tremble at the sight, while we read the inscription, emblazoned in large letters, 'MYSTERY, BABYLON THE GREAT,' written by the hand of St. John, guided by the Holy Spirit of God, on the forehead of the Church of Rome."[48]

A word ought to be mentioned with respect to the influences on Wordsworth and those whom he consulted when researching the commentary. It is perhaps surprising that, while Church Fathers such as Origen and their highly figurative mode of interpretation are common in his exegesis, many modern interpreters also impact his reading. He does not shy away from invoking the names of such modern German exegetes as Vitringa, Gesenius, Hitzig, Delitzsch, and Hengstenberg. He considers Delitzsch's commentary as "excellent"[49] and that of Hengstenberg with approval, since they tend to cohere with his point of view. Moreover, when he does cite with approbation those exegetes who take a more critical approach to the text, it tends to be when they render a translation that is in his favor. He does not shy away from using modern scholars to make his case for him.

Wordsworth's introduction to Isaiah almost immediately characterizes the book in terms of its predictive capacity: "Prophets did not *work* miracles, but (if we may so say) they *spoke* miracles . . . . Their divine mission was proved by the immediate fulfilment of *some* of the prophecies which they uttered, and this fulfilment was a pledge and earnest that their *other* prophecies concerning distant events would be fulfilled also. . . . The Prophets . . . afford additional evidence of God's presence with them."[50] Ultimately, Isaiah "proves that the Gospel holds the first place in the counsels of the Divine Mind."[51] Wordsworth also maintains the traditional view regarding the unity of authorship of the book of Isaiah.[52] What is most interesting in Wordsworth's "Introduction," however, is that, although subtle, he makes a connection between the threat to Israel in the text and to the present-day Church of England. Isaiah came

---

48. Wordsworth, *Union with Rome*, 66.
49. Wordsworth, *Isaiah*, xxi.
50. Ibid., vi-vii.
51. Ibid., ix.
52. Ibid., xvii-xx. He comes back to this issue on p. 113.

> at a time when National Establishments of Religion appear to be threatened, and the condition of some may be, before long, like that of the exiles at Chebar—where every man was thrown on the support of those gifts and graces which he received from spiritual communion with God—it is the duty of all to listen to that prophetic teaching; and while we have the comfort of knowing that the Scriptures will never perish, and the Sacraments will never cease to be administered; and while it is a happy result even of our religious divisions, that there is now no ecclesiastical power on earth which can impair or affect the ancient Creeds, received from a united Christendom.[53]

Wordsworth sees the threat to Israel in terms of a "National Establishment," surely anachronistic, commensurate with a High Church political vision that sees a theological correspondence between Israel and England.

THE CHURCH AT THE EXPENSE OF THE INDIVIDUAL

The impact of ecclesial division upon Wordsworth's exegesis is obvious when placed in the context of his antipathy toward Rome. However, his definition of the Church that he envisions is couched in rather negative terms and is often abstractly articulated; it is *not* the Church of Rome in the modern era. *Neither*, however, is the Church to be conceived of as merely a spiritual (meaning invisible) affiliation of individuals. On this latter point, one can only speculate so far, but it is striking how Wordsworth studiously avoids speaking of the individual believer.

Wordsworth interprets Isaiah in such a way that the Church plays a central role in understanding the meaning of the text. His reading closely parallels that of Pusey's and Newman's view that the *visible* Church must be linked to "carnal" Israel. The ecclesial centrality in Wordsworth's interpretation of Isaiah quickly makes itself clear, and given what has been said thus far, ought not be surprising. Examples abound, but I take as emblematic his commentary on Isa 30:19 ("For the people shall dwell in Zion at Jerusalem: Thou shalt weep no more: He will be very gracious unto thee at the voice of thy cry; when he shall hear it, he will answer thee"). Wordsworth simply states that "this promise is fulfilled in the Church."[54] The commentary on Isa 30:20–26 is entitled "Retrospect of the Prophecy (vv. 20–26.) Its Spiritual Sense." Wordsworth's somewhat brief comments with respect to Christ and the Church are helpful for an understanding of his meaning of "spiritual

---

53. Ibid., xiii.
54. Ibid., 88.

sense," as it becomes clear that it is quite different than that of Robert Payne Smith. "Spiritual," as Wordsworth sees it, does not have to do with a moral or abstract concept, but speaks to a direct connection between Christ and the Church. For the Isa 30 passage, he does not argue against interpreting the text in its application to historical Israel: "This prophecy began to be fulfilled on the return of Israel from Babylon, when they put away their idols." However, he continues to argue that the "larger fulfillment was in the coming of CHRIST. Then the *Lord* had *waited* for many generations to be gracious. . . . Then the people saw their TEACHER, and He established a Visible Church, wherein His Word is preached, and His sacraments are administered in the whole world."[55] I use this text from Isaiah as it is not traditionally understood as a clear reference to Christ or the Church, yet Wordsworth uses it as an occasion to raise the visibility and universality of the Church as well as the sacraments and preaching. Wordsworth's hermeneutic, which brings out the importance of the visible Church, calls for more exploration in the context of his political theology. There is no doubt that Wordsworth has the Church of England front and center in his mind when he thinks of the Church. For instance, Wordsworth has a rather extended discussion of the importance of a national church in his exegesis of Isa 49:23–26, which is the one I note above that is often used to justify a monarchical church. This passage leads Wordsworth to say "That National Establishments of True Religion are pleasing to Almighty God, and bring down His blessings, spiritual and temporal, upon those who maintain them, is evident from such declarations of Holy Scripture such as these . . ."[56] In classic High Church form, Wordsworth argues that

> every Country which has a National Religious Establishment ought to endeavour to improve it; and that any country which has such an Establishment, and does not maintain, but destroys it, falls away from God . . . . Temporal jealously of the spiritual attributes of the Church . . . is fatal to the welfare of States and Thrones. . . . If the United Church of England and Ireland were now allowed to expand herself in all the integrity of her Apostolic doctrine and discipline, with faithful Bishops placed in the great towns and cities of the Realm, then the best interests of the English Monarchy would be promoted, and the loyalty and happiness of the people would be placed on a solid and secure foundation of religion and piety, let "Kings be nursing fathers, and Queens be mothers of the Church of Christ;" and He, who

55. Ibid., 89.
56. Ibid., 145.

> is "King of Kings" will give them His blessing in the world and in another.⁵⁷

It is not until the very end of this passage does Wordsworth makes a connection to the text. It is also interesting to note the highly political tone of his comments. An Evangelical, for instance, would tend to argue that the problem of the Church is a lack of sincerity, earnestness, or personal conviction. At the same time, Broad Churchmen urged the need for freedom of thought. Wordsworth avers that the lack of concrete embodiment of the Church in the nation itself contributes to her downfall.

This verse is illustrative of how High Church political theology bears on his exegesis. And to this extent it is helpful to address the connection Wordsworth makes between the Church and Israel, since it is often the nation of Israel *qua* nation in the Old Testament that provides a model of the Church for many in the High Church. Even more, the pro-Establishment perspective, as represented by Wordsworth, contributes to the breakdown of the uniquely Anglican view of Scripture by narrowing his focus on the protection of the Monarchy for the sake of the Church.

It is significant that Wordsworth has a greater appreciation for the close connection between the Church and Israel than can be found in the other exegetes in this book. For instance, he often refers to Jerusalem as "the mother of the Church." An exemplary case is in his analysis of Isa 60:12 ("For the nation and kingdom that will not serve thee shall perish . . .") Wordsworth says

> It must ever be borne in mind, that the original and well-spring of the Universal Church of Christ was at Jerusalem,—the place where Abraham offered up Isaac in will; the city of David and Solomon; the city of the Temple; the home of Isaiah, and most of the prophets; the place where Christ suffered and rose again from the dead, and where the Holy Ghost came down from heaven. Jerusalem, therefore, ever lives and moves in the whole body of the Church.⁵⁸

This passage speaks to a host of issues regarding the connection between the Two Testaments and the unity of the canon. For now, I focus only on the relation between Israel and the Church. The connection between the two was often ambiguously defined for many in the nineteenth century, especially since a distinction arose between "Israel" and "the Jews," the former being the more ideal form of revealed faith, which had degenerated by the

---

57. Ibid., 146.
58. Ibid., 174.

time of Christ. "Judaism" as such came to be seen in a negative light, as a faith of the ignorant and blinded people who rejected the true Messiah. Nonetheless, Wordsworth has a deep theological interest in maintaining the link wherein Jerusalem gives birth to the Church, for Jerusalem is "not a mere maternal city which is represented by Zion, but something animated with divine breath and life, and far more glorious, extensive, and enduring than any earthly Capital."[59]

In terms of how Wordsworth connects theology and Scripture, he presents a deeply canonical approach to the text that links the Church to Israel through Jerusalem to the heavenly Jerusalem of Revelation. Throughout his commentary the Church participates in Christ as the center of God's plan for the world. That is, Israel was "the Church" of the Old Testament, not yet universalized by the coming of Christ. While Robert Payne Smith also refers to Israel as a "church," there is in Wordsworth's analysis a much greater sense of continuity between Israel and its spiritualization. For Wordsworth, this continuity extends to the realm of practice and form. This was not as prominent as it was for Pusey, for Wordsworth was less forceful on the issue of "ritual." It was a political continuity, as we saw Wordsworth's biblical justification for a nationally established church above. In other words, the Church is not only to be a "spiritual" entity. Another example with more historical grounding can be seen in his exegesis of Isa 62:8,9 ("Surely I will no more give thy corn to be meat for thine enemies . . . . They that have gathered it shall eat it . . . in the courts of my holiness"). Wordsworth finds a felicitous occasion to compose an ode of sorts to the Church and the Eucharist:

> The literal Israel were commanded to consecrate their harvests by bringing the first-fruits and third years' tithes, and dedicating them to the Lord . . . . But the Evangelical Antitype of this is perpetuated and universalized in the Christian Sion, in the courts of the Lord's holiness, especially in the Holy Eucharist, where the faithful offer themselves, and their substance, as a sacrifice to God.[60]

Note that there is no mention here that one biblical image is only a "spiritual" representation of the other. Indeed, it is true that he implies a distinction between "literal" Israel and a subsequent universalization of it. However, it is often the case in the nineteenth century and earlier to consider the external accoutrements of "carnal" Israel to be merely the husk that hides an inner, spiritual and immutable reality. But for Wordsworth Israel serves much more than as a mere precursor for the Church. Israel, with Jerusalem

59. Ibid.
60. Ibid., 180.

as its synecdoche, was chosen as the locus of God's economy of salvation: "Palestine was a theatre in which God's judgments on His own people and on all other Nations were displayed as a spectacle to the eyes of all mankind in successive acts of a great historical drama."[61] This is not to say that he avoids anti-Semitic language, for it is almost inevitable that a theologian of his time would construe Judaism *vis-a-vis* Christianity in terms of Jewish perfidy. For instance, Isa 29:11 says, "the vision of all is become unto you as the words of a book that is sealed," which is justification for Wordsworth's claim that "the prophecies of the Holy Scriptures, which ye Jews hold in your hands, and which ye hear with your ears . . . will be unintelligible to you, who imagine that you alone can see."[62] This is a typical chastisement of the Jews for their unbelief—and note also here that the distinction is made between Israel and the Jews in this quote.

Wordsworth therefore has a strong idea of what the Church is. However, it is also important to note what he says the Church is *not*. It is not exemplified in Rome, and his exegesis of Isaiah bears this out. It is perhaps on this point above all others that an overtly divisive or antagonistic exegesis can be identified. Isa 28 is a description of the woes proclaimed against Samaria and Israel. Wordsworth interprets these woes as signifying the scattering of Israel. When he comes to vv. 3–4 ("The crown of pride, the drunkards of Ephraim, shall be trodden under feet: and the glorious beauty, which is on the head of the fat valley, shall be a fading flower."), the image of a crown serves as an occasion to stage a minor assault on Roman Catholicism. His train of thought is as follows: the word *crown* signifies "purity of religion and worship," to which Roman Catholicism presents the greatest threat:

> You know how busy the emissaries of the Church of Rome have been to take this crown from us; or at least to pick up the diamonds out of it, and to put in false counterfeit ones in their places. They stole away the power of religion, and filled up the room with shadows and fopperies of their own devising. It is the vanity of that Church to think that they adorn the worship of God, when they dress it up with splendour in her service . . . . They dress it up with a multitude of gaudy ceremonies, and make it the smallest part of itself; whereas, its true glory consists, not in pomp, but in purity. . . . There is another Woman [in the Apocalypse], arrayed in purple and scarlet . . . and . . . full of abominations.[63]

61. Ibid., 36.
62. Ibid., 84.
63. Ibid., 79. Wordsworth is quoting a sermon by Archbishop Robert Leighton (1611–84), which was about this passage in Isaiah.

I speak below of the connection of Roman Catholicism in Wordsworth's exegesis to the harlot of the Apocalypse; for now I continue to outline other areas in which his antipathy toward Rome funds his exegesis. The above example is not subtle, but in his exegesis of Isa 46 there is some of the strongest language yet. Verse 5 says, "Sit thou silent, and get thee into darkness... For thou shalt no more be called, The lady of kingdoms." With a more obvious pretext by virtue of the use of the term *lady*, Wordsworth asserts

> There is a spiritual power in Europe which makes a similar claim [of Supreme Lord, as did the King of Babylon]. Its Supreme Ruler calls himself also the "King Vicar;" and when he is crowned, is addressed with these words:—"Know that thou art the father of Princes, and of Kings and the *Ruler of the World*;" ... And its seat is the mystical Babylon—Rome.[64]

A final example that also illustrates his view of Zion as the mother of the Church, Wordsworth comments on Isa 54:1 ("Sing, O barren, that thou didst not bear; ... Cry aloud, thou that didst not travail with child: For more are the children of the desolate than the children of the married wife.") Wordsworth begins by echoing St. Paul's allegory in Gal 4:24–29, that "Jerusalem that is above is free, and she is our mother," after which follows this verse from Isaiah. This leads Wordsworth to an excursus on the Church:

> This truth,— that Zion is the Mother of all faithful people—is very important to its positive character, and also as a safeguard against errors. By it the unity of the Church of Christ with the Church of the Patriarchs is displayed; and the reader is guarded against the heresy of those (such as Marcion and the Manichaeans), who set the Old Testament against the New.... By it we are also defended against a more modern heresy, that which is involved in the assumption of the present Church of Rome calling herself "the Mother of all Churches" ... in defiance of the prophecies of the Old Testament and the history of the New, and in spite of the testimony of Christian Antiquity.[65]

Thus the Church does not subsist in Rome, and in fact Rome usurps what does not belong to it, in Wordsworth's view. Note also his appeals to Christian antiquity via the Patriarchs to support his argument against perceived Roman Catholic claim as the final authority on theological matters.

In terms of what the Church *is* for Wordsworth, there are numerous instances in his commentary where he expounds on the Church. Perhaps

---

64. Ibid., 138.
65. Ibid., 158.

one of his most poetic descriptions is his comment on Isa 60:16 ("Thou shalt also suck the milk of the Gentiles, and shalt suck the breast of kings"). What he says is rather lengthy, but it illuminates his deep reverence for the Church:

> This bright galaxy of splendid imagery serves the purpose of showing that it is not a mere material City which is represented by Zion, but something animated with divine breath and life, and far more glorious, extensive, and enduring than any earthly Capital. The Zion of the Prophet had a local origin in Jerusalem; but she went forth as a living and growing Power, with spiritual vitality and energy, to enfold the World. She is the city set on a hill, which cannot be hid. . . . She is visible to the eyes of all Nations; and all are bound to revere her with humble homage as an august Queen—the Queen at Christ's right hand. . . . She is built on Christ, the Rock of Ages, and the gates of Hell cannot prevail against her. . . . All the faithful of every age and nation are lively stones, built into this Holy Temple,—a Temple ever growing in life and light, and culminating in heavenly glory.[66]

This is a striking description of the Church, but it raises a vital question: what is this entity that is "visible to the eyes of all Nations"? Elsewhere, Wordsworth says,

> There is One Adam, and one Eve; One Christ and One Church; One Husband and One Bride. Zion becomes the Bride by being universalized in the Catholic Church; but she does not cease to be Zion. . . . Wherever the Church is, there Jerusalem is.[67]

When commenting on Isa 65:16 ("Behold, I create new heavens and a new earth: and the former shall not be remembered"), Wordsworth states

> It is always to be borne in mind, in comparing this and other prophecies, that there are *not two Churches* of Christ, but *one Church Universal* in *two different states*—militant here on earth, and to be glorified hereafter in heaven.[68]

Clearly, there is only one Church for Wordsworth, the "Queen at Christ's right hand," and many of his comments appear to bring the Church militant and triumphant very closely together. While he is not unique to Wordsworth, his focus on the *oneness* of the Church in the face of a divided reality

---

66. Ibid. 175.
67. Ibid., 179.
68. Ibid., 188.

cannot but render his conception of the Church as a rather abstract concept. It is very rare in this commentary for Wordsworth to consider the Church beyond an undivided reality. One example is when he speaks to Isa 7:1, where it says, "In that day seven women shall take hold of one man, saying . . . let us be called by thy name." Although it is unusual for Wordworth to be inconsistent, this is one such case. On the one hand, via Origen, he interprets the verse as follows:

> *Seven* is a symbol of universality, see Rev. i.12, where the *seven* candlesticks represent the *Universal Church* . . . . They will embrace the Gospel preached by Him, and will cling to Christ, as very members of His mystical Body, by faith and obedience.

However, on the other hand, when Wordsworth comes to the next passage, "in that day shall the branch of the Lord be beautiful and glorious," he is more circumspect: "though there be many Churches throughout the world, there is but *one Man*—one Husband to them all—Christ."[69] His focus on unity and oneness has now been subtly abandoned for a focus on Christ. In another instance, Wordsworth more directly speaks of intra-ecclesial division in his exegesis of Isa 34:5 ("my sword shall be bathed in heaven: Behold, it shall come down upon Idumea, and upon the people of my curse, to judgment"). He comments

> *Edom* . . . appears before us in Scripture as the unbrotherly Enemy of the people of God in its needs and distresses . . . and is the representative of those persons and Nations who are not wholly alien from the Church of God, but are connected with it by some ties of affinity or consanguinity . . . and represents *Christian* adversaries of Christ.[70]

Wordsworth gives as biblical examples of Ishmael, Herod and, Judas as such adversaries. None, of course, are as such *Christian* examples of enemies, and he does not elaborate on this interpretation.

Wordsworth's exegesis suggests that he would not accept the Roman Catholic Church to be a part of any singular ecclesial reality. What is less clear, however, is the status of the numerous denominations that, by his time, had proliferated throughout England? His solution is not to argue for greater comprehensiveness in the Church of England but he offers no serious consideration of the reality of a fragmented Church. Despite Wordsworth's efforts to argue for an embodied ecclesiology, it is difficult to conceive of his account of the Church as anything other than an idealized one.

69. Ibid., 10.
70. Ibid., 100.

Wordsworth's thinking on the Church is pulled in various directions. First, he attempts to speak of the Church in the same way the Church Fathers do: as a unified, single Church, outside of which are heretics. At the same time, his nationalistic perspective narrows his options for ecclesial referents, essentially becoming parochial. The consequence of such an idealistic view of the Church is often a conflation of the Church militant and triumphant, lacking a depiction that reflects the reality of the Church in the nineteenth century.

Wordsworth's ecclesial position is exemplified by his use of authorities, and it is noteworthy to point out what is missing from his exegesis: there are only two time periods from which Wordsworth primarily draws support—the relatively recent and the very early. There is little or no wrestling with thinkers from the medieval era, or with great exegetes like Thomas Aquinas or even John Calvin. He does no more than object to claims of multiple Isaiah authorship. One can find references to Vitringa, Hengstenberg, or Michaelis on the one hand, and Jerome and Origen on the other. In the case of the former, as mentioned earlier, they tend to be used not as guides to exegesis but as buttresses for his case. Why does Wordsworth avoid medieval commentators, and even makes no mention of the several seventeenth- and eighteenth-century Isaiah exegetes from England that I summarize in Chapter 2? Perhaps it is that Even they were too much influenced by Continental thinkers (recall his displeasure with the Belgic Confession) who did not argue stridently enough for a national Church. Whatever the case, I suggest that this parochialism renders his exegesis unstable, as modern exegetes are used only to lend support to his interpretation, but his ecclesial outlook "pretends" to be that of the Church Fathers.

Even more subtle, but not insignificant, is how Robert Payne Smith and Wordsworth are on opposite ends of the spectrum with respect to the role of the Church and of the individual. Whereas Smith generally considers the Church in a rather disembodied "spiritual" manner, favoring the individual as the interpreter and audience of the text, there is in Wordsworth almost no mention of what would today be called a "personal application" of the text. While in the introduction to this commentary, he says that "true religion is a practical thing, a thing of the heart and of the life. . . . The Temple in which God most delights to dwell, is the human heart,"[71] this is rather the exception that proves the rule. With all that I have discussed regarding the centrality of an ecclesial reading of the text in classical Anglican thinking, Cranmer, Whitgift, and Hooker would not deny the importance of individual appropriation of the Bible. Public reading and common liturgy

---

71. Ibid., xii.

are the *means of* ultimate personal edification; the Church does not merely take on an authoritative interpretive role (at least, not ideally) but it is the space in which the Word (and words) of God are received in the reading of the text *and* the reception of the Eucharist. I would surmise that Wordsworth offers a studious avoidance of the individual precisely in opposition to common Evangelical tendencies to hortatory exposition. In fact, a purely ecclesial interpretation was not a typical way of reading Scripture by the Fathers.[72] While Wordsworth's sermons undoubtedly had parenetic aspects, it is all the more surprising that this is lacking in his exegesis.

ISAIAH, CHRIST, AND THE CANON OF SCRIPTURE

The interpenetration of themes and the close unity between the Old and New Testaments that Wordsworth affirms should not be surprising. The central figure of all of Scripture is Christ. The canon is one because of the One to whom it witnesses. For Robert Payne Smith in the previous chapter and Thomas Kelly Cheyne in the next, making a distinction between the exegetical categories of literary versus spiritual was not difficult. For Wordsworth, however, attempting to do so would be artificial. While I began by discussing the Church, it would be a mistake to assume that ecclesial issues were his only concern. The previous section is illustrative of the point: one cannot abstractly distinguish themes such as christology and ecclesiology out of Wordsworth's exegesis.

I begin by summarizing some claims that Wordsworth makes with respect to Scripture as a unitary canonical witness. I follow with examples of Wordsworth's use of typology and figuration, the traditional hermeneutical and theological orientation to questions of Christian Old Testament interpretation. As the last section began to show, there are many instances where he reads the text explicitly against the Roman Catholic Church. In this context he finds connection between Isaiah and the Apocalypse. Additionally, like Robert Payne Smith, Wordsworth seems to be intermittently unable to avoid reducing prophecy to the one-dimensional concept of evidentiary proof.

In the Preface to the first volume of his commentary on the Old Testament, Wordsworth outlines his view on how the Bible hangs together. Using Augustine's famous dictum that *"in Vetere Testamento Novum latet, in*

---

72. For instance, in his sermon on Ezekiel, Origen says, "If I, who believe in Jesus Christ and have entrusted myself to so great a master, should sin, who will be a father to me?" (Balthasar, *Origen, Spirit and Fire,* 161). Origen interprets the text as addressing himself personally, and by implication, his readers and listeners.

Novo Vetus patet," Wordsworth asserts that "both Testaments are from one and the same Divine Hand, and form one harmonious whole; that the New Testament is enfolded in the Old, and that the Old Testament is unfolded in the New."[73] He sees a parallel intellectual state of affairs in his time as that of Tertullian, whereby there was an eclipse of the importance of the Old Testament. He perceives such threats as originating with the rise of historical criticism—not that he rejects the increased use of biblical criticism as such: he even accepts that "much has been effected by Biblical Criticism for the elucidation of the Sacred Text." However, the

> history of the Old Testament is treated in many ways in our own days as if it were a common history. The history of God's dealing with the Patriarchs and with His chosen People is often classed with the histories of ancient Greece and Rome, and is read and interpreted as such. But wherever it is thus treated, its real meaning is lost; and it is degraded from its true position and dignity, and is exposed to the cavils of Unbelief.[74]

Wordsworth wants to recover a view in which the Old Testament is constitutive of what Scripture is. In his reading of Isaiah, we find him attempting to carry out his belief that

> in order that we may be able to read the Old Testament with benefit, we must begin with the New. We must firmly be built upon the great doctrines of the Christian Creed, especially of the Godhead of Christ, and of the Holy Ghost.... We must listen to the interpretations given [the OT] by Jesus Christ, the Son of God and by his Apostles.[75]

However, it is helpful to also consider how the pressure of more critical readings of the text overshadows his own. In other words, is his aim to maintain canonical unity tainted by apologetic maneuvering rather than christological/ecclesial exegesis?

There is no question that, in terms of scriptural cohesion, Wordsworth desires to maintain a deep connection between Isaiah and the rest of Scripture. He regards Origen as an exegetical exemplar, and a reader of Wordsworth may find his approach particularly "Alexandrian." For instance, when Isa 12:3 says, "with joy shall ye draw water out of the wells of salvation," this reminds Wordsworth of

---

73. Wordsworth, *The Holy Bible in the Authorized Version*, 1:vii.
74. Wordsworth, *Isaiah*, vii.
75. Ibid., viii-ix.

> the Feast of Tabernacles, prefiguring the Son of God tabernacling our flesh (see John i.14, and notes on 1 Kings viii. 65; and Ezra iii.4. Neh. viii.16), Water was drawn from the Pool of Siloam, also a type of Christ ... and was poured on the great altar in the Temple ... on which burnt-offerings (the figures of Christ's perfect sacrifice of Himself) were offered. In like manner, now that Christ is come in our flesh, Who sums up all of these types in Himself, we draw near with joy out of the wells of salvation.[76]

This single phrase from Isaiah functions as the basis of a meditation on numerous connections to the New Testament, but all center on the person and work of Christ. This speaks to the typical view in High Church hermeneutics of the *fecundity* of the text. For instance, the word "water" gives rise to a host of images for a reader with Wordsworth's hermeneutic. This is more than a kind of intertextuality—it is no mere literary device, but is justified by the fact that Christ, by whom and for whom the world was created, is the ontological basis of Scripture, always generative of a kaleidoscope of new meaning, albeit ordered and delimited by the New Testament's use of christological terms.

Typology is an important concept for Wordsworth as he works out how to read Isaiah as a genuine constitutive element of Christian Scripture. It is worthwhile to consider an example of Wordsworth's application of typology from Isa 25–26. These chapters are Hezekiah's songs of praise after victory over his enemy, Sennacherib of Assyria, and his restoration from sickness, a case in which Isaiah was directly involved (2 Kgs 19–20). While Wordsworth does not ignore the historical context, his interest is in how Hezekiah serves as a type of Christ. The connection between Hezekiah and Christ are obvious to him:

> Hezekiah (whose name means "JEHOVAH *strengthens*") ... was a type of CHRIST. ... In his name, in his faith and obedience, in his tears and strong crying to God ... and in his wonderful deliverance, and in that of Jerusalem his city, by means of his faith and prayers ... and also in his personal *resurrection*, as it were, from the dead, on *the third day* ... a resurrection attended by a miracle ... and in the wonderful extension of his life, at a time when as yet he had no son; and in the springing forth from him and from his wife *Hephzi-bah* (i.e. *my delight is in her*), a type of Christ's spouse the Church ... of a seed, from which Christ came ... he prefigured CHRIST, Who came from his

---

76. Ibid., 36.

loins according to the flesh, and Who is the King of the spiritual Jerusalem.⁷⁷

Such theological connections are numerous and the above quote is only a sample. It is relatively rare that Wordsworth attempts to make one-to-one connections between events but christological interpretation serves as a powerful theme in his exegesis. Even the wife of Hezekiah prefigures the Church by her name (via a figural interpretation of the Song of Songs). What is also noteworthy is that he begins this discussion of these two chapters by stating that "this chapter concerns the Universal Church of God,"⁷⁸ indicating the close relationship between Christ and the Church. Given that he also says that "the Victory achieved by God in Christ, dying and rising from the dead, and conquering Sin and Satan, and redeeming His people, will bring *all nations* to adore Him in the spiritual Zion of His universal Church"⁷⁹ Wordsworth's soteriology is as closely or even more closely linked to the Church than it is to justification by faith, the jewel of Protestant theology.

There are moments, however, when these figural interpenetrations are driven neither by a christological nor an ecclesial hermeneutic. Rather, being impacted by the same apologetic mood as Robert Payne Smith, Wordsworth often presents prophecies in such an apologetic mode that the polyvalent quality of the text is denuded. Unlike Smith, however, these are neither as common nor as central to his approach to Isaiah. Nonetheless, this mode of exegesis is significant enough to negatively impact his commentary by its antagonistic stance toward those who challenge his reading. Moreover, like Smith, Wordsworth is unable to attend to deeper meanings within the text precisely because the level of discourse within the milieu of his time is limited to a framework of the text's "supernatural," predictive capacity.

For instance, Wordsworth asks why there is a historical interlude that describes Hezekiah's deliverance from Sennacherib and from his illness. This story is also told in 2 Kgs 19–20, and since there are textual dissimilarities between the two accounts, it serves as a challenge for critics of the Bible. Wordsworth speaks to why such an interlude exists because he wants to argue, for Isaiah's unitary whole, and that it is there for a reason and not the result of a textual insertion by a redactor. His answer is that

> this history is a proof of the prophetical mission and prophetic gifts of Isaiah... .This narrative is part of divinely inspired

77. Ibid., 70–71.
78. Ibid., 70.
79. Ibid., 71.

> Scripture, and has been received as such by the Hebrew Church, and by Christ Himself and His Apostles. It is therefore a *true* history. Hence it was evident that Isaiah was endued by God, in a signal manner, with the gift of prophecy."[80]

This history is justified by the fact that this narrative, in which Isaiah predicts the victory of Israel over Assyria,

> adds new strength to the proof of Isaiah's prophetic mission, and of the Divine origin of Christianity; and they afford conclusive evidence that the *other* great prophecies of Isaiah which yet remain to be fulfilled, namely, those which relate to the Universal Resurrection and Judgment to come, and to an Eternity of future Rewards and Punishments, will be fulfilled also.[81]

In terms of what Wordsworth refers to as "slight textual variations between the narratives," he directs the reader to the work of the relatively more conservative critics, Vitringa and Delitzsch, without further elucidation.[82] There is, of course, no mention of the challenges of other exegetes, all of which speaks to his selective use of authorities. What is important for Wordsworth is that these accurate predictions are "conclusive evidence" and the means of authentication of the "divine origin" of Christianity. On this point and others like it, Wordsworth begins to sound like Robert Payne Smith and does not heed Pusey's warning about using prophecy to prove the faith.

As it does with Robert Payne Smith, so also does Isa 53 offer significant evidence for Wordsworth of the inspiration of Scripture and the truth of Christianity. His approach, however, is a rather dramatic one, with Christ speaking words of warning and comfort at the beginning of chapter 51, followed by the response of "faithful Israel," starting at 51:9. Christ then replies to the faithful in 51:17 to 52:12. This culminates in Isa 53, though Wordsworth at once loses this dialogical/dramatic reading and moves into a more aggressive stance, beginning with the statement that

> this prophecy, which affords the strongest argument of the truth of Christianity . . . was written by Isaiah, and that it foretells the sufferings of Christ . . . is certain, from the sure testimony of the HOLY GHOST, speaking in the New Testament, by the mouth

---

80. Ibid., 104.
81. Ibid.
82. Ibid.

of St. John (xii. 38), of St. Matthew (vii. 17) of St. Luke (xxii. 37. Acts viii. 28–35), and St. Paul (Rom. x. 16).[83]

It is worth mentioning that, contrary to Smith, Wordsworth does not just argue for the truth of the predictive element of this prophecy by showing a one-to-one correspondence between prediction and event. Rather, because of his strong canonical perspective, the witness of the New Testament is sufficient to establish the authenticity of the prophecy. However, there is a strident note in his commentary, in which he warns that

> the pious meditations of the Christian reader need not be disturbed by the speculations of some in later days, who, adopting the sceptical language of a more recent Judaism . . . have endeavoured to wrest this prophecy from the true meaning which has been assigned to it by the Holy Spirit of God, and to apply it to the Hebrew Nation personified (*Eichhorn, Rosenmüller, Hitzig, Hendewerk, Köster*), or to the Order of Hebrew Prophets (*De Wette, Gesenius, Schenkel, Umbreit*) or (with *Bunsen, Ewald* and others) to Jeremiah, or some unknown martyr-prophet.[84]

This is a veritable who's who of primarily German critics of whom Wordsworth disapproves. He subsequently mentions others such as Duthe, Hensler, Michaelis and Stendel as "maintaining the ancient, Scriptural, catholic, and Apostolic interpretation of this prophecy."[85] One the one hand, it is Wordsworth's intent to hold together the two Testaments, the New enlightening the Old; on the other hand, he also finds it necessary to marshal his own coterie of authorities who can, via their own modern critical apparatus, give support to the textual relationship between Isaiah and Jesus of Nazareth. They also serve to prove that, prior to Christianity, the Jews historically believed that this text affirmed a suffering Messiah. Once Christ came, there arose an "apostate" Jewish belief that, in fact, misrepresented the original meaning of the text. Thus, "the *unbelief* of the Jews is an argument in favor of our *belief* in Christianity." Here Wordsworth is alluding to and affirming the apologetic practice of proving that the "original" interpretation of Isa 53 was that of a suffering Messiah, from which Jews deliberately turned away in response to Christianity. He disapproves of critics whom he accuses of participating in this "Jewish" apostasy.

Finally, within the context of biblical canonicity, consider his antipathy toward Roman Catholics. While he makes several connections between

83. Ibid., 153.
84. Ibid.
85. Ibid.

Isaiah and the Apocalypse, one of his more substantial links is that of Babylon and the Roman Catholic Church. Right from the preface, he asserts without reference to any authority that "Babylon typifies another form of Antichristianism—that of Idolatry and Superstition."[86] It is not surprising, given his Protestant prejudice against Roman Catholics, that the mention of Babylon invokes an apostate and superstitious institution. We already know from his *Union with Rome* that he interprets Rome as the antitype of Babylon. It is not surprising, then, that in his *Lectures on the Apocalypse* we find more direct references to the Roman Catholic Church as the harlot of the Apocalypse, which I only briefly mention. For instance, Lecture X is a discussion of the prophecies of Babylon in Revelation, most of which pertains to matters related to the Roman Catholic Church. Wordsworth says

> It cannot be doubted that our most eminent Divines have commonly held and taught that the Apocalyptic prophecies, concerning Babylon, were designed by the Holy Spirit to describe the Church of Rome . . . such as Archbishop Cranmer, Bishops Ridley and Jewel, and the Authors of our Homilies, but they also who followed them in the next, the most learned, Age of our Theology. . . . It may suffice to mention the illustrious names of Richard Hooker and Bishop Andrewes. . . . But after them a new generation arose. This was a race of men more endued with more zeal than knowledge; devoid, for the most part, of reverence for Authority and Antiquity.[87]

He continues, bemoaning the fact that thinkers of this latter generation, in their lack of knowledge, hurl anti-popish epithets without being able to make a distinction between what is "Babylonish" and what is of antiquity. Elsewhere, by way of the letters to the Church of Sardis and Laodicea at the beginning of the Apocalypse, Wordsworth determines that

> it was justly concluded by our Divines, that no desire of Unity on our part, nor reluctance on the part of Rome to cast off her errors, could exempt England from the duty of Reformation; and if Rome, instead of *removing* her corruptions, refused to communicate with England, unless England consented to communicate with Rome in her corruptions, then no love of Unity could justify England in compliance with this requisition of Rome.[88]

---

86. Ibid., xv.
87. Wordsworth, *Lectures on the Apocalypse*, 305–6.
88. Ibid., 314–15.

Therefore, when Wordsworth exegetes Isaiah regarding the Babylonian captivity, he has in mind the Roman Catholic Church. At this point I think it is important to make the observation that at such times he is also being the least "christological" in his interpretation; that is, he intends an argument that legitimates the Church of England, but Christ is no longer the key to this interpretation. It is replaced by an argument that appeals to the primitive Church.

CONCLUSION

This chapter has shown that Christopher Wordsworth's approach to Scripture is one that attempts to mimic that of the Church Fathers in a desire to preserve a "primitive" ecclesial and exegetical form. In comparison with all other nineteenth-century exegetes in this book, his exegetical strategy coheres with a deeply christological reading of Isaiah. Moreover, the centrality of the Church in his exegesis is almost overwhelming—to the point that the Church overshadows *any* role for the individual. And it is on this ecclesial point that the impact of a divided Church can be discerned. Wordsworth was at a time that was at the waning end of the old High Church Hackney Phalanx, whose central theological commitment was the Established Church as the best form of the Apostolic Church. This is in distinction to the Oxford Movement, who were disenchanted with the idea of the state participating in the ecclesial structure. Wordsworth's theopolitical vision becomes most clear when he exegetes Isa 49:23: he regards "national" Israel as the model of the national Church of England. This political vision pushes Wordsworth in numerous theological directions, as his ecclesial instability within a pluralizing culture leads Wordsworth to "pretend" as if there were no other challenges to his ecclesial vision. In his exegesis, he borrows from the Fathers as if they are representatives of the *same* Church that he defends. Or, in order to lend credibility to his apologetic arguments, he selectively employs more recent thinkers.

Wordsworth's approach to the Bible is on many points distinct from Robert Payne Smith's, particularly in the centrality he gives to the Church and a greater emphasis on the physical, embodied reality of ecclesial life. There is also a freer use of allegorical interpretation than most nineteenth-century interpreters; they would regard it as arbitrary or too divergent from the literal meaning of the text. His exegesis is deep, and he consistently aims to connect Isaiah to all of Scripture via typology, key words, and the tradition of antiquity. However, to suggest that his exegesis is unmarred by ecclesial division is to be blind to his deep political commitments, which see the Church in *English*, parochial terms. It is difficult to see, in his construal, what he means when he speaks of the Church as "one," "universal," or catholic, unless he is simply ignoring other ecclesial communities. Thus, what emerges is a nonspecific ecclesiology in his exegesis gives no definition to the role of the individual in its exegesis. This is despite the fact that many of the Church Fathers urged a personal application of the text in their sermons. There appears to be a studious avoidance of the individual in the economy of salvation. His commentary even suggests a form of soteriology in which Christ's only purpose in coming was to bring about the Church.

There are also numerous instances in which Wordsworth uses prophecy as "proof" of the truth of the Christian faith. He does so with less tenacity than Smith, but prophecy and typology are often employed apologetically to disprove those who differ from his interpretation. External sources are then used to show, for instance, that early Jewish exegesis argued for a suffering Messiah and that externally verifiable historical evidence supports the truth of Isaiah's words. It is at this point that Wordsworth's interpretation becomes more one-dimensional.

Finally, Wordsworth is at his most divisive when he uses Isaiah, and its connection with the Apocalypse via the figures of the harlot and Babylon, to speak against the Roman Catholic Church. When he does this, the christological hermeneutic tends to be attenuated and he directs his reading of the scriptural text primarily toward his high disapproval of Roman Catholic practice. This is not an unusual approach for a Protestant in the nineteenth century, but it displays the reality and intractability of ecclesial division.

5

Skepticism Is the "Truest Piety"
Thomas Kelly Cheyne and the Broad Church Exegesis of Isaiah

INTRODUCTION: THOMAS KELLY CHEYNE AND HIS WORK

THE CENTRAL EXEGETE OF this chapter is Thomas Kelly Cheyne, who published a significant commentary on Isaiah. Two central arguments serve as my points of departure. First, although most interpreters made use of new exegetical tools that emerged in the seventeenth and eighteenth centuries, it is Broad Church exegesis that is most defined by philology, historical criticism, and an attempt to avoid theological exegesis. I illustrate this by use of Cheyne's commentary. Second, I make use of Matthew Arnold for reasons other than merely exegetical, which is to show how he is representative of the general "religious" outlook of the Broad Church party. Despite an aim in their exegesis to be free (or "liberalized") from dogma, they cannot help but generate a new set of theological commitments that speak of a general religious *disposition* within humanity, of which the Bible is an evocative expression.

I connect Cheyne to the problem of ecclesial division in the context of his perspective on the role of the Church in the process of exegesis. It is not just the fact that Broad Church exegetes engage in higher criticism of Scripture that identifies them as "divisive." Rather, there is no longer any guarantee of dogmatic certainty in what they saw as a traditional mode of reading Scripture because of the Church's failure to present a coherent theological identity. The tendency is therefore to be highly suspicious of dogmatic schemes in biblical exegesis. But even more significant is a new representation of the nature of Christianity *sub specie aeternitatis*. The Bible, the Church, and most religious practices are rendered in terms of outward, phenomenological expressions of an inner reality that cannot be described in traditional dogmatic categories.

It needs to be noted, however, that despite the fact that much liberal exegesis is "antagonistic" toward traditional or conservative approaches, Broad Churchmen aim at a *defense* of the Christian faith and its revival, seeking to reinterpret belief and religion with an understanding that the world has a new "modern" consciousness. And it is also important to note that they are part of a historical process that begins in the mid-seventeenth century and the irenic exegesis of William Day, Samuel White, and William Chillingworth, as I described in Chapter 2. These latter thinkers, despite their theological conservatism, were innovators in setting out to redefine the process of exegesis, which was to make a distinction between historical textual referents and the theological/ecclesial structure that lies behind them. By the time of the nineteenth century, the theological dimension had generally become, for exegetes like Cheyne, a superfluous mode of engaging with the text. Rather, this was replaced by, for instance, an analysis of the religious sentiment behind the "Israelite" faith.

By the late nineteenth century, England saw a flowering of Old Testament criticism, with several key thinkers who contributed to this growth. "Between 1860 and 1900 . . . the new historical knowledge brought widespread agreement in the main study of the Old Testament, so widespread that it began to penetrate the mind of many educated people."[1] There was a gradual acceptance of German historical-critical theories such as Graf-Wellhausen's documentary hypothesis, a multiple-source theory of the Pentateuch.[2]

---

1. Chadwick, *The Victorian Church*, 2:59.
2. For the English translation of Wellhausen's formulation of the Documentary Hypothesis, see Wellhausen, *Prolegomena to the History of Israel*.

In terms of the history of Isaiah scholarship in England, the commentaries of both S. R. Driver (1846–1914) and of Thomas Kelly Cheyne (1841–1915) were seminal, and each viewed the other as a respected friend. Both were described by many as "being the real Bahnbrecher of our modern British Old Testament research."[3] The *Harvard Theological Review* called Cheyne "one of the most influential English expounders of the new critical views" and stated that "it was his commentary on Isaiah ... that first established him as a scholar of importance."[4] Numerous thinkers in England were imbibing new textual-critical theories, not only within the Church of England, but also in Scotland, including controversial critics such as Robertson Smith.

I focus on Thomas Kelly Cheyne's work on Isaiah, which was described as "revolutionary."[5] Cheyne was a towering intellectual figure, well-versed in Arabic, Hebrew, and other Semitic languages, as well as Jewish commentaries. Most of all, Cheyne was steeped in German historical-critical methods and refers to many well-known critics who had been ignored in England for the most part because of their unorthodox "rationalist" conclusions. Matthew Arnold represents the nineteenth-century concern for the "religious" capacity of the human self. He also published a commentary on Isaiah 40–66 and is illustrative of this religious disposition. The depth of his commentary, however, does not approach that of Cheyne; I use Arnold to indicate the religious outlook that he and Cheyne share. This perspective is, theologically speaking, no longer Christianity, but a new kind of supra-Christian religion, deeply moral, highly individualistic, and suspicious of authority. T. K. Cheyne is the central exegete of this chapter, but I also argue that the religious outlook that Cheyne and Arnold share is compatible with Cheyne's ultimate turn toward a kind of "meta-religion," the Baha'i faith—an image of the natural culmination of an irenic orientation toward dogma, the Bible, and Christianity.[6]

Cheyne's definition of "exegesis" is almost entirely shorn of any sense of theological or dogmatic concern, but also rarely takes on an overtly "antagonistic" tone against one particular group or another. While he was an Anglican priest—and apparently remained so even upon his conversion to

---

3. Whitehouse, "T. K. Cheyne's Founders" 280. *Bahnbrecher* is the German word for "trailblazer" or "pioneer."

4. Toy, "Thomas Kelly Cheyne," 2–3.

5. Chadwick, *The Victorian Church*, 2:105.

6. The Baha'i faith regards all religious founders (e.g, Jesus, Mohammed, Buddha) as messengers participating in the one Source, who is God. All religions are therefore essentially the same.

the Baha'i faith—one searches in vain for more than coincidental affinities to a uniquely Anglican approach to Scripture. His brief mention of Robert Payne Smith and Pusey are respectful, but he clearly sees his method as superior in light of the new approach to the text and the necessity to move beyond the "older" or "traditional" readings of the Bible.

The influence of division can thus be described as an instance of the "tradition" of irenic exegesis, but in a very strong sense. This tradition of reading Scripture led to the development of modern scientific tools that claimed objective discernment of biblical texts. Part of the central theme of this project is to argue that the loss of a cohesive ecclesial identity in the Church in general, and religious violence between competing sects, initiated a crisis of certainty that raised a generation of scholars who attempted to read Scripture in a way that minimized the theological aspect of exegesis. This also led to a theologically "neutral" view of history whereby the text can only be interpreted diachronically, minimizing the place of the Church and its understanding of history and time in typological and figurative modes.

Cheyne was a prolific scholar and published not one, but two commentaries on Isaiah. The first, *The Book of Isaiah Chronologically Arranged*, was written in 1870, intended for inclusion in a much larger work. His longer commentary, *The Prophecies of Isaiah*, was written in 1884 in two volumes and was a significant contribution to Isaiah scholarship. My primary focus is on the latter, supplemented by the former where necessary. The approach in each tends to be similar, though in *The Prophecies of Isaiah* Cheyne at times corrected and changed his mind from his earlier commentary. In addition to these works on Isaiah, he wrote *The Book of Psalms, The Origin and Religious Content of the Psalter, Job and Solomon*, and, in a decisive turn that almost entirely broke away from Anglican orthodoxy, he wrote *Aids to the Devout Study of Criticism*. In a kind of ode to thinkers who brought criticism to bear on the Old Testament, he penned *Founders of Old Testament Criticism*. He also edited the *Encyclopedia biblica*. His last work was *The Reconciliation of Races and Religions* in 1914, after he had become a follower of the Baha'i religion. Attendant to Cheyne's shift away from traditional Christianity was a deep sense of division. He begins *The Reconciliation of the Races* by noting that,

> In the hour of darkest night it is not for us to lose heart. Never was there greater need for men of faith. To many will come the temptation to deny God, and to turn away with despair from the

Christianity which seems to be identified with bloodshed on so gigantic a scale. Christ is crucified afresh today.[7]

Cheyne refers in this passage to the beginning of World War I, which he saw as a religious conflict. Although the violence of religious conflict was a catalyst for new exegetical approaches in the seventeenth century (see Chapter 2), religious violence pressed Cheyne even farther from traditional Christianity. The final solution to religious conflict was to move even beyond "liberal" ideas of religion and to see, as expounded in the teachings of the Baha'i faith, that all religions are one, a final rejection of all ecclesiastical dogma. I construe this move to a kind of "supra-religious" mode that he found embodied in the Baha'i faith as a natural culmination of not only Cheyne's thought, but also that of Arnold. He eschewed the specificity of "dogma" in favor of "certain Oriental conceptions and systems that had been making their way gradually in the Western world. . . . He held that peace among the nations could be secured only through religious union . . . A common faith would make all men brothers."[8]

Cheyne's earlier work on Isaiah does not reflect such a radical shift, but I argue that his turn to modern critical tools is to aim at similar purposes. Previous "theological" readings of Scripture had failed to engender "true" religion, in his view. Thus, the approaches taken by Robert Payne Smith and Christopher Wordsworth are outdated and even prone to cause violence by their theological character. The analysis undertaken in this chapter, however, does not necessarily reveal Cheyne as being "divisive," neither in the manner of Smith's strident attempt to build a bulwark against the encroaching tide of negative exegesis nor in the manner of Wordsworth's efforts to discover the figure of Christ or the Church embedded in every text for the purpose of proving its provenance. Rather, Cheyne, with his painstaking and methodical analysis of the text and his prodigious intellect, aims at taking a "scientific" approach, and hence one which has little need for ecclesiastical interference.

Cheyne was an ordained priest in the Church of England and spent time studying at the University of Göttingen under Heinrich Ewald, whose influence on his study of Isaiah was considerable. His grandfather was Thomas Hartwell Horne, another famous critic from earlier in the century whose own three-volume *Introduction to the Critical Study and Knowledge of the Holy Scripture* (1818) was a standard work. Cheyne was vice-president of St. Edmund Hall, and he was the first to teach the new critical methods of Old Testament study at Oxford. He was rector of Tendring in Essex and

7. Cheyne, *The Reconciliation of Races and Religions*, 2.
8. Toy, "Thomas Kelly Cheyne," 5.

was a member of the Old Testament Revision Company. Near the end of his life, he was the Oriel professor of the interpretation of Scripture and canon of Rochester Cathedral.[9]

MATTHEW ARNOLD AND THE BROAD CHURCH RELIGIOUS CONSCIOUSNESS

The Broad Church is such an amorphous and ill-defined group of thinkers that it is necessary to briefly attend to Matthew Arnold (1822–88), who had a rather passing dalliance with Isaiah in order to give greater definition of a "Broad Church" perspective. Furthermore, my use of Arnold also highlights the role of division in such exegetical positions, in addition to setting up the "religious" background of these exegetes. Matthew Arnold was son of the famous Rugby Headmaster Thomas Arnold (1795–1842) and one of the "founders" of the Broad Church movement.[10] I use Arnold to show the continuities between him and Cheyne in terms of this religious background, which describes a kind of supra-Christian religious consciousness.

Though not a theologian as such, Matthew Arnold was often concerned with religious matters. A poet and literary critic, he was primarily employed as a school inspector. Arnold was a very "religious" person and was initially impressed by the works of his godfather, the Oxford Tractarian John Keble, but he eventually came to reject the Oxford Movement. In comparison with Cheyne, one can sense a much stronger "Romantic" quality to his religious views, opting for the more emotional aspect of religion to balance the "rational."[11] He saw confusion and instability in Victorian society, and wanted "a transformation of the 'dominant idea of religion' through the re-energizing stimuli of culture and poetry."[12] He encouraged the use of German thinkers, who "thought the English clergy unlearned and bound by superstitious dogmas, in comparison with the religious freedom allowed to the clergy of Germany."[13] Arnold was keen to embrace the modern age and to eschew the bondage of previous ecclesial "superstition," rejecting the

---

9. Livingstone and Cross, *Dictionary of the Christian Church*, s.v. "Cheyne, Thomas Kelly (1841–1915)."

10. Jones, *The Broad Church*, 51–128. This is, of course, an arbitrary choice, as I argue that the Broad Church movement is in deep continuity with several traditions of previous centuries.

11. Ibid., 242.

12. Knight and Mason, *Nineteenth-Century Religion and Literature*, 1.

13. Crowther, *Church Embattled*, 48.

validity of "unscientific" ideas such as miracles, while fully embracing the power of religious feeling.

In 1875, Arnold wrote *Isaiah XL–LXVI with the Shorter Prophecies Allied to It*. It was a work that, as Arnold claimed, was "for the benefit of school-children."[14] It does not consist of a new translation, but an attempt to emend the King James Version to render the text in a more readable form. In it he engages directly with Cheyne, even amidst their different exegetical foci, and they make very similar assumptions with one another regarding the nature of Scripture and of religion. Arnold also says quite explicitly what is somewhat more hidden in Cheyne's work, which is that a turn toward modern critical tools is precisely an attempt to assuage the problems raised by a divided Church. Arnold's emendation of the text is not an attempt at a wholesale undoing of the translation of the day. My intent is not to attend to the quality of his choices, but only the principles that fund his approach to such a task.

It is interesting to note Arnold's choice to work only on the chapters that biblical critics refer to as "II Isaiah." With more directness than that of Cheyne's exegesis, he avers that "whatever may be thought of the authorship of the last twenty-seven chapters, every one will allow that there comes a break between them and what goes immediately before them, and they form a whole by themselves."[15] While Arnold does not say that certain parts of Isaiah are to no longer be thought of as Scripture, it would be difficult for him to maintain a traditional approach to Scripture.

The most prominent feature of his view of the text is that it must exhibit the proper *style*, as opposed to fidelity of translation. Here is an issue on which we find Arnold engaging with Cheyne, sometimes quite critically. Lowth's influence is particularly evident in terms of how the text must be viewed as a work of poetry, as a particular literary genre, and as a text of emotive force. Like Cheyne, Arnold acknowledges that "the Hebrew language and genius . . . are seen in the Book of Isaiah at their perfection."[16] Given that Arnold's aim was to improve the "readability" of Isaiah, he notes that "the general reader, who has the bare text of a common Bible and nothing more may perceive that there is something grand in this passage, but he cannot possibly understand it."[17] The "bare text" is no longer, as the Word of God, sufficient to work in the *ecclesia*, and it is not the clergy who participate in the role of explaining possibly problematic readings, but the

14. Arnold, *Isaiah XL-LXVI*, 2.
15. Ibid., 3.
16. Ibid.
17. Ibid., 6.

cultured and the educated, whose skill is to bring out something "grand" within the passage. Cheyne also sees the professional academic as a kind of modern secular priest who is the only one properly able to interpret the text to its readers.

Arnold was influenced by the work of Heinrich Ewald, though he gives greater explicit acknowledgement to Lowth, Vitringa, and "Aben-Ezra" (Abraham Ibn Ezra), who he claims are "the three men who, before the labours of the Germans in our own century, did most to help the study of Isaiah."[18] He praises Lowth for his skill in poetry and literature, but faults him for not exhibiting the right *style* in his translation of the text. When Arnold turns his attention to Cheyne, he is critical of Cheyne's rendering of some of the passages in Isaiah. But it is clear that he is in complete agreement with Cheyne's overall project of critical engagement with the text. Minor textual issues are called into question, but not for theological reasons, but because of their lack of *style*:

> Mr. Cheyne, who, scientific though his object be, nevertheless talks of governing himself in making changes, by "the affectionate reverence with which the Authorized Version is so justly regarded," may be rendering [Isaiah 42:4] with more accuracy when he writes: "He shall not fail nor be discouraged till he have set religion on the earth, and the sea coasts wait for his doctrine." But he must not imagine that he is making a slight change in the rhythm of "He shall not fail ... till he have set judgment in the earth; and the isles shall wait for his law;" for he destroys the balance of the rhythm altogether.[19]

Arnold's concern is the "sentiments" evoked by the poetic rhythm of certain verses. For instance, in his discussion of the propriety of replacing "the Lord" with "Jehovah" in the Psalms, Arnold notes that

> besides the contents which a term carries in itself, we must consider the contents with which men, in long and reverential use, have filled it; and therefore we say that *The Lord* any literary corrector of the English Bible does well at present to retain, because of the sentiments this expression has created in the English reader's mind. ... It is in deference to these pre-established sentiments that we prefer ... for any famous passage of our chapters which is cited in the New Testament, the New Testament rendering, because this rendering ... touches more chords.[20]

18. Ibid., 16.
19. Ibid., 18.
20. Ibid., 14.

The emendations thus reflect Arnold's desire to maintain or improve the style and rhythm of the text, giving precedence to the religious affections the texts evince. It is often *sentiment* that connects the two Testaments together, not a concept of a scriptural canon. Arnold's literary approach does not necessarily preclude any kind of connection to Jesus Christ. Indeed, Arnold accedes, "I admit unreservedly that these prophecies have a scope far beyond their primary historical scope, that they have a secondary, eternal scope, and that this scope is more important."[21] He states that the "secondary application" of Isa 53 must be to Jesus Christ. However, later Arnold discusses the Servant Passages (which include Isa 53) about which he argues that "we all know the secondary application to Jesus Christ, often so striking; but certainly this was not the primary application."[22] Since the theological is seen as "secondary," Arnold directs more attention to possible historical referents and the ostensive original purpose of Isaiah. By the time of Arnold the use of "primary" had become value-laden, the *preferred* sense. Extended suggests that it is optional—even disposable. This is a similar approach in the work of Cheyne.

Given this brief outline of Arnold's approach to the text, I conclude by indicating the role of a divided Church, as Arnold speaks to this more overtly than Cheyne. Referring to his notes that accompany the text, his hope is that the reader will be led to "the more," that luminous *something* that Scripture has to offer;

> that *more* . . . has the advantage of not offering ground for those religious disputes to which a more extended interpretation of the Bible often gives rise . . . and they are the fewer the more the enquiry is conducted in an unassuming and truly scientific manner; when that only is called certain which is really certain, and that which is conjecture, however plausible, is allowed to be but only conjecture.[23]

This is a retreat from any ecclesial, creedal, or communal understanding of the text; as Arnold sees them, they lead to disputes and division. There is more here, however, than a mere turn toward the scientific in order to achieve certainty. Just as we shall see that Cheyne retreats from the contentiousness of dogma toward the Baha'i faith, a religion that embraces all religions, Arnold too takes an approach to religion that is less radical in form, but not in kind. His praise of biblical poetic sentimentality reflects a

---

21. Ibid., 27.
22. Ibid., 29–30.
23. Ibid., 28.

shift away from Christianity proper into religion of another kind. As Vincent Buckley argues, Arnold

> seems also to have the intention of, as it were, redefining religion, so that it is no longer a *bond* between God and man, a bond of which doctrinal formulations are a necessary illumination and expression, but a state of mind. Religion, that is, has its own best guarantee in the state of mind which it is capable of inducing. In a sense, it *is* that state of mind.[24]

This redefinition of religious meaning leads Cheyne to use language of inclusion and unification, while for Arnold, and *for the same reason*, leads to the preservation of Christian language, albeit with the theological content of this language evacuated and replaced by this "state of mind." This affective mode is the inner phenomenon that biblical language merely evokes. Even more, Arnold generally affirmed the moral system that tended to be associated with Christianity; as A. O. J. Cockshut says, "Arnold's system really was religious, though not, in any acceptable, historical sense, Christian. Arnold himself defined religion as 'morality touched with emotion.'"[25] Cockshut's argument is that Arnold is an "emotional conservative," who clung to the language of Christianity and even conservative Anglicanism because of a belief in its evocative power.

Thus Arnold represents the religious landscape for my analysis of Cheyne's commentary. The two thinkers differ on minor textual matters, but they both see the use of scientific tools for exegesis as essential for revealing the meaning of Scripture. Moreover, they both share a perspective on how Scripture evokes the human phenomenon of religious consciousness. Most importantly, I suggest that there is a clear connection between such views and an urge to avoid the divisive nature that dogmatic principles generate. This is less apparent, but no less powerful, in Cheyne's exegesis.

THE STRUCTURE, METHOD, AND INFLUENCES ON CHEYNE'S COMMENTARIES

Cheyne's many years of work on the prophet Isaiah represent a significant achievement in England in advancing a detailed, scholarly engagement with the text. *The Prophecies of Isaiah* comprises his own translation of the text; *Isaiah Chronologically Arranged* provides emendations of the Authorized Version. Each provides critical notes and commentary on the text, though

24. Buckley, "Matthew Arnold," 152.
25. Cockshut, "Matthew Arnold," 171.

the later *Prophecies of Isaiah* is his more "mature" work. Within the critical notes of the text one would have to look very carefully to find his commentary dwelling significantly on theological issues. This is not to say they are absent, but Cheyne is very explicit that he understands the bulk of exegesis to be a philological and historical study of the text.

Cheyne's methodology is to use the most recent discoveries of inscription material, comparative linguistics, and extra-biblical sources as necessary tools for exegesis. Moreover, traditional conceptions of authorship and meaning cannot be predetermined by the weight of ecclesial history. While Robert Payne Smith would no doubt have considered Cheyne's approach to Isaiah as a "negative" one, there is very much a sense of "reconstruction" in Cheyne's work, comprising in Cheyne's mind a very positive effort. There is on the one hand a reconstruction of the *text* as he aims to correct the translation of the 1611 Authorized Version. On the other hand, Cheyne's reconstruction is *historical*, a reconstruction of the events that gave rise to the writing of the book by the author(s). Cheyne's work is emblematic of Hans Frei's point that modern critical hermeneutics tended toward discovering the "ostensive reference" of the text. In the case of Cheyne, this is primarily a historical one, and secondarily of Israelite "religious" consciousness.[26] The meaning of the text is subsumed by philological, historical, and other critical methods.

Despite its erudition, Cheyne's commentary requires a close reading and half-guessed inferences to glean conclusions of significant theological weight, were his final set of essays not offered, in which he puts his theological cards on the table. Similar to Robert Payne Smith, Cheyne often works in two "modes." The primary one in Cheyne's case is that of a historical and philological critic, comprising the vast bulk of his commentary. The second mode is what could very loosely be called theological, though I suggest that it is more accurately called "religious."

Many of Cheyne's exegetical influences were German; however, an English thinker who figures prominently in his commentary is Robert Lowth. This can be seen by Cheyne's attention to the text as a special kind of poetic literature. The level of textual "style" is often determinative of his approach to Isaiah. For instance, Cheyne compares the prophecy against Babylon in Isa 13 and the "taunt" of Babylon in Isa 14, noting that "the poetical merits of the latter are, however, so far superior to those of the former, that I have been led to the conjecture . . . that the Ode was not originally composed to occupy the present position."[27] Or, for Isa 21, which speaks

---

26. See, e.g., Frei, *The Eclipse of Biblical Narrative*, 150.
27. Cheyne, *The Prophecies of Isaiah*, 1:81

of Babylon that "cometh from the wilderness," he observes that "there is no cuneiform evidence that any invasion of Babylon was made from the S.W.; but why should we insist on a literal historical fulfilment? It is a grand poetical symbol which we have before us."[28] This lifting up of the poetic quality of the text parallels the focus on the prophetic author as "genius," to which I attend below. Moreover, he observes that Isaiah's "discourses, at any rate, in the form in which they are now extant, presuppose in their author a high degree of literary cultivation."[29] Cheyne explicitly acknowledges Lowth as the one who "began that aestheticising movement in Biblical criticism which, with all its faults and shallowness and sometimes perhaps irreverence, fulfilled . . . a providential purpose in reviving the popular interest in the letter of the Scriptures."[30]

Heinrich Ewald also had an enormous impact on Cheyne's thinking. For the most part, he sees Ewald's approach to the Bible as exemplary. Ewald represents the turn toward the "reconstruction" of the diachrony of a text and the people of whom it speaks. With respect to Isaiah, Cheyne perceived Ewald's project as having

> . . . the governing idea of reconstruction . . . As an interpreter of the prophets . . . he reminds us somewhat of his master Eichhorn, whose poetic enthusiasm he fully shares. . . . His translation of the prophets has a rhythmic flow. . . . He totally ignores the New Testament; but it is at any rate free from the anti-dogmatic theories of the rationalists.[31]

His latter point is worth highlighting: even those who in England engaged in critical studies of the Bible did not want to be cast as "rationalist," an epithet that could evoke considerable controversy. Yet, neither are there in Cheyne's commentary many references to the New Testament, and even they are frequently vague and merely suggestive. It is not until his Essays at the end of Volume 2 when Cheyne makes explicit mention of a "Christian" interpretation of Isaiah.

There are numerous other influences that bear upon Cheyne's commentaries. Most are German, such as Hitzig, Gesenius, and Delitzsch, but also the Dutchmen Vitringa and Grotius. He speaks with some negativity of Hengstenberg, who, says Cheyne,

---

28. Ibid., 1:127.
29. Cheyne, *Book of Isaiah, Chronologically Arranged*, vi.
30. Cheyne, *The Prophecies of Isaiah*, 2:276.
31. Ibid., 2:279.

> had no historical gifts, and never seems to have really assimilated that doctrine of development which, though rejected by Pietists on the one hand and Tridentine Romanists on the other, is so profoundly Christian.... He was therefore indisposed to allow the human element of inspiration, denied the limited nature of the Old Testament state of revelation, and ... made prophecy nothing but the symbolic covering of the eternal truths of Christianity.[32]

A great deal can be discerned here from his negative view of Hengstenberg's perspective on Scripture, which was an attempt to read Scripture "confessionally," that is, "expressed in terms of the Augsberg Confession."[33] While there is rarely an overtly "divisive" approach to Scripture in Cheyne along the lines of Smith's strident attempt to oppose the "negative critics" of Isaiah, given his disapproval of strongly confessional exegetes such as Pusey and Hengstenberg, one cannot deny that Cheyne is wary of readings that he regards as burdened by the entrapments of ecclesial readings that are informed by "dogma."

Cheyne's choice of thinkers as his primary interlocutors speaks to the highly "historical" form of exegesis and "reconstruction" of which someone like Ewald is representative. The earlier "traditional" shape of biblical hermeneutics conceives of Scripture as revealing the mystery of the world and the relation of God to it and it to God; this includes history, and exegetical approaches developed over the centuries (e.g., tropological, spiritual, etc.) were tethered to the "literal" or "historical" sense of the text.[34] Nonetheless, the historical or grammatical sense did not exhaust the meaning of the text. By the nineteenth century, exegesis enacted a reification of the "historical" sense of the text, for conservatives and critics alike. Christopher Seitz shows how, in Germany, an increased interest in the "religious" sensibilities of Old Testament peoples, led to the prophets drawing greater attention: "the prophets offered the best hope for a solid ground floor in Old Testament religion, on the terms of the kind of rebuilding project being undertaken and the blueprint it was following."[35] This was based on the historical conclusion that many Old Testament texts were written and/or compiled after the Exile; De Wette was one of the key critics who contributed to this shift. He believed that "the prophets are the only figures of the Old Testament ... whose times we can identify clearly and whose circumstances we are

---

32. Ibid., 2:281.
33. Rogerson, *Old Testament Criticism in the Nineteenth Century*, 81.
34. Balthasar, *Origen, Spirit and Fire*, iv.
35. Seitz, *Prophecy and Hermeneutics*, 86.

in a position to feel confident we know."[36] The rest of the narratives were "mythical," by which "de Wette certainly meant unhistorical."[37] Only those texts with verifiable histories, and hence trustworthy, were given greater attention, and the prophets often met these criteria. The mode by which such readings were carried out was also historical, that is, the relation of the text to its immediate historical context and not its place within the larger biblical canon. As we saw with Robert Payne Smith, this also meant a concern for the prophet as a poetic "genius," to be studied in terms of the prophet *qua* individual.[38]

Cheyne's "reconstruction" project resulted in is a re-ordering not only of each prophetic book in the Bible, but also of the chapters within them. For instance, in Cheyne's *Isaiah Chronologically Arranged*, beyond being a commentary on the text, each chapter is rearranged in the order of an externally determined historical sequence. Thus, for instance, his version of Isaiah begins with chapters 2–9:7, but with 9:8 inserted in the middle of Isa 5. Cheyne was thus a participant in a project of historical reordering of the canon, believing that "what really matters is a historical account in which we can track the stages and movement of the prophetic consciousness in its historical particularity and that this is what truly constitutes the achievement of the prophets of Israel."[39] In Cheyne's mind, this "scientific" approach to the text employs externally verifiable truths for interpretation and constitutes the process of "criticism." De Wette, Ewald, and Cheyne never saw themselves offering anything other than a *Christian* reading of the text. In the midst of the reality of a divided Church, new critical tools were regarded as capable of bypassing the need for an ecclesial presence in the process of reading Scripture.

NEITHER CHURCH NOR INDIVIDUAL: A NEW KIND OF PRIEST

From the evidence of his commentary on Isaiah, Cheyne is least open to seeing the Church in any way as constitutive of the exegetical process. Cheyne sought to provide a commentary free from the strictures of ecclesial dogma: this is the meaning of a "critical" commentary. While Cheyne asks in the Preface "where *is* [this] commentary entirely free from theological

---

36. Ibid., 77.
37. Rogerson, *Old Testament Criticism in the Nineteenth Century*, 33.
38. Seitz, *Prophecy and Hermeneutics*, 82.
39. Ibid., 90.

or philosophical bias?"⁴⁰ his aim is nevertheless to raise various "critical issues" because "within my own range of observation it has not received much countenance from the authorities.... As yet we hear little said about these things in the organs of Church and University opinion." His hope is that by introducing these critical tools to the study of Isaiah, "the want of which not only philology, the theology and the Church in general suffer—the application of modern methods to the criticism and exegesis of the Old Testament."⁴¹

Cheyne's exegesis of Isaiah is a deliberate turn away from tradition to a notion that the Church *qua* Church *cannot* read Scripture until it has first engaged with a "critical" approach to the Bible. The Church failed because of an inordinate stress on dogma. He directs his work toward the "English" student:

> The plan which I adopted corresponds to their requirements. Tired of the traditionalism of the older commentators, they seem to ask, not indeed to be kept in complete ignorance of the critical problems and solutions, but to be enabled to study the text in a historical spirit, without . . . being under the dominion of a fixed critical theory. . . . Criticism is the only key to the inner chamber of exegesis.⁴²

Cheyne's definition of "critical" is rather indeterminate, given that he follows this with the statement that "there are some writers who seem only to care for 'the higher criticism;' *I* am not one of those. Pure exegesis has a fascination of its own, and is a great liberalizer of the mind." One could conceive of several definitions of "criticism" even within Cheyne's account. What is clear is that his aim is a "pure exegesis," which is the "liberalizer of the mind." From what is the mind freed? This refers back, I suggest, to Cheyne's above reference to students who are "tired of the traditionalism of the older commentators." Given the nature of Cheyne's own exegetical style, this freedom is from the perceived exegetical suppression of dogma, from which the mind must be freed to explore new theological and historical ideas.

Cheyne is enigmatic about what constitutes a distinction between the "higher criticism" and the "pure exegesis" that he lauds. I would suggest that the shape of this "pure" exegesis maintains the priority of the philological mode of interpretation over the "theological," muting an ecclesial reading of the text. One case where Cheyne makes this argument most forcefully

40. Cheyne, *The Prophecies of Isaiah*, 1:viii.
41. Ibid., 1:x-xi.
42. Ibid., 2:vi.

is in a brief but enlightening engagement with Pusey's interpretation of a word in Isa 52:15, which is translated in the Authorized Version as, "so he will sprinkle many nations." The key word is יַזֶּה [*yazeh*], which Pusey translates as "sprinkle," along with the Authorized Version. Cheyne argues that "through an unfortunate failure in this respect, even Dr. Pusey is unable (be it said with all respect) to state the facts of Hebrew usage accurately."[43] The translation can be the traditional one, meaning that the nations are passively sprinkled, that is, "besprinkled." Another translation is that the nations are in the active accusative mode, being themselves sprinkled out. Finally, by an appeal to cognate Arabic terms, the word can be akin to "startle," the response by the nations at the disfigurement of the Servant of Jehovah. In his notes on the verse, Cheyne prefers to conclude that there is a corruption in the text,[44] but in the philological notes at the end of the commentary, he suggests that the corruption was a change in the original word, which he submits was *yatir*, "to make tremble" or "to startle." The point here is that, for Cheyne, "no word in the whole of the Old Testament so forcibly exemplifies the urgent necessity for keeping the philological department in exegesis separate from the theological."[45] This separation of exegetical modalities, already common in the seventeenth and eighteenth centuries, is a move away from what is perceived as the strictures of ecclesial bondage. Thus disputes can be adjudicated via academic discourse that refer to non-dogmatic, commonly accepted terms.

It is also important to note that Cheyne focuses so closely on a word that has such significant christological import. Although I speak to the christological aspect of Cheyne's exegesis below, the theological implications of his treatment of Isa 52:15 must be mentioned briefly. Surely the fact that Cheyne so forcefully focuses on this word as indicative of the need for structural changes in exegetical practices cannot be merely coincidental with its historical christological impact. Cheyne goes out of his way to offer speculation that a corruption must be present in the text, which leads him to Arabic cognates. It can only be inferred that Cheyne is not merely "objectively" interpreting the text but enacting an agenda to distance it from its theological and christological referents. The point here is not to critique his philological choices, but the method underpinning his interpretation, which is to eschew the theological history of the text and to reconstruct the linguistic and historical background independent of previous (ecclesial) reception history.

43. Ibid., 2:167.
44. Ibid., 2:42.
45. Ibid., 2:166–67.

Contrary to Robert Payne Smith, however, Cheyne does not encourage an individualist reading of the text. His tendency to read the Bible primarily from the perspective of an academic suggests a "communal" exegesis of a different kind, which is one guided not by the Church, but by the rules of modern critical exegesis—the guild. Moreover, given the numerous possible corruptions in the text, the difficulty of Hebrew, and the demand to historically orient the text and author, only those who are well-versed in such methods can interpret effectively. Cheyne, Gesenius, Ewald, and others are priests of another kind, whose ecclesially unbounded analysis, emerging from a "liberalized mind," can correctly mediate the textual meaning that the Church had hitherto avoided, and whose dogmatic allegiances precipitated numerous blind spots. The new tools of historical criticism were enormously successful in finding meanings in the text that the Church in its dogmatic impotence was unable to find. Cheyne was not against the Church *per se* (after all, he was an ordained priest) but thought that a divided Church could be saved and freed from herself by turning to more "neutral" and "scientific" methods of reading her texts.

ISAIAH AND A PHILOLOGICAL/HISTORICAL CANON

From what has already been said, it ought also be clear that in Cheyne's view, there is very little sense in which Isaiah is in any significant way a part of the *one* "word of God," equally subsistent in all parts of the Bible. There is no consistent view of how the Old Testament is to be interpreted in light of the New, nor vice versa, though Cheyne does make a rather feeble attempt at doing so, to which I attend below. If Isaiah can be understood only via a historical understanding and by considering him as a particular individual on this historically constructed timeline, then connections between texts can be made only on the basis of very narrow categories. These categories no longer are construed theologically and therefore the meaning of *exegesis* is transformed into something new. For Cheyne, the categories for determining connections between books were literary/philological, and historical.

I give attention to three central texts in Isaiah that have traditionally been used as keys to linking the book to the entirety of Scripture and have a close relationship to the New Testament. They are Isa 7, especially v. 14, (the birth of Immanuel to the *almah*), Isa 9:6–7 ("he shall be called Wonderful, Counsellor. . ."), and the Suffering Servant passage of Isa 53. This not only to show how *non-canonical* Cheyne's exegesis is but also how, through the application of novel categories to the text, new connections are made once they are free from traditional theological structures, generating a new kind of "canonical" shape. For now, I attend strictly to his commentary without taking into account his subsequent essays that attempt to give a more "Christian" reading of these passages.

Cheyne commences his analysis of Isa 7 with a brief historical background of the text: there was a war between the northern Kingdom of Israel, ruled by King Pekah, and King Rezin of Syria. Cheyne notes that the parallel passages in 2 Kgs and 2 Chr are

> less original than the narrative in Isaiah, especially that of Chronicles, which many critics go so far as to reject as absolutely unhistorical. Nor are they without excuse, not to say justification, considering the difficulty of discriminating between the traditions embodied by the Chronicler, and the adventitious matter due to his predominating regard for edification.[46]

Cheyne agrees with de Wette that "the books of Chronicles are late in composition, and provide no reliable evidence for the religion of Israel in the pre-exilic period."[47] Rather, it was the "adventitious" attempt by someone to render the story in 2 Chr 28 in a manner that seeks to "edify." Thus, Cheyne concludes that Isaiah is more "historically" reliable. He also concludes that an attempt by an author to provide "edification," or theological commentary to a story render it historically questionable. The passage from Isaiah is preferable for its brevity of factual reporting.

Further to his introduction to this chapter, Cheyne comments that

> it will be observed that chap. vii does not claim to be the work of Isaiah. There is also a looseness in the connection, and an occasional *feebleness of style*, which make even the editorship of Isaiah difficult to realise.... Taken together with the very peculiar introduction to chap vii., and the cumbrousness of vii. 17–25, it makes it a very probable conjecture that the whole section vii. i–ix. 7 only assumed its present form long after the original utterance of the prophecies.[48]

Influenced by an aesthetic perspective of the text, Cheyne doubted Isaianic authorship on the basis of its "feebleness of style."

---

46. Ibid., 1:41.
47. Rogerson, *Old Testament Criticism in the Nineteenth Century*, 34.
48. Ibid., 1:42, italics mine.

Cheyne's analysis of Isa 7 argues that the chapter bears evidence of inserted words, scribal errors, and lost passages. Although such claims are not unusual in his commentary, it is notable that they are more frequent here than is typical, for within one chapter—one that is important in Christian usage throughout history—he has questioned the authorship of the text and thrown into question the unity of the chapter itself, suggesting that there was more than one editor. Just as his interpretation of *yazeh* had become such a term of philological focus precisely because of, I suggest, its theological importance, Cheyne also gives greater attention to Isa 7 because of its place in Christian theological interpretation of the Old Testament. These two instances are somewhat subtle but are nonetheless examples of a more "antagonistic" form of exegesis. Cheyne is actively directing his critical tools against passages that have "traditional" theological import.

Cheyne is careful, however, as he approaches the central (theologically and historically speaking) text of v. 14. He translates *almah* unequivocally as "young woman," and he makes one of his enigmatic forays into maintaining a kind of textual "canonicity":

> The prophet sees the woman selected by Jehovah with the inner eye. We need not, however, suppose that he had any other reason for mentioning her than to introduce the naming of the child (comp. Luke i. 60).[49]

This is a strange connection between Luke 1:60 and Isa 7:14. It is not a reference to Mary or Jesus, but to Elizabeth, the mother of John the Baptist, who says, "He shall be called John." While the referent or allusion Cheyne selects is a reference to the naming of a child, his curious choice of this Lukan passage is not clear.

The translation of *almah* as "young woman" is philologically acceptable, but it is traditionally argued to be a direct prophecy of the Virgin Mary. Cheyne, however, is less willing to translate based on such theological predispositions; rather,

> unless the context determines otherwise, we are precluded from going beyond the strict etymological meaning of the word, which is simply, "a woman of mature age." ... As to the details of the interpretation, opinions are and will always be divided. There is no explanation which does not require us to make some assumption not directly sanctioned by the text.[50]

---

49. Ibid., 1:47.
50. Ibid.

The infelicitous use of a triple negative notwithstanding, Cheyne is clear that the philological approach and the immediate historical background determine the interpretation, without recourse to a connection to the New Testament. Cheyne suggests "that the 'young woman' is the mother of the Messiah, whose advent, as Ewald has well pointed out, was expected by Isaiah to synchronise with the Assyrian invasion."[51] Thus, Cheyne conceives of Isa 7 to be "an incomplete summary of Isaianic discourses; or again . . . we may regard this prophecy as the first rough sketch of the Messianic doctrine, to be filled up on subsequent opportunities."[52] This concept of a "messianic doctrine" is a central notion in his interpretation and is helpful to understand Cheyne's view of the connection between the history and Israelite religion. However, he is reluctant to connect this "messianic" doctrine directly to the New Testament, but, at best, does so obliquely.

Cheyne perfunctorily interprets the name "Immanuel" to mean "God is on our side."[53] He does not consider the messianic figure in this text to be *himself* God but to be a sign that God is on the side of his people. He refers to the subsequent description of this messianic figure as one "based on incomplete, though authentic notes" and is therefore not entirely clear. His conclusion is "that something . . . has been lost with regard to Immanuel seems highly probable."[54] There is, however, a more nuanced development to his conception of the "Messianic doctrine," as he continues his analysis of Isa 9, particularly vv. 1–7. The introduction to this chapter is brief, but he notes that it indeed does refer to the Messiah, who "shall appear, and bring the tyranny of Israel's foes to an end. Under him the empire of David shall be restored in an indestructible foundation."[55] The concept of the Messiah is raised in his commentary on v. 3, which says, "you have enlarged the nation and increased their joy." Cheyne notes that "a supernatural increase of the population [is] a common feature in Messianic descriptions."[56] There is therefore no question that Cheyne regards a "messianic" reading of Isa 9 as the correct one, but he is strangely ambiguous as to *what* the reader should understand by the concept of the "Messiah." His analysis often consists only in rendering a summary of the text, rarely moving beyond the confines of Isaiah.

To illustrate, the following lists some of Cheyne's analysis of Isa 9:

51. Ibid., 1:48.
52. Ibid., 1:28.
53. Ibid., 2:49.
54. Ibid., 1:50.
55. Ibid., 1:58.
56. Ibid., 2:59.

> A prince of a new "order" has arisen with supernatural qualities and privileges.... The prophet is unrolling a picture of the future, and each part is introduced with a "factitive" perfect tense. He is designedly vague; the word rendered "child" will serve equally well for a new-born infant . . . and for a youth or young man. . . . It is therefore quite uncertain what interval is to elapse between the birth of the child and his public manifestation as the Messiah.[57]

Since Cheyne considers Isaiah to be a contemporary of Micah, he connects this passage with Mic 5:3–5, which speaks directly about a "son" who will "be our peace when the Assyrians invade." This connection between passages cannot be called a "canonical" one; they are linked only by virtue of the ostensive historical reconstruction of the prophecies. However, there is a *religious* connection in the sense that Scripture is an expression of the religious sentiments of a people, the Israelites. Therefore, this messianic hope that took root in Israel can also be found in other passages as instances of Israel's religious hope, not necessarily as christological referents that underpin a single canon of Scripture. It is a "history-of-religions" approach that is tethered to Cheyne's own view of religion.

Cheyne would consider it an exegesis too influenced by dogma to venture into any kind of canonical interpretation of the text, traditionally conceived, without first reading them within a philological and history-of-religions framework. Cheyne does not *reject* a "Christian" reading of the text, but it does not figure within the purview of a proper commentary. What is rejected, however, is what holds together all of Scripture: that it is constituted by the Word of God, spoken by *the* Word of John 1:1. In Cheyne's view, what gives the text any integrative quality is simply the thing to which it attests on the surface, such as history or an inner religious dimension.

One of the central texts of Isaiah that plays such a crucial role in Christian theology is the "Suffering Servant" passage of Isa 53. It should first be noted that Cheyne, as with most German critical scholars by this period, accepted that this section of Isaiah may not have been written by the same author as that of 1–39. His view is rather ambiguous at times, as Cheyne appears to distance himself from the "higher critics." In *Isaiah Chronologically Arranged* he presents the case for and against the unity of Isaianic authorship. He is more accepting of the conclusion that there was more than one author, and, perhaps strangely, the reason for this is precisely the "Messianic doctrine," which he regards as

---

57. Ibid., 1:60.

so unlike Isaiah that we can hardly avoid ascribing them to some later prophet.... So bold a development of the old Messianic idea cannot possibly have proceeded from Isaiah. It presupposes a spirituality of mind, a sympathy with foreign nations, and an indifference to the claims of the house of David, which can only have arisen during a prolonged separation from the soil of Palestine.[58]

The "development" of this Messianic doctrine is a move away from the Godlike "hero" of Isa 9, toward a suffering Messiah whose bearing is less kingly, and subject to the mockery and the violence of Isa 53. Thus, this is a development of religious sensibilities that "cannot possibly have proceeded from Isaiah," and which indicate a plurality of authorship of the book.

In his later commentary, Cheyne takes a more conciliatory approach to the controversy regarding authorship. In his introduction to Isa 40–66, he says,

From the only admissible point of view—the philological, the problem of the date and literary origin still remains unsettled, for until we know under what circumstances a prophecy was written, portions at least of the exegesis cannot but remain vague and obscure.... I shall leave it an open question whether the book was composed by Isaiah or by some other author or authors, and whether it falls into two, three, or more parts, but not whether it is in the fullest sense of the words prophetic.... Let us now approach with sympathetic minds this Gospel before the Gospel. Though written primarily for the exiles at Babylon, its scope is as wide as that of any part of the New Testament, and New Testament qualifications are required alike in the interpreter and his readers.[59]

This passage offers a strange conflagration of antithetical ideas. Whereas he makes a rather predictable comment that the philological perspective is the only "admissible" one, it is here that Cheyne makes one of his rare explicit connections to Christ in the commentary, the closest he comes to the notion of a canon. He contends that regardless of the historical context of the unknown author, the text has a meaning that "extends" to the coming of the Messiah. Given, however, that his commentary is so rarely christological, this can hardly be viewed as more than a concession to those who want to have some latent theological potential in the text. The next section examines

---

58. Cheyne, *Book of Isaiah, Chronologically Arranged*, xxiii-xxiv.
59. Cheyne, *The Prophecies of Isaiah*, 1:242-43.

Cheyne's allowance of a secondary, "religious," meaning such that this section of Isaiah can be understood as a "Gospel before the Gospel."

The Servant passages in Isaiah are of great interest to Cheyne and he offers an interpretation that leaves open the possibility that Jesus of Nazareth was the fulfillment of the prophecy. Commenting on Isa 42, he says, "I am unable to resist the impression that we have a presentiment of an individual, and venture to think that our general view of 'the Servant' ought to be ruled by those passages in which the enthusiasm of the author is at its height."[60] In other words, Cheyne does not define the Servant as Hezekiah, or collective Israel. The Servant of Isa 53 is an individual: "[he] refers not to the type (the pious kernel of the nation), but to the anti-type (the personal Servant.)"[61] This use of traditional theological language is quite rare in Cheyne's commentary. He also disagrees with contemporaries like Lowth, Henderson, and Alexander that the referent of Isa 53 is a collective understanding of the Jewish people. One of the reasons for Cheyne's view that this is a *person* rather than a symbolic representation of collective Israel is his contention that the book of Job is key to understanding this section of Isaiah. Indeed, there are few other biblical books in all of Cheyne's commentary that have such an influence on his reading of Isaiah as Job. This connection is not the result of such theological concepts as typology or canon. Their affinity is based on the similarity of their style and word-use. It can be said that there is a kind of philological, historical, and religious "canonicity" between Isaiah and Job, meaning that because of the historically reconstituted background and the literary connections between the two texts, each can be used to determine the meaning of the other. Therefore, in his translation of v. 3 ("Despised and *deserted* of men"), Cheyne says, "The Book of Job (a fund of parallels for II Isaiah) supplies us with the best justification of this rendering." Since Job provides such an aid in interpretation, it also drives his conclusion that Isa 53 speaks only of one individual. Arguments supposing that the Servant is symbolic of collective Israel were "probably influenced by Jewish objections to the received Christian application."[62] The point here is that while Cheyne eventually takes a relatively more "conservative" stance in his interpretation of the Suffering Servant as a person rather than as a symbol, the *means* by which he comes to this is via the utilization of non-dogmatic criteria. The mind of the prophet can be discerned only by a historical perspective of the text whereby the only relevant biblical material is that which has been

60. Ibid., 1:263.
61. Ibid., 2:43.
62. Ibid., 2:44.

determined to have been contemporary to the prophet. There is therefore no sense of reading Isaiah "canonically" in Cheyne's commentary.

Cheyne also accepts that the text suggests that the Suffering Servant undergoes a vicarious suffering. It does not make logical sense for him that a group of people, such as all of Israel, vicariously suffer. However, despite the fact that Cheyne appears to come to a relatively non-radical conclusion that this is an individual who suffers on behalf of someone, much of his commentary has to do with the typical concern for paraphrasing the text, discussing the fine points of translation, and other such academic matters. For *whom* the Servant suffers, Cheyne only says, "inasmuch as the Servant, by Jehovah's will, has made himself the substitute of the Jewish nation, it follows that the punishment of the latter must fall upon him. We have no right . . . to find a reference to the imposition of hands on the Sin-offering."[63] At the same time, contradicting this somewhat, Cheyne later says, "may it not be one object of the prophet to show that in the death of the Servant, various forms of sacrifice find their highest fulfillment?"[64] At this point, Cheyne discusses the concept of "satisfaction" within the orbit of Old Testament religion. He notes that Isa 53 speaks of a "guilt offering" rather than a "sin offering." But the former can refer only to an individual and the latter to a group of people. He asserts that "this can only be met by the hypothesis that the Servant is in some mystic and yet real sense identified with Israel; that he embodies all that is high and noble in the Israelitish character, and yet transcends it." This rather unimaginative approach to the text is, however, not entirely Cheyne's set views on the matter. In parentheses, following the above statement, Cheyne adds

> (It would be a still simpler solution to suppose that the distinction between sin-offering and guilt-offering was not very clearly drawn when the prophet wrote; but this would require us to adopt the Grafian hypothesis as to the date of the Levitical legislation. It would be unfair to import the huge difficulties which beset this question into the comparatively simple subject of the exegesis of Isaiah)[65]

While an apparently innocuous parenthetical comment, it is not hard to imagine that the "simpler solution" is the better one in his mind. However, it is not necessary to merely speculate: at the very end of the Essays appended to the commentary, Cheyne offers a series of "Last Words," in which

63. Ibid., 2:46.
64. Ibid., 2:50.
65. Ibid., 2:51. The "Grafian hypothesis" is what is now called the "Documentary hypothesis."

he takes up this very central topic. He comments on Wellhausen's argument that there is no sense of "guilt-offering," to which he responds

> As a commentator on Isaiah I am not called upon to discuss the theory at the root of this bold negation; but I would frankly admit that . . . it is difficult to say why the word אשם [the word translated as "guilt offering] should be particularly used here, and that the "simpler solution" mentioned at the end of my note on the clause (p. 51) commends itself to my judgment. If we adopt it, however, must we take the Grafian hypothesis as to the Levitical legislation into the bargain? We must either do this, or else suppose that this body of laws, though in existence, was not very widely known.[66]

Cheyne is therefore fully willing to accept the Graffian hypothesis, though he does so very indirectly, perhaps out of concern for being criticized.

Recall that a canonical approach to the text does not merely assert that the entire Bible is to be read as a whole—as if it were some synchronic literary theory that guarantees a correct reading if such an approach was utilized—but that the Old and New Testaments together are the Word of God and bear witness to Jesus Christ. There is indeed very little in Cheyne's commentary that considers Isaiah as constitutive of the entire canon of Scripture. As far as the "inner canonicity" of Isaiah is concerned, that is, the arrangement of the present form of the book, I already indicate above that Cheyne regards it as important to render Isaiah in a form that is governed by reconstituted history. In the first Essay that follows the commentary, "The Occasional Prophecies of Isaiah in the Light of History," in a rather rare moment of direct opposition to a specific thinker, Cheyne speaks against Hengstenberg, who proposes "Have we not already in the Book of Isaiah itself an authoritative chronological arrangement?" To this, unsurprisingly, Cheyne disagrees, arguing,

> 1. that it implies the infallibility of the later Jewish editors of Isaiah, and 2. that it regards the prophecies of Isaiah, or at any rate those in the first part, as if they had been sent out into the world singly, whereas internal evidence strongly favors the view that underlying our present book there are several partial collections.[67]

The differences between Hengstenberg and Cheyne, however, are with regard to the issue of textual categorization. For Hengstenberg, the question

---

66. Ibid., 2:307.
67. Ibid., 2:178.

is whether the current form of the text is *authoritative*, an appellation that Cheyne finds problematic, raising questions in terms of whether the text or its editors are "infallible." Within the context of divisive exegesis, Cheyne is wary of terms such as "authority," as it would imply a lack of freedom granted to him as a scholar. For the Church or dogma to determine the meaning of the text is problematic as there are numerous churches that make competing claims to the text. Therefore, he chooses to turn to a standard set of rules to govern his exegesis, namely, historical reconstruction and philology. This is, it bears repeating, more evidence that Cheyne's approach is deeply affected by ecclesial division as he regards the Church, representative of "authority," to have failed at the exegetical task.

A "CHRISTIAN" READING OF ISAIAH

In Cheyne's "Essays Illustrative of the Commentary on Isaiah" that follow his commentary, Cheyne often reveals a great deal more of his own thinking regarding theological issues and Isaiah, which are only hinted at in the commentary proper. We particularly find him attempting to offer a reading that comports in some way with the fact that he is a Christian, amidst giving pride of place to a philological approach to Scripture, and a need for a rigorously historical point of view. Nonetheless, though he is aware that there is controversy about the various approaches to Isaiah, he often disdains what he considers a failed attempt by the Church to determine the meaning of the text. For example, in his discussion of the chronological placement of the Servant passages, he avers:

> It seems to me clear that, though not discordant with the other passages relative to the servant, this obscure and difficult section cannot have been originally intended to follow chaps. xlix. 1–lii.12. *Let any plain, untheological reader be called upon to arbitrate; I have no doubt as to his decision.*[68]

While admittedly Cheyne is referring to an "arbitration" concerning a very specific passage, my contention is that his use of innovative critical tools is also an attempt to arbitrate between opposing readings of Scripture. His contest no longer gives serious weight to tradition, Church, or the authority of Scripture, but uses "nontheological" methods to which all can appeal.

Despite this, in Essay III, "The Christian Element in the Book of Isaiah," Cheyne takes a different tone than that of the rest of his commentary. Here is Cheyne the ordained priest of the Church of England, no mere

---

68. Ibid., 2:190, italics mine.

atheist, but one who desires to give witness to the Christian message in light of the modern era—this too is part of his "reconstruction" project. As his opening to this essay says, "the effort to express this witness anew must now be made; it is useless to repeat what is no longer in harmony with the best knowledge of the age. Apologetic theology must be reformed, and Biblical criticism and exegesis have to aid in preparing the ground."[69] From Cheyne's point of view, he is not the "negative critic" that Robert Payne Smith disdains, but he believes he is participating in defending the Christian faith: *he is an apologist*.

It is in this essay on the "Christian element" in Isaiah that Cheyne concisely states his objective:

> The object of the present work . . . is mainly exegetical, and only indirectly critical; but it is, perhaps, for that very reason important to meet the expectations of any section of its readers with more than usual frankness. For it is emphatically not a party book, but designed to help as many students as possible to a philologically sound view of the text . . . Most English books on Isaiah carry their theological origin on their forefront; this one can hardly be said to do so.[70]

Despite the fact that he does not claim to be part of a "party," it would be difficult to see Robert Payne Smith or Christopher Wordsworth reading his commentary with approval. That he does not want to be associated with a "party" is revealing, for doing so would suggest a set of theological claims, which he is strenuously trying to avoid. Rather, his interpretive methods emerge out of the awareness of the divisiveness inherent in reading Scripture in the modern world. He attempts not to be divisive: "Its scope . . . is not polemical," but

> the essays on Biblical subjects called forth by controversy have seldom been those which have permanently advanced the sacred interests of truth. After spending even a short time on the heavy air of controversial theology, the student is forced to exclaim with a kindred spirit among the prophets, "Oh that I had in the wilderness a lodging-place of wayfaring men!" [Jeremiah 9:2]. . . . Yet the misunderstanding and suspicion which from opposite sides meet the Biblical investigator may well render him as reluctant to publish on questions of the day as Jeremiah was to prophesy. . . . As the preceding commentary will have shown, he belongs to a school of interpretation mainly, at any

---

69. Ibid., 2:191.
70. Ibid., 2:192.

> rate, composed of rationalists. It is true he has come to believe in a definitely Christian interpretation of the Old Testament, but this he thinks should be based entirely upon the obvious grammatical meaning.[71]

Cheyne's conclusion in the midst of controversy is that his "lodging place" of retreat from the division and conflict between different parties is "rationalism." At the same time, he does not reject a Christian interpretation of Isaiah. On the one hand, Cheyne is uncomfortable with the idea of a "Christian" interpretation of Isaiah: "I have ventured to use the phrase 'a definitely Christian interpretation of the Old Testament.' I do not thoroughly like it, no more than I like the distinction between the natural and the supernatural." On the other hand, he continues by stating what is, at first glance, a classic Christian perspective on the Old Testament: "Everything in the Old Testament stands in some relation to Christ, whether 'definitely' or not." His justification of this is instructive, however:

> Every revolution of the ancient heathen world, whether in politics or in thought, is a stage in its journey towards that central event, which is the fulfilment of its highest aspirations. Plato speaks almost as if he foresaw the crucifixion.... It is at least not irrational to maintain that the "prophetic voices" which announce the Messiah in the Old Testament are so definite and distinct, and in such agreement with history, as to prove that God has in very deed revealed himself to Israel ... in a fuller sense than to other nations.... It depends on one's moral attitude towards the two great Biblical doctrines summed up in the expressions "the Living God," and "the God-man Jesus Christ." If you believe heartily in the God of Revelation and of Providence, you are irresistibly impelled to a view of the Scriptures, which ... is none the less in the highest degree reasonable.[72]

Here is a rather broad understanding of what can be seen as a kind of "natural religion," in which the world is so related to this cosmic Christ that there is not a distinction between "general" and "special" revelation. All spheres of creation reveal, and the "moral attitude" of the observer determines its probative value in reference to God's revelatory will. This general revelatory potential of nature itself and its teleological ordering warrant a "reasonable" point of view that Scripture has predictive value, albeit somewhat provisionally. However, the actual nature of Scripture itself has very little ontological bearing in the economy of salvation in Cheyne's account.

71. Ibid., 2:192–93.
72. Ibid., 2:194–95.

Cheyne is aware that a divided Church in the modern era was the cause of numerous conflicting approaches to Scripture. In a passage that highlights the Broad Church appeal to a very real *via media*, he describes this reality and its consequences:

> The torrents of ridicule which have been poured out upon "circumstantial fulfilments" have left a general impression that they can only be admitted by doing violence to grammar and context, which to a modern student is nothing short of "plucking out" his "right eye." Hence many "liberal" theologians have been fain to stunt their religion in favor . . . of their philology. . . . But must there not be some mistake both on the side of the cross-bearers and of the cross-rejecters? Can it be that human nature is "divided against itself," and left to choose between intellectual and religious mutilation? *Here at least scepticism is the truest piety*.[73]

It is revealing to consider Cheyne's understanding of the meaning of "messianic," which, just as with his "Christian" interpretation of Isaiah, there is a similarity between this and his account of the generalized christological presence in Scripture and nature. He writes, "I think I am in harmony with the Biblical writers if I define the word Messiah as meaning one who has received some direct commission from God determining his life's work, with the single limitation that the commission must be unique, and must have a religious character. . . . David was a Messiah. . . . The people of Israel was theoretically a Messiah."[74] Thus, there is a "general" Messiah of which Christ was a kind of "anti-type" in a weak sense. Indeed, with respect to the Psalms, Cheyne concedes that "in some of its details, the traditional Christian interpretation is no doubt critically untenable, but in essentials it seems to me truer than any of the current literary theories."[75] The christological aspect of the text, however, is not grounded theologically, but is demanded by virtue of a certain literary *aporia*:

> It now appears to the author that [literary studies of the Old Testament] supply a sound basis for the "Christian interpretation" at any rate of the Psalter; but this is entirely an after-thought. That there is a mysterious *x* in this wonderful book became clear to the author from a purely literary point of view. Applying the key furnished by the Christian theory, he then found himself in a position to explain this mystery, and was further enabled to

---

73. Ibid., 2:196, emphasis mine.
74. Ibid., 2:198.
75. Ibid., 2:202.

rediscover those peculiar, circumstantial prophecies which are so natural and intelligible upon the Christian presuppositions.[76]

This is a somewhat grudging acceptance of a correspondence between the Old Testament and Christ, and it is only by virtue of an apparent "mysterious x," after historical and philological reconstructions are complete. The Christian interpretation finally fills out the text—only, of course, for those who are so predisposed. But this is not based on any well-defined hermeneutic of Scripture in which the christology *is* the hermeneutic; but it is no better than a secondary interpretation. Indeed, it is only in this essay that Cheyne gives any serious consideration of the christological interpretation of the text. It is the "Christian remainder" that hovers at a rather abstract level, funding a "religious" mode of reading.

Cheyne's view of the New Testament's use of the Old Testament is taken from a history-of-religions point of view, which is that there is a development in the "messianic doctrine" that began in the Haggadic literature. He traces the development of various Jewish conceptions of the Messiah, where, for instance, there was an idea of two "Messiahs," one "Son of David," and the other the "Son of Joseph." One is a Messiah of war and the other of suffering.[77] But Cheyne argues that several factors came to play in the development of this doctrine; while he states, "I believe that the suffering Messiah is, at least germinally, in the Old Testament,"[78] he also states that the meaning of "Messiah" must be expanded to include both kingship and affliction:

> Surely an open-minded reader must allow that the writer of these words [of Isa 52 and 53] identifies the Messianic king with the afflicted teacher and redeemer; that, in a word *both are Messianic*, and that we have to look out for a wider definition of the word Messiah than the pedantry begotten of controversy would allow. That, in fact, the progress of revelation or (if rationalists will not allow this) the progress of religious thought has introduced new elements into the conception of the Messiah.[79]

Cheyne's attempt at distancing himself from the "rationalists" appears somewhat disingenuous. Given his preference for modern approaches to the Bible, Cheyne would prefer to use the image of religious progress, a development of the messianic doctrine that was influenced by many historical forces.

76. Ibid., 2:204.
77. Ibid., 2:218–20.
78. Ibid., 2:221.
79. Ibid., 2:222.

CONCLUSION

Thomas Kelly Cheyne's exegetical work embraces new and modern critical tools, which are brought to bear on Isaiah. This exegetical method further subsists within a religious milieu that conceives of the Bible as an expression of human religious phenomenon, devoid of ecclesially linked dogmatic categories. The consequences of examining the text *qua* text are to avoid historically divisive dogmatic issues in favor of a perception that new strategies bring certainty that Church dogmas had heretofore failed to do. These critical tools are primarily those of historical reconstruction and philology.

The result is a commentary in which there is no role for the Church, for such a divided entity has proven itself unable to come to certainty regarding textual meaning; rather, it is perceived that the Church built many theological "systems" that obscure the text and that only an unbiased modern approach can clarify. This is not to say that Cheyne or Arnold would consider their exegesis of the text as *not* theological, for a proper reconstruction and illumination of the religion of Israel, discovered from the clues of historical methods, is what proper theological exegesis should be.

Just as there is no role for the Church, neither does Cheyne espouse an individualist interpretation along the lines of that of Robert Payne Smith. Those who are able to offer the correct interpretation of Isaiah are those who are properly trained in the skills of philology, the original languages, and history. Moreover, any kind of canonical consideration of Isaiah is of no concern for Cheyne or Arnold. Any connection between Isaiah and other biblical texts is by virtue of the context during which they were written. In terms of a christological reading of the text, both Cheyne and Arnold accept that this is one possible understanding of how to read the text. However, they tend to render such a reading as "secondary." For Cheyne, it is the "mysterious x," the remaining meaning of the text once the reader has carried out all other analyses.

This chapter is not intended to bemoan a "liberal" reading, nor a loss of a uniquely Anglican reading of Scripture *per se*. Rather, it is to argue that the state of reading Scripture in the nineteenth century by the Broad Church party in the Church of England is the consequence of finding new ways to read Scripture that are derived to avoid the divisions that "theological" exegesis elicits. It could be suggested that the move to common principles of exegesis is not a divisive one, but a "peacemaking" one that attempts to avoid division. While this may have been what thinkers like Cheyne thought, it is clear that (i) such a decision—and actually one that at the time was not usually done with such self-consciousness—was a product of ecclesial conflict and therefore was shaped by it, and (ii) it explicitly eschews a hermeneutic considered "traditional" or "dogmatic."

Despite this irenic, putatively non-dogmatic desire that funds their academic and exegetical pursuits, this impulse leads many in the Broad Church party—Cheyne and Arnold as exemplars—to a new set of theological commitments. The ultimate result for Cheyne in his latter years was to become committed to principles informed by the Baha'i faith, which is that all religions are part of a single truth. I suggest that this is the somewhat natural, though by no means inevitable, extension of an irenic exegesis taken to its logical conclusion. If dogmatic commitments are to be avoided (which is in fact impossible), one does not have to become a Baha'i in order to at least implicitly accept that they are merely outward accoutrements of an inward (i.e., spiritual) human phenomenon. Cheyne and Arnold argue for a set of general beliefs, often deeply moral, regarding religion as an anthropomorphic phenomenon. While Cheyne's "conversion" to the Baha'i faith is not inevitable, such a view of Christianity in the Broad Church is similar in kind, if not degree, as is the direct product of a divided and confused Church.

6

English Roman Catholicism and Isaiah
Exegetical Minimalism in a State of Siege

INTRODUCTION: A TEXTUAL AND ECCLESIAL BIFURCATION

In *The English Catholic Enlightenment*, Joseph Chinnici observes that "during the polemics of the Counter Reformation [the] emphasis on the mutual inherence of Holy Writ and Holy Church bifurcated into a dualism that opposed Scripture (written word) to church (custodian of unwritten tradition)."[1] This chapter illustrates that such polemics specifically come to bear on the reading of Scripture in English Catholicism, resulting in an avoidance of exegetical engagement with the Bible. It is also my intention in this chapter to allow some Roman Catholic writings to come into dialogue with the Anglican exegetes of the previous chapters to highlight some of the central themes of this book.

I use Roman Catholic academic journals, devotional literature, and other popular works to show that the effect of this bifurcation has an exegetical parallel to that of the kind of reading offered by the Broad Church party of the last chapter. I situate this within the context, of a response to the breakdown and re-establishment of methods of "certainty." For Broad Churchmen, certainty is achieved methodologically via irenic (that is, non-dogmatic) exegetical strategies, and religiously through an appeal to

---

1. Chinnici, *The English Catholic Enlightenment*, 76.

a common human religious consciousness within. In the case of English Roman Catholicism, the story is exegetically comparable to that of the Broad Church in two ways. First, while there is a nominal belief in the close connection between theology and the text, the practice was to regard the theological referents of Scripture as perfectly congruous with Church practice. The Church continues, but the text itself remains behind and scant theological exegesis is performed beyond using it as a buttress against Protestant polemics, in a kind of "supportive" capacity. Second, Broad Church exegetes sought authority by an appeal to a universal human religious capacity. Roman Catholics, on the other hand, found religious authority in the Church, the only living source of interpretation. Part of this was a reaction against Protestant claims to the sole authority of Scripture. English Roman Catholics frequently portray the Bible as a dangerous book, the unfettered distribution of which was the cause of divisions and errors exemplified in the disparate Protestant churches, effecting confusion regarding how Scripture was to be engaged.

The results of this negative orientation toward Scripture are frequent warnings against biblical engagement in any way akin to that of Protestants, particularly as regards various critical approaches. Theologically, however, English Catholics were in a state of *confusion* as to the relation between the Church and Scripture, leading to several responses. Some Catholics felt that portions of the new critical work pioneered primarily by Protestants were warranted, and despite the official proscription of critical scholars by the *curia*, many referenced such scholars in their reading of Scripture. The confusion regarding the role of Scripture allowed for few options for Roman Catholics. Scripture became relegated to a rather static existence, positioned in a more "supportive" role, as a source for proof-texting Church tradition. This had affinities with Robert Payne Smith's reading of Isaiah as a book to be mined for its proof of the truth of the Christian faith.

It is important to devote this chapter to Catholicism[2] as part of this discussion of division and the nineteenth-century English as Catholicism usually remained by definition the ultimate antagonist for all Protestant thinkers. This attitude toward Catholics by English Protestants emerged out of historical antecedents that shaped religious life in England, with the rise and fall of king and queens with Catholic commitments or sympathies. By the time of the nineteenth century, the Union with Ireland Act of 1800 did not help in allaying fears, with many Catholics moving from Ireland to England. More importantly, right from the emergence of Protestantism in

---

2. For the sake of simplicity, I use the term "Catholic" to refer to "Roman Catholicism," which is to be distinguished theologically from "catholic."

England (and elsewhere), exegesis of the Bible was formed in opposition to Catholicism.

My intent is to provide evidence that the often defensive stance on the part of English Catholics meant that, since the Bible was often the battleground of division, there was an avoidance of serious exegetical engagement with Scripture. Indeed, much of this chapter highlights the difficulty of presenting any significant Catholic analysis of Isaiah. I consider this part of the strength of my argument: as a key book in the history of exegesis, Isaiah is conspicuously absent in English Catholic catechetical and doctrinal literature.

To some extent, the comparison between Catholics and Protestants in England is an unfair one. Even though almost all prohibitions were removed by the Catholic Emancipation Act of 1829, it was not until 1854 that a Catholic could obtain a degree from Oxford, and 1856 for Cambridge. Few Catholics could thus acquire an education in England to be equal to that of Smith, Wordsworth, or Cheyne. There were, however, some opportunities for higher education on the Continent, most notably at Douay, out of which emerged the definitive Roman Catholic English translation of the Bible, the Douay-Rheims Bible. Moreover, much of the work that influenced English Catholic thinking was written in the eighteenth century, particularly the catechetical writings. However, this is not to suggest an absence of polemical engagement prior to the nineteenth century that contributed substantially to theological disarray and decline.[3]

English Catholics saw the divisive nature of Protestantism's reliance on *sola scriptura* and "private judgment" as proof of the errors of granting the Bible such a central place in theology. The effect was that Catholic thinkers often *ignored* the Bible, especially in connection with doctrinal issues. Many became "anti-modernist," resorting to earlier scholastic methods such that "for the anti-Modernists a neo-scholastic formulation of the faith and the faith itself were so identified that they could hardly be separated; to reject the formulation was to reject the faith itself."[4] Other Catholics latched onto the idea that the Bible's perspicacity was so minimal that any critical exegesis would lead to innovation.

---

3. Peter Marshall's discussion of Protestant and Catholic debates surrounding the location and nature of Hell in the intra- and post-Elizabethan era has strong analogies to my contention that ecclesial division attenuated theological exegesis. He shows that, first, the result of many reforms "was perhaps the single most audacious act of theological downsizing in the history of western Christianity" (Marshall, "The Reformation of Hell?," 280). It is yet another form of theological minimization that arose as a result of ecclesial division.

4. Jodock, *Catholicism Contending with Modernity*, 10.

I begin by offering a general overview of the context in which English Catholics lived out their faith. I follow this with an analysis of three kinds of Catholic theological literature. First, I consider influential catechetical works and the course of study for Catholic priests destined for England. Second, I briefly consider two commentaries of a sort, particularly that of Isaiah, namely the *Haydock Bible Commentary* and the comments written in the Catholic translation of the Bible by Bishop Richard Challoner (1691–1781) in the Douay-Rheims Bible. Third, I examine the most predominate English Catholic scholarly journal of the mid- to late- nineteenth century, *The Dublin Review*, and mine it for its contribution to understanding Catholic discourse with respect to Scripture and, where possible, that of Isaiah.

ENGLISH CATHOLICS IN THE NINETEENTH CENTURY

This section describes the intellectual and hermeneutical context in which English Catholics functioned during the nineteenth century. Part of this relates to the broader movements in Catholic Europe (e.g., the *Syllabus of Errors*), but the English instance of Catholic thinking was particularly reactive against Protestant notions of Scripture. This led to an approach that avoided close engagement with the text and confusion about the relation between the Bible and the Church.

The rather consistent Protestant anti-Catholicism resulted in a perspective within the Catholic community that self-identified as a beleaguered minority in England. For this reason, many communities functioned in a "sectarian" manner[5] and an attitude frequently pervaded of rigidity and conservatism that was ineffective in responding to the challenges of modernity. As Watkin argues, "Conservatism and defence ... such has been the presentation of Catholicism from the Reformation to our own time, a presentation inevitably restricted by its historical conditions and therefore unable to prove permanently satisfying.[6] For the most part, Catholic biblical exegesis was impacted by the Counter-Reformation, out of which emerged the Council of Trent,[7] which rejected the idea of *sola scriptura*, as it was

---

5. Questier, *Catholicism and Community,* 3.

6. Watkin, *Roman Catholicism in England,* 13. Note that Watkin is writing from a pre-Vatican II era. At the time of his writing, there was a kind of flowering of Catholic theological interpretation of Scripture, taking into account some of the results of historical-critical study. This was especially ushered in by the work of those involved in *ressourcement*, namely Henri de Lubac, Jean Daniélou, and Yvers Congar. See Mayeski, "Quaestio Disputata," 140–53.

7. Bedouelle, "Biblical Interpretation in the Catholic Reformation," 428–49.

seen to be equivalent to private interpretation—a view not usually denied by Protestants.

It would be a mistake to denote Catholic thought in England—or in Europe for that matter—as monolithic. Indeed, while there were laws that had been inconsistently applied to the Catholic communities since the Elizabethan laws of uniformity, there was a kind of uneasy truce that had emerged between Roman Catholics and Protestants such that English Catholicism, separated from Rome both geographically and culturally, was often practiced in a way that had its own "English" form. It has been suggested that "Anglo-Gallicanism" resulted, born out of suspicions toward papal jurisdictions and a desire to prove loyalty to the monarch of England. After Emancipation in 1829, however, an Ultramontane wing of Catholicism gradually arose, represented by people such as Nicholas Wiseman (1802–65) and former Tractarian Henry Manning (1808–92). They were often in sharp and vitriolic opposition to the relatively moderate "Cisalpines," Catholics who came out of the "Anglo-Gallican" tradition of Douay College. Representatives of this latter "school," were well known people such as John Lingard and Charles Butler.

In the larger Catholic world, there was a strong reaction against the "liberalism" that had been developed primarily by Protestants, an attitude that can be seen most acutely in the *Syllabus of Errors*, released by Pope Pius XI in 1864. The document was not itself a newly formulated one but a conglomeration of papal issuances published previously and characteristic of the perspective of the *curia* at the time. The *Syllabus* comprised 80 statements that the Church opposed, the topics consisting of politics, philosophy, and marriage. Of interest to the present discussion are such condemned statements as that of Proposition 7, "The prophecies and miracles set forth and recorded in the Sacred Scriptures are the fiction of poets, and the mysteries of the Christian faith the result of philosophical investigations . . . In the books of the [Bible] there are contained mythical inventions, and Jesus Christ is Himself a myth;" or Proposition 18, "Protestantism is nothing more than another form of the same true Christian religion . . .;" or Proposition 80, "The Roman Pontiff can, and ought to, reconcile himself, and come to terms with progress, liberalism and modern civilization."[8] These statements (in which Scripture is mentioned only once) shy away from anything that was perceived to be theologically innovative and are made equivalent to Protestant thinking.

In England, the first bishop of the newly restored Roman Catholic hierarchy of 1850, Nicholas Wiseman, while he "gloried in the inventiveness

---

8. Taken from http://www.ewtn.com/library/PAPALDOC/P9SYLL.HTM.

of the times, and sought to attach Christianity to the expansive and progressive qualities of the intelligentsia," nonetheless "saw English Protestantism all round him sinking into liberalism and ultimate scepticism."[9] Such documents as the *Syllabus* can therefore be seen as strong reactions against the perceived heterodoxy of Protestants. While the reaction to the *Syllabus* was predictably rather negative, the reaction of Catholics was mixed. Many considered it a wholesale rejection by the Magisterium of most Enlightenment principles, and for this reason it was hailed or rejected either for its clarity, or its harshness.

There was, at the same time, a struggle over the Bible by Catholics in the *katholische Tübinger Schule* in Germany, which put forth various theories of biblical inspiration in the nineteenth century that had some impact in England. Under the *göttlich-menschlich* formula, there is no competition between human and divine agency in the formation of the canon of Scripture. The Holy Spirit provides specific revelation about events or concepts, but the general rule was that no author writes beyond his or her own human capabilities. "The sacred writer's faculties, far from being immobilized during periods of divine takeover, are hypersensitized for their task, so that while following their ordinary human operational laws, they become empowered to transmit a deeper, divine message."[10] Early pioneers of these ideas included Johann Sebastian von Dey and Johann Adam Möhler.[11] For the Catholic Tübingeners, Scripture emerges out of the Church (rather than vice versa for Protestants, as a rule) and is only one instance among others of the Holy Spirit giving the Church its faith. "Though the written gospel was an expression of the living gospel, it was never a total expression."[12] Moreover, "Christianity was never a religion propagated by writing. A book-religion is a fundamentally individualistic, private affair: each man reads by himself and draws his own conclusions. Christ and the Church have always approached men through preaching, a communal activity."[13] In this instance, the community is not just one of faith in general, but that of the preservatorial office of the Church. Möhler and von Drey, may appear to resemble a rather "liberal" approach to Scripture in their argument that God is not per se the author of Scripture. Yet in their criticism of the Protestant *sola scriptura* principle, they suggest that "every aberration in belief

---

9. Norman, *The English Catholic Church*, 86.

10. Burtchaell, *Catholic Theories of Biblical Inspiration*, 21–22.

11. See Drey, "Grundsätze zu einer Genauen Bestimmung Des Begriffs der Inspiration," 387–411; Möhler, *Symbolik*.

12. Burtchaell, *Catholic Theories of Biblical Inspiration*, 18.

13. Ibid., 19.

could and did appeal to Scripture; thus the further need of an interpreting authority."[14] Therefore, although there are similar sentiments between more liberal Protestants and the Catholic Tübingeners, the ultimate aim of the latter was to grant greater authority to the Church at the expense of Scripture. They did so by employing the same tools of "liberal" academics to call into question Scripture's divine source.

Johann von Kuhn is an ideal representative of this *göttlich-menschlich* model of biblical inspiration.[15] Just as the Chalcedonian formula asserts Christ's dual natures—unconfused and in perfect harmony—so too does Scripture illustrate "the Bible both as God's immediate production and as the literary responsibility of the human authors."[16] This acknowledgement of Scripture's human element meant that "much of what it contains is not the object of faith, for there is much purely human material intercalcated among the items of revelation. Being so thoroughly heterogeneous ... a document, it can never serve by itself as the adequate and exclusive source of faith."[17] Thus, in order to know the entire Word of God, one must see beyond this one instance of the Spirit's work to where God's Word also resides in tradition, the unwritten Word. Burtchaell's central point is that

> The Tübingen Catholics wrought their formula in the forge of controversy. ... Catholics at the time felt themselves challenged theologically at either flank. On the one hand, orthodox Protestantism had laid it down that the exclusive, infallible source of Christian faith was the Bible, and the Bible alone ... On the other hand were the adversaries from the Enlightenment. Christianity as they saw it was one of the more impressive creations of the human spirit, but no more than that. ... To the Protestants they insisted that much of revelation had eluded the New Testament and had to be sought in ancillary Church traditions.[18]

I do not go into more detail on these matters within Germany beyond noting similar controversies n England, though they were not formulated in the same context. Burtchaell notes, however, that John Henry Newman was influenced by some of this thought. Like his German predecessors,

---

14. Ibid., 25.
15. See Kuhn, "Zur Lehre von der Göttlichen Erwählung," 629–70.
16. Burtchaell, *Catholic Theories of Biblical Inspiration*, 26.
17. Ibid., 30. One must immediately note that the Chalcedonian analogy breaks down just at this point. Surely no Catholic would find Christ's human nature unreliable, or make a distinction within the one Person between one act and another without entering into quasi-Nestorian discourse.
18. Ibid., 40–41.

> [Newman] takes the stand on the problematic of Scripture which was typical of the English Liberal Catholics: he admits the obscurities, the contradictions, the insufficiencies of the Bible. Indeed, he underscores them, he brandishes them—and then turns them to his purpose by insisting that they only postulate an infallible interpreter to preside over genuine development and preserve it from deviation.[19]

Thus, there were numerous dedicated Catholics who varied in their opinions regarding Scripture; indeed, as a result of the rather reactionary perspective of the *curia*, there was a general sense of confusion about the relation between Scripture, Church, and doctrine.

CATECHETICAL LITERATURE FOR CLERGY AND LAITY

This section explores some influential writings used for the training of Catholics, both for priests and lay people in England. For each, I look at the general approach to Scripture and its relationship to theology. Where possible, I also explore the function of the book of Isaiah.

Peter McGrail's collation of material on eucharistic preparation between 1568 and 1910, which was used primarily to catechize children, is helpful to get a sense of catechetical preparation.[20] McGrail refers to the well-known *Garden of the Soul* by Bishop Richard Challoner, who was a significant eighteenth-century figure of English Catholicism, as a book that "enjoyed enormous popularity within the English Catholic community.... It was effectively the prayer-book of most English Catholics."[21] Several sections also provide religious instruction. Challoner also penned the popular catechetical work *The Catholic Christian Instructed*. It is interesting to note that much of this material was written before the nineteenth century but was still widely in use. In fact, very little popular catechetical literature was developed in the nineteenth century for English Catholics.

Few English Catholic clergy, let alone the laity, had books that were current; after his visitation to various English parishes in 1855, Bishop Goss notes that "the chief impression one gets from the lists is that the books were old, a feeling that the collections were about a hundred years out of date. There is very little after 1820, and the years most heavily represented are

---

19. Ibid., 69.
20. McGrail, *First Communion*, 19–35.
21. Ibid., 21.

1600–1750."²² The primary catechetical works I examine comprise a catechism by Henry Tuberville that came out of Douay in 1649 and that enjoyed wide use in the nineteenth century: *An Abridgment of the Christian Doctrine with Proofs from Scripture on Points Controverted*. In addition, there was Jacques-Bénigne Bossuet's *An Exposition of the Doctrine of the Catholic Church in Matters of Controversy*, composed in 1668 and reprinted in 1830, interestingly, by members of the Church of England (translator unknown.) Although Bossuet was French, his work had some early impact on English Catholics and caused some controversy when *An Exposition* was translated.²³ I end with an examination of Challoner's *The Catholic Christian Instructed*.

The instruction of the clergy in the nineteenth century used these catechetical works. The details of the curriculum, however, are not always clear:

> It is difficult to ascertain the exact content of the educational scheme at Douai, St. Omer's, and the English College, Rome, after 1750. The extant material relates mostly to the English College, Douai. There the common course of studies for the priesthood took eleven years: a five-year course in the humanities . . . then two years of philosophy and four of theology. The greatest emphasis was on the classics: Cicero, Virgil, Tacitus, Livy, Homer, Thucydides, and Herodotus. The curriculum demanded a thorough knowledge of Greek and Latin and a familiarity with Hebrew.²⁴

Douay's pedagogical material was influenced by Challoner and Bossuet, who were "cited frequently by all of the textbooks, [and] represented an assiduous search for 'pure doctrine.'"²⁵ Peter Doyle notes, however, that by the time of the restoration of the hierarchy, the bishops

> advocated a training which isolated the seminarians from contemporary developments in secular education and which was marked by a deep suspicion of the world; it reflected a very narrow view of theology, and was partly responsible for the failure

---

22. Doyle, "The Education and Training of Priests," 217.

23. Simpson, "Bossuet's Interest in the Church of England," 43–50.

24. Chinnici, *The English Catholic Enlightenment*, 7. Chinnici also states that "the theology course at Douai . . . relied heavily on a study of the sources, Scripture and the patristic tradition" (8), but very little evidence is offered regarding the nature of this scriptural engagement. See also Haile and Bonney, *Life and Letters of John Lingard*, 29–31 in which the course of study is described; Hebrew and Greek are taught, presumably for the purpose of biblical study, but the Bible is not explicitly mentioned.

25. Chinnici, *The English Catholic Enlightenment*, 8.

> to develop a commitment to continuing study after ordination in many of the clergy.[26]

Doyle also observes that the Bishops who set out to establish colleges often considered it an important part of clerical training to be prepared to defend oneself against Protestants.[27] Doyle mentions the nature of biblical teaching:

> A report from St. Edmund's Ware, shows that there, at least, the study of scripture was subordinate to that of dogmatic theology. The same lecturer taught both, and the scripture course consisted mainly of 'an abstract of the rules of scriptural interpretation dictated twice a week.'[28]

The result, argues Doyle, was a "static" form of Roman Catholicism.[29] When Bishop Goss made the visitation I note above, he observed that the clergy possessed books that were rarely related to biblical matters: "While bibles and copies of the New Testament are common, commentaries and works on scriptural interpretation are rare."[30]

Henry Tuberville's *Abridgment of Christian Doctrine with Proofs of Scripture on Points Controverted* illustrates a typically Catholic perspective relating Scripture, doctrine, and the Church. It was often called "The Douay Catechism" and new editions were published well into the nineteenth century, despite its 1649 origin. As can be discerned from the title, the catechism was not merely a tool for teaching Catholic doctrine, but was also apologetically-oriented for the purpose of opposing Protestants. With regard to the *use* of Scripture, the point can be made rather briefly: Scripture is used merely as a "proof" for the various doctrines described. For instance, one of the questions concerns the administration of the Eucharist under only one kind:

> Q. How do you prove it is lawful for the laity to communicate under one kind only?
>
> A. First, because there is no command in scripture for the laity to do it under both, though there be for priests in those words, "Drink ye all of this," *St. Matt.* xxvi. 27, which was spoken to the apostles only and by them fulfilled: for it follows in *Mark* xiv.

---

26. Doyle, "The Education and Training of Priests," 208.
27. Ibid., 210–11.
28. Ibid., 212.
29. Ibid., 213.
30. Ibid., 217.

23, "And they all drank." 2. Out of *St. John* vi. 58, "He that eateth of this bread shall live for ever." Therefore, one kind sufficeth.[31]

Scripture's deployment as a buttress for theological claims is not unusual for a catechism, as most Protestant catechisms use Scripture as a guarantor of doctrinal statements as well. However, the non-contextual deployment of Scripture to affirm ecclesial practice is striking. For instance, consider the series of questions pertaining to contentious issues:

> Q. How do you prove it is lawful to dedicate or consecrate material temples?
>
> A. Out of ... *St. John* x 22, where it is recorded, that *Christ* himself kept the dedication of the temple in Jerusalem, instituted by Judas Maccabeus. 1 *Mac.* iv. 56, 59.
>
> Q. How do you prove it is lawful to adorn churches with tapestry, pictures, and the like?
>
> A. Out of *St. Mark* xiv. 15, where Christ commanded his last supper to be prepared in a great chamber adorned.
>
> Q. What proof have you for the order and number of the canonical hour?
>
> A. For Matins, Lauds, and Prime, that of *Psal.* v. 4. "Early in the morning will I stand up to thee, early in the morning wilt thou hear my voice."
>
> Q. What for the third, sixth, and ninth hours?
>
> A. For the third, out of *Acts* ii. 16. "At the third hour, the Holy Ghost descended on the apostles." For the sixth, out of *Acts* x. 9, "Peter and John went up into the highest part to pray, about the sixth hour." And for the ninth, out of *Acts* iii. 1, "And at the ninth hour Peter and John went into the temple to pray."
>
> Q. What for the Even-song and Complin?
>
> A. That of the *Psalmist*, "Morning and Evening will I declare the works of our Lord."[32]

It is also instructive to consider how the catechism speaks *of* Scripture. In its discussion of the nature of the Church, it argues that "with Catholics it is *essential* and *fundamental* to believe in the Holy Catholic Church; to hear her rather than our own idle fancies; and to abide, in doubts on religion, by the judgment of her Pastors." This is followed by:

---

31. Tuberville, *An Abridgment of the Christian Doctrine*, 82–83.
32. Ibid., 36.

> Q. Is it not possible to settle religious doubts or controversies by private judgment without an infallible tribunal?
>
> A. No; it is not possible. 1st. Because the judgment of most men change and differ one from the other, and especially in matters of Religion, as may be seen in the numberless sects into which those who are not in the Church divide themselves . . .
>
> Q. Why may not the letter of the scripture be a decisive judge of controversies?
>
> A. Because it has never yet been able . . . to decide any one, as the whole world doth experience; all Heretics pretending equally to it, for defence of their novelties and heresies, and no one of them ever yielding to another.
>
> Q. How then can we be assured of the truth in points controverted?
>
> A. By the infallible authority, definition, and proposition of the Catholic Church.
>
> Q. For what end then was the Scripture written, if not to be a decider of controversies?
>
> A. The writing of the Holy Scriptures was for the purpose of the better preserving the revealed will of God, and that by a sensible and common reading of it . . . we might be able to know that God is, and what he is, as also that there is a heaven and a hell, rewards for virtue, and punishment for vice, with examples of both.[33]

This is a remarkable view of Scripture in that orients it in a way that devalues its revelatory character. This is a key example of Richard Popkin's assertion about Catholic tendency, in the midst of debate over the interpretation of Scripture, to assert the interpretive authority of the Church.[34] There is a devaluation of the revelatory power of Scripture beyond these minimalist claims about rewarding people for their deeds and the existence of God. Insofar as doctrine is concerned, beyond these rather fundamental points, the only infallible source for doctrine (and for certainty) resides in the Church. Notwithstanding the irony that this entire catechism attempts to prove doctrine using Scripture, the assertion is that the Bible cannot be turned to in difficult matters.

It is also important to emphasize that the claim that those doctrines listed above can be determined "by a sensible and common reading" of the

---

33. Ibid., 23.
34. E.g, Popkin, *The History of Scepticism*, 14.

Bible differs very little from some forms of deism. Terrence Tilley, argues that the "eclipse of biblical narrative" occurred much earlier than Hans Frei's historical scheme suggests. Tilley shows that combatants of early conflicts between groups such as the Huguenots and Catholics regarded these wars in terms of unfolding historical events that disclose God's providential favoritism of one side over another. This led such Catholic skeptics as Michel de Montaigne (1533–92) to mock

> the self-serving dissymmetry of such theological polemics.... It is this insoluble confrontation over the meaning of events in the biblical narrative that forces a new pattern of discourse.... The eclipse of the biblical narrative for structuring European Christendom begins in the wars of religion in the sixteenth century and in the polemical arguments Protestants and Catholics made against the other; it is not merely the result of the intellectual climate of the Enlightenment, as Frei is often understood to imply.[35]

Tilley argues that "these Christian theologians became pure philosophers in their arguments. Theological particularity was caught in the stalemate and abandoned.... [They] proposed a Christianity completely without mystery, a 'theism' with a god so distant from the world of creation as to deserve the new nomenclature 'deism.'"[36] Most Catholics did not take this route, but there was a disconnect between doctrine and Scripture, and the catechetical passage above suggests as much. Note also that Tilley's argument affirms my claim of the impact of division on these changes. Frei's descriptive account of the "eclipse" of biblical narrative in terms of new intellectual movements omits the more *causal* element of ecclesial division that is generative of a vast array of competing exegetical approaches.

Finally, with respect to the use of Isaiah, I merely list representative references, few as they are, for they indicate that Isaiah is no more central than any other biblical text in the Catholic literature. For instance, the front page of Tuberville's catechism quotes Isaiah 30:21, "This is the way; walk ye in it." The proof of the lawfulness of making pilgrimages to holy places quotes Isa 11:10,[37] and Isa 11:21 establishes the acceptability of making vows.[38] In terms of Isaiah's predictive capacity, Isa 11:10 is used to show that it was predicted that Christ's burial would be with honour ("and his resting

---

35. Tilley, *History, Theology, and Faith*, 72.
36. Ibid., 73.
37. Tuberville, *An Abridgment of the Christian Doctrine*, 53.
38. Ibid., 55.

place will be glorious").[39] This meager use of Isaiah illustrates that it does not figure prominently in theological discourse, at least, not for catechetical material.

Bossuet's *An Exposition of the Doctrine of the Catholic Church in Matters of Controversy* is representative of English Catholic thought, as he influenced many Catholics of a more "Anglo-Gallican" orientation. I limit this discussion to his use and account of Scripture, but it should be immediately pointed out that Isaiah plays no role in this work. Bossuet's statement regarding the relationship between the Bible and tradition ought to be familiar by now:

> Jesus Christ having established His Church by the preaching of the unwritten word, it became the first rule of Christianity; and when the writings of the New Testament were added to it, this word lost none of its authority on that account: therefore we feel bound to receive with the same reverence all that the Apostles taught, whether by writing, or by precept, as St. Paul himself has expressly declared, 2 Thess. ii.15. And it is a certain proof, that when no origin of a doctrine can be traced, and yet it is embraced by the whole Church, it must have come down from the Apostles themselves.[40]

Thus Scripture itself supports the idea of non-scriptural teaching; like most movements of the time—Protestants and Catholics alike—Bossuet aims to uncover what best represents "primitive antiquity."[41] As such, it is only the Church, "the deposit of the Scriptures and of Tradition," who can interpret Scripture; "for by means of Tradition we interpret the true sense of Scripture. . . . It is thus that the children of God acquiesce in the decisions of the Church, believing to have heard by her mouth the oracles of the Holy Spirit."[42] This is the now-familiar Catholic response to Protestant claims that the Holy Spirit speaks infallibly through the text of Scripture. Bossuet's argument against private interpretation is not just that it is theologically problematic—it is *dangerous*:

> [The Church] has neither the means nor the intention of innovating in the least, since she not only submits herself to the Holy Scripture, but the better to silence at once all private interpretations of it, which are too apt to be regarded in the same light as Scripture, she has determined to listen to no other

---

39. Ibid., 16.
40. Bossuet, *An Exposition of the Doctrine*, 37–38.
41. Ibid., 10.
42. Ibid., 38–39.

interpretations but those of the Fathers as regards matters of faith and discipline.[43]

Despite his statement that the Church submits herself to Scripture, the historic, ecclesial interpretation is presented as exhaustive: no further engagement with Scripture is necessary. Moreover, the Bible remains insufficient in informing faith and in fact can be problematic without the interpretive presence of the inspired primitive Church.

Richard Challoner bears some similarities with Bossuet. An important and influential figure for Roman Catholics in seventeenth-century England, he left for Douay at the age of fourteen. Challoner was also a grandfather of sorts to a group who came to be known as the Cisalpines, firmly Catholic, but also just as firmly "English" in their willingness to declare their allegiance to the crown. He participated in the Douay-Rheims revision of the Bible, as well as its commentary, in addition to *The Catholic Christian Instructed*, and the popular devotional manual *The Garden of the Soul*. He also wrote an *Abridgment of Christian Doctrine*, which is similar in form to that of Tuberville. It was often called "The Penny Catechism," and "for countless Catholics it was, in fact, the beginning and end of their doctrinal training."[44] I attend to his larger catechism, as it was written in a state of conflict, in this case with the controversialist and deist Conyers Middleton (1683–1750). The latter had written a popular book, arguing that putatively non-biblical practices in the Roman Church derive from pagan customs. Although Challoner did not write the catechism in order to refute Middleton, he added a response to him in the preface.[45]

While the exchange is an interesting one, I examine only those passages that bear on issues of the Bible. As with many catechisms, *The Catholic Christian Instructed* is structured in question/answer format but, more importantly, it is formulated with the complaints of Protestants in mind. Challoner had a particularly acute interest in the liturgical effectiveness of the Catholic Church and vigorously defended the theological integrity of her practices. He aimed to show that no practice contradicts Scripture, but also that such church ceremonies not mentioned in the Bible are justified by their ancient provenance.

There are two aspects of Challoner's understanding of Scripture that reflect a typical English Catholic attitude in the nineteenth century, ultimately working to attenuate the importance of the Old Testament in general and Isaiah in particular. First, is the deeply functionalist role of the Bible in

43. Ibid., 39.
44. O'Donovan, *The Venerable Bishop*, 20.
45. Burton, *The Life and Times*, 1:99–100.

his scheme. As in other Catholic contexts, Challoner's reading of Scripture is not *exegesis*, but rather a positioning of Scripture in a supportive role to prove that Catholic practices accord with Scripture. For instance, Challoner offers several "proofs" for the real presence of Christ in the Eucharist; John 6 is one of them, out of which he argues that when Jesus talks of eating his flesh and drinking his blood, he refers to the partaking of the elements in Communion.[46] Or, in a specifically directed question against the Quaker practice of not baptizing everyone,

> Q. How do you prove against the quakers that all persons ought to be baptized?
>
> A. From the commission of Christ, St. *Matt. xxviii* 19. *Go teach all nations baptizing them in the name of the Father, and of the Son, and of the Holy Ghost.*[47]

In a most interesting example of expressly antagonistic exegesis of Scripture, Challoner uses the book of Revelation against Martin Luther. In a section where he discusses various religious orders, he mentions that of St. Augustine. Challoner then adds

> From this order Luther apostatized in the 16*th* century, and like the dragon, Revel. xii. ver. 4. "drew with him the third part of the stars of heaven, (that is, great numbers of religious of all denominations) and cast them to the earth."[48]

Nothing is added to this and while such an explicitly antagonistic use of Scripture is not frequent, Catholics are apparently no less reticent than Protestants in using Scripture against their opponents in a simplistic, proof-texting context.

Second, it is instructive to note that Challoner generally avoids figurative or spiritual readings of Scripture in favor of a "literal" interpretation. The implication for this is a distrust of potential ambiguities of meaning in favor of clear and distinct referents in literal interpretations. Whereas in earlier ages, the figurative reading of the Bible was a crucial component in exegesis, we now find the following:

> Q. Why do you take these words of Christ at his last supper according to the letter, rather than in the figurative sense?

---

46. Challoner, *The Catholic Christian Instructed*, 62.
47. Ibid., 32.
48. Ibid., 212.

> A. You might as well ask a traveller why he chuses [sic] the high road, rather than to go by by-paths with evident danger of losing his way.... In interpreting scripture the literal sense of the words is not to be forsaken, and a figurative one followed without necessity; and that the natural and proper sense is always to be preferred.[49]

The phrase "without necessity" is important. The figurative sense is perceived as extraneous and abstract, and certainly one not sufficient in controversial matters and pressed further from the literal sense. This "without necessity" suggests it is an interpretation that goes beyond the literal. This is not to say that Challoner disapproves of figural interpretation in certain warranted instances. He concedes,

> in certain cases, when a thing is already known to be a sign or figure of something else, which it signifies or represents, it may indeed, according to the common laws of speech and the use of the scripture be said to be such or such a thing; as in the interpretation of dreams, parables, and ancient figures.[50]

Challoner's intent is a reading of Scripture according to a proper understanding of its variegated literary forms. For the most part, however, he describes the reading of the Bible in terms of its most "obvious" sense; if this is not sufficient, then one can turn to the infallible interpretation of the Catholic Church. Whereas a figural reading in the early Church was an *essential* (thus necessary) part of how Scripture was to be read—this was the major way of relating the Two Testaments together—Challoner, while not rejecting such a reading, denies it as a fundamental aspect of exegesis. There is a diminishment of Scripture's multifaceted influence in favor of clear and distinct concepts, shorn of the layered fecundity attributed to it in earlier eras. With this diminishment of figuralism comes a similar decrease in importance granted to the Old Testament.

Attending briefly to Isaiah, There are times that Challoner employs Isaiah, but, as with most other texts, it functions only as support for Catholic practice and teaching. For instance, Isa 53, 58, and 60 are quoted in support of various prayer times, yet Challoner does not speak of any christological significance in the same Isa 53 passage.[51]

While Challoner has a deep knowledge of Scripture, the above analysis of his catechism indicates the strong bifurcation, as mentioned by Chinnici

---

49. Ibid., 54.
50. Ibid., 60.
51. Ibid., 236–37.

at the beginning of this chapter, between Church and Scripture. Thus, Challoner indicates his agrees with the claim of Scripture's *insufficiency* for faith and this this view arises out of the matrix of controversy with Protestants.

POPULAR CATHOLIC BIBLICAL COMMENTARIES

While there were no significant scholarly Catholic commentaries on Isaiah, two resources that were used by many English Catholics warrant mention. The first is the translation of the Bible many Catholics had in their homes, namely, the Douay-Rheims version. In the nineteenth century, these Bibles usually contained comments written by Bishop Challoner or ones to which were additionally appended notes by Rev. Leo Haydock. There is not a great deal of exegesis; however, some interesting points can be noted. For instance, Challoner introduces Isaiah by saying,

> This inspired writer is called by the Holy Ghost, the great prophet (Ecclesiasticus 48, 25), from the greatness of his prophetic spirit, by which he hath foretold so long before, and in so clear a manner, the coming of Christ, the mysteries of our redemption, the calling of the Gentiles, and the glorious establishment, and perpetual flourishing of the church of Christ: insomuch that he may seem to have been rather an evangelist than a prophet.[52]

Thus, Challoner's view of Isaiah is that it reads like a gospel of sorts. Note also that both the Church and Christ are important referents in the text. Bearing in mind, however, Challoner's preference to minimize figural reading, this is, I suggest, a moment of concession that supports the general Catholic perspective on Isaiah without significant exegetical depth. Where there is some exegetical engagement with Isaiah, Challoner's interpretation is often directed against Protestants. For instance, for Isaiah 2:18 ("And idols shall be utterly destroyed") he argues,

> This was verified by the establishment of Christianity. And by this and other texts of the like nature, the wild system of some modern sectaries is abundantly confuted, who charge the whole Christian church with worshipping idols for many ages.[53]

From Challoner's perspective, in order for this prophecy to be rightly fulfilled, the Catholic Church must be the referent the prophet held in view:

---

52. Challoner, *The Holy Bible*, 676.
53. Ibid., 677.

being the more ancient of the two rival Christian groups, Catholicism is *ipso facto* the true Church as opposed to Protestantism.

What I refer to as The Haydock Bible maintains Challoner's notes, but has additional introductions and comments interspersed with those of Challoner that allow for more insight into early nineteenth-century thinking with respect to Scripture. Father Leo Haydock (1774–1849) had spent some time in the English College at Douay, but left during the French Revolution. He served as general prefect and master of schools. Though he was well educated, he was not an academic as such. He did, however, spend some time studying on his own, especially during a time when he was forbidden to say mass for eight years.

In the Preface, Haydock lists the commentators whom he uses in his notes. It is interesting that he includes many Protestants, such as Calvin, Grotius, Luther, and Wesley, in addition to some other Jewish thinkers. He marks all non-Catholics with a †, noting that as "perhaps men of learning . . . have *erred from the faith which was once delivered to the Saints*, and can therefore be consulted only as Critics, or to be refuted."[54] He also says that

> though we have occasionally consulted some of the heterodox versions and commentators, in points of criticism; yet it has been with fear of deception, and we have dwelt upon the works of Catholic authors, both with greater pleasure and advantage. . . . In all these things let us stick invariably to the doctrine of the Church, and receive the bread which she breaks for her little ones with gratitude and submission.[55]

Haydock is cautious about which biblical critic he allows into his comments and their views must always submit to the rule of the Church. What is interesting, however, is his willingness to refer to Protestant writers at all, especially those who are critical of the text. Moreover, these Protestant critics comprise most of the more recent commentaries on Isaiah to which he refers—unsurprising, given the scarcity of Catholic exegetical contributions. Therefore, Haydock, in a more conservative mode, reflects what I show in more detail below in the case of *The Dublin Review*: the aridity of Catholic exegesis is such that Catholics eventually have no choice but to refer to Protestant writings.[56]

---

54. Haydock, *Haydock's Catholic Family Bible*, xi.

55. Ibid., x.

56. A mention of some of the Catholic dictionaries in the late nineteenth and early twentieth centuries indicates this turn toward Protestant critical works, even as they at times reject the conclusions. For instance, William Addis' *Catholic Dictionary*, though it does not have an entry on Isaiah, does have one on the "Canon of the Scriptures."

In his introduction to the Prophets in general, Haydock states that "all the sacred writings refer ultimately to him [Jesus], who is the end of the law (Rom 10.4)... Their predictions are the most convincing proof of its divine origin Is. 41.23. They contain many things clear, and others obscure; having, for the most part, a literal and a mystical sense."[57] Furthermore, unlike Challoner, Haydock provides a commentary on Isa 7:14, offering a standard argument in favor of *alma* meaning a virgin, summoning St. Jerome for support.[58] For Isa 9:6–7, he objects to Grotius' translation of "Wonderful, Counsellor, God the Mighty" as "the consulter of the strong God," suggesting that despite Grotius' opposition to non-Trinitarian Socinians, "he too often sides with them."[59] Of Isa 53, Haydock once against assembles the standard, but remarkably brief, statements made by Challoner, Calmet, and Jerome that it is about the Passion of Christ.[60]

Thus Haydock provides a kind of "commentary of commentaries," at times raising minor points of controversy in translation, and in this sense his book was an aid for the English Catholic to get a handle on some exegetical matters. The end result, however, is that, despite its popularity, this can hardly be called a "commentary" in comparison to that of Cheyne or Wordsworth; it is even less so a "theological commentary," for it does little more than repeat traditional doctrine with no significant elaboration. For example, there is the usual predictive aspect of prophecy with scant attention given to figuration. There is some mention of Israel as the figure of the Church;[61] what this means beyond the image of shadow to fulfillment, Haydock provides no elaboration.

This discussion of catechetical literature and popular Catholic commentaries gives a sense of the exegetical state of affairs for most English Catholics. Three themes emerge from this analysis, and on which I give more detail below. First, is the claim that the Bible is a dangerous book, which, if

---

There are some references in this section to the historical critics Gustav Volkmar and Franz Delitzsch, as well as a disapproving note about William Robertson Smith (Addis, *A Catholic Dictionary*, 107–9). There is also the French *Dictionnaire de la Bible* by Fulcran Grégoire Vigouroux (1837–1915), the first secretary of the Pontifical Biblical Commission. Even though the author was not English, the *Dictionnaire* was used by English Catholics and it is remarkable how conversant he is with the critical work of scholars such as Koppe, Eichhorn, Hitzig, Driver, and Duhm (Vigouroux, *Dictionnaire de la Bible*, 946–84). While he disagrees with many of their conclusions, the very fact that *these* commentators are his interlocutors is significant.

57. Haydock, *Haydock's Catholic Family Bible*, 1015.
58. Ibid., 1022.
59. Ibid., 1024.
60. Ibid., 1064–65.
61. E.g., ibid., 1056.

allowed to be the only source of doctrine and subjected to private interpretation, the result would be confusion, division, and splintering into an array of competing doctrinal claims. Protestantism is, in such a view, proof of this claim. Second, Scripture is oriented in what I refer to as a "supportive role" for the dogmatic claims of the Church. That is, there is an exegetical flattening of the text that minimizes figural readings, seeking textual support for doctrine in a way that conceives of Scripture in a rather static mode. Third, the lack of exegetical engagement by English Catholics meant that people such as Leo Haydock, who wanted to provide some exegetical commentary, had no recourse but to consult with Protestant critical work.

CATHOLIC BIBLICAL ENGAGEMENT: THE CASE OF *THE DUBLIN REVIEW*

In what follows, I explore various articles in *The Dublin Review* as a representative journal of English-speaking Catholic attitudes toward Scripture. This journal was a prominent, English Catholic journal that began early in the nineteenth century, and it allows us to trace its responses to events of that time. I continue with the themes I raise in the previous two sections, namely, Scripture's danger, the use of Scripture as a support for ecclesial dogma, and, later in the life of *The Dublin Review*, a move toward reading liberal Protestant modes of exegesis.[62]

The consistent Catholic perspective was that Protestant failure to engage Scripture in a way that maintained orthodoxy was proof that any exegesis, without being linked to the structures of the Catholic Church, results in exegetical and theological confusion. This is a rather rigid following of the Council of Trent's decree that

> no one, relying on his own skill, shall ... presume to interpret the said Scriptures contrary to that sense which holy mother Church,—whose it is to judge of the true sense and

---

62. It is a legitimate question to ask why this recourse was to *liberal* Protestant exegetical strategies. Why not Evangelical? The Evangelical hermeneutical approach was too virulently anti-Catholic. But, more importantly, some Catholics considered Evangelical exegesis an over-simplification of the text to its apologetic function that, on this point, too closely resembles that of Catholicism. While a liberal Protestant like Cheyne also theologically flattens the text, there is no doubt that the force of his historical, linguistic, and philological analysis provides a deep complexity that was liberating for some Catholics. There was also the important point that the liberal deconstruction of the text, and how form and redaction criticism reveal the deep diversity of the sources, shows that the Bible is unreliable on its own. Interpretation therefore necessitates ecclesial guidance.

interpretation of the holy Scriptures,—hath held and doth hold; or even contrary to the unanimous consent of the Fathers; even though such interpretations were never (intended) to be at any time published. . . . And wishing, as it is just, to impose a restraint, in this matter, also on printers . . . [not to] print, without the license of ecclesiastical superiors, the said books of sacred Scripture, and the notes and comments upon them of all person indifferently.[63]

John Sandys-Wunsch argues that the effect was either to choose "between the impossible problem of making the fathers of the church agree among themselves about biblical interpretation or . . . [to accept] an increasing emphasis on the authority of the papacy."[64] The statement by Trent reveals a perspective that regards an unfettered access to the Bible as a dangerous idea, and this sentiment can be seen consistently in the articles of *The Dublin Review*.

The Dublin Review was founded in 1836 by Nicholas Wiseman, Michael Joseph Quin, and Daniel O'Connell. Despite its name, it was situated in London and is therefore representative of English Catholic thought, albeit from a more Ultramontane perspective, given Wiseman's influence. An article in its inaugural issue Renn Dickson Hampden's famous Bampton Lectures of 1832.[65] This lecture incensed both Newman and Pusey as they thought Hampden's lectures argued that there was no doctrine in Scripture, and that "faith" and "creeds" are distinct.[66] The writer in *The Dublin Review* considers Hampden's apparent rejection of the Trinity and the sacraments, among other doctrines, as representative of Protestants who reflect the "strait to which the right of freedom in religious opinion, on the one side, and the exacted submission to subscription on the other, have, by alternate

---

63. Waterworth, *The Canons and Decrees*, 19–20.

64. Sandys-Wunsch, *What Have They Done to the Bible?*, 46.

65. Hampden, *Scholastic Philosophy Considered*.

66. See Turner's account and Newman and Pusey's attempt to block Hampden's accession as Regius Professor of divinity in Turner, *John Henry Newman*, 207–55. Tod Jones lists several of the statements that generated theological furor (Jones, *The Broad Church*, 84–87). Typically, the matter had to do with Dickson's apparent inability to affirm the truth of central Christian doctrines. A classic statement he makes with respect to the Trinity is "the truth itself of the Trinitarian doctrine emerges from these mists of [scholastic] human speculation . . . No one can be more convinced than I am, that there is a real mystery of God revealed in the Christian dispensation . . . But I am fully sensible, that there is a mystery attached to the subject, which is not a mystery of God" (Hampden, *Scholastic Philosophy Considered*, 146). Elsewhere he declares, "Strictly to speak, in the Scripture itself there are no *doctrines*" (ibid., 374).

and repeated blows, driven the theological science of the Establishment."[67] With respect to the Oxford Movement, despite its vitriolic opposition to Hampden, the author of this article sees the Tractarians as "a species of mythological protestantism; which, like the Homeric deities, was invisible save occasionally as a thin vapoury phantasm appearing amidst the turmoil of controversial warfare."[68] Of Protestantism in general, the author offers a final invective:

> if two contending parties arise in the Protestant Church, the one is driven to tax the other with Socinianism, and that other retorts with the accusation of popery. It only confirms what every Catholic must feel, that the rejection of the principle of authority necessarily leads, theoretically at least, to the rejection of all mystery, and so to Socinianism, while its adoption obliges its supporter to reason on principles purely Catholic.[69]

If only the debaters would, muses the author, set aside their antipathy toward "popery" and consider authority rightly, they would come to the Catholic position.

It is remarkable that no mention is made of Scripture in the article, even though much of the criticism of Hampden has to do with his claim about the Bible. Rather, for the *Dublin Review* author, when authority is invoked, it is in the context of the Magisterium. This absence of significant engagement with Scripture is also reflected in an article published in the same volume, *Declaration of the British Catholic Bishops*, which states that although the Church has never "forbidden or discouraged the reading or the circulation of authentic copies of the sacred Scriptures," nonetheless,

> when the reading and the circulation of the Scriptures are urged and recommended as the entire rule of faith, as the sole means by which men are to be brought to the certain and specific knowledge of the doctrine, precepts, and institutions of Christ; and when the Scriptures so read and circulated are left to the interpretation and private judgment of each individual: then such reading, circulation, and interpretation, are forbidden by the Catholic church, because the Catholic church knows that the circulation of the Scriptures, and the interpretation of them by each one's private judgment, was not the sole means ordained by Christ for the communication of the true knowledge

---

67. "The Oxford Controversy," 253. For quite some time, the authors' articles were written anonymously.
68. Ibid., 254.
69. Ibid., 256.

of his law.... The unauthorized reading and circulation of the Scriptures, and the interpretation ... by private judgment, are calculated to lead men to contradictory doctrines on the primary articles of Christian belief ... which cannot be part of the uniform and sublime system of Christianity ....[70]

Two points are noteworthy from this passage that run as common threads throughout Catholic censure against Protestant biblicism. First is the very clear idea that the "right to private judgment" is the *cause* of ecclesial breakdown and its legitimacy must be denied. One can attach many meanings to this term. From the Catholic perspective, it was not *necessarily* individualism that was problematic, but *private* interpretation, the view that either an individual or a group of people can read Scripture, unimpeded by any extrinsic rule. Without the Church providing the correct interpretation and approved translation, the potential result is as many errors and sects as there are readers of the text.

Note also the rejection of the Protestant claim that in Scripture alone is found the "entire rule of faith" and doctrine. While the Tractarians also chafed under what they viewed to be a wooden Protestant doctrine of *sola scriptura*, the Catholic perspective suggests that doctrine can be formed extra-biblically. Therefore, this statement by Catholic bishops asserts a separation between doctrine and Scripture. Since in England, there *was* no official Catholic authority as such to grant an *imprimatur* to new translations and scriptural notes, the effect was to locate Scripture in a more devotional mode without permitting an exegesis that engaged with the theology of the Church.[71] In other words, with the lack of any official Catholic authority in England to provide the guidance needed for interpretation, serious exegetical engagement was not carried out beyond the level of popular devotional literature.

Many articles in subsequent issues of *The Dublin Review* bear out these two points. In an article that praises the work of Maynooth College and defends it against many charges leveled by Protestants,[72] there is the rather terse comment that "many passages of the Old Testament ... which the Protestant practice places, without any disguise of language, in the

---

70. "Declaration of the Catholic Bishops" 270–71.

71. There were the Vicars Apostolic, but England was divided into large sections with very little oversight; their bishoprics were titular, and they were considered bishops *in partibus infidelium*. Vicars Apostolic exist today, such as the Vicariate Apostolic of Alexandria of Egypt, Arabia, and Istanbul, Turkey.

72. Maynooth College was set up in Ireland in order to provide for the education of priests in 1795 because they were unable to receive such education in the universities of that country.

hands of all, without distinction of age or character, are susceptible of, and *have actually suffered*, similar perversion at the hands of the infidel and the blasphemer."[73] In a review of various lectures given by Wiseman, an article briefly argues that his biblical criticism succeeds in fending off that of such people as Griesbach. In Wiseman's hermeneutical approach, he "shows how the principles of this science have been known and applied in the earliest ages of the Church . . . [and] . . . how the progress of this study has conduced to the vindication of the ancient fathers of the Church."[74] The article praises how Wiseman "proceeds to point out the importance of this study in relation to polemical theology."[75] It is noteworthy that it is not even *apologetics* as a form of defense of the faith against unbelievers, but a "polemical" theology that aims to show which church is the true one.

In 1837, *The Dublin Review* examined a lecture given by the Tractarian John Keble, "Primitive Tradition recognized in Holy Scripture." The author of the article is intrigued to consider the views of "a small body of youthful, learned" clergy who "have seized . . . a territory not their own, but of our legitimate possession."[76] The article's central concern is Keble's summary of the relationship between the Church and Scripture. Keble asserts the Church's subordination to Scripture, and that the individual must submit to the authority of the Church in matters of faith and doctrine. Keble's thus attempts to deny the right to private judgment, but also to subsume the Church under the infallible rule of Scripture, so that the Church cannot say anything more than what is in the Bible. Keble, however, does concede a point on which the Catholic reviewer latches. Given that the canon of the New Testament took some time before it was complete, there was a period during which there was a "tradition" that was sufficient for salvation apart from Scripture; this was "the good treasure entrusted to you" of 2 Tim 1:14. The reviewer finds fault in Keble's suggestion that this pre-scriptural *oral* tradition was somehow abrogated by *written* Scripture: "A right clearly conferred, and not limited by, or made dependent on, contingent events, requires a clear abrogation before it ceases. Traditional, authoritative teaching, *was* clearly appointed; the substitution of Scripture *never* was."[77]

What is remarkable about the nature of this discussion, and an indicator of the deeply divisive nature of theological discourse, is that *there is no*

---

73. "Maynooth College," 152. While I select relevant material from *The Dublin Review* to illustrate my point, it should be noted that articles pertaining to Scripture are very rare.

74. "Science and Revealed Religion," 324.

75. Ibid., 323.

76. "The High Church Theory of Dogmatical Authority," 46.

77. Ibid., 51.

mention of a text that the "primitive" Church most certainly had in hand—the Old Testament! One could ask of both Keble *and* his Catholic interlocutors why they seem to omit a discussion of the Old Testament as the Scripture at the time of the "primitive" Church, in which Isaiah already played a prominent doctrinal role. The entire discussion is overshadowed by matters of "authority" and the order of priority between the Church and Scripture.[78] This is one of the central themes of this project: to show that in the fallout of a fractured Church is a focus on competing doctrinal claims—in this case, Church authority vis-à-vis Scripture—and the occlusion of the text itself.

The conclusion of the critic in *The Dublin Review* is therefore predictable: Scripture is not sufficient, neither for historical reasons (there was, in his view, no Scripture in apostolic times) nor for textual ones (nowhere does Scripture argue it is all-sufficient, nor do the early Fathers of the Church). The culprit for the Church of England's woes, ultimately, is the reliance on private scriptural interpretation. The Catholic Church, the author continues, maintains a consistent doctrine *and* tradition, each of which has equal authority.

Warnings against private judgment are constant in *The Dublin Review*. For instance, eight years later, a lengthy article decries how private judgment "has formed one of the most powerful impelling causes of the Romeward progress of [Protestants],"[79] for, in their view, it is essentially equivalent to Rationalism.[80] Another article aims to suggest that the Catholic Church did in fact publish numerous Bibles and polyglots prior to the Reformation and, further, that "in nine-tenths of the European states, no popular version existed when they embraced Protestantism."[81] The fact that many received Protestantism without ever having a Bible highlights the point that "the reading of Scripture, therefore, has not promoted Protestantism."[82] The intimation is that Protestantism is less a biblical reformation of the Church than a heresy that is fundamentally schismatic, leading the faithful astray. Claims to a retrieval of pristine Christianity are false because Protestantism

---

78. This is a particularly salient point—the indispensability of the Old Testament in the formation of Christian doctrine—made in Seitz, *The Character of Christian Scripture*. There was *not* only oral preaching that sustained the early Church; rather, Christ's life, death, and resurrection were seen as carried out "according to the Scriptures" (cf. Rom 16:26, 1 Cor 15:3–4, Luke 24:25–27).

79. "Dewar's German Protestantism," 403.

80. Ibid., 405.

81. "The Bible and the Reformation," 441.

82. Ibid., 449. The author also makes the salient point that, even when there may have been a Bible, many could not read.

has moved away from the age-old practices and ecclesial structures that guarantee its faithfulness.

In an 1838 article on the *Tracts for the Times*, a Catholic perspective is offered on the Oxford Movement and its hopes for renewal in the Anglican Church. The author asks, "Will they succeed in their work? We firmly believe they will; nay, strange to say, we hope so. As to patching up . . . the English Church, it is beyond human power."[83] The Church of England's "foundations" are crumbling under the effect of the Reformation:

> It will be a curious and unexpected result of such mighty convulsions in the religious and political world . . . that the great safeguards of revealed truth should have been pulled down; the stable foundation of divinely appointed regiment in the Church plucked up; rites and ceremonies coeval with christianity abolished; practices come down from the first ages discontinued and discountenanced . . . And yet all this must be called a "godly work of reformation," that same "Reformation" signifying a re-pristination of primitive christianity![84]

What is especially pertinent is the perception that the Reformation was merely the alteration of the rites and ceremonies of the Church. This is the bulwark to which the author clings. In addressing the nature of Catholic "reform" at Trent, the author speaks of amendments to acknowledged laxity in certain "religious practices."[85] There is considerable self-satisfactory sentiment in the author's observation that the Tractarians finally appreciate the importance of ancient Church practice and the damage the Reformation wrought. Some in the Church of England, in this view, are finally coming around to what Catholics have always held to be essential to the faith. In a rare instance when Isaiah is used in such an article, it is employed for rhetorical purposes, and it is only a phrase from Isa 34:11: "the line of confusion, and the stone of emptiness."[86] Many of the articles continue along similar lines, often decrying Protestant insistence on the right to private judgment.[87] The *Dublin Review* contributors are of course astute enough to know that private judgment is in practice rather ephemeral: "it must be plain that this principle extends only to bringing different sects into existence; and that, as soon as they are in being, and have established articles of faith . . . it can

---

83. "Tracts for the Times," 308.
84. Ibid., 309.
85. Ibid., 326.
86. Ibid., 334.
87. See, e.g., "Dr. Honinghaus' Protestant Evidences of Catholicity," 277–301 and "The Philosophy of the Rule of Faith," 273–336.

no longer be allowed by them."[88] Therefore, even Protestants have "popery" of sorts, guiding statements from which one cannot dissent if they wish to remain in the "sect." Catholic "popery" is therefore merely more consistent and open about its stance on ecclesial authority. While Protestants contend that the Pope has arbitrary and tyrannical power, the history of the Church of England, whose head is the monarch, tells of numerous illustrations of equally tyrannical and despotic application of power.[89] No direct engagement with Scripture is offered by the authors of these articles in *The Dublin Review*, however, despite the claim that the Catholic Church is the true "owner" of Scriptures.[90] There is no exegetical meditation of biblical texts and very frequent polemical screed-like writings against Protestants and their religious failures. Equally frequent are articles that defend either the Real Presence of Christ in the Eucharist, the acceptability of praying to saints, or the importance of the Virgin Mary.

Part of the reason for Scripture's danger is its high level of complexity, always at risk in the Catholic mind of engendering erroneous interpretations. While the contributors to *The Dublin Review* hesitate to point out actual biblical contradictions or inaccuracies, they indicate Scripture's inherent opacity:

> Holy Scripture is a book of unfathomable depth, as well as of inexhaustible riches. It is possible that not a single chapter of it has yet been fully explored. A single text is often so many-sided that it reveals meaning beneath meaning, as it is more and more deeply searched. For this reason the mystical interpretation of Holy Scripture has ever been insisted on by Catholic theologians, as well as the literal. But if isolated individuals are to interpret it, they cannot trust themselves to a method of interpretation. . . . . It is the apostolic Church only that can interpret Scripture.[91]

While this is a rich perspective on Scripture, English Catholics rarely carried out this scriptural vision by providing its people with the means to traverse its dangerous waters. Indeed, in the early Church, it was often the case that biblical complexity was the *cause* of biblical commentary, from

---

88. "Arbitrary Power—Popery—Protestantism," 6.

89. Ibid., 31. See also "The Reformation the Result of Tyranny," 1–27, which is directed against the role of the Established Church and the government in its actions against Roman Catholics.

90. A later article states that "those who are alien to the Church have *purloined* the Scriptures. . . . The protestant world can never establish its right to hold, disseminate, or read the Scriptures" ("Christ, the Church, and the Bible," 320–21).

91. "The Philosophy of the Rule of Faith," 317–18.

which new insights were gleaned. Instead, these English Catholic leaders warned people away from the text in light of Protestant error.

When the issue of the Bible is raised in *The Dublin Review*, it is also always in the context of opposing the views of Protestant opponents. One rare case of minor exegesis can be provided. In an article that praises the work of (Catholic) Bishop Kenrick for his translation of the four Gospels, it states that "it is intended to vindicate that Catholic Vulgate, and shew its superiority to the Anglican."[92] It contends that

> if we would only take full possession of scripture, and place it before those who love, or affect to love, it, in its true and catholic light ... we should easily convince our adversaries that ours is the only religion of Scripture, and our inheritance is its interpretation.[93]

The article proceeds to show how Jesus used parables in his teaching, such as that of the sower (Mark 4:3–9). Even in this exegesis, Protestantism is the referent in that the parable shows the dangers of false sects, the weeds in the parable: "Protestantism is essentially Donatist, whether in its high-church theory of branch separation from the trunk, or in its lowest evangelical idea of an invisible elect church."[94] Thus, in this rare instance of actual biblical exegesis, it is performed highly antagonistically.

Thus far, I have followed the discourse of Catholic thought from approximately 1836 and into the next several decades. Two central, interpenetrating themes speak to how English Catholics are inhibited from a deep exegetical engagement with Scripture. First, the Protestant tendency to form numerous sects is proof that Scripture as the sole source of doctrine is a dangerous idea. Second, the idea of a "right" to private judgment is rejected as it is seen to diminish the importance of the visible, authoritative Church, bringing into question the certainty of the historic faith. An unintended but significant result was a paucity of serious biblical engagement. This exegetical dearth finally led to a positive engagement with biblical critics despite official curial proscriptions. The result, strangely, is an approach to Scripture that has some similarity to that of T. K. Cheyne of Chapter 5.

Later articles of *The Dublin Review* begin to wrestle more with the pervasiveness of critical biblical scholarship. In general, it continues to maintain its conservative spirit in the nineteenth century, maintaining that Moses was the author of the Pentateuch and that "inspiration" meant that

---

92. "The Parables of the New Testament," 181.
93. Ibid., 184.
94. Ibid., 203.

God was the author of Scripture, as Trent and Vatican I state.[95] However, in concluding my analysis of *The Dublin Review* articles, an essay in three parts called "The Church and the Bible" stands out for its distinctively new orientation that differs from the conservative stance that is typical of most contributions. These essays were written in response to the encyclical *Providentissimus Deus* and composed by the Catholic scholar Friedrich von Hügel (1852–1925).[96] They are additionally instructive because they refer to Isaiah. Though an Austrian by birth, von Hügel resided in England from the time he was fifteen; he was also viewed by many as a "modernist" and therefore his contributions to *The Dublin Review* can in some ways be seen as a departure from its more conservative roots. He offers a Catholic way to negotiate the rough waters of theological orthodoxy and biblical criticism in the late nineteenth century. Of the article, Burtchaell says that von Hügel "strove to arrange some sort of armistice between pope and scholars."[97] His first article asserts that, with respect to revelation, "the communication of Revelation by God to its minister was, of course, always mental, and never by writing."[98] He agrees with Lessing that Christianity existed prior to the writing of its sacred texts. In other words, he asserts a compatibility between the (liberal) Lessing and Catholic doctrine. The Church rests on more than the Bible; there is a history, a "religion" beyond the boundaries of a written document. And this document is also fully open to be subjected to various critical methods that, for instance, reveal that one synoptic gospel is reliant upon another.[99] Von Hügel does not hesitate to employ the works of "liberal" critics to support his arguments. He contends that "Revelation and a Church are practically identical, but . . . Revelation and Scripture are not; that the former are necessary, the latter but contingent consequences of man's creation. . . . The relations between the necessary Church and contingent Scripture are necessarily twofold, and must ever be kept carefully distinct."[100]

---

95. See, e.g., Howlett, "The Mosaic Authorship of the Pentateuch," 264–81, which criticizes S. R. Driver's account of the formation of the Pentateuch, as well as Van den Biesen, "The Authorship and Composition of the Hexateuch," 40–65.

96. *Providentissimus Deus* was released in 1893 by Pope Leo XIII, and it has to do with the study of the Scriptures. Generally seen as a conservative document, it warns against what it refers to as "Rationalists" emerging from what is a thinly veiled reference to Protestant thinkers.

97. Burtchaell, *Catholic Theories of Biblical Inspiration*, 194.

98. Hügel, "The Church and the Bible," 323.

99. Ibid., 333–36.

100. Hügel, "The Church and the Bible: The Two Stages of Their Interrelation" 306.

Von Hügel's second essay speaks to the nature of the Old Testament and prophecy, in which he refers directly to Isaiah, though relatively briefly. Like Robert Payne Smith, who used the tools of the critics in order to prove the truth of his case, von Hügel takes a rather similar stance, arguing "not as to what the Church . . . rightly claims from direct Catholic believers about [these prophecies], but as to what we can, within the bounds of Theistic principles and of ordinary historical proof . . . [use] as solid arguments in favor of such Christian and Catholic beliefs."[101] He freely quotes from a wide assortment of "modern" interpreters, from Ernest Renan, to William Robertson Smith.

Von Hügel's consistent theme with regard to the Old Testament is that of "development." We may find Christ within the Old Testament, yet it is "defective" since it falls short of Christ.[102] Thus there is a shift away from a kind of "prophetic" mode of time, a non-linear correspondence between events, to the modern conception of cause-and-effect, progress, and development. Using Jesus' parable of the grain of mustard seed he presents this development: "First, the potent seed of Mosaism, and then the blade, so fresh and hopeful, of Prophetism, and then the hard, protective ear of Legalism, and at last the full corn, the Bread of life, Christianity."[103] There is a similarity here to Cheyne; there was Mosaism or Prophetism, or, we could call, in general, various forms of Israelite "religion" that bear glimmers of messianic expectation. Jesus then claimed these prophecies for himself, and Paul continued in these applications. "And the New Testament expressly requires us to find in the Old Testament this slow divine education, not only as to legal matters, that Law which Our Lord Himself has expressly taught us that He came 'to fulfil,' Matthew v. 17. . . . But also as to prophecy, which He came to fulfil in the same sense as He fulfilled the Law."[104] Finally, citing Newman and Alfred Loisy in support, about Isaiah von Hügel states that "catholic scholars are coming to admit . . . a deutero-Isaiah,"[105] though it is doubtful that this was as yet a majority opinion among Catholic scholars at the time. Insofar as the fulfillment of prophecy is concerned, he approvingly offers a long quote from Wellhausen of "the striking fulfilment of some of their predictions concerning the near future,"[106] by which he means a local fulfillment, not directly referring to Christ. From Wellhausen, he also sug-

101. Ibid., 307.
102. Ibid., 312.
103. Ibid.
104. Ibid., 329.
105. Ibid., 321.
106. Ibid., 322.

gests that Deutero-Isaiah emerged to show that Cyrus would not be the final instrument by which Israel would be saved. In this section of the book, there is "the reality, persistence and progressive purification of the Messianic expectation."[107] Like Cheyne, he sees a change in "Israelite religion" (not his term) out of which emerged a hope for a figure who would save them.

How does von Hügel connect the two Testaments together? He borrows from the thought of another non-Catholic liberal scholar, Adolf von Harnack, asserting that Jesus and especially Paul were steeped in rabbinical thought when using the Old Testament. Thus Paul used this mode of reading the Old Testament to develop a theology that incorporated texts such as Isaiah: "Development and economy apply, as to the whole Old Testament, so also to the Messianic prophecies and to their New Testament interpretation."[108] The Old Testament is in this sense a kind of pedagogical instrument used judiciously by Jesus and other New Testament writers:

> And the New Testament expressly requires us to find in the Old Testament this slow divine education, not only as to legal matters, that Law which Our Lord Himself has expressly taught us that He came 'to fulfil,' Matthew v. 17 . . . but also as to prophecy, which He came to fulfil in the same sense as He fulfilled the Law.[109]

The use of Isaiah and other Old Testament prophets was thus "but a sifting and utilising of the religious language of the times, a language simply necessary and legitimate and true in the strict sense and for the limited purpose in which Our Lord and His apostles used it."[110] Note the similarities between Cheyne and von Hügel: although their respective conclusions differ; each draws from an acceptance of a critical approach to the text. For von Hügel, the nature of Scripture is analogous to the two natures of Christ: divine and human, what we saw earlier as the *göttlich-menschlich* model. Therefore,

> the inlitteration of the Spirit is as real in the one case, as the Incarnation of the Son is in the other. Our Lord's body weighed a particular weight on His mother's arm. . . . The Spirit's letter is composed of such and such documents of a definite age and length and literary complexion. In both cases the Faith tells us

---

107. Ibid., 324–25.
108. Ibid., 328.
109. Ibid., 329.
110. Ibid., 331.

that Reason can thus observe and register, and bids Reason to do so as far as possible.[111]

We see support here for Chinnici's bifurcation: there are the words of Scripture *as text*, to which can be applied all the methods of scientific exploration. Then there is *doctrine* that transcends these words, the object of ecclesial theologians. At the end of his last article, von Hügel ends on a personal note, which indicates that it is not primarily the Bible from which doctrine proceeds:

> Only through what I may keep and gain in common with the truly humblest of my fellows, can my soul's ear be won to the divine harmonies of the Spirit in Scripture, and of that "God-gifted organ-voice" of all men, the testimony, teaching and authority of the Catholic Church.[112]

These *Dublin Review* articles reveal that for many decades of the nineteenth century, much is spoken *about* the Bible in English Catholic circles with very little engagement with it. As a result of the inherently divisive nature of Protestantism, funded by the doctrine of individual private judgment, Catholic scholars were discouraged from providing commentaries on the Bible. The conservative statements of the *curia* regarding the dangers of the Bible led to confusion about its nature, generating within Roman Catholicism various competing perspectives. There were ultramontane conservative thinkers like Wiseman who upheld the generally protective attitude. There were at the same time Catholics such as the Cisalpines and liberal Catholic scholars such as von Hügel who were willing to challenge the text without relating it to ecclesial doctrine. Amidst confusion was an impetus to seek for a way to engage Scripture amidst exegetical aridity. And many like von Hügel found a perceived resolution in the thought of Protestant liberal scholars.

In the Catholic context, for liberals and conservatives alike, there is a truth that is somewhere "behind" or "beyond" the text, embodied by the Church. But especially acute in the nineteenth century is the frangible quality of ecclesial definition. These articles give evidence of a hermeneutical parallel with Broad Church thinkers like Cheyne, who see a kind of amorphous religious consciousness behind the text.

---

111. Hügel, "The Church and the Bible (Part 3)," 283.
112. Ibid., 304.

CONCLUSION

This analysis has been rather disparate by necessity, using catechisms, commentaries, and journal articles to explore the ways that division impacts Catholic exegesis of Scripture in England. There are no definitive commentaries on Isaiah in England by Roman Catholics, and therefore I have selected from several sources to illustrate my claims. The data reveal few instances of direct engagement with Scripture, but considerable instances of conflict even within the Church as to the Bible's nature. This arises out of confusion generated by the response of the Church to fissiparous Protestantism that typifies the dangers of unlimited biblical access and the right of private judgment.

The Magisterium, the Vicars Apostolic, and the eventual Bishops in England conceived of the Bible in terms of its dangers to the laity. The Church is not only the ultimate arbiter of doctrinal matters, but the one who pronounces what such doctrines are. Scripture then functions in a kind of supportive, secondary mode, a buttress of doctrinal claims. But it also implies that doctrine resides somewhere "above" the text, guaranteed by an infallible Church. Effectively, exegesis was regarded as superfluous: all necessary doctrines had already been determined. Meanwhile, thinkers like von Hügel grappled with the relation between the Bible, doctrine, and the Church. The reactive nature of the Magisterium created confusion regarding how to respond to the challenges of modern approaches to the text. Since the level of engagement with the Bible was so minimal, thinkers like von Hügel felt it necessary to turn to the critical methods of Protestant liberals. This can also be seen in the work of someone like Leo Haydock, who, albeit in a negative mode, consulted critical Protestant works. Thus there was very little engagement with the biblical text itself, and even less that of Isaiah.

7

Conclusion
The Despair of Ecclesial Biblical Retrieval

BRINGING IT ALL TOGETHER: A LAMENT

THIS PROJECT IS A kind of exegetical genealogy with one central theme: the impact of ecclesial division on the exegesis of Isaiah in the Church of England. The thesis is that the fragmentation of the Church is so profound, and so *theologically* foundational to exegesis in England, that a unitary meaning of "theological exegesis" is rendered incomprehensible. This chapter briefly summarizes the findings of the previous chapters and the way that ecclesial division is *constitutive* of their interpretation. I end with a discussion of more global ecclesial implications, for ecclesial division is just as profound as it is in the Church of England. The "selfhood" of the Church contains within it so many deep self-contradictions that various projects of exegetical retrieval are in a state of "despair," defined in ecclesially-transposed Kierkegaardian language. I cannot here offer a "solution" to the problem of ecclesial despair other than by offering this as a description of the state of the Church's identity.

A secondary but equally important goal of this project is to challenge the "standard" account of modern exegesis in which scientific discoveries and new historical methods present a set of serious oppositions to the reliability of the Bible and to traditional exegesis. This is a subset of the "religion versus science" paradigm that asserts an incompatibility between the two.

The narrative of this book is one in which the vociferous conflicts in the Church over dogma generated modes of reading Scripture that lessened the dogmatic scope of exegesis. These new, methodological, self-consciously non-theological approaches in favor of historical, philological, and other kinds of exegesis set aside theological referents as functionally separate from the text. For instance, even for a conservative exegete like William Day (see Chapter 2), figurative and typological forms of exegesis became reduced to a "secondary" meaning. The engine of ecclesial division began a secularization of exegesis as a distinct task from dogmatic theology. If this conclusion—emerging from my analysis of Isaiah—is correct, then the central issue regarding Scripture and exegesis has less to do with the putative challenges issued by science to the "reliability" of Scripture, and more with the way that Church division brings her relation to Scripture into question. The problem has to do with failed ecclesiology, not with the Bible.

Before presenting a summary of my findings, an important observation must be made: the number of Isaiah commentaries written by people from the Church of England is remarkably sparse. There are virtually no Evangelical Church of England Isaiah commentaries available. For this reason, for Robert Payne Smith, who did not publish a commentary, I could only employ his lectures. Nor was Christopher Wordsworth's commentary written as a result of any particular expertise with Isaiah but was part of a larger biblical commentary. And, there simply were *no* Roman Catholic commentaries on Isaiah in England at the scholarly level. Thus, Cheyne's work on Isaiah is a considerable *tour de force* for someone from the Church of England. But what can we make of this nineteenth-century dearth of engagement by Anglicans with Isaiah in a scholarly mode? I would like to offer three likely reasons from a theological perspective. First, there simply was less interest in the "Jewish" Scriptures at the time, which was a function of prevailing notions of "progressiveness," where humanity had little need for the writings of a "primitive" people. Hermeneutically, this is informed by a form of neo-marcionism that offers a diminished view of the Old Testament in comparison with the New. Second, for Evangelicals and High Church exegetes (both in their eighteenth-century and Tractarian forms), close critical engagement with the Old Testament was minimal precisely because of new, non-English, critical work that was applied to the Old Testament. In the eyes of many in England, this work carried out a destructive agenda directed against what they considered as biblical orthodoxy. Thinkers such as Johann S. Semler (1725–91) and J. D. Michaelis (1717–91) were part of a group of Old Testament exegetes who, "at the turn of the [eighteenth] century... had been brought up Pietists, and both had moved away from Pietism under the influence of English Deism."[1] This avoidance of Isaiah and of the Old Testament in general by more conservative parties was in order to circumvent critical challenges. Finally, historically, Isaiah was considered as a crucial "bridge" between the two Testaments in Christian theology. Yet, with a diminution Old Testament importance also came an equally strong attempt by more conservative elements of the Church to maintain the connection between the two Testaments. Isaiah was seen as central in this apologetic stance. However, many of these same biblical conservatives did little else by way of deeper exegesis. In other words, Isaiah is often *quoted* as a proof text but rarely *commented on* in a deeply theological manner.

My analytic method is based on the claim that the historical roots of the Church of England have a deeply biblical basis, out of which emerge three central themes: (1) the reading of Scripture *in common* within the Church and the Church under the judgment of Scripture; (2) the Bible as constitutive of the *one* Word of God in its entirety; and (3) the christological centrality of biblical interpretation as the key to understanding the Bible. I refer to these themes as comprising the touchstone of Anglican hermeneutics in order to illustrate the ways that various interpreters cohere or diverge from this vision. I also employ the emerging movements of humanism, spiritualist traditions, and skepticism as discursive and categorical aids as kinds of exegetical "tools" of division.

In Chapter 3, Robert Payne Smith presents Isaiah in terms of its apologetic, probative value in ensuring the truth of Christianity. As such, Smith engages in a vigorous attack against those who challenge the prophetic, supernatural essence of the book. In doing so, Smith places himself in an exegetical situation whereby he can only engage in this task in terms defined by his opponents. Smith also employs the tools developed in earlier centuries by irenic exegetes against those who have come to opposite conclusions, *but who employ the same tools.* Thus, whereas the irenic reading was formulated in the seventeenth- and eighteenth-century climates for the purpose of avoiding theologically contentious exegetical matters, Smith *alleges* a clear, rational, and objective reading that accords with Christianity, arguing that supernaturalist presuppositions are the *sine qua non* of proper biblical exegesis. The proof of their success is revealed in the contradictory conclusions of the "negative critics," as opposed to the consistent ones of those with these supernaturalist presuppositions.

Discourse informed by spiritualist traditions marks Smith's exegesis. As regards the Church, there is no way to identify an embodied reality to which Smith refers when he speaks of the Church. Indeed, Smith's prevailing

---

1. Rogerson, *Old Testament Criticism*, 16.

themes relate to the centrality of the individual and the working out of his or her free will. Scripture is not the constitutive bedrock of a *common* ecclesial reality; rather, the Church is incidental to the process of exegesis, and rarely a coherent referent. Part of this is a response to Roman Catholic disparagement of private judgment in matters to do with Scripture. With regard to biblical canonicity, Smith employs modern tools that direct his attention to the Prophet Isaiah *qua* individual literary genius. This exegetically prescinds from a Bible held together in the unity of God's providential ordering of the history to which it bears witness. Moreover, while there is a connection between the two Testaments for Smith, the relation is one of abrogation in which the carnal, outward faith of Israel is subsumed and overcome by the coming of Jesus of Nazareth. But Smith says little that offers a definitive account of the nature of the Church, aside from representing a new spiritual reality that had been at the core of "Jewish" religion, previously enmeshed in outward liturgical practices that no longer have theological significance for true religion. The value of Old Testament exegesis is therefore greatest in its predictive function, leading ineluctably to a form of progressivism, a story of the growth of human spiritual awakening.

In terms of the christological aspect of Smith's exegesis, the elements of evidentiary proof and spiritual references continue to dominate. Christ is certainly an important referent, but only in the context of Isaiah's function of foretelling the future and proving the supernatural, and hence divine, source of the Bible. Deeper typological and figural interpretation, regarded in early Anglicanism as the connective tissue of Scripture, shaped by the figure of Christ, is absent.

Smith's exegesis is therefore intrinsically bound to the reality of a divided Church. It takes on an "antagonistic" form in that he gave these lectures in order to directly oppose new critical challenges to Isaiah. For an Evangelical like Smith, who identifies with a group so committed to the centrality of Scripture, there is no deep theological approach to Isaiah other than in its ability to provide proof to those who disparage it. In doing so, the arguments proposed by his opponents shape the form of his exegesis. Moreover, the Church is minimized in favor of individual, private interpretation, Christ is present only as a purely future referent, and the entire Old Testament is perceived within a supercessionist theology.

In Chapter 4, I turn my attention to Christopher Wordsworth's commentary on Isaiah as an instance of "old" High Church party exegesis, in distinction to that of the Tractarians. The theme that serves as the focus of my analysis, and which is central to understanding the role of ecclesial division in High Church exegesis is the ecclesio-political vision of an "English" Church that powered the vision of Wordsworth. While his confessional commitments are superficially identical to those of Smith, Wordsworth's notion of the "one, holy, catholic Church" is so narrowly focused on the national Church of England that it is difficult to speculate on his conception of "catholic." High Church identity can be seen as shaped by a response to the modern challenge of pluralism. As regards Wordsworth's interpretation of Isaiah, there is the expected vitriolic disparagement of Roman Catholicism, not only because he merely reflects a typical Protestant sentiment, but because of his view that they are distinctly un-English. They are unworthy participants in the Establishment that is to give succor to its Church.

The exegetical impact of this politically-infused reading is a radically different approach to the same texts than that of Robert Payne Smith. There considerably more focus on the Church's concrete particularity, namely, in a nationally established form. Wordsworth sees a biblical parallel between the "national" religion of Israel and that of England, employing Isa 49:23 in the same way as earlier High Church divines. Conversely, however, despite Wordsworth's apparent emulation of the Church Fathers, he has little to say about the text's tropological impact on the believer. Any moral or individual applicative meaning is eclipsed by the centrality of his ecclesial/political concerns.

Where Wordsworth's interpretation bears strong affinities with Robert Payne Smith's is his strongly apologetic mode of exegesis. Like Smith, he appeals to sources that support his theological claims, or he appeals to statements by such ancient figures as Origen and Jerome. While Wordsworth's claims to the unity and canonicity of all of Scripture are made more explicit than Smith's, he frequently resorts to the mere defense of biblical passages of disputed interpretations.

Thomas Kelly Cheyne's exegesis is by most accounts inimical to that of both Smith and Wordsworth, though it too has certain parallels with them. Cheyne's work is the culmination of a religious disposition that employs irenic exegetical tools. This leaves theological matters at the periphery in order to apply the power of this non-dogmatic, irenic exegesis. This led, in later years, to his embrace of the Baha'i faith, which purportedly accepts *all* religions as merely siblings of the same human phenomenon—the most irenic form of ecumenism. Of the three tools of division to invoke, humanism, and skepticism, the latter two best characterize his exegetical influences. This is proven by the fact that almost all of his interpretive strategy is directed at philological matters and historical/textual reconstruction; at the same time, he studiously avoids most theological issues in favor of *religious* ones. That is, Cheyne explores the religious history of Israelite faith, as an instance of a certain anthropological phenomenon. This historical reconstruction is the humanist side of his exegesis, but, more subtly, in response to the skepticism engendered by the perceived failure of dogmatic religion, Cheyne regards his religious orientation of explicit skepticism as the most theologically accurate (and thus certain) form of faith.

It should come as no surprise that Cheyne's exegesis gives virtually no role for the Church, precisely because this entity has failed to provide certainty—indeed, dogmatic commitments only generate strife and division. This ecclesial lacuna generates a new kind of textual mediation, one offered by the professional scholar. There is little room for the personal piety that an individual reading of the Bible entails, and an even stronger dislike of any reference to the tradition of biblical exegesis that accords with the Anglican touchstone. Cheyne is deeply embedded in the Broad Church tradition of reading the Bible that is suspicious of ecclesial, and thus dogmatic, exegesis.

At the same time, Cheyne is theologically reserved, as was often the case with biblical exegetes in nineteenth-century England. There was a well-established bifurcation of biblical commentary between textual/philological analysis and theological interpretation. Cheyne primarily engages in philological and historical reconstruction of the text, with some rare excurses on theological matters, and only explicitly done in an appendix. With regard to the unity of Scripture, Cheyne attempts to maintain a connection, however feeble, between Isaiah and some of the events in the Gospels. There is, however, no significant sense in which Scripture functions theologically as one canon in Cheyne's approach.

Cheyne does not deny that Isaiah is "Christian" Scripture, and, as such, attempts to sketch out the historical referents of the text *and* the religious meaning of the "messianic doctrine" embedded within it. He presents this as an idea that historically emerged as a spark in the religious consciousness of Israel and grew in anticipative power. In purely *historical* terms, therefore, it is perfectly acceptable to read certain passages as "messianic prophecies," namely, expressions of the expectation of Israelite religion and politics. In Cheyne's reconstruction, this religious idea is concomitant with the notion that Israelite prophets were heralds of monotheism as a new religious orientation.

When Cheyne speaks directly to a "Christian" reading of Isaiah, this is the closest he comes to a christological reading of Scripture. In many ways, Cheyne's own dogmatic commitments have moved so far from the Anglican touchstone that the term "christological" has almost no theological meaning. Nonetheless, he wants to defend the Christian faith and rejects claims that he is one of the "negative critics" against whom Robert Payne Smith contends. In point of fact, he is just as committed to an apologetic stance as

Smith, though for Cheyne, he wants to update Christian theology to be in accord with modern academic assumptions about history, texts, and science. In christological terms, Cheyne certainly does not want to *deny* that there is room within Isaiah to permit some form of Christian understanding of the text. But the nature of this is highly abstract; he refers to any non-historical, "religious" referent as a "mysterious *x*."[2] Thus, while such a christological hermeneutic was necessary in early Anglican biblical theology, for Cheyne and his colleagues, it is secondary, even only a mere *possibility*.

Chapter 6 examines the state of Roman Catholic exegesis in England. All Protestant parties (though not necessarily all individuals of these parties) regarded Roman Catholics as the epitome of "priestcraft," superstition, and the heretical development of non-biblical theological doctrine. Given these accusations, it is necessary to outline the exegetical path that English Roman Catholicism follows in the nineteenth century.

Roman Catholic exegesis, in its response to Protestant polemics, is an equally acerbic discourse. Much Roman Catholic literature derides the vapidity of a reliance on the Bible alone as the source of doctrine and the ecclesial life. As a counter to the Protestant insistence on biblical sufficiency, English Roman Catholics resort to practicing a wooden ecclesial reading that is as equally lacking in its richness and textual inter-connectivity as its Anglican counterparts. Emerging from this polemical context is a reading that has little resemblance to classic Western exegesis from Origen through to the Middle Ages. In other words, because of Protestant focus on Scripture, Roman Catholicism distances itself from deep scriptural interpretation. Left in the hands of the laity, the Bible is a dangerous book, generative of schism, heresy, and confusion. In the specifically English case, much Roman Catholic exegesis functions with a somewhat sectarian mindset, in a kind of siege mentality. Thus, in addition to the educational limitations imposed on them, English Roman Catholics produced few significant commentaries on Scripture.

I present the Catholic perspective in terms of the Bible's *danger* and its *insufficiency* for faith without the Church providing the role as sole protector and interpreter. Much of the Catholic approach ignores the Bible. Controversies occur at a high level, namely, around concepts such as biblical sufficiency and the right of private judgment rather than direct engagement with the text itself. I consider how the Catholic journal *The Dublin Review*, catechetical devotional literature, and the specific case of the *Haydock Bible Commentary* address the Bible and its exegesis. The clearest factor for which

---

2. Cheyne, *The Prophecies of Isaiah*, 2:204.

many Roman Catholic polemics strive, almost painfully, is to offer certainty in Mother Church.

My construal points out a parallel between Broad Church biblical engagement and that of English Roman Catholics. The Broad Church's search for certainty by engaging the tools initiated by irenicism, led exegetes such as Cheyne to minimize or "flatten" Scripture in order to extract historical data. Scripture's relation to dogmatic claims by the Christian faith is minimal. Similarly, English Catholicism assumes that the Church embodies a perfect correlation with the theological intent of Scripture. Therefore, the Bible becomes a kind of relic to be left behind, as the Church is the sufficient pedagogue. This conclusion, however, is one I make as an inference of what is said in their literature and the dearth of biblical engagement. It would certainly not be an explicit claim that any Roman Catholic would make, nor would Cheyne claim that his exegetical practice was "untheological."

THE CHURCH OF ENGLAND: A PARABLE OF THE CHURCH CATHOLIC?

After having spent the bulk of this book analyzing very specific instances of Isaiah's interpretation, is it possible to begin a process of turning our analytical lenses to more analysis of the Church as a whole? Can we begin to consider what it means to engage in the process of exegesis in the midst of the *current* reality of a divided Church?

This attempt is a brief foray, a tentative step that can only intimate the potential for further consideration. I begin this step by using Origen's exegesis of Ezek 16 to indicate an exegetical approach to Scripture that is absent from modern purview, namely, a view that God's judgment rests on a divided Church, just as it did on a divided Israel. This takes into account several features that were missing from almost all the exegetes in the previous chapters. First, the Church is spiritually coupled with the notion of Israel; but the concept of "spiritual" in this case is not in opposition to "carnal" Israel. Second, there was a definitive understanding of what "the Church" meant at the time of Origen. This was a historical context when it was not generally conceivable that there were many separate "churches" to challenge catholicity. Third, the text can have numerous referents, what I refer to elsewhere as the textual *fecundity*—christologically shaped—whereby the meaning is not exhausted when an interpretation is offered.

In this chapter I also use Kierkegaard's and his concept of *despair* as applied to an individual who is unable to integrate the disparate facets of the whole self, transposed in terms of an *ecclesial self*. By a brief examination of some current attempts at an ecclesial retrieval of the Bible, I suggest that they are, at bottom, projects of resignation and ecclesial despair. By way of Reinhard Hütter's concept of pathos and suffering, I suggest that the beginning of a solution to exegesis in a rent Church is to *suffer* the divine text.

Origen (c.184–c.253) was one of the most influential exegetical figures in Christian antiquity and this influence is particularly notable in his use of figuralism and typology. Origen's application of these exegetical and theological tools can be seen by examining his sermons on Ezekiel. Consider Ezek 16, which speaks of Jerusalem as a harlot. The prophet uses striking imagery; in verse 25 he writes, "You ... degraded your beauty, spreading your legs with increasing promiscuity to anyone who passed by." It is perhaps not surprising that this passage is rarely addressed in sermons today.[3] In the eighteenth century, John Wesley's *Explanatory Notes Upon the Old Testament* interprets "Jerusalem" of v. 1 to be "the whole race of the Jews."[4] Given our experience with much English thought, few would have disagrees with this interpretation. Not so with Origen; on the one hand, he knows that Ezekiel *qua* individual prophet *meant* to refer to the Jewish people. He therefore affirms the historical referents of the texts. Yet, on the other hand, there is not a theological "mysterious *x*" for Origen that hovers above this "historical" interpretation, whereby the literal or historical is "set aside." Origen states that "we should know that everything that is said about Jerusalem applies to all people in the church."[5] He connects this to Jesus' weeping over Jerusalem in Luke 20, saying, "If [Jesus] had reason to weep over Jerusalem, he will have much more reason to weep over the church, built to be a house of prayer but become, through shameful greed and luxury of some (and are not leaders of the people among them?!) a den of thieves."[6] And while Origen continues to speak, as does Ezekiel, of Jerusalem as a whore, in his mind he maintains that the Church is also part

---

3. The fact that the Revised Common Lectionary leaves out this verse indicates that sections of the Bible are too "problematic" for modern ears. E.g., with respect to the incestuous rape of Tamar by her half-brother, see Knetsch, "Tamar's Tale," 33–48.

4. Wesley, *Explanatory Notes Upon the Old Testament*, 2318.

5. Balthasar, *Origen, Spirit and Fire*, 161.

6. Ibid., 159

of the textual referent. For Origen, the Church is at once the perfect bride of the Apocalypse, yet also beset by sinners from within its own boundaries. Of these people, it is therefore "give[n] the name 'church' to this whole mixture of just and unjust."[7] For Origen, there is only one Church; there indeed may be "factions" within this Church —even sinners who misinterpret the Scriptures. But there are not numerous "churches"—the *one* Church is under God's judgment. Origen, because of his hermeneutical orientation, can utilize such "obscure" passages as Ezek 16 and exegetically affirm the reality of a *corpus permixtum*, not the *multa corpora*, so facilely regarded as acceptable since the Reformation.

Origen's notion of Scripture's judgment on the body of the Church is an interpretive approach to Old Testament exegesis that is missing from all exegetes in this book—except Nehemiah Rogers. This lack is equally true for those whose agenda is either to retrieve patristic interpretation (e.g., Wordsworth and the Roman Catholic tradition) and those who regard themselves as the true inheritors of Reformation principles (e.g., Robert Payne Smith and Thomas Kelly Cheyne.) For the former, the problem is resolved either, as in the case of Roman Catholicism, by a forceful and repetitive claim that there has only ever been one Church, or a complete disengagement with the reality of numerous competing ecclesial bodies, as with the old High Church party. In the case of the latter, Smith "spiritualizes" the Church to such an extent that its concrete "incarnation" in the world is almost imperceptible. And for Cheyne, it must be said rather perfunctorily that he has no concern with the Church as such.

Recall from Chapter 2 that Nehemiah Rogers' *Song of the Vineyard* is the only exegesis of Isaiah that employs a robust ecclesial reading in which the Church itself comes under the judgment of the Bible—a necessary but often ignored corollary of the Protestant principle of *sola scriptura*. Indeed, as I have shown with Origen, this is not only a Protestant interpretive principle, for God's judgment on the Church was an important part of Origen's interpretation. Rogers is not merely participating in a project of retrieval (as I suggest Wordsworth is), but stands within a larger "reform" tradition, in which the Church of England was a part. Origen, too, was engaged in his own attempt at "reform" in his interpretation of Scripture.

After Origen, but before the Reformation, amidst warring states and a powerful Church, this exegesis of judgment was rare, though not entirely absent. In the early thirteenth century, Francis of Assisi (1181–1226), despite his dedication to obeying ecclesial authorities, saw the form of Jesus' life as given not just in its material poverty, but as the poverty taken on by

---

7. Ibid., 158.

the Word made flesh; he regarded this as the example, biblically informed, that he and his followers were to emulate.[8] This was a call for ecclesial reform, a turn toward the enfleshed Word who himself lived in poverty. In other words, despite Francis' obedience to Church authority, Scripture, for him, critiqued a Church that had moved away from the One who gives it its body and which is also the figural embodiment of that same One. A little over a hundred years later came John Wycliffe (1328–84), whose opposition to the Church was more brazen. He had several theological concerns, but much of his agitation was directed against the papacy's failure to serve the laity. He thought that the Church should not be a monetarily rich entity holding temporal power.

These are rather fleeting instances in which the Bible is interpreted as pronouncing judgment on the Church. It was not until the Reformation that this notion was revived. Yet this often devolved into a form of judgment against one part of the Church—the Roman Catholic Church, or the radical reformers, and vice versa. The common Protestant recourse was to avoid concrete ecclesial definition in favor of an "invisible" Church. In doing so, there is little influence that this Origenist aspect of scriptural ecclesial judgment can have on the Church body as a whole, as it is explicitly divided into the true, "invisible," Church, or an ill-defined conglomerate of opposing factions. The early scriptural vision of the Church of England maintains the hermeneutical tradition of Origen, Francis, and Wycliffe. This tradition in Anglicanism is less explicit than Origen's claim of ecclesial whoredom, but I suggest that it can be found, for instance in Article 20 of the Prayer Book:

> The Church hath power to decree Rites or Ceremonies, and authority in Controversies of Faith: and yet it is not lawful for the Church to ordain any thing that is contrary to God`s Word written, neither may it so expound one place of Scripture, that it be repugnant to another. Wherefore, although the Church be a witness and a keeper of Holy Writ, yet, as it ought not to decree any thing against the same, so besides the same ought it not to enforce any thing to be believed for necessity of Salvation.

The Church is thus not only the "keeper of Holy Writ," but also subjected to it. As William Covell (*d.* 1613) says in his commentary on Hooker's doctrine of Scripture in 1603:

> Touching therefore the authoritie of the Church, and the scriptures ... we say, that we are taught to receive it, from the authoritie of the Church; we see her judgment; we heare her voice;

---

8. Thompson, *Francis of Assisi*, 86.

> and in humilitie subscribe unto all this; ever acknowledging the Scriptures to direct the Church, and yet the Church to afoord (as she is bound) her true testimony to the Scripture.[9]

Unfortunately, the overwhelming pressures of ecclesial division from the Puritans and other movements curtailed the hermeneutical force of this aspect of exegesis in the confusion of competing theological and exegetical claims.

While this has been a highly specific book in that it considers only the exegetical works of Anglicans in England—and primarily those of Isaiah—I suggest that what we find is an indication of the problematic nature of maintaining a cohesive Christian exegetical vision since the Reformation. The Church of England's reception history of Isaiah serves, *mutatis mutandis* and *ceteris paribus*, as a kind of parable for the state of biblical exegesis up to the twenty-first century. Theological *cohesiveness* is lacking, which is to say, a stable theological understanding of what the Bible *is*, its ontological location within the economy of God's providential ordering of history. Indeed, in a riven Church, this is not possible. I am not arguing for normative uniformity of exegesis—such a thing has never existed. But this lack of cohesiveness is tethered to ecclesial division. With this in mind—that the "ecclesial self" is a non-integrated entity—I invoke, for the purpose of illustration, Kierkegaard's concept of despair as applied to various contemporary projects of connecting Scripture to the Church. This comprises publications by Matthew Levering, Christian Smith, Robert A. Oden, Roland Boer, and Stephen Fowl.

Despite their laudable contributions, recent exegetical efforts that outline various solutions to the problem of theological exegesis, in my construal, function within the *despair* of the ecclesial self. Indeed, they can be nothing but projects of despair. To be in despair within the context of the ecclesial self, and in reference to biblical exegesis, means to work as a conflicted self, offering theories of reading Scripture that cannot resolve the non-integrated self of the Church. The primary reason for this is a lack of serious recognition that a crucial element of the Church's identity is Scripture, and if this identity is limned in confusion, then so is exegesis.

There are many attempts to offer a solution to the difficulty of holding together the exegetical reality of bifurcation into textual analysis and theological extraction. They often have to do with "recovery" projects that locate the Bible in its "proper" theological/ecclesial location. I argue, however, that the Church must live in the mode of *suffering*, which is to learn to endure, to live within the text and under its judgment. To be in this mode is a way

---

9. Covell, *A Iust and Temperate Defence*, 33–34.

of *being-in-the-world* (that is, a *way* of being; this is not an ontological statement per se) rather than a grasping at new exegetical methods that cannot hold together the divided ecclesial self.

I borrow the distinction between *despair* and *suffering* from the Kierkegaardian tradition, especially as he uses them in *Fear and Trembling* and *The Sickness Unto Death*. The dilemma that Kierkegaard addresses is the disjunction between universal principles of reason that can be *known* and the individual who must come to know these things in a particular way. For Kierkegaard, the self is "a relationship to the juxtaposed 'contradictory factors' of finite and infinite, temporal and eternal, necessity and freedom."[10] This particularly modern problem sees the self unable to hold together these contradictory factors. The result is that every individual is in despair, unless he or she can succeed, like Abraham in his response to the ultimate call to sacrifice his son Isaac, to become a "knight of faith."[11] Despair is a state in which the self is unassimilated, incomplete. Yet, there is no doubt that Abraham *suffered* in his struggle to "suspend the ethical" and follow God's call.

With respect to the Bible, there is a kind of ecclesial existential crisis and my intent is to give more meaning to the term *despair* than a state of mind; rather, despair characterizes the whole exegetical process. Indeed, it is quite an obvious fact that a divided Church is, in general, in a state of universal despair, as her component members cannot be theologically integrated. When Kierkegaard says that *everyone* (except the "true" Christian) exists in a state of despair, he does not speak of a *feeling*, that everyone subjectively experiences a loss of hope or direction in life, but that, even in the midst of (counterfeit) happiness, their *existence* is in a state of despair. When the Church was a true "self"—when its referent was to a singular body—it suffered, but it was not in despair.

In terms of *suffering*, I employ the thought of Reinhard Hütter in his book *Suffering Divine Things*. Here is a more constructive vision of the Church in which he describes its *pathos*:

> Christian faith under the conditions of modernity experiences itself in a two-fold difference: on the one hand in the context of the split in Western Christendom, and on the other with respect to a modernity that understands itself to be post-Christian. This double difference makes ecclesiological self-reflection necessary in a way quite unknown to pre-Reformation Christianity. . . . Theology has two choices. It can continue to take its orientation largely from a comprehensive concept of reason . . . Or theology

---

10. Mooney, *Knights of Faith and Resignation*, 69.
11. Kierkegaard, *The Sickness Unto Death*, 32–33.

can understand itself directly and explicitly as "poesis," that is, a "construction," its creator being the religious subject who within the framework of its theological constructions conceptualizes certain ... religious experiences and makes these experiences communicable.... The other alternative would be *explicitly pneumatological* as well as *ecclesiological* prolegomena to Christian theology ... a development of the pathos that makes Christian theology plausible as a distinct Church practice.[12]

Elsewhere, Hütter defines pathos as "'suffering, undergoing' as opposed to 'doing.' ... The reference is ... to the 'other' of action, that which determines or defines a person prior to all action, in all action, and against all action, that which only a person can *receive*."[13] Referencing Martin Luther, Hütter shows that this reception, this undergoing of the action of another, is the *hearing* that is faith, the hearing of "the word."[14] Hütter's scope is larger than that of biblical exegesis, but I would like to work within the mode of what I call the ecclesial call to the suffering of Scripture as its primary *poesis*. The Church must *suffer* the divine word spoken in order to commence a move out of the enigma of despair, in which the ecclesial self is fragmented into opposing corporeal shards.

The following considers recent theological efforts that pertain to Scripture and the Church, indicating how each works in the mode of despair by not sufficiently holding together the various interpretive elements sufficiently. The Church is in most cases an indefinable quantity, and therefore these models *resign* themselves to division as a norm. In so doing they ultimately fail to articulate an integrated ecclesial self, because such a self does not exist. I begin with a book intended for a popular audience written by Christian Smith, written from an Evangelical Protestant perspective. He notes that the central Protestant claim to *sola scriptura* often leads to an untenable position of "biblicism." This runs from the absurd to the more serious reality that out of a staunch biblicism emerges "the problem of interpretive pluralism."[15] At the end of his book, Smith suggests a more robust model for a "true" Evangelical reading of the Bible. He suggests that there must be a new "christological key" to understanding Scripture whereby "a Christocentric reading of the Bible ... simply says that all topics both

---

12. Hütter, *Suffering Divine Things*, 22–23.
13. Ibid., 29–30.
14. Ibid., 31.
15. Smith, *The Bible Made Impossible*, 16–26.

addressed in the Bible and not must be read and considered through the logic of the gospel of Jesus Christ."[16]

What, however, of the Church? Who are the readers, and in what context is Scripture read in this christological key? This "christological key" is certainly not a new one, as it is constitutive of early Anglican exegesis, which should be clear from my analysis in this book. The very fact that Smith needs to assert this reading in the midst of the Evangelical community who identifies with the proclamation of the *euangelion* of Jesus Christ is itself indicative that something is deeply problematic with the state of exegesis.

Christian Smith cannot be read apart from his follow-up book, *How to Go from Being a Good Evangelical to a Committed Catholic in Ninety-Five Difficult Steps*. No longer does Smith argue for Evangelicalism, but for the virtues of Roman Catholicism. He recognizes the pitfalls of interpretive plurality that obtain in the Protestant tradition. Smith believes that the "security" found in modern Evangelicalism betrays a feeling that it is "flat, even empty, about supposedly having it all figured out."[17] A sense of mystery attracted him to the Catholic tradition (and its lack in Protestantism that drove him away). Smith explicitly rejects the objection that he is merely exchanging one form of certainty for another—biblical inerrancy for an infallible Church. I am therefore not about to argue that Smith's arguments directly parallel those of Roman Catholics in nineteenth century England. However, it is curious that in one of his "steps" he mentions that there are indications that the Great East-West Schism of 1054 will be overcome and result in "a genuinely global catholic communion," and later refers to the breaking apart of the Anglican Communion.[18] But more importantly, his central concerns have to do with the nature of the Church and the personal struggle he went through—*yet Scripture does not figure prominently in his discussion*. One of the few points when Scripture exerts its power on Smith is when he reads passages that warn against division:

> Something or other hits you that makes you notice in a new way how thoroughly and deeply the visible Christian church is divided.... Scores of biblical passages calling for Christian unity and harmony and condemning church division and schism start coming to mind (e.g., Rom 15:5–6, 16:17; 1 Cor 1:10–13, 3:3–4, 11:18–19, 12:12–26; Eph 4:2; Phil 2:2,14, 4:1; 1 Pet 3:8, 2; 2 Tim 2:23–24.)[19]

16. Ibid., 103.
17. Smith, *How to Go*, 35.
18. Ibid., 163, 181.
19. Ibid., 28.

The suggestion in this passage is that a turn toward Rome is one toward Christian unity and harmony. However, the unity Smith achieves is merely a nominal one. It essentially resorts to a claim that Catholicism obeys Scripture more than any other ecclesial community. However, is not ecclesial pathos also a requirement for Roman Catholics? While cataloguing the suffering he endured under Protestant absurdities, does a move toward the Catholic Church avoid God's Word spoken to a Church under judgment? I suggest that Smith instantiates a move from one state of ecclesial despair to another in the sense that he avoids the apparent absurdities of Protestantism by a retreat to another ecclesial form in which the disintegration of the Church is less apparent—or it is essentially ignored. Yet the reality of the broken body remains. Exegetically, the tradition remains within Catholicism that this Church most closely corresponds to the biblical model of Church. That is, Catholic doctrine is the same as that intended by Christ and Scripture. This, however, is no different than the claims of a host of other Protestant "sects." It is almost always the case today that a new denomination forms with the intent of better representing the "true" form of Christ's Church.

A more direct approach to exegesis is *Participatory Biblical Exegesis* by Roman Catholic scholar Matthew Levering. I consider this in dialogue with Protestant Stephen E. Fowl's *Engaging Scripture*. Both suggest a "way" to read the Scriptures as a response to the domination of the historical-critical method in the academy that leaves out the uniquely Christian guidelines that historically played such an important role. Levering asks a question that goes to the heart of the matter: "what happens to the texts of Scripture when read through the lens of the synagogue or the Church, rather than solely through the perspectives of the academy?"[20] Indeed, this is what this book explores, but I consider this reading in terms of discontinuous refractions through a broken lens.

Fowl's answer is that "scriptural interpretation should shape and be shaped by the convictions, practices, and concerns of Christian communities as part of their ongoing struggle to live and worship faithfully before God."[21] Levering's analysis of Fowl's work goes to the root of the problem: "Fowl cannot identify any actual Christian communion that possesses . . . the ability to read Scripture authoritatively as a Church."[22] Indeed, it is only in a footnote that Fowl directly addresses the issue of what he interchangeably refers to as the Church and the "Christian community." He says,

---

20. Levering, *Participatory Biblical Exegesis*, 90.
21. Fowl, *Engaging Scripture*, 62.
22. Levering, *Participatory Biblical Exegesis*, 130.

> I am not ... willing to make global judgments about any particular type of group. Using the phrase "Christian community" both allows me to include the church and allows for the possibility of considering a wide range of groupings that might not be strictly churches, but still manifest the relevant communal characteristics to find my arguments of value.[23]

With respect to the relation between the individual and the Church, Fowl wishes for some kind of authority invested in the Church as this interpretive community. But he does not—and in the terms he has set out, *cannot*—speak of the relation between the Bible and this Church/community. This is the greatest weakness of his argument, for the Church in Fowl's account is a disembodied self, an amalgam of communities, many of whom, he neglects to seriously consider, read the Bible antagonistically against each other. He attempts concrete specificity in interpretation, but it is hard, ultimately, to consider Fowl's proposals as anything but merely methodological ones, resigned to the "universal." This is the kind of despair, therefore, in which Fowl struggles, namely, to deny the Church its identity in terms of its concrete particularity with respect to biblical exegesis.

Levering also offers a salve for the destructive effects of the historical-critical method. In his "participatory" approach, his is, more than Fowl's, a "retrieval" project in favor of "patristic-medieval exegetical practice."[24] A "truly ecclesial biblical interpretation" is by the "Spirit-constituted Church."[25] In Levering's case, given his frequent choice of exegetes (e.g., Thomas Aquinas, Henri de Lubac) and his interaction with the Pontifical Biblical Commission, he clearly intends that the ideally constituted Church is the Roman one, though he does not say so explicitly. As with Fowl, Levering's most revealing statement on the Church is in his engagement with some of the work of N. T. Wright in a footnote. He approvingly cites Wright's support for the communal context of interpretation but critiques his assertion of the necessity of teaching by "the church's accredited leaders." Levering responds, "Who accredits them, how do they receive this accreditation, and what does their accredited status mean for the practice of cruciform obedience ... in the Church?"[26] No Protestant-in-general can answer these questions, but they are, of course, very clearly addressed in the Roman Catholic tradition.

But more importantly, Levering's retrieval project disregards the Origenist interpretive tradition. What if the Church herself *cannot* actively

---

23. Fowl, *Engaging Scripture*, 2.
24. Levering, *Participatory Biblical Exegesis*, 148.
25. Ibid., 138.
26. Ibid., 255.

participate in God's economy because of its riven body? Thus, cruciform obedience would need to be cast in terms of *suffering* the divine judgment on the people of God. There is no definable Church that can act as an agent in this figural history, except only as shaped by the state of Christ's body on Holy Saturday, or the people of Israel in Babylon. Both Fowl and Levering see a fitness between the Church as presently constituted and the exegetical outputs that emerge from it, but this fitness is far from clear. Thus, Levering and Fowl exemplify *despair* in the sense that the account they offer no stable, or integrated, underlying ecclesial structure, or self. Both assert exegetical practices carried out by a non-integrated agent.

There are other retrieval projects of a sort from the "non-orthodox" side. In such cases, resignation to the irretrievable quality of the ecclesial self results in wresting the Bible away from the perceived strictures placed on *any* sense of ecclesial reading; often this is reminiscent of Cheyne's approach. For instance, consider *Rescuing the Bible* by Roland Boer. His position becomes clear when we discover from *whom* the Bible is to be rescued, namely, "from the clutches of the religious and political right, its most systemic abusers."[27] In its place, Boer argues for a "new secularism" in which "religion and secularism are entwined like two strands of a rope. . . . This is to the benefit of both."[28] Boer's work is indeed a "manifesto," self-consciously in the Marxist tradition. Though his sights are fixed on right-wing American political abuses of the Bible, he has no interest in considering any positive role for the Church. The Church is only a hindrance to the revolutionary power of Scripture. A similar work, *The Bible Without Theology* by Robert A. Oden, is likewise highly critical of the history of interpretation in which theology plays a central role. He argues that

> theologically governed biblical scholarship wishes to imply that what makes Israel's religion unique is . . . the presence of revelation—of divine guidance that is subtle, complex, and often almost hidden but that remain unexampled. . . . Hence comparative religion in the instance of the religion of the Hebrew Bible is strictly speaking impossible . . . A whole range of potential historical and comparative questions is at the outset so removed by the theological tradition that questions at the center of a variety of academic disciplines . . . go unasked.[29]

---

27. Boer, *Rescuing the Bible*, 1.
28. Ibid., 23.
29. Oden, *The Bible Without Theology*, 154–55.

Oden's worry is that the "theological tradition" suppresses an authentically academic reading of Scripture—a comparative-religion or history-of-religions orientation.

Boer and Oden resemble Cheyne in their disparagement of the role of the Church or of a interpretive theological tradition; it is not a disparagement of "religion" itself. They both engage in "rescue" projects, not just to wrest Scripture out of the clutches of an irresponsible Church, but to generate new projects for recovering its "true" meaning. For Boer, it is a new alliance between the secular and the religious; for Oden, it is a Bible free from theology. There is no end to this generation of new projects; from Levering to Oden, all have their roots in the historical process and exegetical habits in which the role of Scripture inexorably becomes highly contested in a fissiparous Church. This project shows how deeply this confusion is rooted in the theological divisions of the sixteenth and seventeenth centuries.

I am suggesting that *all* exegetical projects reside in the existential state of despair because of the dismantling of the ecclesial self by the theologically divisive struggles. I should make it clear that I am not fundamentally pointing to the fact that there are numerous disagreements between believers. Rather, the *historical roots* of theological antagonism have generated the exegetical "traditions" of irenic, philological, apologetic, and outright antagonistic exegesis that have intrinsically shaped the nature of the exegetical task. These methodological developments eclipse historically deeper theological modes of exegesis.

A tentative step toward addressing this problem is to seek out a new existence for the Church, the direction of pathos, of *suffering the divine text*. For the Word of Christ, present within the very words of Scripture, speak words to his unfaithful people, to whom he says "the idols among the smooth stones of the ravines are your portion; indeed, they are your lot" (Isa 57:6). I suggest, perhaps ominously, that the Quest for Methodology, the minimization of theological meaning within the text that hides the presence of the Word spoken, is "the portion," "the lot," of the present Church. Theological thought perhaps needs to reconsider the distinction between the *ecclesia militans* and *triumphans*, and revive the concept of the third notion of the Church, the *ecclesia penitens*, traditionally denoting suffering Christians in Purgatory. Or, to avoid altering this traditional definition, I suggest *ecclesia passione* as it evokes the image of the Passion of Christ, the One who was broken, whose very body, like the Church, lay dead at the hands of his own people.

This book has no claim on a solution to the loss of the ecclesial "self" and its attendant exegetical quandaries. Yet I suggest that the Church (by whatever definition) needs to subject itself to a kind of *epoché*, that is, a kind of suspension of *poesis* in the mode of devising new methodological solutions to exegetical disparity. Of new methodological approaches there is no end, yet the call of Luther to *oratio*, *meditatio*, and *tentatio* with respect to Scripture remains an imperative. This is another way of saying that the Church undergoes the pathos of a text that presents the Church today with a great question mark. If we follow Origen's exegesis of Ezekiel, which describes the unfaithful spouse as a figure of the Church, then this question mark etched on the Church is one of identity. When most Churches every week throughout the world proclaim the notion of a "catholic" Church in the Apostles' Creed, the problem is not just that there is no longer any consistency in the definition of the term: it is either rendered incomprehensible, or comprehensible only in the terms defined by that particular community.

On these matters, I digress into areas of pure ecclesiology rather than exegesis, but the two are inextricably linked. For now, the answer to the question that Scripture directs to the Church eludes her. Neither can I provide one, other than to suggest that the implications of this project are that the exegetical task is currently one of despair. A kind of "therapy" for the Church (if I remain in a Kierkegaardian/psychological mode) is an acceptance that the Church and theological exegesis are currently in a mode of despair—the first step of repentance. A way out is not to seek "new" exegetical strategies, but to find a way to live under the text, to simply read Scripture and enjoin the Church to endure the Word spoken to it.

The problem of ecclesiological division is not the same as the issue of *pluralism*. The Church has historically dealt with cultural and even theological differences, at times successfully and at other times with great failure. The Eastern Rite of the Roman Catholic Church permits clergy to marry, and England itself, at the time of Augustine of Canterbury, was permitted liturgical leeway. *Pluralism* is not the same phenomenon as *division*. Despite a surge of interest in ecumenism, the fact remains that not only does a great deal of intransigence remain on all sides of various theological debates; the shape of our discourse, exegetical tools, acceptable modes of logic, and even culture itself—that is, what we call *modernity*—is the product of centuries of division. This is part of the story I have told in this book. This is not one of a Church beset on all sides by the rise of the New Science. Indeed, the works of Newton, Darwin, *et. al.* would not have been perceived to be nearly as threatening as they had, if the context in which this discourse was carried out has not been so inflammatory.[30] The Quest for Certainty, the search for new methodologies, the emergence of protestant poetics, philology,

---

30. This is also the contention of Brad S. Gregory in his magisterial, though more general work in comparison to mine, Gregory, *The Unintended Reformation*.

the minimization of prophetic referents, and a strict dichotomy between "natural" and "supernatural" categories all emerge out of a swiftly splitting Church struggling with her own identity. Modernity did not "happen" to the Church; the Church is a fundamental part of the history of the West. Nor is it that one can make a univocal assertion that the Reformation "caused" modernity: historical causation is notoriously problematic concept, as human affairs are complex and multifaceted. It would be an error, therefore, to overstate my case and claim that a divided Church is the singular agent in the rise of new scholarly readings of the Bible. I am not unearthing a secret historical fact that is key to uncovering a new, revisionist history of the Reformation. There is, however, a need to give attention to this aspect of the modern narrative. The Bible is such an immensely foundational document to much of the world's history, that surely changes in how it is read must parallel new theological paradigms.

Bibliography

Addis, William E. *A Catholic Dictionary: Containing Some Account of the Doctrine, Discipline, Rites, Ceremonies, Councils, and Religious Orders of the Catholic Church.* London: Kegan Paul, Trench, 1884.

Alexander, Joseph Addison. *Commentary on the Prophecies of Isaiah.* Edinburgh: Andrew Elliot and James Thin, 1865.

Allchin, A. M. "The Theological Vision of the Oxford Movement." In *The Rediscovery of Newman: An Oxford Symposium*, edited by John Coulson and A. M. Allchin, 50–75. London: Sheed & Ward, 1967.

Andrewes, Lancelot. "A Summary View of the Government Both in the Old and New Testament; Whereby the Episcopal Government of Christ's Church is Vindicated." In *A Pattern of Catechistical Doctrine and Other Minor Works of Lancelot Andrewes.* Library of Anglo-Catholic Theology, The Works of Lancelot Andrewes 6. Oxford: John Henry Parker, 1846.

"Anglican Claim of Apostolical Succession." *The Dublin Review* 7 (August 1839) 139–80.

"Arbitrary Power—Popery—Protestantism." *The Dublin Review* 8.15 (February 1840) 1–55.

Arnold, Matthew. *Isaiah XL-LXVI: With the Shorter Prophecies Allied to It.* London: Macmillan, 1875.

Aston, Nigel. "Horne and Heterodoxy: The Defence of Anglican Beliefs in the Late Enlightenment." *The English Historical Review* 108/429 (October 1993) 895–919.

Augustine, Saint. *On Christian Doctrine.* Translated with an introduction by D. W. Robertson. Library of Liberal Arts 80. New York: Liberal Arts Press, 1958.

Auksi, Peter. "Reason and Feeling as Evidence: The Question of 'Proof' in Tyndale's Thought." *Reformation* 4 (1999) 1–20.

Balfour, Ian. *The Rhetoric of Romantic Prophecy.* Cultural Memory in the Present. Stanford: Stanford University Press, 2002.

Balthasar, Hans Urs von, ed. *Origen, Spirit and Fire: A Thematic Anthology of His Writings.* Washington, DC: Catholic University of America Press, 1984.

Barbeau, Jeffrey W. "Coleridge, Christology, and the Language of Redemption." *Anglican Theological Review* 93/2 (Spring 2011) 263–82.

Bartlett, Robert. *The Natural and the Supernatural in the Middle Ages: The Wiles Lecture Given at the Queen's University of Belfast, 2006.* The Wiles Lectures. Cambridge: Cambridge University Press, 2008.

Bedouelle, Guy. "Biblical Interpretation in the Catholic Reformation." In *A History of Biblical Interpretation: The Medieval Through the Reformation Periods*, edited by Alan J. Hauser and Duane F. Watson, 2:428-49. Grand Rapids: Eerdmans, 2009.

"The Bible and the Reformation." *The Dublin Review* 3 (October 1837) 428-52.

Boer, Roland. *Rescuing the Bible*. Blackwell Manifestos. Malden, MA: Blackwell, 2007.

Bonney, Edwin, and Martin Haile. *Life and Letters of John Lingard, 1771-1851*. London: Herbert & Daniel, 1911.

Bossuet, J. B. *An Exposition of the Doctrine of the Catholic Church in Matters of Controversy*. London: James Darling, 1830.

Boyer, Paul. *When Time Shall Be No More: Prophecy Belief in Modern American Culture*. Studies in Cultural History. Cambridge, MA: Harvard University Press, 1992.

Bromiley, Geoffrey William. *Thomas Cranmer, Theologian*. New York: Oxford University Press, 1956.

Brueggemann, Walter. *The Book That Breathes New Life: Scriptural Authority and Biblical Theology*. Minneapolis: Fortress, 2005.

———. *Theology of the Old Testament: Testimony, Dispute, Advocacy*. Minneapolis: Fortress, 1997.

Buckley, Vincent. "Matthew Arnold: Poetry as Religion." In *Matthew Arnold: A Collection of Critical Essays*, edited by David J. DeLaura, 150-67. Englewood Cliffs, NJ: Prentice-Hall, 1973.

Burtchaell, James Tunstead. *Catholic Theories of Biblical Inspiration Since 1810: A Review and Critique*. London: Cambridge University Press, 1969.

Burton, Edwin H. *The Life and Times of Bishop Challoner (1691-1781)*. 2 vols. London: Longmans, 1909.

Calmet, Augustin. *Commentaire Littéral sur Tous les Livres de l'Ancien et Nouveau Testament*. Paris: Chez Pierre Emery, 1707-22.

Carter, Grayson. *Anglican Evangelicals: Protestant Secessions from the Via Media, c. 1800-1850*. Oxford Theological Monographs. Oxford: Oxford University Press, 2001.

Chadwick, Owen. *The Victorian Church*. Ecclesiastical History of England. London: A. & C. Black, 1971.

Challoner, Richard. *The Catholic Christian Instructed in the Sacraments, Sacrifices, Ceremonies and Observances of the Church by Way of Question and Answer*. Baltimore: G. Dobbin and Murphy, 1809.

———. *The Garden of the Soul: Or, a Manual of Spiritual Exercises*. London, 1775.

———. *The Holy Bible : Translated from the Latin Vulgate and Diligently Compared with the Hebrew, Greek and Other Editions in Divers Languages with Notes by Bishop Challoner*. New York: Douay Bible House, 1941.

Cheyne, Thomas Kelly. *The Book of Isaiah, Chronologically Arranged; an Amended Version with Historical and Critical Introductions and Explanatory Notes*. London: MacMillan, 1870.

———. *The Prophecies of Isaiah, a New Translation with Commentary and Appendices*. New York: Whittaker, 1888.

———. *The Reconciliation of Races and Religions*. London: A. & C. Black, 1914.

Childs, Brevard S. *Old Testament Theology in a Canonical Context*. Philadelphia: Fortress, 1985.

———. *The Struggle to Understand Isaiah as Christian Scripture*. Grand Rapids: Eerdmans, 2004.

Chillingworth, William. *The Religion of Protestants, a Safe Way to Salvation*. London: G. Bell & Sons, 1888.
Chinnici, Joseph P. *The English Catholic Enlightenment: John Lingard and the Cisalpine Movement, 1780–1850*. Shepherdstown, WV: Patmos, 1980.
"Christ, the Church, and the Bible." *The Dublin Review* 42/84 (June 1857) 317–63.
Christlieb, Theodore. *Modern Infidelity and the Best Methods of Counteracting It: A Paper Read at the New York Conference of the Evanglical Alliance*. London: Elliot Stock, 1874.
Christman, Angela Russell, and Michael J. Hollerich. *Isaiah: Interpreted by Early Christian and Medieval Commentators*. Translated and edited by Robert Louis Wilken. The Church's Bible. Grand Rapids: Eerdmans, 2007.
Clarke, Adam. *The Holy Bible: Containing the Old and New Testaments: The Text Carefully Printed from the Most Correct Copies of the Present Authorised Translation, Including the Marginal Readings and Parallel Texts: With a Commentary and Critical Notes Designed as a Help to a Better Understanding of the Sacred Writings*. London: Printed for Joseph Butterworth, 1810–17.
Cockshut, A. O. J. "Matthew Arnold: Conservative Revolutionary." In *Matthew Arnold: A Collection of Critical Essays*, edited by David J. DeLaura, 168–80. Englewood Cliffs, NJ: Prentice-Hall, 1973.
Collins, Anthony. *The Scheme of Literal Prophecy Considered; in a View of the Controversy, Occasion'd by a Late Book, Intitled, A Discourse of the Grounds and Reasons of Christian Religion*. London: Printed by T. J., 1726.
Conybeare, W. J. *Essays Ecclesiastical and Social*. London: Longman, Brown, Green and Longmans, 1855.
Covell, William. *A Iust and Temperate Defence of the Fiue Books of Ecclesiastical Policie: Written by M. Richard Hooker: Against an Vncharitable Letter of Certain English Protestants (as They Tearme Themselues) Crauing Resolution, in Some Matters of Doctrine, Which Seeme to Ouerthrow the Foundation of Religion, and the Church Amongst Vs*. London: Printed by P. Short for Clement Knight, dwelling at the signe of the holy Lambe in Paules church-yard, 1603.
Crowther, M. A. *Church Embattled: Religious Controversy in Mid-Victorian England*. Library of Politics and Society. Newton Abbot: David & Charles, 1970.
Dawley, Powel Mills. *John Whitgift and the Reformation*. The Hale Lectures. London: Black, 1954.
Day, William. *An Exposition of the Book of the Prophet Isaiah*. London: Printed by G. D. and S. G. for Ioshua Kirton, 1654.
"Declaration of the Catholic Bishops, the Vicars Apostolic, and the Coadjutors in Great Britain." *Dublin Review* 1 (May 1836) 265–78.
DeLaura, David J., ed. *Matthew Arnold: A Collection of Critical Essays*. Spectrum Book Twentieth Century Views. Englewood Cliffs, NJ: Prentice-Hall, 1973.
"Dewar's German Protestantism." *The Dublin Review* 19/38 (December 1845) 401–33.
Dickson, Donald R. "The Complexities of Biblical Typology in the Seventeenth Century." *Renaissance and Reformation* 23/3 (1987) 253–72.
Douglas, Brian. "Pusey's 'Lectures on Types and Prophecies in the Old Testament': Implications for Eucharistic Theology." *International Journal of Systematic Theology* (2012) 194–216.
Doyle, Peter. "The Education and Training of Roman Catholic Priests in Nineteenth Century England." *Journal of Ecclesiastical History* 35/2 (April 1984) 208–19.

"Dr. Honinghaus' Protestant Evidences of Catholicity." *The Dublin Review* 7/14 (November 1839) 277–301.

Drey, Johann Sebastian von. "Grundsätze zu einer Genauen Bestimmung Des Begriffs der Inspiration." *Theologische Quartalschrift* 2 (1820) 387–411.

Ehrman, Bart D. *The New Testament: A Historical Introduction to the Early Christian Writings*. New York: Oxford University Press, 2008.

English, John C. "John Hutchinson's Critique of Newtonian Heterodoxy." *Church History* 68/3 (September 1999) 581–97.

Farrar, F. W. *History of Interpretation*. Grand Rapids: Baker, 1961.

Fowl, Stephen E. *Engaging Scripture: A Model for Theological Interpretation*. Challenges in Contemporary Theology. Malden, MA: Blackwell, 1998.

———. "Further Thoughts on Theological Interpretation." In *Reading Scripture with the Church: Toward a Hermeneutic for Theological Interpretation*, edited by A. K. M. Adam and Kevin Vanhoozer, 125–30. Grand Rapids: Baker Academic, 2006.

Frappel, Leighton. "'Science' in the Service of Orthodoxy: The Early Intellectual Development of E. B. Pusey." In *Pusey Rediscovered*, edited by Perry Buter, 1–33. London: SPCK, 1983.

Frei, Hans W. *The Eclipse of Biblical Narrative: A Study in Eighteenth and Nineteenth Century Hermeneutics*. New Haven: Yale University Press, 1974.

Frere, Walter Howard, and Charles Edward Douglas, eds. *Puritan Manifestoes. A Study of the Origin of the Puritan Revolt. With a Reprint of the Admonition to the Parliament and Kindred Documents*. London: Society for the Preservation of Christian Knowledge, 1907.

Gadamer, Hans-Georg. *Truth and Method*. London: Sheed and Ward, 1989.

Gillespie, Michael Allen. *The Theological Origins of Modernity*. Chicago: University of Chicago Press, 2008.

Goulburn, E. M., et al. *Replies to "Essays and Reviews."* With a preface by the Lord Bishop of Oxford, letters from the Radcliffe Observer, and the Reader in Geology in the University of Oxford. New York: Appleton, 1862.

Gray, Robert. *A Key to the Old Testament and Apocrypha: In Which is Given an Account of Their Several Books, Their Contents, and Authors*. Dublin: Printed for Messrs. P. Byrne, A. Grueber, W. M'Kenzie, J. Moore and W. Jones, 1792.

Greenfield, Robert Harvie. "'Such a Friend to the Pope.'" In *Pusey Rediscovered*, edited by Perry Buter, 162–84. London: SPCK, 1983.

Greer, Rowan A. *Anglican Approaches to Scripture: From the Reformation to the Present*. New York: Crossroad, 2006.

Gregory, Brad S. *The Unintended Reformation: How a Religious Revolution Secularized Society*. Cambridge, MA: Belknap, 2012.

Gurses, Derya. "Academic Hutchinsonians and Their Quest for Relevance, 1734–1790." *History of European Ideas* 31 (2005) 408–27.

Haig, Alan. *The Victorian Clergy*. London: Croom Helm, 1984.

Hampden, Renn Dickson. *The Scholastic Philosophy Considered in Its Relation to Christian Theology, in a Course of Lectures Delivered in the Year MDCCCXXXII*. Hereford: J. Head; London, Simpkin, Marshall, and Co., 1848.

Harris, Khim. *Evangelicals and Education: Evangelical Anglicans and Middle-Class Education in Nineteenth-Century England*. Foreword by David Bebbington. Studies in Evangelical History and Thought. Carlisle, UK: Paternoster, 2004.

Harrison, Peter. *The Bible, Protestantism, and the Rise of Natural Science*. Cambridge: Cambridge University Press, 1998.
Haydock, Leo. *Haydock's Catholic Family Bible and Commentary*. New York: Printed by Edward Dunigan and Brother, 1859.
Hayes, John H., and Frederick C. Prussner. *Old Testament Theology: Its History and Development*. London: SCM, 1985.
Hefling, Charles, and Cynthia L. Shattuck, eds. "Introduction: Anglicans and Common Prayer." In *The Oxford Guide to the Book of Common Prayer: A Worldwide Survey*. New York: Oxford University Press, 2006.
Henderson, Ebenezer. *The Book of the Prophet Isaiah, Translated from the Original Hebrew*. London: Hamilton, Adams, 1857.
"The High Church Theory of Dogmatical Authority." *The Dublin Review* 3 (July 1837) 43–79.
Hofstetter, Michael J. *The Romantic Idea of a University: England and Germany, 1770–1850*. Romanticism in Perspective. Houndmills, UK: Palgrave, 2001.
Holyoake, G. Jacob. *Rationalism: A Treatise for the Times*. London: J. Watson, 1845.
Hooker, Richard. *Of the Laws of Ecclesiastical Polity*. Folger Library Edition of the Works of Richard Hooker 1–4. Cambridge, MA: Belknap, 1977–82.
Horne, George. *A Commentary on the Book of Psalms*. London: T. Nelson and Sons, 1776.
———. *Sixteen Sermons on Various Subjects and Occasions*. London: Printed for J. Cooke, Oxford; and G. G. and J. Robinson, Paternoster Row; by J. Cundee, 1800.
Horne, Thomas Hartwell. *An Introduction to the Critical Study and Knowledge of the Holy Scriptures*. Philadelphia: Published by E. Littell; sold also by Wilder & Campbell, New York; and Cummings, Billiard, & Co., Boston, 1825.
Horsley, Samuel. *Critical Disquisitions on the Eighteenth Chapter of Isaiah*. London: J. Robson, 1799.
Howlett, J. Aidan. "The Mosaic Authorship of the Pentateuch." *The Dublin Review* 109 (April 1892) 264–81.
Hügel, Friedrich von. "The Church and the Bible." *The Dublin Review* 115 (October 1894) 313–41.
———. "The Church and the Bible: The Two Stages of Their Interrelation." *The Dublin Review* 116 (April 1895) 306–37.
———. "The Church and the Bible: The Two Stages of Their Interrelation (Part 3)." *The Dublin Review* 117 (October 1895) 275–304.
Hull, John M. "Isaac Watts and the Origins of British Imperial Theology." *International Congregational Journal* 4/2 (February 2005) 59–79.
Hütter, Reinhard. *Suffering Divine Things: Theology as Church Practice*. Grand Rapids: Eerdmans, 2000.
Idestrom, Rebecca. "Elizabeth Wordsworth: Nineteenth Century Oxford Principal and Bible Interpreter." In *Recovering Nineteenth-Century Women Interpreters of the Bible*, edited by Christiana de Groot and Marion Ann Taylor, 181–200. Society of Biblical Literature Symposium Series 38. Atlanta: Society of Biblical Literature, 2007.
Ingalls, Ranall. "Richard Hooker as Interpreter of the Reformed Doctrine of Sola Scriptura." *Anglican and Episcopal History* 77/4 (2008) 351–78.
Jasper, David. "Pusey's 'Lectures on Types and Prophecies of the Old Testament.'" In *Pusey Rediscovered*, edited by Perry Buter, 51–70. London: SPCK, 1983.

Jay, Elisabeth, ed. *The Evangelical and Oxford Movements*. Cambridge English Prose Texts. Cambridge: Cambridge University Press, 1983.

Jodock, Darrell, ed. *Catholicism Contending with Modernity: Roman Catholic Modernism and Anti-Modernism in Historical Context*. Cambridge: Cambridge University Press, 2000.

Johnson, Dale A. "Popular Apologetics in Late Victorian England: The Work of the Christian Evidence Society." *Journal of Religious History* 11/4 (December 1981) 558–77.

Jones, Tod E. *The Broad Church: A Biography of a Movement*. Oxford: Lexington, 2003.

Jowett, Benjamin. "On The Interpretation of Scripture." In *Essays and Reviews*, edited by J. Parker, 330–433. London: John W. Parker, 1860.

Katz, David S. *God's Last Words: Reading the English Bible from the Reformation to Fundamentalism*. New Haven: Yale University Press, 2004.

———. *The Jews in the History of England, 1485–1850*. Oxford: Clarendon, 1994.

Kidder, Richard. *A Demonstration of the Messias, In Which the Truth of the Christian Religion is Defended, Especially Against the Jews*. London: By J. H. for W. Rogers, 1699.

Kierkegaard, Søren. *Fear and Trembling; Repetition*. Edited and translated with introduction and notes by Howard V. Hong and Edna H. Hong. Princeton: Princeton University Press, 1983.

———. *The Sickness Unto Death: A Christian Psychological Exposition for Upbuilding and Awakening*. Translated with an introduction by Walter Lowrie. Princeton: Princeton University Press, 1941.

Knetsch, Robert L. "Tamar's Tale: Elizabeth Hands as a Protofeminist Theologian." In *Strangely Familiar: Protofeminist Interpretations of Patriarchal Biblical Texts*, edited by Nancy Calvert-Koyzis and Heather E. Weir, 33–48. Atlanta: Society of Biblical Literature, 2009.

Knight, Mark, and Emma Mason. *Nineteenth-Century Religion and Literature: An Introduction*. Oxford: Oxford University Press, 2006.

Knott, Edward. "Christianity Maintained." In *Christianity Maintained. Or a Discouery of Sundry Doctrines Tending to the Ouerthrovve of Christian Religion: Contayned in the Answere to a Booke Entituled, Mercy and Truth, or, Charity Maintayned by Catholiques*. Saint-Omer: English College Press, Permissu superiorum, 1638.

Kuhn, Johann von. "Zur Lehre von der Göttlichen Erwählung." *Theologische Quartalschrift* 20 (1838) 629–70.

Lake, Peter. *Anglicans and Puritans? Presbyterianism and English Conformist Thought from Whitgift to Hooker*. London: Unwin Hyman, 1988.

———. "Presbyterianism, the Idea of a National Church and the Argument from Divine Right." In *Protestantism and the National Church in Sixteenth Century England*, edited by Peter Lake and Maria Dowling, 193–224. London: Croom Helm, 1987.

Lane, Calvin. "Before Hooker: The Material Context of Elizabethan Prayer Book Worship." *Anglican and Episcopal History* 74/3 (2005) 320–56.

Larsen, Timothy. *Crisis of Doubt: Honest Faith in Nineteenth-Century England*. Oxford: Oxford University Press, 2006.

———. *A People of One Book: The Bible and the Victorians*. Oxford: Oxford University Press, 2011.

Laud, William. *The Works of the Most Reverend Father in God William Laud, D.D.* Oxford: John Henry Parker, 1860.

Legaspi, Michael C. *The Death of Scripture and the Rise of Biblical Studies.* Oxford Studies in Historical Theology. Oxford: Oxford University Press, 2010.

Leith, John H., ed. "A Fruitful Exhortation to the Reading and Knowledge of Holy Scripture." In *Creeds of the Churches: A Reader in Christian Doctrine, from the Bible to the Present,* 231–38. Atlanta: John Knox, 1982.

Levering, Matthew. *Participatory Biblical Exegesis: A Theology of Biblical Interpretation.* Reading the Scriptures. Notre Dame: University of Notre Dame Press, 2008.

Lewalski, Barbara Kiefer. *Protestant Poetics and the Seventeenth-Century Religious Lyric.* Princeton: Princeton University Press, 1979.

Lindbeck, George A. *The Nature of Doctrine: Religion and Theology in a Postliberal Age.* Philadelphia: Westminster, 1984.

Livingstone, F. L., and E. A. Cross, eds. *Dictionary of the Christian Church.* Peabody, MA: Hendrickson, 2007.

Lowth, Robert. *Isaiah: A New Translation; with a Preliminary Dissertation and Notes Critical, Philological, and Explanatory.* London: Printed by J. Nichols for J. Dodsley, 1778.

———. *Lectures on the Sacred Poetry of the Hebrews.* Translated by G. Gregory. London, 1787.

Maltby, Judith. *Prayer Book and People in Elizabethan and Early Stuart England.* Cambridge Studies in Early Modern British History. Cambridge: Cambridge University Press, 1998.

Mandelbrote, Scott. "English Scholarship and the Greek Text of the Old Testament, 1620-1720: The Impact of Codex Alexandrinus." In *Scripture and Scholarship in Early Modern England,* edited by Ariel Hessayon and Nicholas Keene, 74–93. Burlington, VT: Ashgate, 2006.

Marshall, Peter. "The Reformation of Hell? Protestant and Catholic Infernalisms in England, c. 1560–1640." *Journal of Ecclesiastical History* 61/2 (April 2010) 279-98.

Mather, F. C. *High Church Prophet: Bishop Samuel Horsley (1733–1806) and the Caroline Tradition in the Later Georgian Church.* Oxford: Clarendon, 1992.

Mayeski, Marie Anne. "Quaestio Disputata: Catholic Theology and the History of Exegesis." *Theological Studies* 62 (2001) 140–53.

"Maynooth College." *The Dublin Review* 2 (December 1836) 129–68.

McGrade, A. S. "Richard Hooker on Anglican Integrity." *Anglican Theological Review* 91/3 (Summer 2009) 417–31.

McGrail, Peter. *First Communion: Ritual, Church and Popular Religious Identity.* Liturgy, Worship, and Society. Burlington, VT: Ashgate, 2007.

McKim, Donald K., ed. *Dictionary of Major Biblical Interpreters.* Downers Grove, IL: InterVarsity, 2007.

———. "The Functions of Ramism in William Perkins' Theology." *Sixteenth Century Journal* 16 (1985) 503–17.

Metzger, Bruce M., and Bart D. Ehrman. *The Text of the New Testament: Its Transmission, Corruption, and Restoration.* New York: Oxford University Press, 2005.

Milbank, John. "Hume *Versus* Kant: Faith, Reason and Feeling." *Modern Theology* 27/2 (April 2011) 276–97.

Miller, J. Barrett. "The First Book of Homilies and the Doctrine of Holy Scripture." *Anglican and Episcopal History* 66/4 (1997) 435–70.

Moloney, Raymond. "De Lubac and Lonergan on the Supernatural." *Theological Studies* 69/3 (Spring 2008) 509–27.

Mooney, Edward F. *Knights of Faith and Resignation: Reading Kierkegaard's* Fear and Trembling. SUNY Series in Philosophy. Albany: State University of New York Press, 1991.

Moorman, John R. H. *A History of the Church in England*. London: A. & C. Black, 1976.

Möhler, J. A. *Symbolik: Oder Darstellung der Dogmatischen Gegensätze der Katholiken und Protestanten Nach Ihren Öffentlichen Bekenntnisschriften*. Mainz: F. Kupferberg, 1832.

Newman, John Henry. "The Christian Church a Continuation of the Jewish." In *Sermons Bearing on Subjects of the Day*, 180–98. New York: Appleton, 1844.

———. "The Principle of Continuity Between the Jewish and Christian Churches." In *Sermons Bearing on Subjects of the Day*, 199–217. New York: Appleton, 1844.

———. "Tract 83: Advent Sermons on Antichrist." In *Tracts for the Times, Volume V*, edited by Members of the University of Oxford, 1–54. London: Rivington, 1840.

Nichols, Aidan. *The Panther and the Hind: A Theological History of Anglicanism*. Foreward by Graham Leonard. Edinburgh: T. & T. Clark, 1993.

Niculescu, Mihai Vlad. *The Spell of the Logos: Origen's Exegetic Pedagogy in the Contemporary Debate Regarding Logocentrism*. Gorgias Eastern Christian Studies 10. Piscataway, NJ: Gorgias, 2009.

Nockles, Peter Benedict. *The Oxford Movement in Context: Anglican High Churchmanship, 1760–1857*. Cambridge: Cambridge University Press, 1994.

Norman, Edward. *The English Catholic Church in the Nineteenth Century*. Oxford: Clarendon, 1984.

Null, Ashley. "Thomas Cranmer and the Anglican Way of Reading Scripture." *Anglican and Episcopal History* 75/4 (2006) 488–526.

———. "Thomas Cranmer's Theology of the Heart." *Anvil* 23/3 (2006) 207–17.

Nye, Stephen. *A Letter of Resolution Concerning the Doctrines of the Trinity and the Incarnation*. London, 1691.

Oden, Robert A. *The Bible without Theology: The Theological Tradition and Alternatives to It*. New Voices in Biblical Studies. San Francisco: Harper & Row, 1987.

O'Donovan, Patrick. *The Venerable Bishop Dr Richard Challoner, Sometime Vicar Apostolic of the London District, 1691–1781*. London: Westminster Cathedral, 1981.

O'Neill, J. C. *The Bible's Authority: A Portrait Gallery of Thinkers from Lessing to Bultmann*. Edinburgh: T. & T. Clark, 1991.

Orr, Robert R. *Reason and Authority: The Thought of William Chillingworth*. Oxford: Oxford University Press, 1967.

Overton, John Henry, and Elizabeth Wordsworth. *Christopher Wordsworth, Bishop of Lincoln*. London: Rivington, 1888.

"The Oxford Controversy." *The Dublin Review* 1 (May 1836) 250–65.

"The Parables of the New Testament." *The Dublin Review* 27/53 (September 1849) 181–227.

Patrick, Symon, and William Lowth. *A Critical Commentary and Paraphrase on the Old and New Testament and the Apocrypha*. Philadelphia: Carey and Hart, 1846.

Penner, Myron Bradley. *The End of Apologetics: Christian Witness in a Postmodern Context*. Grand Rapids: Baker Academic, 2013.

Pfizenmaier, Thomas C. *The Trinitarian Theology of Dr. Samuel Clarke (1675-1729): Context, Sources, and Controversy.* Studies in the History of Christian Thought 75. Leiden: Brill, 1997.

"The Philosophy of the Rule of Faith." *The Dublin Review* 35/70 (December 1853) 273-336.

Popkin, Richard H. *The History of Scepticism from Erasmus to Descartes.* Berkeley: University of California Press, 1979.

Prickett, Stephen. *Words and the Word: Language, Poetics, and Biblical Interpretation.* Cambridge: Cambridge University Press, 1986.

Pusey, E. B. *An Historical Enquiry Into the Probable Causes of the Rationalist Character Lately Predominant in the Theology of Germany: To Which is Prefixed a Letter from Professor Sack, Upon the Rev. H. J. Rose's Discourses on German Protestantism; Tr. from the German.* London: Printed for C. & J. Rivington, 1828-30.

Questier, Michael C. *Catholicism and Community in Early Modern England: Politics, Aristocratic Patronage, and Religion, c. 1550-1640.* Cambridge Studies in Early Modern British History. Cambridge: Cambridge University Press, 2006.

Radner, Ephraim. *The End of the Church: A Pneumatology of Christian Division in the West.* Grand Rapids: Eerdmans, 1998.

Rawlinson, George. *Isaiah.* Exposition and homiletics by George Rawlinson; homilies by various authors. The Pulpit Commentary. London: Kegan Paul, Trench, 1887.

"The Reformation the Result of Tyranny." *The Dublin Review* 41/81 (September 1856) 1-27.

Reno, R. R. *In the Ruins of the Church: Sustaining Faith in an Age of Diminished Christianity.* Grand Rapids: Brazos, 2002.

Reventlow, Henning Graf. *The Authority of the Bible and the Rise of the Modern World.* Philadelphia: Fortress, 1985.

Rogers, Nehemiah. *The Wild Vine: Or an Exposition on Isaiah's Parabolicall Song of the Beloved: Isa. 5. 1, 2, 3, Etc.* London: E. Brewster, 1632.

Rogerson, J. W. *Old Testament Criticism in the Nineteenth Century: England and Germany.* Philadelphia: Fortress, 1985.

Rose, Hugh James. *The State of the Protestant Religion in Germany: In a Series of Discourses Preached Before the University of Cambridge.* Cambridge: Printed by J. Smith; for J. Deighton & Sons. And sold by C. and J. Rivington, and G. B. Whittaker, 1825.

Rundle, Elizabeth. *The Early Dawn; or, Sketches of Christian Life in England in the Olden Time.* New York: Dodd, Mead, 1864.

Sandys-Wunsch, John. *What Have They Done to the Bible? A History of Modern Biblical Interpretation.* Collegeville, MN: Liturgical, 2005.

Sawyer, John F. A. *The Fifth Gospel: Isaiah in the History of Christianity.* New York: Cambridge University Press, 1996.

"Science and Revealed Religion." *The Dublin Review* 2 (April 1837) 293-329.

Seitz, Christopher R. *The Character of Christian Scripture: The Significance of a Two-Testament Bible.* Studies in Theological Interpretation. Grand Rapids: Baker Academic, 2011.

———. *Figured Out: Typology and Providence in Christian Scripture.* Louisville: Westminster John Knox, 2001.

---. *The Goodly Fellowship of the Prophets: The Achievement of Association in Canon Formation*. Acadia Studies in Bible and Theology. Grand Rapids: Baker Academic, 2009.

---. *Prophecy and Hermeneutics: Toward a New Introduction to the Prophets*. Studies in Theological Interpretation. Grand Rapids: Baker Academic, 2007.

Simpson, R. S. "Smith, Robert Payne (1818–1895)." In *Oxford Dictionary of National Biography*. Oxford: Oxford University Press, 2004.

Simpson, Sparrow W. J. "Bossuet's Interest in the Church of England." *American Church Quarterly* 26 (1929) 43–50.

Smith, Christian. *The Bible Made Impossible: Why Biblicism is not a Truly Evangelical Reading of Scripture*. Grand Rapids: Brazos, 2011.

---. *How to Go from Being a Good Evangelical to a Committed Catholic in Ninety-Five Difficult Steps*. Eugene, OR: Cascade, 2011.

Smith, George Adam. *The Book of Isaiah*. The Expositor's Bible. London: Hodder & Stoughton, 1893–95.

Smith, R. Payne. *The Authenticity and Messianic Interpretation of the Prophecies of Isaiah Vindicated in a Course of Sermons Preached Before the University of Oxford*. Oxford: J. H. and J. Parker, 1862.

---. *Daniel I-VI: An Exposition of the Historical Portion of the Writings of the Prophet Daniel*. London: James Nisbet, 1886.

---. *The Mosaic Authorship and Credibility of the Pentateuch*. Present Day Tract 15. London: Religious Tract Society, 1883.

---. *Prophecy: A Preparation for Christ: Eight Lectures Preached Before the University of Oxford in the Year 1869*. London: Macmillan, 1871.

---. *The Third Part of the Ecclesiastical History of John Bishop of Ephesus*. Oxford: Oxford University Press, 1860.

Sprunger, Keith L. "John Yates of Norfolk: The Radical Puritan Preacher as Ramist Philosopher." *Journal of the History of Ideas* 37/4 (December 1976) 697–706.

Stafford, Richard. *The Cause and Cure of Divisions or, The Way and Means for All Christians (However They Are Distinguished or Named) to Come to Unity*. London: N.p., 1699.

---. *The Exceeding Great Comfort and Benefit of Having Walked Before God in Truth and with a Perfect Heart and of Having Done That Which is Good in His Sight Set Forth in Several Discourses on Isaiah 38:2,3*. London: Ralph Simpson, 1699.

---. *An Exhortation to All Dissenters to Return to the Church of England*. London: D. Poplar, 1695.

Stansell, Gary. "The Poet's Prophet: Bishop Robert Lowth's Eighteenth-Century Commentary on Isaiah." In *"As Those Who Are Taught": The Interpretation of Isaiah from the LXX to the SBL*, edited by Claire Mathews McGinnis and Patricia K. Tull, 223–42. Society of Biblical Literature, Symposium Series 27. Atlanta: Society for Biblical Literature, 2006.

Strype, John. *The Life and Acts of John Whitgift, the Third and Last Lord Archbishop of Canterbury in the Reign of Queen Elizabeth*. 3 vols. Oxford: Clarendon, 1822.

Sundberg, Walter, and Roy A. Harrisville. *The Bible in Modern Culture: Baruch Spinoza to Brevard Childs*. Grand Rapids: Eerdmans, 2002.

Targoff, Ramie. *Common Prayer: The Language of Public Devotion in Early Modern England*. Chicago: University of Chicago Press, 2001.

Taylor, Charles. *A Secular Age*. Cambridge, MA: Belknap, 2007.

Thompson, Augustine. *Francis of Assisi: A New Biography*. Ithaca, NY: Cornell University Press, 2012.

Tilley, Terrence W. *History, Theology, and Faith: Dissolving the Modern Problematic*. Maryknoll, NY: Orbis, 2004.

Tindal, Matthew. *Christianity as Old as the Creation, or, The Gospel, a Republication of the Religion of Nature*. London, 1730.

Toulmin, Stephen. *Cosmopolis: The Hidden Agenda of Modernity*. New York: Free Press, 1990.

Toy, Crawford Howell. "Thomas Kelly Cheyne." *The Harvard Theological Review* 9/1 (1916) 1–6.

"Tracts for the Times." *The Dublin Review* 4 (April 1838) 307–35.

Treier, Daniel J. *Introducing Theological Interpretation of Scripture: Recovering a Christian Practice*. Grand Rapids: Baker Academic, 2008.

Tuberville, Henry. *An Abridgment of the Christian Doctrine with Proofs from Scripture on Points Controverted by Way of Question and Answer, Composed in 1649*. Dublin: James Duffy, 1851.

Tulloch, John. *Movements of Religious Thought in Britain During the Nineteenth Century*. St. Giles' Lectures. New York: Scribner, 1885.

Turner, Frank M. *John Henry Newman: The Challenge to Evangelical Religion*. New Haven: Yale University Press, 2002.

Turner, Philip, and Ephraim Radner. *The Fate of Communion: The Agony of Anglicanism and the Future of a Global Church*. Foreword by Stanley Hauerwas. Grand Rapids: Eerdmans, 2006.

Tyndale, William. *The Obedience of a Christian Man*. Edited and with an introduction and notes by David Daniell. Penguin Classics. New York: Penguin, 2000.

Van den Biesen, C. "The Authorship and Composition of the Hexateuch." *The Dublin Review* 112 (January 1893) 40–65.

Varley, E. A. *The Last of the Prince Bishops: William Van Mildert and the High Church Movement of the Early Nineteenth Century*. Cambridge: Cambridge University Press, 1992.

Vigouroux, Fulcran. *Dictionnaire de la Bible: Contenant Tous les Noms de Personnes, de Lieux, de Plantes, d'Animaux Mentionnés dans les Saintes Écritures, les Questions Théologiques, Archéologiques*. Encyclopédie Des Sciences Ecclésiastiques 5. Paris: Letouzey et Ané, 1912.

Voak, Nigel. "Richard Hooker and the Principle of Sola Scriptura." *The Journal of Theological Studies* 59 (April 2008) 96–139.

Wallace, Dewey D., Jr. "Via Media? A Paradigm Shift." *Anglican and Episcopal History* 72/1 (2003) 2–21.

Walsh, Marcus. "Profession and Authority: The Interpretation of the Bible in the Seventeenth and Eighteenth Centuries." *Journal of Literature and Theology* 9/4 (1995) 383–98.

Waterworth, J., trans. *The Canons and Decrees of the Sacred and Oecumenical Council of Trent Celebrated Under the Sovereign Pontiffs, Paul III, Julius III, and Pius IV*. London: Burns and Oats, 1848.

Watkin, E. I. *Roman Catholicism in England, from the Reformation to 1950*. Home University Library of Modern Knowledge. London: Oxford University Press, 1958.

Watkins, C. S. *History and the Supernatural in Medieval England*. Cambridge Studies in Medieval Life and Thought 66. Cambridge: Cambridge University Press, 2007.

Watson, Duane F., and Alan J. Hauser, eds. *A History of Biblical Interpretation*. Vol. 2, *The Medieval Through the Reformation Periods*. Grand Rapids: Eerdmans, 2009.

Wellhausen, Julius. *Prolegomena to the History of Israel*. Translated by J. Sutherland Black. Edinburgh: A. & C. Black, 1885.

Wesley, John. *Explanatory Notes Upon the Old Testament*. Bristol: Printed by William Pine, 1765.

Whiston, William. *The Accomplishment of Scripture Prophecies, Being Eight Sermons Preach'd at the Cathedral Church of St. Paul's in the Year MDCCVII at the Lecture Founded by the Honourable Robert Boyle, ESQ*. Cambridge: Cambridge University Press, 1708.

White, Samuel. *A Commentary on the Prophet Isaiah, Wherein the Literal Sense of the Prophecy is Briefly Explained*. London: Printed by J. B. for Arthur Collins, 1709.

Whitehouse, O. C. "T. K. Cheyne's *Founders of Old Testament Criticism*." *The Thinker* 4 (1893) 279–82.

Whitgift, John. *An Answere to a Certain Libel Intituled, An Admonition to the Parliament*. London, 1572.

———. *The Defense of the Answere to the Admonition Against the Reply of TC*. London, 1574.

———. *The Works of John Whitgift, D. D.* Edited by Rev. J. Ayre. Cambridge: Cambridge University Press, 1851–53.

Williams, Isaac. *Tracts 80 and 87, On Reserve in Communicating Religious Knowledge*. London, 1838.

Wordsworth, Christopher. *The Holy Bible in the Authorized Version. V. 1, Genesis and Exodus*. London: Rivingtons, 1866.

———. *The Holy Bible in the Authorized Version. V. 5, Isaiah, Jeremiah, Lamentations, and Ezekiel*. London: Rivingtons, 1871.

———. *Lectures on the Apocalypse: Critical, Expository, and Practical: Delivered Before the University of Cambridge*. Hulsean Lectures. London: Francis & John Rivington, 1849.

———. *On the Inspiration of the Holy Scripture: Or, On the Canon of the Old and New Testament, and on the Apocrypha: Twelve Lectures, Delivered Before the University of Cambridge*. Philadelphia: Herman Hooker, 1854.

———. *Union with Rome: "Is not the Church of Rome the Babylon of the Book of Revelation?"* With a prefatory note by C. J. Casher. London: C. J. Thynne & Jarvis, 1924.

Zabriskie, Alexander, ed. *Anglican Evangelicals*. Philadelphia: The Church Historical Society, 1943.

Index

Aaronic Priesthood, 37–38, 70
Abel, 124
Abelard, Peter, 59
Abraham, 139, 233
Abrogation of oral tradition by Scripture, 211
Abrogation, of the Old Testament, 98, 103, 116, 224
Accuracy of biblical translation, 74–75, 162, 170
Accuracy of Scripture (historically or prophetically), 60, 108, 150
Ad Fontes, 16
Adam, 29, 143
Adiaphora, 30
Aesthetic dimension of Scripture, 51–52, 74, 76–78, 166
Affective dimesion of Scripture, 74, 76, 84, 95–96, 162–64
Ahaz, 58, 100–101, 110, 112
Alexander, Joseph Addison, 85, 116, 177
Alexandrian Interpretation of Scripture, 147
Allchin, Arthur Macdonald, 126–27
Allegorical interpretation, 48, 56, 60–61, 63–65, 77–78, 99, 110–11, 115, 142, 153
Almah, 58, 100–101, 171, 173, 206
Amos, 55
An Abridgment of the Christian Doctrine with Proofs from Scripture on Points Controverted, 195–97, 199
Anabaptists, 26–27

Anagogical interpretation of Scripture, 63, 110
Andrewes, Bishop Lancelot, 37–38, 41, 70, 126, 152
Anglican "factions," 3, 78–81
Anglican Communion, 2, 8, 235–36
Anglican reading of Scripture, 5–8, 13–41, 60
Anglicanism and Isaiah, 85–86, 222–23
Annunciation, 40
Antagonistic interpretation of Scripture , 4, 28, 61–62, 73, 78, 82–83, 116, 136, 141, 173, 202, 215, 224, 239
Antichrist, 26, 125
Antitype, 59, 140, 152
Apocalypse (Book of Revelation), 132, 141–42, 146, 152, 154, 230
Apocrypha, 86, 132
Apologetic interpretation of Scripture, 52, 71–74, 83, 87–88, 91, 93, 98, 102, 107–9, 112, 115–16, 121, 128, 130, 132, 147, 149, 151, 153–54, 181, 196, 207, 211, 223, 225–26, 239
Apotheosis (of the author), 74
Aquinas, St. Thomas, 63, 82, 91, 145, 237
Archetype, 124
Arianism, 27, 65, 120
Arimathea, Joseph of, 134
Aristotle, 17
Arnold, Matthew, 155, 157, 159–64, 185–86

Askesis, 2
Assisi, St. Francis, 230–31
Assyria, 68, 100, 148, 150, 174–75
Atheism, 72, 89, 125, 181
Atonement, 112
Augsburg Confession, 37, 167
Augustine, St., 14–15, 25, 63, 81, 87, 146, 202, 240
Auksi, Peter, 16–17
Authorial genius, 74
Authorial intent, 78, 100
Authority of natural reason or feeling, 17, 46, 50, 61, 188
Authority of Scripture, 19, 22, 30, 35, 46, 50, 65, 97, 104, 134, 180, 200, 212
Authority of the Church, 19, 45, 61, 93, 96–97, 113, 134, 142, 180, 188, 193, 198, 208–12, 214, 219, 231, 237

Babylon, 113, 136, 138, 142, 152–54, 165–66, 176, 238
Baha'i faith, 157–59, 163, 186, 225
Balfour, Ian, 75
Balthasar, Hans Urs von, 146, 167, 229
Bampton Lectures, 6, 84, 95, 208
Baptism, 19, 53
Baptist, St. John, 9, 40, 173
Barth, Karl, 11
Belgic Confession, 133, 145
Bentley, Richard, 63
Bifurcated exegesis, 36, 109, 187, 203, 219, 226, 232
Blake, William, 135
Boer, Roland, 232, 238–39
Bossuet, Jacques-Bénigne, 195, 200–201
Boyle Lectures, 65
Broad Church, 3, 77–79, 81, 95, 119, 126, 129, 135, 139, 155–56, 160, 183, 185–88, 219, 226, 228
Brueggemann, Walter, 5, 11
Buckley, Vincent, 164
Burtchaell, James Tunstead, 192–93, 216
Butler, Charles, 91, 191

Calmet, Antoine Augustin, 81, 206
Calov, Abraham, 51–52
Calvin, John, 19, 24, 45, 52, 109, 145, 205
Calvinism, 19, 24–25, 33, 35, 120
Canon of Scripture, 8, 14, 30–36, 41–43, 47, 53, 55, 77, 97–107, 117, 133, 139–40, 146–47, 151, 163, 168, 171–73, 175–79, 185, 224–26
Carnality (bodliness) of the Church, 127, 130, 153
Carnality of the Old Testament, 104, 106, 108, 111, 117, 137, 140, 224, 228
Caroline Divines, 18, 62, 120–21, 123–24
Cartesian epistemology, 15, 29
Cartwright, Thomas, 24–26, 32
Catcott, Alexander, 121–22
Catechetical literature, 37, 189–90, 194–95, 197–201, 203, 206, 227
Catholicity of the Church, 1, 25, 132, 154, 225, 229
Chalcedonian forumula, 193
Challoner, Richard, 190, 194–95, 201–6
Charles I, 42, 44, 55, 62, 79, 124
Cheyne, Thomas Kelly, 56, 81, 99, 132, 146, 155–86, 215, 217–19, 222, 225–28, 230, 238–39
Childs, Brevard, 9–10, 51, 81, 116–17
Chillingworth, William, 42–47, 49, 51, 94, 156
Chinnici, Joseph, 187, 195, 203, 219
Christ and his Passion, 124, 150, 206, 239
Christ as figure or type, 38–39, 59, 110, 114–15, 124, 148, 159, 183, 224
Christ as Logos (Word) in Scripture, 39, 47, 60, 115, 119, 122, 148, 150, 239
Christ as predicted in the Old Testament, 47–48, 56, 59, 68, 86, 88, 92, 103, 108, 114, 117, 138, 163, 204, 217, 224
Christ as the connection between the Testaments, 12, 41, 47, 53, 55,

67, 84, 98, 104, 106, 129, 146–47, 179, 182, 184, 217
Christ in the Eucharist, 202, 214
Christ, the Church as the form of, 37, 40, 126–27, 133, 138, 140, 143–44, 148, 192
Christendom, 15, 17, 71, 125, 137, 199, 233
Christian Evidence Society, 91, 95
Christological interpretation (hermeneutic) of Scripture, 8, 10, 14, 36–39, 41, 48, 55–56, 58–59, 68, 70, 108–15, 127, 147, 149, 153–54, 170, 175–76, 183–85, 203, 223–24, 226–27, 234–35
Christology, 8, 41, 43, 85, 146, 184
Chronicles, 172
Chronological arrangement of the text, 179–80
Chrysostom, John St., 10
Church militant, 54, 143, 145
Cicero, 195
Circumcision, 70
Cisalpines, 191, 201, 219
Clerical education, 84, 196
Cockshut, A.O., 164
Codex Alexandricus, 63
Coleridge, Samuel T, 6, 96, 126, 128
Collins, Anthony, 47–50
Comma Johannem, 48
Communal reading of Scripture, 14, 28, 34, 94, 163, 171, 192, 237
Conformity, 18, 22, 28, 30, 32
Congar, Yves, 190
Conscience, 17, 22, 29, 44–46, 62, 83, 88, 97
Constantinople, 63
Conybeare, William, 78
Corporeal, 55, 234
Corpus Permixtum, 25, 27, 230
Covell, William, 231–32
Covenant, 114
Coverdale's translation of the Bible, 39–40
Cranmer, Thomas, 8, 13, 19–23, 27–28, 30–32, 34, 37, 40–42, 60, 71, 93–94, 97, 131, 145, 152
Cromwell, Oliver, 62

Crucifixion, 182
Curia, 188, 191, 194, 219
Cyrus, King of Persia, 218

Daniel, 11, 83, 127–28, 208
Daniélou, Jean, 190
Darbyism, 106
Dawley, Powel Mills, 19, 23, 26–27, 31
Day, William, 44, 52, 55–63, 65, 69, 71, 76, 78, 85, 89, 102, 156, 222
De Wette, Wilhelm Martin, 151, 167–68, 172
Deism, 43–44, 47, 49–50, 62, 101, 120, 123–24, 199, 201, 223
Delitzsch, Franz, 136, 150, 166, 206
Descartes, 16–17
Despair (of modern exegesis), 7, 221, 229, 232–34, 236–40
Diachronic approach to the text, 11, 158, 166
Disciplinarians, 23
Disenchantment, 90, 153
Dispensationalism, 106
Divided Church, 1–2, 15, 25, 49, 53, 63, 76, 93, 97, 102, 119, 125, 131, 143–44, 153, 161, 163, 168, 171, 183, 185–86, 224, 228, 231, 233, 235, 241
Divisiveness, 12, 54, 78, 93, 104, 113, 131, 181
Doctrine, 15, 18, 30, 37, 45–46, 48–49, 61, 80, 86, 91, 106, 110, 112, 115, 117, 124, 128, 130, 138, 147, 162, 167, 182, 194–201, 205–12, 215–16, 219–20, 227, 231, 236
Documentary hypothesis, 156, 178
Dogma, 6, 31, 79, 98, 155, 157, 159–60, 163, 167–69, 175, 180, 185, 207, 222
Dogmatism, 47, 135
Donatist, 215
Donne, John, 64
Douay-Rheims translation, 189–90, 201, 204
Doyle, Peter, 195–96
Dualism, 89–90, 187
Duhm, Bernhard, 85, 206
Easter, 40

Ecclesia Anglicana, 18, 23
Ecclesia Militans, 239
Ecclesia Penitens, 239
Ecclesial Embodiment, 16, 103, 126, 131–32, 139, 144, 153, 219, 223, 231
Ecumenism, 1, 49, 62, 69, 225, 240
Edwardine Homilies, 20
Egypt, 210
Ehrman, Bart, 5, 48
Eichhorn, Johann Gottfried, 75, 151, 166, 206
Election, 16, 24–25, 27, 39, 94, 98, 106, 122, 125–26, 215
Elizabeth I, 18, 23–24, 80, 132, 173, 189, 191
English Roman Catholicism, 3–4, 7, 13, 16–17, 21, 44–45, 50, 63, 80–81, 124, 132–33, 151–52, 187–220, 222, 227–28, 230
Enlightenment, 14, 36, 42–43, 62, 117, 121, 187, 192–93, 195, 199
Epistemology, 15, 17, 29, 44, 90
Epoché, 239
Erasmus, Desiderius, 16–17, 48
Erastianism, 120, 122
Eschaton, 15, 103, 106, 124–25
Eton, 56
Eucharist (Communion), 23, 26, 129, 140, 146, 194, 196, 202, 214
Evangelicalism, 3, 16, 21, 77–79, 82–84, 91, 93, 96, 105, 109, 119, 126, 130, 135, 139, 146, 207, 215, 222, 224, 234–35
Evidence for Christianity, 36, 62, 86, 88–89, 91–92, 94–95, 108–9, 119, 130, 136, 150, 154, 172, 179
Ewald, Heinrich, 87, 151, 159, 162, 166–68, 171, 174
Exegetical minimalism, 88, 95, 187–220, 222
Experiential-expressive mode of religious discourse, 128
Ezekiel, 98, 146, 229, 240
Ezra, 148, 162

Fanaticism, 95
Farrar, Frederick, 6

Fecundity of Scripture, 47, 64, 66–67, 98, 110, 128, 148, 203, 229
Figuralism, 8, 39, 41, 63, 66, 85, 103, 106–7, 110, 119, 126, 136, 146, 158, 202–3, 206, 222, 229
Fiore, Joachim of, 15
Foretelling of prophecy, 97, 150, 204, 224
Form Criticism, 109, 112
Fowl, Stephen, 11, 232, 236–38
Free will, 95–97, 117, 224
Frei, Hans, 101–2, 111, 165, 199
Frere, Walter, 24–25, 31–32
Fulfilment of prophecy, 40, 71, 88, 91–92, 96, 106, 115, 126, 128, 136, 138, 166, 177–78, 182–83, 206, 217

Gadamer, Hans-Georg, 14
Gallicanism, 191, 200
Geneva, 45
Genius of the prophet figure, 74, 76, 87, 98–99, 161, 166, 168, 224
Gesenius, Wilhelm, 85, 87, 136, 151, 166, 171
Gospel, 9–10, 35, 56–57, 70–71, 85, 106, 113, 122, 126, 136, 144, 176–77, 192, 204, 215–16, 226, 235
Göttlich-menschlich formula, 192–93, 218
Grace, 35, 124, 126
Graffian hypothesis, 179
Greer, Rowan A., 6–7, 44
Gregory of Nyssa, 10
Gregory, Brad S., 6, 240
Griesbach, Johann Jacob, 211
Grotius, Hugo, 51–52, 65, 67–68, 166, 205–6

Habits, 27, 36, 239
Hackney Phalanx, 119, 122–24, 153
Hampden, Renn Dickson, 208–9
Harnack, Adolf von, 218
Harrison, Peter, 60–61, 78
Haydock Bible, 190, 204–7, 220, 227
Heaven, 62, 107, 122, 125, 139, 143–44, 198, 202

Hebrew, 51–52, 57, 59, 63, 65, 67, 72, 74–76, 78, 84–85, 87, 100, 121–22, 150–51, 157, 161, 170–71, 195, 238
Hegstenberg, Ernst Wilhelm, 116, 130, 136, 145, 166–67, 179
Hell, 143, 189, 198
Henderson, Ebenezer, 86, 177
Henry VIII, 19
Herbert of Cherbury, 49
Herder, Johann Gottfried, 75
Herodotus, 195
Heterodoxy, 60, 120, 122, 131, 192, 205
Hexapla, 74
Hexateuch, 216
Hezekiah, 68, 148–49, 177
High Church interpretation of Scripture, 3, 118–54, 211, 222, 224–25, 230
Hitzig, Ferdinand, 136, 151, 166, 206
Homer, 195, 209
Hooker, Richard, 8, 13, 28–30, 34–36, 41–42, 71, 152, 231
Horne, George, 120, 122–24
Horne, Thomas Hartwell, 86, 159
Horsley, Samuel, 123–25
Hügel, Friedrich von, 216–20
Huguenots, 199
Hulsean Lectures, 132
Humanism, 8, 14, 16, 18, 45, 48, 50, 63, 70, 223, 225
Hutchinson, John, 121–22
Hutchinsonianism, 74, 120–23
Hütter, Reinhard, 229, 233–34

Ibn Ezra, Abraham, 162
Idestrom, Rebecca, 132
Immanuel, 58–59, 171, 174
Incarnation, 23, 38–39, 41–42, 48, 110, 126, 218, 230
Individual and the interpretation of Scripture, 4–5, 8, 13, 16–18, 20–23, 27–28, 30, 32, 37, 41, 44, 46–47, 61, 66, 71, 79–80, 82–83, 85, 93–97, 107–8, 116–17, 121, 133, 135, 137–46, 153–54, 157, 171, 185, 192, 209–11, 214, 219, 224–26
Inerrancy, 235
Infallibility, 6, 36, 45–46, 100, 121, 179–80, 193–94, 198, 200, 203, 211, 220, 235
Insufficiency of Scripture, 32, 194, 201, 204, 227
Interiority, 21
Interregnum, 42
Intertextuality, 148
Ireland, 80, 138, 188, 210
Irenaeus, 10
Irenic exegesis, 1, 4, 6–7, 42–43, 56, 61–62, 66, 69, 74, 78, 82–83, 91, 98, 116, 156–58, 186–87, 223, 225, 228, 239
Isaac, 65, 121, 128, 135, 139, 233
Isaiah exegesis in the seventeenth century, 51–77
Ishmael, 144
Islam, 49

Jacobinism, 125
Jacobins, 120
Jacobites, 120
Jasper, David, 126–29
Jeremiah, 59, 67, 70, 87, 98, 151, 181
Jerome, St., 10, 66, 145, 206, 225
Jesuits, 44, 66
Jesus of Nazareth as textual/prophetic referent, 8–9, 59, 72, 96, 106–7, 109–12, 122, 151, 177, 224
Job, 158, 177
Jowett, Benjamin, 109, 131
Judas, 144, 197
Judgment of the Church by Scripture, 23, 54, 223, 228, 230–32, 236, 238

Kant, Immanuel, 90
Katz, David, 63, 66, 73–74
Keble, John, 160, 211–12
Kennicott, Benjamin, 74
Kidder, Richard, 52, 71–73, 76, 86, 102–3, 114
Kierkegaard, Søren, 221, 229, 232–33, 240

Kneeling, 26, 28
Knetsch, Robert L., 229
Koran (Qur'an), 133
Kuhn, Johann von, 193

Laicization, 18, 41
Lapide, Cornelius à, 66
Larsen, Timothy, 79, 127–28
Latitudinarianism, 44, 47, 51, 62, 94, 123–24
Laud, William, 52, 79, 120
Lauds, 169, 197
Lectionary, 22, 40, 229
Legaspi, Michael, 4, 43, 50, 62, 75, 77
Lessing, Gotthold Ephraim, 75, 216
Levering, Matthew, 232, 236–39
Lewalski, Barbara, 61, 63–64
Liberal, liberalism, 3, 50, 79–80, 82, 96, 98, 100, 103, 125–27, 130, 135, 156, 159, 169, 171, 183, 185, 191–94, 207, 216, 218–19
Lindbeck, George, 128
Lingard, John, 191, 195
Linguistics, 50, 62, 122, 128, 165, 170, 207
Literal interpretation of Scripture, 48, 56–57, 63–65, 67–68, 76, 92, 99–102, 108, 110–11, 113–14, 126, 140, 153, 166–67, 202–3, 206, 214, 229
Liturgy, 10, 18–19, 21–22, 26–28, 31–32, 34, 37–38, 40–41, 70–71, 97, 120, 126, 131, 145, 201, 224, 240
Locke, John, 91
Logos, 38–39, 41, 108, 110–11
Loisy, Alfred, 217
Low Church, 3, 78–79
Lowth, Robert, 51–52, 65, 72, 74–78, 85–87, 95, 161–62, 165–66, 177
Lowth, William, 52, 72
Lubac, Henri de, 90, 190, 237
Luther, Martin, 4, 17, 23, 45, 51, 202, 205, 234, 240
Lutheranism, 19, 37, 51

Manichaeans, 142
Manning, Henry, 191
Marcionism, 142, 222

Mary, Queen, 23, 25
Mary, St., 49, 59, 173
Mather, F.C., 120, 124–25
Matins, 40, 197
Maynooth, 210–11
Mcgrail, Peter, 194
Medieval, 10, 63–64, 82, 89, 145, 237
Meditatio, 240
Melancthon, Philip, 45
Messianic doctrine, 174–76, 184, 226
Metzger, Bruce, 48
Micah, 175
Michaelis, Johann David, 43, 75, 145, 151, 222
Milbank, John, 90
Miracle, 86, 88–89, 91–92, 136, 148, 161, 191
Moab, 66
Modernism, 5
Modernity, 15, 91, 189–90, 233, 240–41
Mohammed, 157
Möhler, Johann Adam, 192
Monotheism, 226
Montaigne, Michel de, 199
Morality, 16–17, 20, 35, 39, 43–44, 46–47, 71, 79, 83–84, 105–6, 108, 110, 113, 125, 138, 157, 164, 182, 186, 225
Mosaism, 217
Moses, 37, 71–73, 110, 121, 215
Mystical interpretation of Scripture, 51, 56, 102, 122, 206, 214

Natural (vs. supernatural), 5, 88–90, 92, 109, 129, 182, 241
Natural religion, 44, 50, 121, 182
Nehemiah, 37, 52, 58, 60, 69, 77, 102, 230
Nestorian, 193
Newman, John Henry, 118, 123, 125–26, 130–31, 137, 193–94, 208, 217
Newton, Isaac, 15, 44, 65, 121–22, 240
Nicaea, 63
Nicholas, Aidan, 191, 208
Niculescu, Mihai, 38–39
Nockles, Peter, 119–23, 130
Non-conformist, 85, 91

index 261

Nonjurors, 124
Null, Ashley, 21, 93–94
Nunc Dimittis, 32
Nye, Stephen, 48–49

Obedience of a Christian Man, 17
Oden, Robert, 232, 238–39
Origen, 10, 38, 74, 136, 144–47, 167, 225, 227–31, 237, 240
Orthodoxism, 128, 130
Oxford Movement (Tractarians), 3, 79, 84, 118–34, 153, 160, 191, 209–11, 213, 222, 224

Paley, William, 91, 122
Pantheism, 121
Papacy, 208, 231
Parochialism, 79, 145, 154
Participatory exegesis, 236–37
Pathos, 229, 233–34, 236, 239–40
Patrick, Simon, 52, 72, 81
Pattern, 16, 37–38, 40, 70–71, 110, 199
Paul, St., 9, 33, 68, 106, 132, 142, 151, 200, 217–18
Penner, Myron Bradley, 91
Penny Catechism, 201
Pentateuch, 79, 84, 156, 215–16
Perspicacity of the Bible, 23, 189
Philology, 4, 43, 48, 50–51, 59–60, 62, 64–65, 67, 69, 71, 74, 78, 85, 87, 89, 98, 116, 155, 165, 169–71, 173–77, 180–81, 183–85, 207, 222, 225–26, 239–40
Pietism, 62, 167, 222
Plato, 182
Pluralism, 7, 225, 234, 240
Poesis, 234, 240
Poetic dimension of Scripture, 51, 74, 78, 143, 162–63, 165–66, 168
Polemical, 36, 46, 63, 77, 84, 101, 116, 131, 181, 189, 199, 211, 214, 227
Polemics, 187–88, 199, 227–28
Political dimension of exegesis, 2, 25, 38, 77, 79–80, 118–54, 213, 224–26, 238
Polysemous meaning, 60, 102
Popery, 209, 214

Popish, 24–27, 32, 79, 152
Popkin, Richard, 16–17, 61, 198
Postfigural, 124
Prayer of General Confession, 22
Preaching, 22, 31, 33–34, 36, 41, 94, 134, 138, 192, 200, 212
Prediction, 8, 41, 56, 65, 88, 92, 103, 107–10, 115, 128, 150–51, 206, 217
Prefiguration, 96, 124, 148–49
Presbyterianism, 24, 38
Presuppositions, 15, 88–89, 92, 116, 128, 184, 223
Preterist, 103
Preternatural, 98
Prickett, Stephen, 75–76
Priestcraft, 61, 120, 227
Primitivism, 26, 131, 133
Private interpretation of Scripture, 18, 47, 79–80, 119, 191, 200, 207, 210, 224
Private judgment, 95, 133, 135, 189, 198, 209–13, 215, 219–20, 224, 227
Probative function of prophecy, 72, 117, 129, 182, 223
Progressivism, 6, 224
Proof, 21, 29, 63, 81, 83, 86–88, 90–91, 95, 102, 108, 114, 117, 131, 146, 149–50, 154, 188–89, 195–97, 199–200, 202, 206–7, 215, 217, 223–24
Prooftexting, 202
Prophet as spiritual hero, 98, 115
Prophetism, 217
Protestant poetics, 55, 61, 63–65, 78, 98, 240
Providentissimus Deus, 216
Proximal interpretation of prophecy, 52–53, 66, 81, 99, 111
Pseudospiritualist, 130
Purgatory, 106, 239
Puritanism, 15–16, 19, 23–29, 31–38, 42, 44, 46, 49–50, 52, 55, 62–63, 70, 78–80, 94, 232
Pusey, Edward Bouverie, 118, 123, 126–31, 134, 137, 140, 150, 158, 167, 170, 208

Pyrrhonic scepticism, 17, 36

Radner, Ephraim, 2
Ramée, Pierre de la, 31
Ramism, 31, 35
Rape, 229
Rationalism, 15–16, 29, 36, 43, 46, 62, 74, 78–79, 100, 111, 114, 121, 128, 157, 160, 166, 182, 184, 212, 216, 223
Rawlinson, George, 85
Reason, 17, 28–29, 35–36, 44, 46–47, 66, 90, 182, 209, 218–19, 233
Recusants, 62, 80, 124
Reformation, 1, 4–6, 14–19, 21, 23, 26–27, 31, 36, 61, 63, 70, 77, 80, 83, 89, 133, 152, 187, 189–90, 212–14, 230–33, 240–41
Reimarus, Hermann Samuel, 43
Religious affections, 17, 36, 51–52, 93, 95–96, 163
Reno, R.R., 2
Repentance, 240
Repristination, 16, 19, 26–27, 44–45, 48, 70, 74, 78, 133, 213
Reserve, 128–29
Resignation, 229, 233, 237–38
Ressourcement, 190
Revelation, 4, 6, 10, 36, 48, 104, 121, 128–30, 140, 152, 167, 182, 184, 192–93, 202, 216, 238
Reventlow, Henning Graf, 15–16, 46, 50
Rezin of Syria, 58, 172
Rhetoric, 16, 75, 122
Ritualism, 131
Rochester, 124, 160
Rogers, Nehemiah, 52–55, 57–58, 60–61, 69, 77–78, 102, 230
Rogerson, John, 43, 50, 131, 167–68, 172, 223
Roman Catholic Emancipation, 80, 122, 189, 191
Romanticism, 6, 52, 74–78, 126, 160
Rose, Hugh James, 130
Royalism, 52, 119–20

Sacraments, 15–16, 25, 31, 39, 126, 134, 137–38, 208
Salvation, 6, 16, 21, 24, 30, 33, 35, 44, 46, 59, 69, 80, 83, 114, 134, 141, 147–48, 154, 182, 211, 231
Sandys-Wunsch, John, 208
Satan, 149
Sawyer, John F. A., 9–10, 85
Scepticism, 8, 14, 16–17, 151, 155, 157, 159, 161, 163, 165, 167, 169, 171, 173, 175, 177, 179, 181, 183, 185, 192, 198, 223, 225–26
Schisms, 27, 47, 54, 93, 125, 212, 227, 235
Schleiermacher, Friedrich, 130
Scholasticism, 17
Science, 3, 5, 15, 44, 92, 121, 130, 209, 211, 221–22, 227, 240
Sectarian, 80, 107, 190, 227
Secular, 75, 90, 195, 239
Secularization, 123, 222
Seitz, Christopher, 98–99, 105, 128, 167–68, 212
Selfhood, 221
Seminarians, 195
Semiosis, 11, 64
Sennacherib, 148–49
Sensus Plenior, 129
Sentiment, 49, 120, 156, 162–63, 175, 193, 208, 213, 225
Shear-jashub, 101
Sin, 25, 40, 88, 125, 146, 149, 178
Smith, Christian, 232, 234–36
Smith, John, 64
Smith, Robert Payne, 56, 81–117, 119, 128, 138, 140, 145–46, 149–51, 153–54, 158–59, 165, 167–68, 171, 181, 185, 188–89, 217, 222–27, 230
Smith, Robertson, 157, 206, 217
Socinianism, 206, 209
Sola Scriptura, 36, 45–46, 55, 63, 80, 189–90, 192, 210, 230, 234
Song of the Vineyard, 52–58
Sophistry, 16–17
Soteriology, 149, 154
Spinoza, Baruch, 73

Spiritualist traditions, 8, 14–16, 18–19, 25, 45, 71, 103–4, 126, 129–30, 223
Stafford, Richard, 44, 52, 69–71
Sublimity, 56, 59–60, 76, 210
Suffering, 10, 48, 54, 67, 73, 92, 103, 112–14, 124, 150–51, 154, 171, 175–78, 184, 229, 232–34, 236, 238–39
Sundberg, Walter, 14–15
Supercessionist, 224
Supernaturalism, 5, 86, 88–92, 94, 111, 116, 149, 174–75, 182, 223–24, 241
Superstition, 29, 152, 160, 227
Synchronic, 179

Tacitus, 195
Targoff, Ramie, 21–22, 30, 32, 34
Taylor, Charles, 90
Te Deum, 40
Temple, 139, 143, 145, 148, 197
Tentatio, 240
Tertullian, 10, 147
Textualization of Scripture, 43, 65
The Book of Isaiah Chronologically Arranged, 158
The Dublin Review, 190, 205, 207–16, 219, 227
Theological exegesis, 1, 3–4, 11–12, 43–44, 50, 60, 76, 83, 94, 107–9, 115–16, 155, 185, 188–89, 221, 232, 240
Theological minimalism, 45, 62, 69–71, 81, 88, 228
Theotokos, 49
Tradition vs. Scripture, 44–45, 47, 49, 66–67, 70, 75–77, 96, 156, 158–59, 165, 169, 172–73, 175, 177, 180, 183, 186–88, 193, 195, 200, 211–12, 226, 235–36, 239
Thesaurus Syriacus, 83
Tholuck, August, 130
Thucydides, 195
Tilley, Terrence, 199
Tindal, Matthew, 49–50
Toleration, 42, 50, 62, 73
Toulmin, Stephen, 15, 61

Tradition of the Church (as historically practiced), 2, 6, 9–10, 14–15, 27, 30, 40–41, 48, 52, 56, 58, 73, 81, 91, 103, 112–14, 116, 122, 129–30, 136, 138, 146, 153, 161, 167, 170–71, 206, 221, 231, 237–39
Treier, Daniel, 11
Trinitarian, 44, 48, 66, 91, 206, 208
Trinity, 38, 40, 48–49, 63, 93, 121, 208
Tropes, 56–57, 63–65
Tropological interpretation, 63, 167, 225
Tuberville, Henry, 195–97, 199, 201
Tulloch, John, 6
Typology, 8, 63–64, 66–67, 69, 73, 106–7, 110, 114–15, 119, 126, 146, 148, 153–54, 177, 229
Tyranny, 44, 50, 127, 174, 214

Ultramontane, 191, 208, 219
Unbelief, 73, 83, 90, 92, 135, 141, 147, 151
Uniformity, 19, 22, 42–43, 45, 47, 49, 51, 53, 55, 57, 59, 61, 63, 65, 67, 69, 71, 73, 75, 77, 79, 81, 191, 232
Unitarianism, 48–49, 132
Univocal referent, 53, 67–68, 98, 241
Ursinus, Zacharias, 68
Urtext, 74

Vatican, 190, 216
Vermittelungstheologie, 130
Vestiarians, 23
Vicars Apostolic, 210, 220
Virgil, 195
Virgin, 10, 48, 58–59, 100, 110, 173, 206, 214
Vitringa, Campegius, 75, 85–86, 136, 145, 150, 162, 166
Vulgate, 63, 75, 215

Wallace, Dewey D., 18, 24
Walsh, Marcus, 50, 75
Warburton, William, 122
Weber, Max, 90
Wellhausen, Julius, 156, 179, 217
Wesley, John, 78, 205, 229

Whiston, William, 52, 56, 65–66, 68–69
Whitgift, John, 8, 13, 19, 23–28, 30–34, 36–37, 41–42, 60, 71, 93, 97, 131, 145
Wilcox, Thomas, 24–25
Williams, Isaac, 128
Wisdom, 28–29, 34–36
Wiseman, Nicholas, 191, 208, 211, 219
Word of God, 8, 12, 14, 20, 23, 30–31, 33, 35–38, 40–41, 47, 81, 94, 97, 102, 110, 119, 121, 133, 161, 171, 175, 179, 193, 223
Wordsworth, Christopher, 81, 85, 118–23, 128, 131–54, 159, 181, 189, 206, 222, 224–25, 230
Wordsworth, William, 118
Wright, N.T., 237

Yazeh, 170, 173

Zacharias, 68
Zwingi, Ulrich (Huldrych), 19, 23, 26

www.ingramcontent.com/pod-product-compliance
Lightning Source LLC
Chambersburg PA
CBHW071247230426
43668CB00011B/1617